“As branches of Christ the true [illegible] flesh. Andrew Hofer provides a p[illegible] of the abundant particularity of the enfleshed Word in patristic preaching. The seven Church Fathers traced in *The Power of Patristic Preaching* serve as worthy exemplars for our own engagement with the Word today. Patristic retrieval must always turn back to the place where Hofer so deftly takes us in this book: to Christ as the vine from whom the branches derive their life. Deeply rooted in the Word, this book does what it claims the patristic preachers did, namely, to offer us the incarnate presence of Christ.”

— HANS BOERSMA —

Saint Benedict Servants of Christ Chair in Ascetical Theology, Nashotah House

“An orator is a master of the word. A preacher is a servant of the Word. The present book shows in inspired and inspiring ways how the Word incarnates Himself every time He is speaking through His servants by presenting seven of the greatest preachers of the ancient Church as timeless models. Each and every present-day preacher of the Word should turn to this volume for inspiration.”

— HUBERTUS DROBNER —

Professor of Church History and Patrology, Theologische Fakultät Paderborn

“The faith of the preacher has to be purified, like the lips of Isaiah, so that his words will engage with the divine incarnation and consequent human deification. His listeners are to experience the Word in their own flesh. This is no simple matter. How is it to be attained? Studying seven outstanding Fathers of the Church, Andrew Hofer tries to detect and explain their underlying multifaceted involvement with God. This book will nudge today’s preacher to an inner conversion.”

— WOJCIECH GIERTYCH, OP —

Theologian of the Papal Household

“In Hofer’s learned yet eminently accessible study, we encounter seven great patristic preachers who, despite their human faults, powerfully communicated the Word made flesh in their own flesh to empower their hearers to live more Christ-like lives, in which God with the least of us is made visible. *The Power of Patristic Preaching* is a rich exploration that will inspire today’s proclaimers and hearers of the Word to embody more fully Christ’s presence in the world.”

— JENNIFER HERDT —

Gilbert L. Stark Professor of Divinity and Professor of Religious Studies, Yale University

THE POWER OF PATRISTIC PREACHING

Patristic Theology

THE POWER OF PATRISTIC PREACHING

THE WORD IN OUR FLESH

ANDREW HOFER, OP

Foreword by PAUL M. BLOWERS

The Catholic University of America Press
Washington, D.C.

Imprimi Potest:
Very Reverend Kenneth R. Letoile, OP
Prior Provincial
Province of Saint Joseph

Nihil Obstat:
Reverend John Baptist Ku, OP
Censor Deputatus

The paper used in this publication meets the minimum requirements of American National Standards for Information Science—Permanence of Paper for Printed Library Materials, ANSI Z39.48–1984.

∞

Cataloging-in-Publication Data on file at the Library of Congress

Printed in the U.S.A.

ISBN: 978-0-8132-3653-7

Book design by Burt&Burt
The interior is set in Warnock Pro and Meta Sans Pro

To Our Lady, Queen of Preachers

"And how does this happen to me,
that the mother of my Lord should come to me?"

—Elizabeth (Luke 1:43)

CONTENTS

ACKNOWLEDGMENTS

I owe gratitude to the Calvin Institute of Christian Worship for accepting me among their inaugural cohort of fourteen Vital Worship Teacher-Scholar grant recipients (2019–20). These grants are made possible by the generous support of Lilly Endowment Inc.; my grant funded my sabbatical in 2019–20 when I wrote some chapters of this book.

For that sabbatical year, I gladly acknowledge the warm hospitality of the Dominican community at Blackfriars, Oxford where I was a visiting lector of the studium in the Michaelmas 2019 term. I owe special thanks to Simon Gaine, OP, David Goodill, OP, and Robert Gay, OP. I was a visiting fellow at Yale Divinity School in that academic year's spring semester before the coronavirus pandemic dramatically curtailed movement. For my time at Yale, I thank especially Gregory Sterling, Jennifer Herdt, Jan Hagens, and Timothee Goselin. I also thank Paul Blowers and Matthew Levering for recommending my application to be a visiting fellow and for their support of my work. Matthew has repeatedly encouraged my work over the past two decades, and to Paul I owe much for also accepting the invitation to write the book's foreword. I am grateful to Jonathan Kalisch, OP, and the Dominican brethren in New Haven during my time at Yale.

I must give thanks to my previous Prior Provincial Kenneth R. Letoile, OP, for his permission to have a sabbatical and for granting the *Imprimi Potest* after the recommendation of the deputed censor, John Baptist Ku, OP. Also, I owe much to my former Prior, Jacob Restrick, OP, my present Prior, Jordan M. Turano, OP, and the brethren of my home, St. Dominic Priory in Washington, DC, and to my confreres and other colleagues over the years at the Pontifical Faculty of the Immaculate Conception, Dominican House of Studies, especially John A. Langlois, OP, Thomas Petri, OP, Dominic M. Langevin, OP, and Dominic Legge, OP.

I thank all my brothers and sisters in the Order of Preachers who have shown me what it means to have the life of a preacher. I thank especially my formators and teachers from many years ago, particularly Ambrose Eckinger, OP, Vincent Wiseman, OP, and the now deceased John Burke, OP, who taught me the history of preaching as well as how to preach. I also thank all my students in the religious life of preachers; I learn from my students. In a special way, I thank the contemplative nuns whose prayers and penance support preaching.

I owe debts to many librarians, especially those of the Dominican House of Studies, the University of Notre Dame, the University of Oxford, and Yale University.

I must express appreciation for all who assisted my writing this book. I thank most especially John Baptist Ku, OP, and Sebastian White, OP, for their regular corrections and suggestions on drafts. Others who have assisted include: Joseph P. Amar, Francis Belanger, OP, John C. Cavadini, Irenaeus M. Dunlevy, OP, Adam Eitel, Peter Fegan, OP, Douglas Finn, Hieromonk Gregory Hrynkiw, Sr. Mary Martin Jacobs, OP, Norbert Keliher, OP, David V. Meconi, Abbot Austin G. Murphy, OSB, Jonah Teller, OP, Joseph P. Wawrykow, Jeff Wickes, Robin Darling Young, participants of my Thomistic Institute lecture on "Chalcedonian Christology for the Poor" at the

Dominican House of Studies on October 5, 2012, participants of the Profound Preaching workshop, "St. Augustine's Preaching for Today," at Mundelein Seminary's Liturgical Institute on October 30, 2015, participants of the "Medieval Lunch" series on February 25, 2020 at Yale University, and the Dominican nuns of the Monastery of Our Lady of Grace in North Guilford, CT who asked me to give classes on Patristic Preaching in August 2021. The book has been influenced in several ways by the life and teaching of Brian E. Daley, SJ.

Two supportive reviewers of my manuscript encouraged its publication at The Catholic University of America Press. John C. Cavadini and Thomas Clemmons, co-editors of the Patristic Theology series at the press, and their board welcomed this book into their new series. John Martino, Brian Roach, Trevor Crowell, and others behind the scenes at The Catholic University of America Press, especially the editorial board, worked for the book's production. I thank them all.

I am grateful to the journal editors for permission to use "Origen on the Ministry of God's Word in the *Homilies on Leviticus*," *Nova et Vetera* (English edition) 7, no. 1 (2009): 153–74 as a basis for adaption in this book's Chapter 1 and to use "The Humble Speech of the Lord: Revelation and Conversion according to St. Ephrem," *Pro Ecclesia* 17, no. 2 (2008): 224–42 as a basis for adaption in this book's Chapter 2.

I am also grateful for the permission to use many quotations of published translated material analyzed in this book. Specifically, I gratefully acknowledge permission from The Catholic University of America Press for use of its Fathers of the Church series; New City Press for use of its Works of Saint Augustine; St. Vladimir's Seminary Press for use of its Popular Patristics Series, especially what I use most, Gregory the Great's *Book of Pastoral Rule*, translated with an introduction by George E. Demacopoulos (Crestwood, NY: St. Vladimir's Seminary Press, 2007); the Center for Traditionalist

Orthodox Studies for Gregory the Great's *Homilies on Ezekiel*, translated by Theodosia Tomkinson, with an introduction by Archbishop Chrysostomos of Etna, 2d ed. (Etna, CA: Center for Traditionalist Orthodox Studies, 2008); and Brian E. Daley, SJ, for use of his translations in *Gregory of Nazianzus*, Early Church Fathers (London: Routledge, 2006), reproduced by permission of Taylor & Francis Group. All rights reserved.

In a special way, I thank Joseph Trigg for giving me in advance of publication his translation of Origen's recently discovered Greek *Homilies on the Psalms*, now found in the Fathers of the Church series of The Catholic University of America Press. I am also grateful to Robert G. T. Edwards for sharing with me his dissertation and subsequent *Providence and Narrative in the Theology of John Chrysostom* before its publication with Cambridge University Press in 2023.

I acknowledge in gratitude Braxton Silva for compiling the bibliography, Garrett Peters for formating the manuscript and beginning the index, and Gerard McNair-Lewis for finishing the index in their Thomistic Institute research assistance.

More personally, I want readers to know of my immeasurable gratitude to my family, especially my nine older siblings and my parents, Jim and Loretta Hofer. I learned my love of the Bible from my dad and my love of the saints from my mom. I am happy that I could write this book that extols what I learned from them to love. My dad passed on March 21, 2021, and I pray that he who was so dedicated to the Word made flesh may share in the glory of his resurrection.

I dedicate this book to the disciple who most knew what it was like to have the Word take flesh and to proclaim the greatness of the Lord in word and deed.

ABBREVIATIONS

AAS	*Acta Apostolicae Sedis*
AKThG	Arbeiten Kirchen– und Theologiegeschichte
ABR	*American Benedictine Review*
ACT	Ancient Christian Texts
ACTI	Augustine in Conversation: Tradition and Innovation
alt.	altered translation
ARAM	*ARAM Periodical*
ArSt	*Aramaic Studies*
ATA	*Augustine through the Ages: An Encyclopedia*
AugStud	*Augustinian Studies*
BA	The Bible through the Ages
BAC	The Bible in Ancient Christianity
BCCT	Brill's Companions to the Christian Tradition
BETL	Bibliotheca Ephemeridum Theologicarum Lovaniensium
BHG	Bibliotheca Hagiographica Graeca (3rd ed.)
BJS	Brown Judaic Studies
BR	*Biblical Research*
ByzAu	Byzantina Australiensia
CAEC	Critical Approaches to Early Christianity
CCL	Corpus Christianorum Series Latina

CCT	Challenges in Contemporary Theology
CH	*Church History*
chap.	chapter
CJA	Christianity and Judaism in Antiquity
CLA	Christianity in Late Antiquity
CollAug	Collectanea Augustiniana
Com	*Communio: International Catholic Review*
CPG	Clavis Patrum Graecorum
CPHST	Changing Paradigms in Historical and Systematic Theology
CSCO	Corpus Scriptorum Ecclesiasticorum Orientalium
CSEL	Corpus Scriptorum Ecclesiasticorum Latinorum
CSS	Cistercian Studies Series
CTM	Calwer Theologische Monographien
CWS	Classics of Western Spirituality
DEC	*Decrees of the Ecumenical Councils*
DR	*Downside Review*
DRLAR	Divinations: Rereading Late Ancient Religion
ECF	The Early Church Fathers
EChr	*Early Christianity*
ep.	epistle
EW	Eusebius Werke
FC	The Fathers of the Church: A New Translation
FTECS	Foundations of Theological Exegesis and Christian Spirituality
HeyJ	*Heythrop Journal*
hom.	homily
ICEL	International Commission on English in the Liturgy
IPM	Instrumenta Patristica et Mediaevalia
JECS	*Journal of Early Christian Studies*
JEH	*Journal of Ecclesiastical History*

JHI	*Journal of the History of Ideas*
JHS	*Journal of Hellenic Studies*
JLA	*Journal of Late Antiquity*
JR	*Journal of Religion*
JRS	*Journal of Roman Studies*
JSSS	Journal of Semitic Studies Supplement
JTS	*Journal of Theological Studies*
LCL	Loeb Classical Library
MelTheo	*Melita Theologica*
MoTh	*Modern Theology*
MST	Mediaeval Sources in Translation
NDST	Notre Dame Studies in Theology
NPNF	Nicene and Post-Nicene Fathers
OCCT	Orthodox Christianity and Contemporary Thought
OChr	*Oriens Christianus*
OCM	Oxford Classical Monographs
OECS	Oxford Early Christian Studies
OECT	Oxford Early Christian Texts
or.	oration
OSHT	Oxford Studies in Historical Theology
OTRM	Oxford Theology and Religion Monographs
OW	Origenes Werke
PL	Patrologia Latina
PMS	Patristic Monograph Series
PO	Patrologia Orientalis
PPS	Popular Patristics Series
ProE	*Pro Ecclesia*
PTMS	Princeton Theological Monograph Series
PTS	Patristische Texte und Studien
RevBen	*Revue Bénédictine*
RevSR	*Revue des Sciences Religieuses*

s.	sermon
SC	Sources Chrétiennes
SCH	Studies in Church History
SE	*Sacris Erudiri*
SEC	Studies in Early Christianity
SGKA	Studien zur Geschichte und Kultur des Altertums
SJT	*Scottish Journal of Theology*
SLA	*Studies in Late Antiquity*
SPM	Stromata Patristica et Mediaevalia
ST	*Storie e Testi*
StPatr	*Studia Patristica*
STAC	*Studien und Texte zu Antike und Christentum*
STT	*Studia Traditionis Theologiae*
SST	Studies in Systematic Theology
SuppVC	Supplements to *Vigiliae Christianae*
TCH	Transformations of the Classical Heritage
Thom	*The Thomist*
tr.	*tractatus* (sermon)
Trad	*Traditio*
TS	*Theological Studies*
TTH	Translated Texts for Historians
TU	*Texte und Untersuchungen*
TV	*Teología y Vida*
VC	*Vigiliae Christianae*
vol.	volume
WGRW	Writings of the Greco-Roman World
WSA	Works of Saint Augustine: A Translation for the 21st Century
ZAC	*Zeitschrift für Antikes Christentum*

FOREWORD

by Paul M. Blowers

The late Henri de Lubac, SJ (1896–1991), one of the most esteemed historians of patristic and medieval biblical exposition, noted that early Christian commentators and preachers focused themselves supremely on "the Fact of Christ," God's ultimate revelatory intervention, "which in its unique individuality has multiple repercussions [and] dominates history and is the bearer of all light as of all spiritual fecundity." At a time when many modern scholars had dismissed Origen, in particular, as an exotic ancient exegete and preacher, or as the quintessential hellenizer of the untainted gospel, de Lubac compellingly argued, to the contrary, that this prolific Alexandrian, far from merely miring himself in Platonic metaphysical speculations, was first and foremost devoted to discovering in the Scriptures "traces of the living Word, personal, incarnate, life-giving."

That Fr. Andrew Hofer, OP, standing in the distinguished tradition of the Dominican "Order of Preachers," has begun his rich monograph on patristic preaching with none other than Origen is therefore thoroughly appropriate. As Fr. Hofer signals early on, Origen was convicted that the Word incarnate must also be "enfleshed" in the preacher of the Christian gospel. Preaching is a thoroughly sacramental action, a medium for the living Word to indwell the preacher and extend the life of the Word beyond the ambo or pulpit. Such is actually a widespread conviction in early Christian homiletics: the Word is present simultaneously in the scriptural texts, in the preacher, in the preacher's words, in the liturgical rites, and is furthermore making a bid to take up residence in the respondent hearers of the proclamation. Fr. Hofer takes us deep into this theology of preaching in the early church, as represented in some of its most eloquent and incisive exponents.

For the seven patristic orators profiled here, the same Christ the Word who, in the beginning, mediated God's work of creating the world, who created flesh, and who recreated flesh in his own incarnation as the New Adam also inaugurated the "ministry of the Word" as a ministry of ongoing formation of human beings according to the image of God in which they were originally created and, more specifically, according to the ultimate and perfect Image of God, Jesus Christ. Pastoral preaching in the context of worship was clearly integral to this ministry of moral and spiritual formation, opening up audiences to the fuller horizons of their faith and couching gospel mandates in terms of fashioning exemplary virtues, both dispositional and performative, that would accompany and manifest Christ's indwelling of believers. Fr. Hofer expertly demonstrates how each of his representative patristic homilists homed in on a particular virtue or character trait manifesting a Christian's growth in Christoformity: holiness (Origen), humility (Ephrem the Syrian), purity of mind and faith (Gregory Nazianzen), hope of salvation (John Chrysostom), passionate love of God and neighbor (Augustine of Hippo), love of the poor (Pope Leo the Great), and recognition of our own weakness and vulnerability before God (Pope Gregory the Great). Each one of these homilists of course covered a broad range of overlapping Christian virtues in their preaching, but Fr. Hofer's highlighting their respective emphases makes for a rich and well-rounded presentation of their aggregate witness.

Another merit of this study is Fr. Hofer's emphasis on how the preaching of each one of his seven homilists was informed—both positively and negatively—by experience of all manner of existential storms and stresses in their own lives. This would require a book of its own, of course, but this book wisely takes biographical factors into serious account. These formative preachers were themselves formed in the refiner's fire of life and of ministry. Sometimes their experience is off-putting to modern audiences. Fr. Hofer notes the virulent polemic against Jews in Ephrem's preaching (the same could be said of John Chrysostom), which has in its background the severe and sustained antipathies between Christian and Jewish communities in various parts of the late ancient Mediterranean world. But more often crisis served to anneal preaching. Origen had experienced the martyrdom of his father Leonides, alienation from his native bishop (Demetrius of Alexandria), and resistance from critics of his use of allegorical interpretation of Scripture. Eventually Origen himself was thrown into prison and tortured in Palestine, the injuries from which hastened his death. This cumulative suffering and experience, however, worked to positive effect in helping this exceedingly erudite Christian intellectual to relate the gospel to audiences of persons of variant levels of spiritual maturity and biblical understanding. Fr. Hofer has showcased, ironically, how Origen's *Homilies on Leviticus*, on historically one of the most difficult canonical books for Christians to find edifying, occasioned his skills as a "spiritual" interpreter to help his audiences envision how the Word was "incarnate" in the seemingly most obdurate of scriptural texts.

Ephrem was formed within the deeply ascetically-oriented Christianity of the Syriac Christian tradition, a literary and liturgical tradition in which God was understood as already sacramentally present in creation but quintessentially so in the incarnate Word. Ephrem saw how the only means of reciprocally approaching this God was through a humble and penitent life, and he himself died while caring for plague victims in 373. Like many ascetically inclined persons of his time, Gregory Nazianzen agonized over his call to the priesthood, and experienced life as an unrelenting refiner's fire, which shows through in his orations and his poetry alike. The monk John Chrysostom likewise contended with his ordination and experienced his fair share of internal ecclesiastical controversy yet left an immense legacy of convicting and encouraging audiences with his extensive exegetical sermons. Augustine spent a lifetime pondering and experiencing the mystery of divine love, and his eloquent *Homilies on 1 John* register the fruits of his labor to know the God who "is love." Guiding churches through the external storm of the collapse of the Roman Empire in the West, Pope Leo the Great meanwhile turned his listeners to the imperatives of care for the poor and the lowly within the Church. From an elite family in Rome, the monk-turned-pope, Gregory the Great, had seen Italy in the dark days of a sustained plague and other upheavals, even serving a term as prefect of Rome before becoming a monk. He had been a papal negotiator with the Byzantine Church, and experienced firsthand the gradual and destabilizing alienation between Rome and Constantinople. Gregory was perfectly suited to articulate the scandalous gospel of strength-through-weakness mirrored in his deeply incarnational preaching and pastoral profile.

Fr. Hofer's book achieves something unique, a combination of close historical-critical scholarship and subtle hagiography, a task some historians might think impossible. The sainthood of these seven patristic preachers comes out not in overly idealized portraits but in the concreteness of their ministries and the power of their own words. Thankfully, Fr. Hofer beautifully bridges the horizon of these ancient preachers with the horizon of contemporary preachers and audiences alike. This "magnificent seven" are enabled a pulpit here to speak afresh to the ecumenical church, to all believers who still long passionately to experience Christ's presence in word, in sacrament, and in life. This is a book of retrieval and ressourcement par excellence, and it will doubtless endure as one of the definitive works on early Christian preaching.

Paul M. Blowers
Milligan University

INTRODUCTION

THE POWER OF PATRISTIC PREACHING

The Word in Our Flesh

We live in an age acutely sensitive to hypocrisy. Those Christians who have stayed in the pews look for authenticity and transparency in the Church only to be discouraged time and again by insincerity and opacity. The sins and scandals of their leaders have racked one Christian community after another. From fear of losing more members of congregations already shrinking, some preachers stop teaching what their listeners would count as "hard" (Jn 6:60), but this makes them inconsistent with the Gospel entrusted to them. Meanwhile, their people suffer tremendously from all sorts of hardships, including the world's indiscriminate disease and sin's discriminating injustice. Suffering without faith in the God who is with us can make us turn to resentment, self-pity, and despair.

"What's the good of my having become a Christian?" Augustine of Hippo once asked in a homily. He most likely said this on the eleventh of September in the year AD 410, which means that he would have delivered this sermon less than three weeks after the Goths sacked Rome.[1] Augustine asks the question to give voice to those who are tempted to leave the Church. Why are they tempted? They see themselves afflicted as all other people—regardless of the Christian faith. What is more, some see that others have much greater prosperity *without* the faith. Augustine assumes the position of the skeptic: "Has it made me any better off than one who isn't a Christian, than that one who doesn't believe in Christ, than that other one who blasphemes my God?" For Augustine, the prophet Isaiah offers a response: "All flesh is grass, and all the honor of the flesh as the flower of the field. The grass has withered, the flower fallen (Is 40:6–7 cf. 1 Pt 1:24)." Augustine comments: "So has everything perished then? Let it not be! 'But the Word of the Lord abides forever' (Is 40:8 cf. 1 Pt 1:25)." "Look, the grass has perished," continues Augustine, "Do you want to avoid perishing? Hold fast to the Word."[2]

Many of us who have been called to evangelize and build up the Church by life and speech want to address the frustrations that upset so many people. We want them to experience the Word through our speaking and living, and we also—sinful, broken creatures ourselves—want to hold fast to the Word. We proclaim from the depths of our being, "Jesus is Lord" (1 Cor 12:3). "The Word became flesh" (Jn 1:14), *our* flesh, weak flesh that passes like the grass of the field. Put to death for our sins, he is risen for our salvation. We want to give witness to his love and mercy for the world. "For we do not preach ourselves," says St. Paul, "but Jesus Christ as Lord, and ourselves as your slaves for the sake of Jesus" (2 Cor 4:5). Will those tempted to leave find in our lives and ministry Christ himself, the one who took on the form of a slave and died for our

1 Augustine, *Sermon* (hereafter *s.*) 33A.3 (CCL 41, 420; WSA III/2, Hill, 162). The critical edition dates the sermon to 410, following A. Kunzelmann, "Die Chronologie der Sermones des hl. Augustinus," in *Miscellanea Agostiniana*, vol. 2 (Rome: Studi Agostiniani, 1931), 417–520, at 501. Edmund Hill reminds the reader that the dating of this sermon (and many others) is a matter of conjecture, but this sermon does have the September 11th date, without a year, in the sermon title.

2 *S.* 33A.3 (CCL 41, 420; WSA III/2, Hill, 162 [alt.]).

sake (cf. Phil 2:7)? Will we be with them in their questioning and pain? Will we express to them by speech and action, "Hold fast to the Word"? Will we lift them up to God in the silent prayer of our hearts?

This book ponders the mystery of Christ's life in us as preached by the power of the Spirit in the early Church. It does not pretend to be a complete overview of patristic preaching. For example, it does not provide a collation of rhetorical rules from Christians in late antiquity about how to preach, as important as such rules might be. One of the greatest Latin orators of his age, Augustine says in his *On Christian Teaching* that such rhetorical rules "should not be looked for from me, either in this work or in any other."[3] Rather than being a how-to compendium of homiletics, the book serves as a resource to show the power of patristic preaching conveying the Word in our weak flesh—a wondrous, multi-faceted divine mystery to be lived by hearer and proclaimer of the Word today.[4] *In patristic preaching, we find the Word in our flesh.*

Indeed, by attending to the lives and words of early Christian preachers, we can discern essential elements of how the Word, who uniquely became flesh, takes the flesh of preachers so that those who hear them may experience in the sacramental life the power of the same Word in their own flesh. Origen of Alexandria once asked in a sermon, "What good is it if I should say that Jesus has come in that flesh alone which he received from Mary and I should not show also that he has come in this flesh of mine?"[5] While teach-

3 *On Christian Teaching* 4.1.2 (CCL 32, 117; WSA I/8, Hill, 201).

4 Robert Wilken writes that the early Christian "mission was to win the hearts and minds of men and women and to change their lives." See Robert Louis Wilken, *The Spirit of Early Christian Thought: Seeking the Face of God* (New Haven: Yale University Press, 2003), at xiv. For an Evangelical recognition of Wilken's summation, see Bryan M. Litfin, *Getting to Know the Church Fathers: An Evangelical Introduction* (Grand Rapids, MI: Brazos Press, 2007), 15.

5 Origen, *Homilies on Genesis* 3.7 (SC 7bis, 140; Heine, 101 [alt.]). For consistency throughout this book, all pronouns in reference to God will be presented in lowercase, even those taken from published sources.

ing on the covenant of circumcision in Genesis 17, Origen ponders what God says there: "Thus my covenant will be in your flesh as an everlasting covenant" (Gn 17:13).[6] How is that true for the Christian Church? Origen believes that Christians now have what was given to Abraham long ago; the covenant is not merely in name and word, but in deeds. This Alexandrian preacher considers a verse from 1 John, "Every spirit that confesses that Jesus has come in the flesh is from God" (1 Jn 4:2), with the words of Saint Paul in 1 Cor 4:20: "The kingdom of God is not in speech, but in power." The Word became flesh in the womb of the Virgin Mary in order to come with power into our lives. Origen declares: "I show the covenant of God to be in my flesh, if I shall have been able to say in accordance with Paul that 'I am crucified with Christ; and I no longer live, but Christ lives in me' (Gal 2:20), and if I shall have been able to say, as he said: 'But I bear the marks of my Lord Jesus Christ in my body' (Gal 6:17)."[7] Without the enfleshment of the Word in Origen himself, the incarnation would be in vain for him. But if this enfleshment does occur, if he shows this Word in his life and preaching, he has a deified life, with its share of Christ's suffering, and others too may experience through him the everlasting covenant of God. Nearly 1,800 years later, Origen's preaching still inspires. It inspires me, and it has inspired this book.

Plan for the Book

This book delves into the lives and words of seven Fathers as exemplars for those of us today who are listeners and proclaimers of the Word. Seven chapters guide the reader through a select examination of seven preachers (three Greek, one Syriac, and three Latin)

6 The Scriptures are quoted in translation usually based on the texts used by individual preachers in the early Church. The *New American Bible, Revised Edition*, approved by the Administrative Committee of the United States Conference of Catholic Bishops, is also used and may appear in modified form.

7 Origen, *Homilies on Genesis* 3.7 (SC 7bis, 140–42; Heine, 101).

from the third through the sixth Christian centuries. They had lives patterned on Christ's life, and can show those dedicated to the Christian faith's proclamation ways of living Christ's life in different times and places.

The definite particularities of narrating lives, virtues, and exemplarism, discussed much in recent moral philosophy and theology, will enable us to lay claim to the Word found in preachers in early Christianity. Linda Zagzebski, for example, offers an exemplarist moral theory based on people's admiration for the hero, the saint, and the sage.[8] For our study of patristic preaching, the Word made flesh is the exemplar of exemplars whose influence is not merely ethical but sacramental and graced, and for that reason this work can be compared with the "Christocentrism of the virtues" proposed in Livio Melina's *Sharing in Christ's Virtues.*[9] Among other major contributions he has made to moral philosophy, Alasdair MacIntyre ponders practical reasoning made by rational agents as seen through narratives of select lives in his recent *Ethics in the Conflicts of Modernity: An Essay on Desire, Practical Reasoning and Narrative.*[10] Such recent interest can inspire us in a theological retrieval of patristic preaching for the Church's needs.

8 Linda Trinkaus Zagzebski, *Exemplarist Moral Theory* (New York: Oxford University Press, 2017).

9 Livio Melina, *Sharing in Christ's Virtues: For a Renewal of Moral Theology in Light of Veritatis Splendor*, translated by William E. May (Washington, DC: The Catholic University of America Press, 2001), especially his reflection on Bonaventure's "Christocentrism of the virtues" in 128–34. I have learned from Patrick Clark's Thomistic appropriation of Zagzebski and Melina. See Patrick M. Clark, *Perfection in Death: The Christological Dimension of Courage for Aquinas* (Washington, DC: The Catholic University of America Press, 2015), especially chapters 6 and 7. For a response to Clark's work, see Stephen J. Pope, "Christocentric Exemplarism and the Imitation of Jesus," *New Blackfriars* 101 (2020): 301–10.

10 Alasdair MacIntyre, *Ethics in the Conflicts of Modernity: An Essay on Desire, Practical Reasoning and Narrative* (New York: Cambridge University Press, 2016). That book's chapter 5 gives four narratives of Vasily Grossman, Sandra Day O'Connor, C. L. R. James, and Denis Faul. MacIntyre writes, "All four led untypical lives, confronting issues that many of us never confront. But each by their choices throws light on the everyday choices of everyday modern life. There is, of course, a certain arbitrariness in my picking out these four, but my aim is no more than to illustrate the part that narratives of others play in our understanding of practice" (244).

John Henry Newman, who knew patristic preaching well, extols the necessity of definiteness in preaching. "Definiteness," Newman asserts, "is the life of preaching." He continues:

> A definite hearer, not the whole world; a definite topic, not the whole evangelical tradition; and, in like manner, a definite speaker. Nothing that is anonymous will preach; nothing that is dead and gone; nothing even which is of yesterday, however religious in itself and useful.[11]

In this book's arrangement of themes, the featured preachers show forth a transformation in their lives and the lives of their people based on the Word who comes to be enfleshed in abundant particularity.

Moreover, in order to say something definite we must admit that we cannot say everything. This book's study of seven preachers, each with a particular emphasis, poses many constraints that require significant omissions of preachers and topics. For example, we will not devote chapters to the Cappadocian brothers Basil the Great and Gregory of Nyssa or the Italian preachers Ambrose of Milan and Peter Chrysologus of Ravenna. The preachers chosen, and the themes studied in the following chapters, also cannot do justice to all the essential aspects of the Christian faith received and proclaimed.

In order to foster connections between a spectrum of readers with the early Church, each chapter starts with a brief biblical reflection from a recent prominent Christian leader. This introduction prepares us to go back to the particularity of an early Christian preacher and behold the Word in his flesh for us. After this review of receiving his life and preaching, we then study select examples of what that preacher contributes toward the chosen aspect

11 John Henry Newman, chap. 6, "University Preaching," no. 7 in *The Idea of a University*, introduction by Don Briel and afterword by Christopher O Blum (Tacoma, WA: Cluny Media, 2016), 310.

of Christian life featured. While each chapter can be read as an independent study, the chapters proceed both chronologically and thematically in a sequence for the book's overarching argument.

We begin with Origen of Alexandria (d. 253/4) and the purpose of the Word's coming to us: holiness. The life of Christ is holiness in the flesh. He is our sinless great high priest, who sacrificed himself for the sake of sinners. The most prolific preacher before the Council of Nicaea (325), Origen preached sixteen *Homilies on Leviticus* to lead his people to their priestly baptismal dignity of being united to the Word in worship. The purpose of the incarnation is here with Origen's preaching on Leviticus at the beginning of our study: sharing in the Word's own holiness through worship. We also see this same approach in Origen's newly discovered Greek *Homilies on the Psalms*, the most exciting patristic discovery made yet in the twenty-first century. From this consideration of holiness in worship as the goal of Christian life, the successive chapters display a deifying virtue, or transformative power for excellence, of the mystery of the incarnation shining forth in the life and words of the preacher.[12] Holiness is seen in the graced life of virtues, divinizing us by the power of the Spirit to be in Jesus Christ, the Son of God the Father.

Chapter 2 moves to examine Ephrem the Syrian (d. 373), exposing his emphasis on the humility of divine speech and the preacher's imitation of that humility for the conversion of others. The Word incarnate communicates humility in the flesh; we cannot attain holiness without that humility. While the other six chapters focus on Greek and Latin traditions, this single chapter dedicated to the greatest Syriac Father manifests that the Gospel is not bound by the dominant Greek and Latin cultures of the Roman Empire. Jesus

12 The term "virtue" for many early Christian preachers indicates how we are deified or transformed. For example, Warren Smith writes, "The Christian life for Ambrose is a virtuous life. The possibility for the true virtue of Christ's followers is created by the grace of baptism. The *conversio* of baptism is the entrance to a new *conversatio*, no longer earthly, but *in caelis*." See J. Warren Smith, *Christian Grace and Pagan Virtue*, 223; cf. Phil 3:20.

himself spoke in a way with which Syriac Christians as fellow Semites identify. Their holy ones express Jesus' speech and life, especially in their humble suffering, as witness for our conversion. In God's providence, it is through the Word's humility that the world may, in the humility of repentance, be converted.

The next two chapters consider two of the "Three Holy Hierarchs" in Orthodox tradition.[13] Whereas we focus on the Word's humility to convert us in Ephrem's chapter, here we consider first how that Word makes us think in new ways. We learn from Gregory of Nazianzus (d. 389/90), the Theologian, and his understanding of the Word's purification of our rational nature through right faith. The Word purifies our mind in the flesh. Unlike the apostate Emperor Julian, who denied the reasonableness of Christians and forbade them to teach Greek literature, and the heretic Apollinarius of Laodicea, who did not believe that the Word assumed a rational soul in becoming flesh, Gregory instructs, in his cultured way of imitating and furthering the best of Greek rhetoric, that the Word takes up a human mind for our healing. By faith, we can believe in who God is: Father, Son, and Holy Spirit.

We then turn to our other featured Holy Hierarch, John Chrysostom (d. 407), declared patron of preachers by Pope Pius X in 1909. Chrysostom's *On the Priesthood* recounts many difficulties that await the priest in ministry, and Chrysostom wants the priest to rely on Christ. By turning to examples of his preaching on the hope of salvation, we find that Chrysostom gives a vision of the life-and-death importance of living an authentic Christian life in view of heaven while experiencing daily struggles on earth.

After these four Fathers of the East, we turn West for the final three, with the first being Augustine of Hippo (d. 430). In imitating

13 Tradition relates that John Mauropos in the eleventh century dreamed that Basil the Great (of Caesarea), Gregory the Theologian (of Nazianzus), and John Chrysostom told him of their concord and that people should not quarrel over ranking them. A new feast of these Three Holy Hierarchs, on January 30, was then established to confirm their unity.

Christ, Augustine can show us how the incarnation gives us love in the flesh, a love that the preacher is to communicate by word and deed. When reflecting on Ezekiel's prophecy concerning the shepherds of Israel, Augustine asks himself "Why do I preach?" He answers: "Is it for any other intention than that we may live together with Christ? This is my passion! This is my honor! This is my possession! This is my joy! This is my glory! . . . I don't want to be saved without you."[14] In this chapter we highlight Augustine's *On Christian Teaching*, his hugely influential text on how to treat Sacred Scripture, and his *Homilies on the First Letter of John*, some of his most beloved preaching.

From this basis of love, the next preacher we consider is Leo the Great (d. 461). While Leo is most renowned for his Christological doctrine, in many of his 97 extant sermons he exhorted the faithful to love through almsgiving. The Word takes our impoverished human nature to enrich it. He loves the poor in the flesh. Leo, who had served as archdeacon of Rome with the special responsibility of caring for the poor, now as the city's bishop preaches, "Let no human being be thought worthless to a human being, nor should that nature which the Creator of things made his own be despised in anyone."[15] Leo offers a striking portrait of a world transformed and charged with incarnational grandeur.

Chapters 3 through 6 feature "faith, hope, and love," the three things that Paul names at the end of 1 Corinthians 13. After the patristic era, tradition will call them the theological virtues. The greatest of these is love, as Paul tells us (1 Cor 13:13), and so the book has a double consideration there, with love itself in Augustine's chapter and love of the poor and the weak in Leo's chapter. Granted that early Christian preachers insisted on the wholeness of loving God with all that we are and all that we do, they often turned

14 Augustine, *s.* 17.2 (CCL 41, 238; WSA III/1, Hill, 367 [alt.]).

15 Leo the Great, *tr.* 9.2 (CCL 138, 35; Freeland and Conway, 40 [alt.]).

the attention of their listeners to those around them in great need. But why should faith, hope, and love be so prominently featured in a book on patristic preaching? Augustine selected these three to answer the question of what worship is: "God is to be worshiped with faith, hope, and love."[16] Early Christian preachers constantly emphasized the connection of the liturgical worship within the church building and the lived worship of people's lives. It is, after all, the same worship.[17]

Finally, after this review of patristic preaching's goal of holiness, the humility for repentance, faith, hope, and love, in Chapter 7 we will look with Gregory the Great (d. 604) at preachers accepting their own vulnerabilities. The Word shows us what it means to have weakness in our flesh. Just as the incarnation occurred in weakness, so our deification occurs in weakness. Gregory's *Book of Pastoral Rule* is the most famous guide for the formation of the clergy in the West, and it concludes by strongly sounding our human limitations. In the incarnation, the Word was made weak, and Gregory urges clergy after their preaching to return to themselves and know their weakness. Gregory knew his. Through his *Homilies on Ezekiel*, we will also see how he opens up a biblical vision for the lives of preachers: In accepting their weakness, they are called to both the heights of contemplation and the sufferings of this world.

In summary, we see that the Word was made flesh and is in the flesh of preachers for the flesh of their hearers . . .

(1) in holiness as our goal (Origen)
(2) in humility for the Word to come down to our lowly level for our repentance (Ephrem)
(3) for purifying our minds in faith (Gregory of Nazianzus)

16 See Augustine, *Enchiridion* 1.3 (CCL 46, 49; WSA I/8, Harbert, 274).

17 For reflections on the variety of meanings "worship" has today, see John D. Witvliet, "Pedagogical Reflections on Changing Uses of the Term 'Worship,'" *Worship* 95, no. 1 (2021): 4–11.

(4) for letting the hope of salvation direct our life in its struggles (John Chrysostom)
(5) out of love for us to be like God who is love (Augustine)
(6) in loving the poor and the weak so as to give mercy to those most in need (Leo the Great)
(7) in weakness that we would receive God's mercy when accepting our own miseries (Gregory the Great)

Jesus himself is the uniquely perfect, definite expression of how to live a fully human life because he alone is the divine Word made flesh. All those in Christ express his inexhaustible mystery, like branches on their vine (cf. Jn 15:1–17). By the power of Christ's Spirit at work in their lives, they imitate him, resemble him, or participate in him—to varying degrees. Early Christians came quickly to recognize his mother, the Virgin Mary, as privileged in closeness to him.[18] She proclaims, "All generations will call me blessed" (Lk 1:48). The early preachers featured here are outstanding in holiness. We must not forget, however, that they are sinners. Augustine, in recounting how even the saints of the Scriptures sinned—explicitly omitting the Virgin Mary—imagines that all of them in unison say the words of John: "If we say, 'We are without sin,' we deceive ourselves, and the truth is not in us" (1 Jn 1:8)."[19]

Given that common sinfulness, this book gives voice to the Word communicated through the brokenness of early preachers, both those featured and through them other Christians. We repeatedly encounter weakness, ignorance, and sin in different ways when we recover the lives and words of these preachers. Arguably the

18 The Gospel accounts of Luke and John most prominently show the mother of Jesus as faithful disciple. For a reconsideration of the early and widespread attention to Mary, see Stephen J. Shoemaker, *Mary in Early Christian Faith and Devotion* (New Haven, CT: Yale University Press, 2015).

19 Augustine, *On Nature and Grace*, 36.42: "Piety demands that we admit that she was without sin"; WSA I/23, Teske, 245. In removing Mary from a discussion of sin, Augustine grants Pelagius's point of not speaking of her committing sin as something commonly held.

most influential scriptural exegete in Christian history, Origen was dismissed as a fanciful wordsmith by some congregants who were turned off by his strange allegories, and his home diocese's bishop contested Origen's ordination to the priesthood. In an Origenist controversy three centuries after his death, he was officially condemned.[20] Ephrem, like so many Fathers, railed against the Jews in a way that is absolutely unacceptable. Scholars repeat that Robert Bellarmine, Jesuit theologian and saint, thought of Ephrem as "obviously more pious than learned."[21] Gregory of Nazianzus exposes how other clergy hurt him, and some think that his incessant speech about himself is politically self-serving. John Chrysostom preached long, very long (which for some is the worst sin in preaching), and was repeatedly dismissed this past century by scholars as moralistic and simplistic.[22] Chrysostom's bitter opponents during his life included Theophilus of Alexandria, Cyril's uncle who led the Synod of Oak that deposed Chrysostom. Augustine was a teenage father who, many years later at his mother's bidding, abandoned his son's mother—much to his heart's sorrow— in order to be betrothed to a wealthy girl. He could not wait for her marrying age, and so took up a mistress before his baptism.[23] During his ministry, Augustine engaged with originality against one opponent

20 Council of Constantinople II (553), after Emperor Justinian's own condemnation of Origen ten years earlier. Regarding Origen's legacy in the West, it should be better known that Thomas Aquinas took far more interest than any other medieval scholastic in Origen, with 1,093 explicit references, at times in praise and at other times in censure. See Jörgen Vijgen, "Aquinas's Reception of Origen: A Preliminary Study," in *Thomas Aquinas and the Greek Fathers*, eds. Michael Dauphinais, Andrew Hofer, OP, and Roger Nutt (Ave Maria, FL: Sapientia Press, 2019), 30–88.

21 See *St. Ephrem the Syrian: Selected Prose Works*, translated by Edward G. Mathews, Jr. and Joseph P. Amar, FC 91 (Washington, DC: The Catholic University of America Press, 1994), 4n3, where we see the remark's occurrence in R. Payne Smith, "Ephraim the Syrian," in *Dictionary of Christian Biography* (London, 1880) 2:140 and in "St. Ephraem, Doctor of the Church," in *Butler's Lives of the Saints*, eds. H. Thurston and D. Attwater, rev. ed. (New York: 1956) 2:574.

22 For examples, see David Rylaarsdam, *John Chrysostom on Divine Pedagogy: The Coherence of his Theology and Preaching*, OECS (Oxford: Oxford University Press, 2014), 2–3.

23 Augustine, *Confessions* 6.15.25.

after another—ensuring enemies in his own day and through the centuries.[24] Leo the Great, hated by those following the Eutychian heresy during his life and held responsible by some for ecclesial divisions over Christ's unity, is said today not to have recognized the personhood of the poor.[25] Gregory the Great began a reform that privileged monks over the non-monastic clergy and set forth an ascetic agenda for clerics. A backlash occurred within the Roman clergy against Gregory's reform.[26]

While these preachers give us reason to admire them and draw us to the Word incarnate, not a single one was or is now universally recognized as perfect. Preachers in every age have their faults and, frankly, opponents. Jesus, after all, certainly had opposition to his public ministry, and he was put to death on a cross. In the first centuries after his resurrection, the early Church was no golden era where all preachers delivered breathtaking homilies to rapt and obedient listeners all the time.[27] But it does give evidence of outstanding preachers and even, at times, attentive listeners who can be studied. All those committed to evangelization and catechesis, if they want to claim continuity with those earliest traditions of Christianity, would do well in following how these preachers, in so

24 For analysis of the three main controversies (Manichean, Donatist, and Pelagian), see Gerald Bonner, *St. Augustine: Life and Controversies*, 3rd ed. (Norwich: Canterbury, 2002).

25 See Bronwen Neil, chap. 5 "Leo I on Poverty," in *Preaching Poverty in Late Antiquity: Perceptions and Realities*, eds. Pauline Allen, Bronwen Neil, and Wendy Mayer, AKThG (Leipzig: Evangelische Verlagsanstalt, 2009), 171–208, at 202.

26 George Demacopoulos finds that the scholarly reconstruction of organized resistance to Gregory during his papacy does not have sufficient historical grounds, but that later sources, such as Gregory's ninth-century Roman biographer John the Deacon, tell us of resistance. Demacopoulos writes that "we are on steadier ground to see those expressions of inner-Roman clerical partisanship to be a debate about the value of Gregory's ideas and legacy rather than evidence of a contemporaneous and organized opposition to it." See George E. Demacopoulos, *Gregory the Great: Ascetic, Pastor, and First Man of Rome* (Notre Dame, IN: University of Notre Dame Press, 2015), 123.

27 For a sobering assessment of the variety of preaching in the early Church and the Middle Ages, see R. Emmet McLaughlin, "The Word Eclipsed? Preaching in the Early Middle Ages," *Trad* 46 (1991): 77–122.

many ways brilliant in the virtues, communicated Christ's life to those listening to them.

For the underpinnings of this argument, we now consider the three touchstones that run through the book's argument: incarnation, deification through the virtues, and proclamation. In each, while the Word takes center stage, so to speak, it is by the power of the Holy Spirit that this mystery unfolds for our salvation to the glory of God the Father. For just as by the Holy Spirit did the Virgin Mary conceive the eternal Word, the Son of God, so too by that Holy Spirit, the Spirit of adoption given to us who are not the eternal Son, do we come in the sacramental life into Jesus Christ and receive the life of his virtues. Only by the Spirit's descent at Pentecost are the first disciples aflame to proclaim Christ to every nation, for "no one can say, 'Jesus is Lord,' except by the Holy Spirit" (1 Cor 12:13).

Incarnation, Deification through the Virtues, and Proclamation

Incarnation

"It seems a truism to say that Christology—the interpretation of the person of Jesus in the light of the Christian canon of scripture, and of the tradition which receives it—is what early Christianity, at its heart, is all about," observes Brian Daley.[28] Early Christians reflected on Christ's incarnation as summing up the *oikonomia*, God's saving plan (cf. Eph 1:10). In this divine plan we are called in Christ to experience the mystery of the most holy Trinity as Father, Son, and Holy Spirit: one eternal, all-wise, all-loving God. The Word's

28 Brian E. Daley, SJ, "Christ and Christologies," in *The Oxford Handbook of Early Christian Studies*, eds. Susan Ashbrook Harvey and David G. Hunter (Oxford: Oxford University Press, 2008), 886–905, at 886.

enfleshment in the mysteries of salvation reveals the Trinity. Sent by the Father, the Word incarnate preached, healed, suffered, died, and rose from the dead. The early Christians committed their lives to the risen Lord. "There was a time in the life of the Church when Easter was, in a way, everything," posits Raniero Cantalamessa.[29]

Remembered weekly on Sunday before becoming an annual feast, the resurrection of Christ led to the Father's giving us the Holy Spirit. In this way, Jesus, who has brought our humanity to the bosom of the Father in heaven, draws us into company with him forever. By the power of the Holy Spirit, we come to know Christ and are led back to the Father. The incarnation, then, should not be thought of as only the particular act of the Word's taking flesh from a virgin in Nazareth. It is rather that one's life in the flesh, whose actions and sufferings lead us to contemplate and praise the most holy Trinity.

Under the pressure of confusions and heresies, such as the extremes of thinking that Christ was a divine being who merely seemed to be human or was a mere human with some special connection to the divine, Christians came to denounce error and celebrate the truth of God's closeness to us in flesh. Beginning in the fourth century, the ecumenical councils concerned themselves not with variants of scriptural texts, but rather with variants of scriptural interpretation about who Jesus is. In Jesus Christ, we find one who is God with the Father as his Son, and who lives and reigns with him in the unity of the Holy Spirit. That one took upon himself our humanity for our sake to die and rise for us. He, the eternal Word of the Father, did not come so as to dwell in a prophet or saint when he was made flesh. Augustine, in his *De Trinitate*, makes this fundamental distinction between the holy ones and Jesus:

29 Raniero Cantalamessa, *Easter in the Early Church: An Anthology of Jewish and Early Christian Texts*, edited and translated by James M. Quigley, SJ, and Joseph T. Lienhard, SJ (Collegeville, MN: Liturgical Press, 1993), 1.

> For the Word in flesh [*verbum in carne*] is one thing, and the Word made flesh [*verbum caro*] another, that is, the Word in man [*verbum in homine*] is one thing, the Word made man [*verbum homo*] another.[30]

Indeed, distinguishing the Word made flesh from the Word in the flesh of prophets and other holy men and women has great importance.[31] With precision, Cyril of Alexandria differentiates Jesus from his saints when he proclaims, "the Word of God the Father was hypostatically united to the flesh."[32] This unique hypostatic union means that the eternal Son, who is the Power and Wisdom of God, assumed humanity, that is, united that humanity to his own hypostasis or person. With Cyril and the conciliar tradition, we can affirm: "the Word of God suffered in the flesh, was crucified in the flesh, and tasted death in the flesh, becoming the first-born from the dead, although as God he is life and life-giving."[33] The truth of the incarnation is made manifest when the Holy Spirit guides the Church to proclaim by word and deed Christ's cross and resurrection.

Through their exegetical work, early Christians came to develop Christological terminology that would become more and more precise about what can, and what cannot, be known about Jesus Christ.[34] Certain terms, such as person, nature, and union, came to prominence because of theological controversies. But as much

30 *On the Trinity* 2.6.11 (CCL 50, 94; McKenna, 63 [alt.]).

31 For an earlier Greek example, see Athanasius's letter to Maximus, *ep.* 61.2 (PG 26:1087C): "Therefore, that rash saying of theirs is not good, that the Word of God came to enter a holy man (*for this occurs in each of the prophets and of other saints*), lest it would appear that he is born and again dies in each one. . . . We are deified not by sharing in the body of some [mere] man, but by receiving the body of the Word himself." My translation.

32 Second anathema of Cyril's *Third Letter to Nestorius* (*DEC* 1, 59; McGuckin, *Saint Cyril of Alexandria and the Christological Controversy*, 273).

33 Twelfth anathema of Cyril's *Third Letter to Nestorius* (*DEC* 1, 61; McGuckin, *Saint Cyril of Alexandria and the Christological Controversy*, 275). The fifth ecumenical council, Constantinople II (553), claimed this *Third Letter's* twelve chapters, or anathemas, for its own teaching. This council, in turn, issued fourteen anathemas (*DEC* 1, 114–22).

34 See Andrew Hofer, OP, "Scripture in the Christological Controversies," in *The Oxford Handbook of Early Christian Biblical Interpretation*, eds. Paul Blowers and Peter Martens (Oxford: Oxford University Press, 2019), 455–72.

as Christians used abstract terms and concrete images, they also recognized the inadequacy of those terms and representations, and indeed of all our words in attempting to express fully the mystery of God's incarnation. No word or image could adequately capture who Christ is in the life-changing experience of encountering him and being transformed by his Spirit.

Deification through the Virtues

It is not the incarnation alone that escapes full definition. Early Christians recognized that words could not adequately describe the saints who communicate the presence of God. In the summer of 431, during the Council of Ephesus dedicated to articulating the mystery of the incarnation, Cyril of Alexandria began his homily in praise of St. John the Evangelist in this way: "All words fall short of the renown and glory of the saints, for, as it is written, they 'became stars in the cosmos, offering the Word of life' (Phil 2:15–16)."[35] Such is the glory of deification. Concluding his recent *God Visible: Patristic Christology Reconsidered,* the most important overview of early Christology available, Brian E. Daley writes:

> Jesus Christ, in his own person, is the realization of God's plan for a straying humanity since the beginning. And the point of that plan is the inclusion of humanity, the reciprocal placement of humanity "in" Christ and Christ "in" humanity, through and in the community of disciples, in the assumed shape of Christ's own life: a life darkened now also by suffering, as his was, but pointed towards resurrection, towards what the Fathers of East and West call divinization, and so towards a growing participation in the same Mystery. The saving reality of Christ is God made present in our midst: "God with us." It is God visible—our brother.[36]

35 Cyril of Alexandria, Homily given at Ephesus on St. John the Evangelist's Day, in *Homiliae Diversae* II (PG 77:985D–987A; McGuckin, *Saint Cyril of Alexandria and the Christological Controversy,* 280 [alt.]).

36 Brian E. Daley, SJ, *God Visible: Patristic Christology Reconsidered,* CPHST (Oxford: Oxford University Press, 2018), 280.

As Daley makes apparent, a study of the incarnation leads us to divinization. God became one with us so that we might be one with him. God is eternally Father, Son, and Holy Spirit, no more and no less. God the Father gives us the Holy Spirit to conform us to Christ and make us, in the words of Scripture, "partakers of the divine nature" (2 Pt 1:4), even to the point of being called "gods" (Ps 82:6, Jn 10:34). Several different ways of expressing deification were at work in early Christianity, and they have had their twists and turns in developments and suppressions in different communities through the centuries.[37]

In the 180s, Irenaeus offers formulas to show the reciprocity between incarnation and deification, such as his extolling "Jesus Christ our Lord, who on account of his immense love became what we are so that he would perfect us to be what he is."[38] Clement of Alexandria, writing around the end of Irenaeus's life, has an abundance of formulations of deification. For example, he says that when one perfectly imitates the heavenly teacher one becomes "a god going about in the flesh."[39] In 363, Gregory of Nazianzus, following upon a long theological deification discourse grounded in Scripture and attentive to cultural needs, was the first to use the

37 See *The Oxford Handbook of Deification*, eds. Paul L. Gavrilyuk, Andrew Hofer, OP, and Matthew Levering, forthcoming. With its introduction and forty-four chapters by scholars throughout the world, this will be the most comprehensive resource for the theology of deification available.

38 *Against Heresies* 5, prologue (SC 153, 14; my translation).

39 Clement, *Stromateis* 7.101.4 (SC 428, 304); cf. Norman Russell, *The Doctrine of Deification in the Greek Patristic Tradition*, OECS (Oxford: Oxford University Press, 2004), 121. About this phrase, Russell quotes Benjamin Drewery's remark that it is an "absurd picture of the perfect Christian." Russell, *Doctrine of Deification*, 126; cf. Benjamin Drewery, "Deification," in *Christian Spirituality: Essays in Honour of Gordon Rupp*, ed. Peter Brooks (London: SCM Press, 1975), 33–62, at 61. Russell goes on to describe Clement's understanding of the gods made so through deification: "The gods are the baptized in whom the Logos dwells, and also those who through the practice of philosophy have mastered the passions and become like God" (139). For an argument about Clement's setting up a contrast of loves and deifications (pagan and Christian) useful for evangelization in his time and ours, see Andrew Hofer, OP, "Clement of Alexandria's *Logos Protreptikos*: The Protreptics of Love," *ProE* 24, no. 4 (2015): 498–516.

Greek word *theōsis*, which became the standard term.[40] What has been acclaimed as its first definition, strictly speaking, does not occur until Dionysius the Pseudo-Areopagite (c. 500). Dionysius says, "Deification (*Theōsis*) is attaining likeness to God as far as possible and union."[41] Created in the image of God, human beings are re-created to resemble God even much more wonderfully during this life by grace and ultimately in the glory of heaven. Theological schools in later eras will differentiate accounts of transformation in Christ. As helpful as those clarifications may be, such was not the preoccupation of Christians in the first centuries of the Church. To quote the fourth-century Latin bishop Hilary of Poitiers, "We needed that God should become flesh and dwell in us [*habitaret in nobis*], that is, by the internal assumption of the flesh of one, he might abide within all flesh [*universae carnis incoleret*]."[42] Patristic preaching vividly conveys the early Christian experience of being taken up into Christ himself in a variety of ways (even by the same preacher) such that deification escapes precise definition.

Deification occurs most fundamentally in the sacraments and prayer of the Church gathered together for worshiping God.[43] Christians have always stressed life-changing rituals that effect what they signify. When one is baptized, one is washed clean of all sin and punishment due to sin, and one enters Christ by receiving the new life of grace. Leo the Great says, "The body of the reborn

40 Gregory of Nazianzus, *or.* 4.71 (SC 309, 184). Cf. Russell, *Doctrine of Deification*, 214. A related term, *apotheōsis*, had previous currency.

41 Pseudo-Dionysius, *Ecclesiastical Hierarchy* 1.3 (Heil and Ritter, 66; Luibheid, 198 [alt.]). Cf. Russell, *Deification in the Greek Patristic Tradition*, 1.

42 Hilary, *On the Trinity* 2.25 (CCL 62, 61; my translation, cf. McKenna, 55). See the discussion of J. Beumer's account of Hilary's quotation in Ellen Scully, "The Assumption of All Humanity in Saint Hilary of Poitiers' *Tractatus super Psalmos*," Ph.D. diss., Marquette University, 2011, p. 10; cf. Russell, *Doctrine of Deification*, 327.

43 For accessible essays, see *Divinization: Becoming Icons of Christ through the Liturgy*, ed. Andrew Hofer, OP (Chicago: Hillenbrand Books, 2015).

becomes the flesh of the Crucified."[44] Cyril of Jerusalem preaches on the Eucharist in this way:

> With perfect confidence, then, we partake as of the body and blood of Christ. For in the figure of bread his body is given to you, and in the figure of wine his blood, that by partaking of the body and blood of Christ you may become of one body and blood with him. For when his body and blood become the tissue of our members, we become Christ-bearers and, as the blessed Peter said, "partakers of the divine nature" (2 Pt 1:4).[45]

The baptismal and Eucharistic mystery transforms and unites mortals to God who became one of us.

Because of this mystery, early Christians understood that they could find Christ in their graced brothers and sisters in particular ways. The Apostle Paul confesses, "I will not dare to speak of anything except what Christ has accomplished through me to lead the Gentiles to obedience by word and deed" (Rom 15:18). The mystery Paul experienced is now also experienced in his listeners. As we later read in the Letter to the Colossians, the mystery hidden for ages but now made manifest is "Christ in you" (Col 1:27). As should be emphasized, all the baptized are to be Christ's presence and show him in the world. Some are blessed with extraordinary gifts to fulfill this, and do so in ways that are celebrated by the Christian community as exemplary. Martyrs and ascetics offer us privileged forms of this witness, and scholarly literature has given us insight into why the early Christians exalted them.[46] Those who proclaim the Word

44 Leo the Great, *tr.* 63.6 (CCL 138A, 387; Freeland and Conway, 276 [alt.]).

45 Cyril of Jerusalem, *Mystagogical Catecheses* 4.3 (SC 126bis, 136; McCauley and Stephenson, 2.181–82 [alt.]).

46 For martyrs, see Candida Moss, *The Other Christs: Imitating Jesus in Ancient Christian Ideologies of Martyrdom* (New York: Oxford University Press, 2010). The genre of the *Passio* can contain acts of preaching, fulfilling Mt 10:19. Writing on the *Passio Sebastiani*, Kate Cooper observes, "[T]he martyr was the quintessential Christian preacher, uniquely able, in his or her complete sacrifice of flesh, to the Word, to serve as the medium of what might be called divine ventriloquism." See Kate Cooper, "Ventriloquism and the Miraculous:

to the assembly would show another privileged form of deified life. Gregory of Nazianzus sets forth the sublimity of becoming a priest in leading the sacred liturgy:

> Who can mold, as clay-figures are modelled on a single day, the defender of the truth, who is to take his stand with angels, and give glory with archangels, and cause the sacrifice to ascend to the altar on high, and share the priesthood of Christ, and renew the creature, and set forth the image, and create inhabitants for the world above, and even, greatest of all, to be a god and be godmaking?[47]

If one heard that an ordained priest was called a "god," one might think that this is the height of what is today called clericalism.[48] But the point of becoming a priest, for Gregory, is deification—to make others gods. As we will see in Chapter 3, Gregory described that priestly deification especially through faith's purification, a healing of the mind by the priest's life and speech.

Conversion, Preaching, and the Martyr Exemplum in Late Antiquity," in *Signs, Wonders, and Miracles*, eds. Kate Cooper and Jeremy Gregory, SCH 41 (Woodbridge: Boydell and Brewer, 2005), 22–45, at 22–23. Ignatius of Antioch's *Letter to the Romans* offers a very early (c. 107) non-canonical account of the martyr as imitator of Jesus. Also, see how even Stephen's martyrdom imitates Christ's death in Acts 7:54–8:1. For a very influential study on ascetics as the locus of supernatural power in the fifth and sixth centuries and with a focus on Syria, see Peter Brown, "The Rise and Function of the Holy Man in Late Antiquity," *JRS* 61 (1971): 80–111. Brown has offered retrospective assessments of this work, such as in his "The Rise and Function of the Holy Man in Late Antiquity, 1971–1997," *JECS* 6, no. 3 (1998): 353–76. The desert tradition would become renowned for holy lives who would "give a word" so that others may live. See, for instance, *The Sayings of the Desert Fathers: The Alphabetical Collection*, translated by Benedicta Ward, rev. ed. (Kalamazoo, MI: Cistercian Publications, 1984).

47 Gregory of Nazianzus, *or.* 2.73 (SC 247, 186; Browne and Swallow, 220 [alt.]).

48 The use of the term "clericalism" has many forms. In *Evangelii Gaudium*, Pope Francis writes against "excessive clericalism" that keeps the laity away from decision-making in the Church. See Pope Francis, *Evangelii Gaudium*, Apostolic Exhortation on the Proclamation of the Gospel in Today's World (2013), no. 102. The most recent *Ratio Fundamentalis Institutionis Sacerdotalis* from the Congregation for Clergy, "The Gift of the Priestly Vocation" (2016), mentions clericalism once, with scare quotes: "Consequently, future priests should be educated so that they do not become prey to 'clericalism', nor yield to the temptation of modelling their lives on the search for popular consensus" (no. 34).

In patristic preaching, vivid language of deification resounds with respect to the status or office of an individual, but that does not necessarily mean that the one with the status or office is true to the deifying grace offered. All the baptized, including the ordained, ascetics, preachers, virgins, the married, the widowed, miracle workers, and so on, have a privileged—one could even say "deified"—classification in different ways. For example, the Christian husband and wife provide an image of the union of Christ and the Church, for "the two become one flesh" (Gn 2:24). But Christian marriage does not necessarily mean that particular husbands and wives, or any other of the baptized, have the grace of deification sanctifying their souls. Christians understand something of the horror of sin, such as in the image of a branch on the vine that does not bear fruit (Jn 15:6). For example, Augustine's theological developments in debates with the Donatists, about ecclesiastical office and ministering the sacraments, and with the Pelagians, about grace and daily living, would show how a bishop could still validly ordain even if he were a sinful traitor to the Church, and how one who is baptized could still be a Christian even after falling into sin. There can be a great difference between a name or office and the reality within the heart. Even martyrs, certainly the most exalted classification in early Christianity, if they do not have love, do not bear witness to the deifying love of Christ—and so they would have no reward (cf. 1 Cor 13:3). Moreover, even those who proclaim the Word do not necessarily have the Word at work through the grace that makes them pleasing to God. "Many people will say to me on that day," says Jesus, "'Lord, Lord, did we not prophesy in your name?' (Mt 7:22; cf. Phil 1:15–18)" Jesus says solemnly that those who prophesy, but who do evil, will hear from him, "I never knew you" (Mt 7:23). They may have a holy title and transmit God's holiness and not be true themselves to what they receive and pass on.

Yet those who proclaim the good news are meant in grace to convey by both speech and action the Word in their very flesh.

Moreover, the deification of the Christian takes place over time and is evidenced through the virtuous life, especially in humility and through growth in the three greatest virtues: faith, hope, and, above all, love. Paul Blowers explains in his book of early Christian sources titled *Moral Formation and the Virtuous Life*:

> One of the monumental legacies of the early church in its witness to later centuries of Christians is the conviction that a Christian is formed over time through multiple means and disciplines, and not simply validated in a single, momentary act of obedience or intellectual assent.[49]

Early Christians repeatedly went to church in order to participate in the sacramental life and worship God, which could include preaching. A preacher, in a special way, continually directed his hearers' attention to the Word of God proclaimed so that they may become daily more humble, faith-filled, hopeful, and loving by the power of the Spirit. Preachers could be of great assistance to the deified transformation of their hearer's lives, as we will see in each chapter's focus in this book. We now turn to the proclamation of preachers conformed to the Word incarnate.

Proclamation

The first preaching about Christ occurred as an outgrowth of the experience of Jewish disciples of Jesus giving testimony to him. The words of Andrew to his brother Simon Peter, "We have found the Christ" (Jn 1:41), exemplify the earliest apostolic joy that bursts into expression. These words anticipate the confession of faith after the descent of the Holy Spirit, in which the Christ must be

49 Paul M. Blowers, ed. *Moral Formation and the Virtuous Life*, Ad Fontes: Early Christian Sources (Minneapolis: Fortress Press, 2019), 1.

understood through his cross and resurrection in fulfillment of the Scriptures (cf. 1 Cor 15:1–5). All disciples are to confess with their lips that Jesus is Lord and believe in their heart that God raised him from the dead in order to be saved (cf. Rom 10:9–10). Proclaiming Jesus is a common Christian gift and duty; various ordained and prophetic offices contributed in special ways to the spread of the good news. The earliest Christians were no doubt influenced by their Jewish experience, as we see for example in Paul's Sabbath proclamation of Jesus in the synagogue of Antioch in Pisidia (Acts 13:14–43). And, after experiencing rejection, Paul turned from the synagogue to speak to the Gentiles (Acts 13:44–49), and even in the Areopagus of Athens (Acts 17:22–31).

Early Christian terminology for preaching varies considerably, and some terms are ambiguous as to the precise significance they held for their early communities. "Preaching" should not be here identified solely with a homily given by the ordained at the Eucharist. In the middle of the second century, Justin Martyr records that the presider of the Eucharist preached after the reading of the Word of the Lord.[50] The Eucharistic homily has a privileged position in preaching, and we can find early restrictions regarding who may preach to support that eminent place.[51] Yet many texts we call

50 "Then, when the reader has stopped, the president, in an address, makes admonition and invitation of the imitation of their good things." Notice the emphasis on imitation of the readings heard. See *Justin's Apology on Behalf of Christians*, 67.4 (Minns and Parvis, 258–59). For a brief overview, see Jeremy Driscoll, OSB "Preaching in the Context of the Eucharist: A Patristic Perspective," *ProE* 11, no. 1 (2002): 24–40; and, by implication to early Christian preaching from a patristics scholar with a broader thesis here, Geoffrey D. Dunn, "Aristotle and the Art of Preaching," *Worship* 72, no. 3 (1998): 220–35, which Dunn reviews, updates, and expands upon in his "Cicero and the Sermon: Further Reflections on the Art of Preaching," *Australasian Catholic Record* 97, no. 1 (2020): 45–58. Also, see Geoffrey D. Dunn, "Rhetoric in the Patristic Sermons of Late Antiquity," in *Preaching in the Patristic Era: Sermons, Preachers, and Audiences in the Latin West*, eds. Anthony Dupont, Shari Boodts, Gert Partoens, Johann Leemans (Leiden: Brill, 2018), 103–34.

51 For example, Possidius records in the *Life of Augustine*, chap. 5 that Bishop Valerius of Hippo, who ordained Augustine a priest, gave him permission to preach in his presence, something which was unknown in North Africa, but would soon be followed by other bishops granting that faculty to certain priests. As for the present *Code of Canon Law* for the Latin Church, can. 767 §1 stipulates. "Among the forms of preaching, the homily,

sermons or homilies were not given in a Eucharistic liturgy. When Basil the Great, as Archbishop of Caesarea in Cappadocia, preached his homilies on the six days of creation, he did so both in the morning and the evening. He did not have two Eucharistic liturgies each day. It is often unclear if some extant records of early homilies came from Eucharistic liturgies or other types of prayer. Sometimes we may not even know that a homily was orally delivered, as our only sources are written documents, not audio recordings.

We have records of patristic preaching difficult to classify with many unknowns. The Syriac tradition has metrical homilies, not to mention didactic hymns, and certain texts seem to blur the distinction between liturgy and school.[52] Do these not fall within the broader tradition of preaching? A memorable Sunday hymn can do more than a sermon for achieving the praise of God and the sanctification of the people by instruction (two traditional marks of preaching). In fact, Ambrose says of his own people who sang his hymns to praise the Trinity that they "all became teachers [*magistri*], who had scarcely been able to be disciples."[53] On Christ's promise, "Where I am, there also will my servant [*minister* in the Latin translation] be" (Jn 12:26), Augustine preaches, "Do not think that this is only about good bishops and clerics. You also in your own way minister to Christ, by living well, by giving alms, by preaching [*praedicando*] his name and doctrine in what you are able."[54]

One reason liturgical homilies were preserved was so that they could be read at future liturgies. Also, a bishop may have composed a homily, and asked one among his clergy to deliver the homily at a service for a particular reason, such as illness or absence. On such

---

which is part of the liturgy itself and is reserved to a priest or deacon, is preeminent; in the homily the mysteries of faith and the norms of Christian life are to be explained from the sacred text during the course of the liturgical year."

52 Jeffrey Wickes, "Between Liturgy and School: Reassessing the Performative Context of Ephrem's Madrāšê," *JECS* 26, no. 1 (2018): 25–51.

53 Ambrose, *Sermon against Auxentius* 34 (PL 16:1018A; de Romestin, 436 [alt.]).

54 Augustine, *Homilies on the Gospel of John* 51.13 (CCL 36, 445; FC 88, Rettig, 279 [alt.]).

occasions, who preached, the bishop who composed or the one who spoke the words? What if a secretary composed a homily and the bishop spoke the words? Augustine, for his part, sought for clergy to have model sermons available that could be memorized and delivered if the clergy did not themselves have the wisdom to compose homilies.[55]

To a certain extent, as early Christian preaching developed it was shaped by the ambient Gentile cultures. Christians today may be unaware of the ways in which early preachers might resemble their non-Christian counterparts in oratory. For example, Dio of Prusa, a rhetor and philosopher who died c. 120, and John, the Bishop of Constantinople who died in 407, are each nicknamed "Chrysostom" ("Golden Mouth"). Social emphases on the pursuit of wisdom and public speech provided the setting for a Christian molding of what it means to be a preacher.[56] Early Christians, nonetheless, never forgot that the first preachers were fishermen, not classical philosophers. Gregory of Nazianzus, in eloquent Greek style, claims that he speaks like a fisherman, not like Aristotle.[57] Gregory and so many other prominent bishops, who would be considered elites in society, did have excellent philosophical and rhetorical training to communicate the faith of fishermen. When Ambrose wanted to write a book on the offices of the Church, he explicitly imitated Cicero's *On Offices* for his own work of the same

55 Cf. Augustine, *On Christian Teaching* 4.29.63. Augustine's only caveat in this situation was that no deception should occur.

56 Two important studies are Peter Brown, *Power and Persuasion in Late Antiquity: Towards a Christian Empire* (Madison, WI: University of Wisconsin Press, 1992), and Averil Cameron, *Christianity and the Rhetoric of Empire: The Development of Christian Discourse* (Berkeley and Los Angeles: University of California Press, 1991).

57 Gregory of Nazianzus, *or.* 23.12 (SC 270, 304). For a similar example in the Latin West, see Leo the Great, *ep.* 164.2, to Leo Augustus: "When he [the Lord Jesus Christ] was about to call all nations to the light of faith, he did not choose those who were to serve in preaching the Gospel from philosophers and orators, but selected those who were to make him known from the lowly and from fishermen. Otherwise, heavenly doctrine, which was filled with power, might seem to require the help of words" (PL 54:1149B; Hunt, 258 [alt.]).

title.[58] Fourth and fifth-century Christian treatments of the bishop or priest emphasized, in varying ways, the duty to preach, its difficulty, its salvific importance, and its role in leading others to the deified life modeled by the preacher.[59] As Paul Kolbet has amply demonstrated, Augustine adapts the classical practice of "psychagogy," guiding the soul through words for healing and elevation, in his preaching.[60]

In order to appreciate how it is the *life* of the preacher that has a fundamental role in preaching, we can, by comparison, briefly consider a few models from the Greek and Roman cultures outside of Judaism and Christianity. Doing so helps us see how widespread was the ideal of having a speaker whose character supported his words. Also, we can see more clearly how Christianity claimed a more divine modeling than what was proposed by their non-Christian counterparts.

For many dialogues by Plato, the figure of Socrates is the model philosopher. Socrates lives and speaks in a humble, unassuming way to get others to know (and to know that they do not know) what life is about. Socrates can get behind the masks and the self-illusions that people have. Unlike his opponents, he speaks as he lives. Take the example of the *Apology* when Socrates defends his life against false accusation. There he proclaims, "I will give you powerful proofs of this, not mere words, but what you honor more—actions. And listen to what happened to me, that you may be convinced that I would

58 See *Ambrose: De Officiis*, edited with an introduction, translation, and commentary by Ivor J. Davidson, 2 vols. OECS (Oxford: Oxford University Press, 2002). For an adroit appraisal of how Ambrose uses non-Christian sources to serve his theology of the baptismal life, see J. Warren Smith, *Christian Grace and Pagan Virtue: The Theological Foundation of Ambrose's Ethics*, OSHT (New York: Oxford University Press, 2010).

59 For some examples that will be considered in this book, see Gregory of Nazianzus, *or.* 2, *On His Flight*; John Chrysostom, *On the Priesthood*; Augustine of Hippo, *s.* 46 *On Pastors*, and *On Christian Teaching*'s Book 4; Gregory the Great, *Book of Pastoral Rule* and *Homilies on Ezekiel.*

60 Paul R. Kolbet, *Augustine and the Cure of Souls: Revising a Classical Ideal* (Notre Dame, IN: University of Notre Dame Press, 2010). For an important early use of the term "psychagogy," see Plato, *Phaedrus* (261a).

never yield to any one, if that was wrong, through fear of death, but would die rather than yield."[61] Socrates himself became, for some of the first Christians, a pre-Christian witness to a life according to divine reason (*logos*).[62] His execution showed how his life and words had a truth uniting them. Others, on the other hand, have only empty words in rhetoric but do not have the character to support their words.

Like some non-Christian counterparts in late antiquity, Augustine and other highly trained Christian orators ridiculed rhetoric for being a matter of proud persuasion independent of truth, sought merely for money and fame.[63] Admittedly, you can find the unscrupulous among orators of antiquity (as you also can among early Christian priests). Yet as Christians continued an anti-rhetoric discourse, many ancients did place great importance on the speaker's character as a constitutive element of rhetoric. They recognized that a speaker cannot be persuasive if in his very speech his listeners think that his life does not correspond with his words.

Rhetoric, by Aristotle's accounting, consists of three principal factors: the character of the speaker (*ēthos*), moving the emotions of listeners (*pathos*), and the subject matter of the speech (*logos*).[64] About the first, Aristotle says "moral character (*ēthos*) constitutes the most effective means of proof."[65] Aristotle himself holds that this character is evinced through the speech itself, that is, it is not about the audience's former knowledge of the speaker's way of life.

61 Plato, *The Apology* 20 (32a) (LCL 36, 114; Fowler, 115).

62 For example, Justin Martyr, *Justin's Apology on Behalf of Christians* 5.4 and 46.3–5 and *Second Apology* 10.

63 For one of many examples, see *Confessions* 1.18.29. For an overview of Augustine on rhetoric, see Catherine Conybeare, "Augustine's Rhetoric in Theory and Practice," in *The Oxford Handbook of Rhetorical Studies*, ed. Michael J. MacDonald (Oxford: Oxford University Press, 2017), 301–11.

64 Aristotle, *Rhetoric* 1.2 (1856a).

65 Aristotle, *Rhetoric* 1.2.4 (1856a) (LCL 193, 16; Freese, 17).

Rhetorical training came to emphasize a more well-rounded virtuous life. Near the end of the first century A.D., Quintilian's formation program for orators says only the "good man" (*vir bonus*) may be an orator.[66] He propounds the virtuous life and favors a noble simplicity for the life of an orator:

> If excessive care for a landed estate, undue anxiety about family property, a passion for hunting, or days spent in the theatres take much time from study (and time spent on anything else is time lost to study!), what are we to think will be the effect of desire, avarice, and envy, rampant thoughts of which disturb even our slumbers and our dreams? Nothing is so preoccupied, so many-faceted, so mauled and torn apart by so many different emotions, as an evil mind.[67]

And yet Quintilian says what Augustine thought to be horrible: "However—hard as this seems when it is first stated—rational consideration may also lead a good man, in his defense of his cause, occasionally to want to cheat the judge of the truth."[68]

In different ways through the centuries, we see tensions between the philosopher and the sophist, a term that means "a wise one." The word was sometimes used ironically for a paid teacher of eloquence rather than for one who lives by and gives truth. These tensions provoked many attempts at a solution, not least in the era called the Second Sophistic during the first centuries of the

66 For Quintilian's reliance on the elder Cato in seeing the ideal orator as the *vir bonus*, see *Institutio Oratoria* 12.1. For studies, see Alan Brinton, "Quintilian, Plato, and the 'Vir Bonus,'" *Philosophy & Rhetoric* 16, no. 3 (1983): 167–83, and Michael Winterbottom, "Quintilian and the *vir bonus*," reprinted in *Papers on Quintilian and Ancient Declamation*, eds. Michael Winterbottom, Antonio Stramaglia, Francesca Romana Nocchi, and Giuseppe Russo (New York: Oxford University Press, 2019), 3–15.

67 Quintilian, *Institutio Oratoria* 12.1.6–7 (LCL 494, 5.200; Russell, 5.201).

68 Quintilian, *Institutio Oratoria* 12.1.36 (LCL 494, 5.214; Russell, 5.215). Some Fathers are aligned more with Quintilian than Augustine on this point. See Boniface Ramsey, OP, "Two Traditions on Lying and Deception in the Ancient Church," *Thom* 49, no. 4 (1985): 504–33.

Christian period.[69] Contemporary orators were compared to classical models and standards of eloquence and virtue. Representative of the Second Sophistic, Philostratus of Athens writes at the beginning of his early third-century *Lives of the Sophists*: "I have written for you in two Books an account of certain men who, though they pursued philosophy, ranked as sophists, and also of the sophists properly so called."[70] Philostratus thought that a "philosophical rhetoric" had developed that combined with eloquence the best of philosophy, without the philosophical tricks and snares.[71] Similarly, the late fourth-century Eunapius begins his *Lives of the Philosophers and Sophists* by extolling Xenophon, the great student of Socrates, as "unique among all philosophers in that he adorned philosophy not only with words but with deeds."[72] Observe that both Philostratus and Eunapius narrate lives here to introduce their cases for the bridging of what was held in classical tension. We should study the great early Christian preachers of the third through sixth centuries within the cultures in which they lived in order to appreciate the commonality with their non-Christian contemporaries and, lest we forget, their distinctiveness.[73]

69 For an overview of the Second Sophistic, both regarding its leading persons, with Philostratus's *Lives of the Philosophers* having prominence, and the variety of approaches and meanings in secondary scholarship, see Tim Whitmarsh, *The Second Sophistic*, Greece & Rome: New Surveys in the Classics, no. 35 (Oxford: Oxford University Press, 2005).

70 Philostratus, *The Lives of the Sophists*, preface (LCL 134, 2; Wright, 3).

71 For his introduction of "philosophical rhetoric," see *The Lives of the Sophists*, Book 1 (LCL 134, 4; Wright, 5).

72 Eunapius, *The Lives of the Philosophers and Sophists*, introduction (LCL 134, 342; Wright, 343).

73 See Aaron P. Johnson, "Early Christianity and the Classical Tradition," in *The Oxford Handbook of the Second Sophistic*, eds. Daniel S. Richter and William A. Johnson (Oxford: Oxford University Press, 2017), 625–38. With an emphasis on literary production, Averil Cameron writes, "Through *Lives*, Christian writers could present an image not only of the perfect Christian life but also of the life in imitation of Christ, the life that becomes an icon." See Cameron, *Christianity and the Rhetoric of Empire*, 143. For the Second Sophistic context of preaching in the first four Christian centuries, see chap. 1, "Philosophical preaching in the Roman world," in Jaclyn L. Maxwell, *Christianization and Communication in Late Antiquity: John Chrysostom and His Congregation in Antioch* (New York: Cambridge University Press, 2006), 11–41.

Most importantly, we should acknowledge that in their distinctive proclamation early Christians looked to the life of Jesus Christ. He is the incarnate Word who suffered, died, and rose for our salvation. They testified to him and wanted to communicate his life through their lives and words. Christ himself in the Gospel accounts draws attention to his preaching as the very reason for his mission. We can think of such examples as Mk 1:38 ("Let us go on to the nearby villages that I may preach there also. For this purpose have I come") and Jn 18:37 ("For this I was born and for this I came into the world, to testify to the truth"). Unlike those of his opponents, Jesus' words proceed perfectly from his life. Jesus tells his disciples to listen to the words, but not to follow the example of the scribes and the Pharisees: "For they preach but they do not practice" (Mt 23:3). In his life, death, and resurrection, Jesus does that to which all his words—in fact, all the words of Scripture—point (Rom 10:4, 2 Cor 1:20). He shows the way of not simply proclaiming the Scriptures, but having them fulfilled in our ears (Lk 4:21).

The first generations of disciples knew the importance of having a life conformed to the Word in order to live and speak well. James commands, "Be doers of the Word and not hearers only, deluding yourselves" (Jas 1:22). The First Letter of John exhorts, "Children, let us love not in word or speech but in deed and truth" (1 Jn 3:18). While the early Christians echo familiar wisdom sayings of antiquity, they express in a particular way what they experienced in their own day as the fullness of life and word coming together in Jesus. Granted that Jesus can be proclaimed "whether in pretense or in truth" (Phil 1:18), the great preference is for truth. Augustine, who argued against the Donatist insistence on the purity of their clergy for the efficaciousness of the sacraments, also held that the lives of preachers mattered enormously for the proclamation of the Gospel.[74]

One's life—more so than one's word—can show others how God has revealed a transformed life for us to live. Augustine confirms this, teaching that a preacher's "form of living is as an abundance of speaking" (*eius quasi copia dicendi forma vivendi*).[75] Looking back on the holy ones of preceding centuries, Gregory the Great preaches: "In the life of the saintly fathers, we ought to understand what is in the book of Sacred Scripture."[76] In an essay on women in patristic preaching, Agnes Cunningham concludes: "[T]he fathers who preached to and about women came to recognize 'mothers of the church' whom they were able to love and admire. In these women, they saw exemplified the simple truth that 'the most effective and sublime speech' is the life of the preacher. The greatest sermon is the proclamation of the earliest Christian kerygma: God became human so that human beings—women as well as men—might become divine."[77] After reviewing preaching as spiritual leadership in Origen, Augustine, and Gregory the Great, Brian Daley concludes, "In the homily, God himself acts through both his word and his preacher to transform us."[78]

74 Cf. Augustine, *On Christian Teaching* 4.27.60 (CCL 32, 164). See discussion in Chap. 4 below.

75 Augustine, *On Christian Teaching* 4.29.61 (CCL 32, 165).

76 Gregory the Great, *Homilies on Ezekiel* 1.10.38 (CCL 142, 163; Tomkinson, 205 [alt.]). Cf. Gregory's final words of his prologue to the *Dialogues*, which set forth the stories of the saints of Italy. Bronwen Neil recently observed about early Christian hagiography: "The life of the early Christian saint was by its very nature an allegory of Scripture." See Neil, "Hagiography," in *The Oxford Handbook of Early Christian Biblical Interpretation*, eds. Blowers and Martens, 303–14.

77 Agnes Cunningham, SSCM, "Women and Preaching in the Patristic Age," in *Preaching in the Patristic Age*, ed. Hunter, 53–72, at 70. Cunningham quotes Yngve Brilioth, *A Brief History of Preaching* (Philadelphia: Fortress Press, 1965), 51, and in a note's final sentence refers the reader to Hugo Rahner, SJ, *A Theology of Preaching* (New York: Herder & Herder, 1968).

78 Brian E. Daley, SJ, "Using the 'Art of Arts': Preaching as Spiritual Leadership in the Early Church," in *Preaching as Spiritual Leadership: Guiding the Faithful as Mystic and Mystagogue*, ed. Michael E. Connors, CSC (Chicago: Liturgy Training Publications, 2021), 34–50, at 50.

The centuries of the patristic era, in proclaiming the life of Christ, looked in a special way to the lives of biblical figures, those who eminently embodied the Word of God. Early preachers read and preached Scripture, and wanted to emulate the lives and writings of the prophets and apostles.[79] Scriptural models ceaselessly recur in early Christian preaching to show how word and life come together in the new life that shares in God's own nature. Early Christians referred to the proclamations recorded in Scripture, not as mere texts, but as voices of persons who witness to Christ in life and word. We hear the Word through their voices. Persons, not books, are the true Christian "classics" that communicate the Word, and they become exemplars for others' lives.[80] Ultimately, all the prophets and apostles proclaimed the crucified and risen Lord. This emphasis on the risen life differs considerably from the classical models of declamation held up by non-Christian figures, even if they have many commonalities, e.g., invoking assistance from above; holding persons in reverence over texts; employing the rhetorical devices of *prosopopoeia* (assuming the voices of persons for dramatic effect) or of *ekphrasis* (painting vivid word pictures of persons and things for an audience to "see"). By the power of the Holy Spirit, the great preachers put on the form of Christ's own

79 Peter Martens writes, "Holy texts went hand in hand with holy readers. As we peer more closely into early Christian exegetical cultures, we detect a mimetic relationship between texts and their readers. The goal of interpretation was brought into conformity with what was thought to be the animating goal of Scripture's authors: the communication of a message of salvation. As brokers of salvation, intermediaries who stood between the cryptic words of God and the people of God, interpreters fashioned themselves as agents who extended and clarified the original revelation for the benefit of new communities of faith. Yet interpretation was not only in service of salvation. It was also expressive of it, and thus, indicative of another symmetry between sacred text and sacred interpreter. Exegesis was conditioned by the interpreter's morality, doctrinal credentials, adherence to the precedents set by venerable (often apostolic) authorities, by a range of exegetical virtues, and by the dynamics of prayer and divine response." See Peter W. Martens, "Ideal Interpreters," in *The Oxford Handbook of Early Christian Biblical Interpretation*, eds. Blowers and Martens, 149–65, at 162.

80 Peter Brown writes that in late antiquity books were "to produce persons; any other function was considered vaguely ridiculous." See Peter Brown, "The Saint as Exemplar in Late Antiquity," *Representations* no. 2, Spring (1983): 1–25, at 1.

crucified and risen life left by the prophets and apostles, and their example helped fashion the lives of the people who listened to them, by the same Spirit.[81]

Ambrose of Milan, for instance, gives instruction to a newly elected bishop, expected to steer the ship of the Church by the rudder of faith. His counsel illustrates the reliance on scriptural models to preach Christ himself.[82] The Church, tossed about by the waves of the sea in the world's storms, sails smoothly on the rivers that have "lifted up their voice" (Ps 93:3). "These are the rivers," says Ambrose, "that flow from the belly of the one who has drunk from Christ and who has received from the Spirit of God (cf. Jn 7:38). Therefore, these rivers, since they redound with spiritual grace, lift up their voice." Ambrose continues with the observation that a stream runs through the holy ones as a torrent (cf. Is 66:12), and gives joy to the soul (cf. Ps 45:5): "And whoever has received from this river, just as John the Evangelist, or just as Peter and Paul, lifts up his voice. For just as the apostles have diffused the voice of the Gospel's preaching in a melodious proclamation even until the ends of the world, so also does that one who begins to preach the Lord Jesus." Ambrose applies this to his letter's recipient: "Therefore, drink from Christ, so that your sound may also go forth."[83]

As we see in Ambrose's counsel, early preachers learned from biblical models how to receive and proclaim Christ. The whole Bible proclaims Jesus Christ, the Son of God through whom all things were made, who was born of the Virgin Mary among the people

81 Peter Gemeinhardt, "Teaching the Faith in Early Christianity: Divine and Human Agency," *VC* 74, no. 2 (2020): 129–64. Gemeinhardt concludes, "Late antique writers knew that, because divine agency is involved, human agency is at the same time rendered possible *and* limited" (163).

82 *Ep.* 2, Ambrose to Constantius of Claterna (PL 16:879A–888A; in "From a letter by Saint Ambrose, bishop," Office of Readings, December 7, *The Liturgy of the Hours*, ICEL, vol. 1, 1218–19). For a study that includes this letter, see Rita Lizzi, "Ambrose's Contemporaries and the Christianization of Northern Italy," *JRS* 80 (1990): 156–73, especially 159–60 and 166.

83 *Ep.* 2.2 (PL 16:879C–880A; ICEL [alt.], 1218–19).

that God elected. Jesus preached, suffered, died, and rose so that what he is by nature, we may become by grace. That is the Gospel for all nations, the mystery of "Christ in you" (Col 1:27) proclaimed throughout the Scriptures. Because the whole Bible is about Christ, the early preachers found exemplars in the Old Testament, such as in Abraham, Moses, David (as the Psalms are ceaselessly cited in Christological fulfillment), Isaiah, Jeremiah, Ezekiel, and Jonah. In a study on the virtue of magnanimity, for example, Warren Smith writes that Ambrose "was following the New Testament convention pioneered by Paul of appealing to the faith of Israel's patriarchs as models for Christian faithful living."[84]

From the New Testament, John, Peter, and Paul, the three chosen in Ambrose's counsel to a new bishop, stand out among Christ's disciples as exemplars for preachers of the first Christian centuries. Although writers such as Origen, Eusebius of Caesarea, and Jerome did pay keen attention to questions similar to recent interests regarding historicity, many early homilies present these New Testament saints without doubts about the correspondence between their literary representations in the New Testament and extra-biblical traditions and their historical identities.[85]

For many early Christian preachers, John is the brother of James, the beloved disciple among the Twelve, the Evangelist and author of three letters and the Book of Revelation, who was not martyred, but lived to be an old man.[86] According to a tradition recorded by Jerome, John in his old age used to preach over and

84 J. Warren Smith, *Ambrose, Augustine, and the Pursuit of Greatness* (Cambridge: Cambridge University Press, 2020), 110.

85 Following Epiphanius and Philaster, Augustine says the Alogi (the Wordless ones) reject John's Gospel and Apocalypse, and they do not think that these are John's authentic writings. See Augustine, *On Heresies* 30.

86 Eusebius records that in the second-century Papias differentiates John the presbyter from John the apostle. See Eusebius, *Ecclesiastical History* 3.39.

over again the words he wrote in his first letter, "Little children, love one another."[87]

Peter, Andrew's brother, is the apostle listed first among the Twelve, and he received a unique authority among the early brethren. Peter is believed to have been the Bishop of Antioch before becoming the Bishop of Rome, where he was martyred. According to a Syriac tradition, Peter declares at his martyrdom, "[I]f I am crucified with my head downward, then I will remember his sufferings for my sake. My mouth and my eyes will kiss the places of the nails with which the feet of the body of God the Word were crucified."[88] In addition to the portrayal of Peter that we find in the four Gospel accounts, the Acts of the Apostles, and some of Paul's letters, tradition identifies him as the author of two canonical epistles.

Paul is the "vessel of election" (Acts 9:15) who becomes the focus of the narrative of Acts and who authored many epistles (including the Letter to the Hebrews according to many early preachers), and whose writings are explicitly ranked among the Scriptures by Scripture itself in 2 Pt 3:15–16. He was martyred in Rome. In the second century, many traditions circulated about Paul's life and preaching, as was the case for John and Peter, in a broad range of communities of varying doctrine and practice. At the beginning of the third century, Tertullian rejected the apocryphal account of Paul's "allowing women to teach and baptize" (*licentiam mulierum docendi*

87 "The blessed John the Evangelist lived in Ephesus until extreme old age. His disciples could barely carry him to church, and he could not muster the voice to speak many words. During individual gatherings he usually said nothing but, 'Little children, love one another.' The disciples and brothers in attendance, annoyed because they always heard the same words, finally said, 'Teacher, why do you always say this?' He replied with a line worthy of John, 'Because it is the Lord's commandment and if it alone is kept, it is sufficient.'" See Jerome, *Commentary on Galatians*, translated by Andrew Cain, FC 121 (Washington, DC: The Catholic University of America Press, 2010), 260 (from Book 3, on Gal 6:10).

88 History of Shimeon Kepha the Chief of the Apostles, cap. 34, in *The Ancient Martyrdom Accounts of Peter and Paul*, translated with an introduction and notes by David L. Eastman, SBL 39 (Atlanta: SBL Press, 2015), 115. For comments on this passage, see David L. Eastman, *The Many Deaths of Peter and Paul*, OECS (Oxford: Oxford University Press, 2019), 8.

tinguendique).[89] In the late fourth century, among many Fathers of the Church, most famously John Chrysostom, an intense devotion to Paul as the preeminent model of Christ's life and preaching arose.

Paul Blowers writes, "For the early churches, Christian morality was neither merely dictated by experts nor reduced to an exclusive, exhaustive list of behavioral axioms. Rather, it was inculcated over the course of time as believers were admonished to imitate paragons of moral excellence."[90] By keeping in mind these three holy paragons of John, Peter, and Paul, we will be better able to consider the Word in the flesh of patristic preachers in their own exemplarity for our studies on the inseparable themes of incarnation, deification, and proclamation. Following upon the New Testament witness lived out in the subsequent centuries of the early Church, we too can be blessed to repeat the apostolic awareness that "we hold this treasure in earthen vessels" (2 Cor 4:7).[91] We go back to patristic preachers and their words to continue the apostolic faith.[92]

89 Tertullian, *On Baptism* 17 (Evans, 36–37).

90 Blowers, *Moral Formation and the Virtuous Life*, 4.

91 This book has been assisted by the example of Brian E. Daley. In an interview, he was asked what his favorite Scripture passage was and why. He replied: "I suppose I would have to pick 2 Cor 4:7–12, where St. Paul speaks of the 'earthen vessels' in which we carry the treasure of the Gospel we preach. As we go on with our ministry, most of us come to discover both our own fragility and inadequacy, and also the transforming effect on even our words and our work of "the life of Jesus" within us. We witness to the Gospel as much by our weaknesses as by our teaching." See interview with Sean Salai, SJ, "Life after Richard McBrien: Q&A with Father Brian E. Daley, SJ," January 28, 2015, America magazine, https://www.americamagazine.org/content/all-things/life-after-richard-mcbrien-qa-father-brian-daley-sj accessed on November 19, 2019.

92 In his approach to *ressourcement*, Yves Congar enlists the support of Pope Pius XII's *Humani Generis* (1950), no. 21: "Theologians ceaselessly ought to go back to the sources of divine revelation. By studying the sources, the sacred sciences keep growing fresher, while speculation that neglects to go all the way back to the study of the deposit of revealed faith becomes sterile, as experience shows us" (*AAS* 42 [1950]), p. 568). See Yves Congar, OP, *True and False Reform*, translated by Paul Philibert, OP (Collegeville, MN: Liturgical Press, 2011), 39–40n35. "The way forward in Christian theology is often seen, paradoxically," Brian Daley writes, "as beginning in 'a return to the sources.' This is not just a sentimental exercise in antiquarianism. It is based on the realization that our faith and our life as a Church are rooted in our collective memory—that it is by reflecting on our history as a people that we discover the presence of our God." See Brian E. Daley, SJ, Foreword to Michel Fédou, SJ, *The Fathers of the Church in Christian Theology*, translated by Peggy Manning Meyer (Washington, DC: The Catholic University of America Press, 2019), xi.

UNITING THE AUDIENCES OF THIS BOOK

I have written this book primarily for hearers and preachers of the Word, all those committed to evangelization and building up the Church. Secondarily, I offer it for all students of early Christian theology and practices. I do so as a Catholic priest in the Order of Preachers, the Dominicans, and as a theologian who specializes in early Christian (and Thomistic) studies. I love patristic preaching, but this book is more than a statement of personal passion. I think it is needed, first for Christian contemplation and ministry and then for the academy's study of early Christianity. In my choice to speak primarily to an audience focused on the Church's ongoing contemplation and ministry, my concern is for the people who deserve to receive the Word through the lives and speech of preachers and all those in ministry. I also have a concern that the academy's use of the lives and texts from the early Christian era do not resemble the dissection of what is dead. Rather, our academic study is to be helpful for ourselves and for others to praise the Word expressed in definite lives and words through the ages. "Indeed," as Hebrews tells us in enfleshment imagery, "the Word of God is living and effective, sharper than any two-edged sword, penetrating even between soul and spirits, joints and marrow, and able to discern reflections and thoughts of the heart" (Heb 4:12).

Similarly, Carol Harrison expresses her concern regarding the academy's study of early sermons, using the example of how we treat a Picasso self-portrait. "Like the modern tendency to hang the paintings of great artists in splendid isolation on the wall of a gallery," writes Harrison, "we tend all too readily to separate sermons out from their liturgical context and treat them as free-standing texts." Harrison continues, "As a result, we can easily overlook the fact that they were always, by definition, part of an act of worship: they were delivered in a physical building; from a particular position; at a specific point in the service; framed by set readings from Scripture; by prayers and appointed psalms; and were part of a multi-sensory encounter with God which involved sight, smell, taste and touch as well as hearing."[93]

Since the Second Vatican Council, the Roman magisterium has repeatedly recommended the Fathers as a resource for the ministry and life of priests, especially with regard to scriptural interpretation and preaching.[94] Commenting on a passage from Pope Benedict XVI's *Verbum Domini* in a lecture, Daniel Cardinal DiNardo observed:

> At the heart of the sacramentality of the word is the mystery of the Incarnation, the "Word Made Flesh." The reality of the mystery is in the flesh of the Word, that through words and deeds, we can come to light, to understanding, and to transformation. Thus Christ is present and speaks to us in the proclamation of the Word. As the unpacking of that word, preaching participates performatively in this "sacramentum." This is the power of patristic preaching as it is consciously aware of being drawn to the Word of God and admonishing and instructing God's people to be transformed. The outer word humbly begs the Word that works within to bring illumination and transformation.[95]

93 Carol Harrison, "Worship as the Beginning and End of Preaching," in *Praedicatio Patrum: Studies on Preaching in Late Antique North Africa*, eds. Gert Partoens, Anthony Dupont, and Shari Boodts, IPM 75 (Turnhout: Brepols, 2017), 201–17, at 202.

94 *Instruction on the Study of the Fathers of the Church in the Formation of Priests*, Congregation for Catholic Education, November 10, 1989; *Directory for the Ministry and Life of Priests*, New Edition, Congregation for Clergy, February 11, 2013, no. 63; *Homiletic Directory*, Congregation for Divine Worship and the Discipline of the Sacraments, June 29, 2014, nos. 4, 25, and 32. Here is one example, taken from the *Homiletic Directory*, no. 25: "Familiarity with the writings of the Fathers can greatly aid the homilist in discovering the spiritual meaning of Scripture. It is from the Fathers' preaching that we learn how profound is the unity between Old Testament and New. From them we can learn to detect innumerable figures and patterns of the Paschal Mystery that are present in the world from the dawn of creation and that further unfold throughout the history of Israel that culminates in Jesus Christ. It is from the Fathers that we learn that virtually every word of the inspired Scriptures can yield unexpected and unfathomable riches when pondered in the heart of the Church's life and prayer. It is from the Fathers that we learn how intimately connected is the mystery of the biblical Word to the mystery of the sacramental celebration."

95 Daniel Cardinal DiNardo, Archbishop of Galveston–Houston, "Preaching with the Fathers of the Church," the Annual Carl J. Peter Lecture, January 13, 2013, North American College, Rome, www.pnac.org/the-seminary/the-carl-j-peter-lecture/cardinal-dinardos-lecture/,

Recognizing this ongoing sacramental mystery of preaching has resonance far beyond a Catholic seminary.

In fact, when expressing the essence of Christian life and ministry, many Christians of diverse traditions and states of life have turned to the preaching of the early Church. For example, in the preface to his proposed project of translating Chrysostom's homilies into French, John Calvin writes: "That I share a common concern with Chrysostom is unquestionably more than adequate justification for me, because I am just imparting to ordinary people what he wrote specifically for ordinary people."[96] Christian leaders and the lay faithful from generation to generation turn to the Fathers of the Church not for something esoteric or merely academic, but for the basic insights of the faith that will assist them, their help to others in the Church, and those they want to draw into the Church. We have seen an increasing interest in patristic preaching on the part of Anglican, Catholic, Evangelical, Lutheran, Methodist, Orthodox, Reformed and many other Christian communities. Walter Burghardt, a Jesuit theologian who admirably sought to unite patristic studies with Christian preaching, comments on what amazed him about patristic preaching:

> The Fathers rarely divorced their search for God's truth from the living people for whom God spoke his truth. For them, theology was not an arcane discipline, done up ivory towers or behind ivied walls. Their theology was itself a spirituality, to be communicated in vibrant speech to pulsing people. . . . The Fathers saw themselves as men of the Bible; they were primarily interpreters of the word.[97]

---

accessed on June 27, 2021. Cf. Pope Benedict XVI, *Verbum Domini*, Post-Synodal Apostolic Exhortation on the Word of God in the Life and Mission of the Church, no. 56. Also, see *Verbum Domini*, no. 37.

96 Quotation translated in Rylaarsdam, *John Chrysostom on Divine Pedagogy*, 2.

97 Walter J. Burghardt, SJ, *Preaching: The Art and the Craft* (Mahwah, NJ: Paulist Press, 1987), 195.

God sent these great preachers of the early Church not to some ideal Christian communities that never existed, but to real ones burdened with pain. Those preachers were weak sinners themselves, but God called them and transformed them to share in his own nature. We need deified preachers and hearers today. Many Christian communities are ill; some are collapsing. Comparing the ministry of the Word to a physician's healing work, John Chrysostom extols the unique power of preaching:

> When all is said and done, there is only one means and only method of treatment available, and that is teaching by word of mouth. That is the best instrument, the best diet, and the best climate. It takes the place of medicine and cautery. When we need to cauterize or cut, we must use this. Without it all else is useless.[98]

Chrysostom's stress on preaching may surprise us today. That is even more reason to go back to early Christian sources to learn what preaching, or even human life, means. Gregory of Nyssa preaches: "the human voice was fashioned for one reason alone—to be the threshold through which the sentiments of the heart, inspired by the Holy Spirit, might be translated clearly in the Word itself."[99] Do we understand that our talking is to be either with God or about God?[100] After quoting "In speaking much you will not escape

98 John Chrysostom, *On the Priesthood* 4.3 (SC 272, 144; Neville, 115). For the late antique use of "healing" in medicine, philosophy, and therapy for the soul, and John's use at the end of his life and how it illustrates his entire ministry's concern, see Wendy Mayer, "The Persistence in Late Antiquity of Medico-Philosophical Psychic Therapy," *JLA* 8, no. 2 (2015): 337–51.

99 Gregory of Nyssa, *Homily 7 on the Song of Songs*, on Sg 4:4, translated in Cameron, *Christianity and the Rhetoric of Empire*, 15. For a different translation of this passage, with the facing Greek text, see *Gregory of Nyssa: Homilies on the Song of Songs*, translated with an introduction and notes by Richard A Norris, Jr., WGRW 13 (Atlanta: Society of Biblical Literature, 2012), 244–47.

100 The founder of the Order of Preachers, Dominic de Guzman, is said to have spoken only with God or about God, which became the model for his preachers; e.g., Testimony of William of Monferrato (Aug. 7, 1233), the Testimony of John of Spain (Aug. 10, 1233), the Testimony of Paul of Venice (Aug. 16, 1233), and Primitive Constitutions of the Order

sin" (Prv 10:19) when he concludes his *On the Trinity*, Augustine exclaimed to God, "O would that I were to speak only by preaching your Word and by praising you!"[101] We can marvel and apply what we hear from early preachers for the needs of the Church today.[102] Encouraged by how Thomas Aquinas in the Order of Preachers collected together and arranged preaching and commentary from the holy doctors for the *Catena Aurea*, the Golden Chain on the four Gospel accounts that continues to be of service for preaching over seven centuries later, I want this book to show how the lives and words of these early teachers of the faith can guide Christian living and ministry in our own times.[103]

Moreover, I offer this book not only to those in the work of evangelization and building up the Church, but also to students of early Christianity in the academy. Interest in patristic preaching naturally follows upon the burgeoning scholarly attention to patristic exegesis; much early Christian work on the Bible served the purpose of communicating to others the "hidden treasure" in the scriptural field.[104] Preaching occupies an enormous place in our access to the early Church. Carol Harrison begins her astutely original book on listening in the early Church with this observation:

---

of Preachers II, 31 in *Early Dominicans: Selected Writings*, translated by Simon Tugwell, CWS (New York: Paulist Press, 1982), 70, 75, 82, and 467.

101 *On the Trinity* 15.28.51 (CCL 50A, 534; McKenna, 524 [alt.]).

102 For a seven-fold application to a post-Christendom context, see Craig A. Satterlee, "Patristic Principles for Post-Christendom Preaching," *Liturgy* 25, no. 4 (2010): 18–29.

103 The Congregation for Divine Worship's *Homiletic Directory*, no. 25 says, "The *Catena Aurea* of St. Thomas Aquinas remains a splendid tool for accessing the riches of the Fathers." For a proposal to access the riches of the Fathers through Aquinas for the theological academy, see Andrew Hofer, OP, "Conclusion: Reading Thomas Aquinas and the Greek Fathers Together for the Renewal of Theology," in *Thomas Aquinas and the Greek Fathers*, eds. Dauphinais, Hofer, and Nutt, 303–30.

104 For a recent book on how patristic interpreters shared a "sacramental" vision of Christ's real presence in the Old Testament, see Hans Boersma, *Scripture as Real Presence: Sacramental Exegesis in the Early Church* (Grand Rapids, MI: Baker Academic, 2017). For an earlier study formative in my life, see Jody L. Vaccaro, "Digging for Buried Treasure: Origen's Spiritual Interpretation of Scripture," *Com* 25, no. 4 (1998): 757–75.

> It would not be a wild overestimate to suggest that around two-thirds of the early Christian texts which we now read were originally spoken, rather than written, and were intended for hearers, rather than readers. They sounded, resonated, and impressed themselves upon the mind and memory through the ear rather than the eye. A significant part of this literature consists of sermons, which were often delivered *ex tempore* and recorded by a secretary, perhaps for later revision.[105]

Those committed to the academic discipline of early Christian studies constantly work with the extant records of early preachers. Can we listen to those voices for the needs in the theological academy today? Lewis Ayres counsels, "When we listen to the Patristic Church, we must certainly hear voices that are every bit as philosophically complex as those that modernity offers, but many of those same Patristic voices struggle not only to defend, but to call us back to the direct language of the faith and to rest there. This is a voice that the modern theological conversation desperately needs to hear."[106] This book's chapters give pertinent references to scholarship on individual preachers and their communities for academic interest. Much work remains to be done.

Wendy Mayer is one recent scholar whose groundbreaking research opens up new lines of inquiry. In a recent essay on early Christian biblical interpretation, Mayer recognizes that new approaches "call us to embark on a complete reframing of what we think interpreting the Bible means in the context of preaching/catechesis." She finds that the oral and performative communication of Scripture was aimed at "effecting the transformation of the

105 Carol Harrison, *The Art of Listening in the Early Church* (Oxford: Oxford University Press, 2013), 1.

106 Lewis Ayres, "Seven Theses on Dogmatics and Patristics in Catholic Theology," *MoTh* (2022): 38, no. 1 (2022): 36–62, at 62. Ayres concludes on that page: "We show the beauty of the Christian tradition not only by apologetic ahistorical arguments, but by showing the mystery of the tradition, its warts and beauty, through exhibiting its explanatory power, its slow development, and the people that it has transformed." I want this book to contribute toward Ayres's goal.

whole human person." She demonstrates this is by showing how preachers like Origen, Augustine, and Chrysostom communicate a "holistic way of looking at biblical interpretation." That way "calls us to extend our sights beyond the liturgical context to consider the way in which the Christian person was transformed (or not) through hearing the truths of Scripture communicated in spiritual instruction—that is, to view the life of the Christian person itself as embodied biblical interpretation."[107] Mayer has elsewhere observed that "the study of early Christian homiletics, still in its infancy, has much to yield the sensitive investigator as it is explored in more scientific and novel ways in the years to come."[108] It is to be lamented, nevertheless, that the work of such fine scholars as Mayer in the areas of early Christian exegesis, theology, and preaching has not yet made its influence felt on Christian theologians as a whole—let alone those who may lay claim to the power of patristic preaching for preaching and evangelization today.[109]

In short, this book offered for Christian ministry today and studies of early Christian theology and practice interweaves study of the incarnation, deification through the virtues, and proclamation through a focus on essential themes in seven early Christian preachers. By the mercy of God, we can behold the breathtaking beauty of the mystery of the Word expressed in the frailty of human life. We can recapture the early Christian sense of the Word dwelling within our lives. Listen to the second-century *Epistle of Barnabas*:

107 Wendy Mayer, "Catecheses and Homilies," in *The Oxford Handbook of Early Christian Biblical Interpretation*, ed. Paul Blowers and Peter Martens (Oxford: Oxford University Press, 2019), 242–54, at 251.

108 Wendy Mayer, "Homiletics," *The Oxford Handbook of Early Christian Studies*, ed. Susan Ashbook Harvey and David G. Hunter (Oxford: Oxford, 2006), 565–83, at 579.

109 Matthew Levering comments, "[D]espite the impressive historical gains contributed by contemporary patristics scholarship, it appears that today's generation of Catholic and Protestant theologians and biblical scholars has less knowledge of patristic theology and exegesis than preceding generations." See Matthew Levering, "Retrievals in Contemporary Theology," in *The Oxford Handbook of Early Christian Biblical Interpretation*, eds. Blowers and Martens, 723–40.

> God truly dwells in our dwelling-place—that is, in us. How? The word of his faith, the call of his promise, the wisdom of his righteous decrees, the commandments of his teaching, he himself prophesying in us, he himself dwelling in us. . . . For the one who longs to be saved looks not to the man but to the One who dwells and speaks in him.[110]

The beneficiaries of the Word's action in these early preachers include us today in a Church that is hurting. We need silence to be able to hear that Word. To understand the Word's action in our flesh better, we begin in Chapter 1 to hear from Origen that the Word was made flesh—and we come to marvel at our goal of sharing in the Word's own holiness.

110 *Epistle of Barnabas* 16.10, in *The Apostolic Fathers: Greek Texts and English Translations*, ed. and trans. J. B. Lightfoot and J. R. Harmer, rev. and updated, Michael W. Holmes (Grand Rapids, MI: Baker, 1999), 319. Cf. Ignatius of Antioch, *Letter to the Ephesians* 15.3. For a use of the passage from *Barnabas* to consider that the one who converts Justin Martyr represents Christ for Justin, see my "The Old Man as Christ in Justin's *Dialogue with Trypho*," *VC* 57, no. 1 (2003): 1–21.

CHAPTER 1

ORIGEN OF ALEXANDRIA

The Word in Our Flesh for Our Holiness

The Word made flesh places his holiness in us. In his exhortation on the baptismal life, Peter reminds his listeners of God's call in Leviticus: "as he who called you is holy, be holy yourselves in every aspect of your conduct, for it is written, 'Be holy because I am holy'" (1 Pt 1:16; cf. Lv 11:44 and 19:2). The incarnation fulfills the Law in making effective what God commands: holiness in us. By the grace of God, we can repent of our sins and become like him in praise.

In 2011, when concluding a catechetical series on the saints, Pope Benedict XVI offered this meditation on Christian holiness: "In Christ, the living God made himself close, visible, audible and tangible so that each one might draw from his fullness of grace and truth (cf. Jn 1:14–16)." Benedict continues:

> Therefore, the whole of Christian life knows one supreme law, which St Paul expresses in a formula that recurs in all his holy writings: in Jesus Christ. Holiness, the fullness of Christian life, does not consist in carrying out extraordinary enterprises but in being united with Christ, in living his mysteries, in making

> our own his example, his thoughts, his behavior. The measure of holiness stems from the stature that Christ achieves in us, in as much as with the power of the Holy Spirit, we model our whole life on his.[1]

From Benedict XVI's articulation of holiness in Christ Jesus, we enter our study of incarnation, deification, and proclamation with the book's only featured preacher not called a saint in Christian tradition: Origen of Alexandria (d. 253/4).

The Word in Origen's Flesh for Us

Among early Christian preachers, Origen holds a prominent place. Less than three months after signing *Sacramentum Caritatis*, wherein we are told that, "[g]iven the importance of the word of God, the quality of homilies needs to be improved," Benedict XVI devoted two Wednesday general audiences to catechesis on this "true 'maestro.'"[2] On April 25, 2007, in reviewing aspects of Origen's life and his theological achievement, Benedict XVI proposed that Origen offers "a perfect symbiosis between theology and exegesis."[3] Benedict highlighted Origen's careful reading of Scripture, textual work in his *Hexapla* (a "sixfold" edition of the Old Testament, which at times had even more than six comparative texts in columns), and systematic commentaries. He then spoke of the Alexandrian doctor's preaching. "[E]ven before his ordination to the priesthood,"

1 Benedict XVI, Wednesday General Audience on Holiness, April 13, 2011. http://www.vatican.va/content/benedict-xvi/en/audiences/2011/documents/hf_ben-xvi_aud_20110413.html. Accessed April 24, 2020. Each chapter begins with a statement on the chapter's biblical theme in patristic preaching from a recent Christian preacher. By doing so, it links a recent Christian witness to our early Christian exploration, without a claim of identity in approach.

2 Pope Benedict XVI, general audience in St. Peter's Square, April 25, 2007. Translation found in "Origen: life and work," *L'Osservatore Romano*, Weekly Edition in English, May 2, 2007, p. 12, and *Sacramentum Caritatis* no. 46.

3 Pope Benedict XVI, general audience, April 25, 2007.

he said, "Origen was deeply dedicated to preaching the Bible and adapted himself to a varied public. In any case, the teacher can also be perceived in his *Homilies*, wholly dedicated as he was to the systematic interpretation of the passage under examination, which he analyzed step by step in the sequence of the verses."[4] In the following week's address, Benedict XVI continued his reflection on Origen, this time focusing on Origen's doctrine on prayer and the Church. For the latter, he selected Origen's ninth homily on Leviticus, and particularly his teaching on the priestly holiness of all the faithful contained therein.[5] Since Origen has been given as a model, we can return to see what his life and preaching were like.

Eusebius provides us with many details of Origen's life and instruction, which take up much of his *Ecclesiastical History*'s Book 6.[6] Origen came from an ardent Christian family in Alexandria. His father Leonides knew that the divine Spirit dwelt within his son, who showed a gift in wanting to know the deep meaning of Scripture. When a persecution broke out and his father was captured, Origen's mother hid the boy's clothes so that he would not leave home and join his father. Instead, Origen wrote his imprisoned father this message: "Take care not to change your thinking on account of us."[7] After his father's martyrdom, Origen, in his eighteenth year, presided over catechesis and attracted many disciples by his love of Scripture and his philosophical life of asceticism. In his excessive zeal, Origen went so far as to castrate himself, Eusebius tells us.[8] On this account, according to Eusebius's telling, Origen's

4 Pope Benedict XVI, general audience, April 25, 2007.

5 Pope Benedict XVI, general audience, May 2, 2007. Translation found in *L'Osservatore Romano*, Weekly Edition in English, May 9, 2007, p. 3.

6 For a comparison with Porphyry's *bios* of Plotinus, see Arthur P. Urbano, chap. 3, "Plotinus and Origen: Biography and the Renewal of Philosophy," *The Philosophical Life: Biography and the Crafting of Intellectual Identity in Late Antiquity*, PMS 21 (Washington, DC: The Catholic University of America Press, 2013), 125–62.

7 Eusebius, *Ecclesiastical History* 6.2 (EW 2.2, Schwartz, 520; Williamson, 240 [alt.]).

8 Eusebius, *Ecclesiastical History* 6.8.

bishop, Demetrius of Alexandria, who had admired Origen's faith and bade him to be even more devoted to instruction, later turned against him. Origen had gone to live in Palestinian Caesarea, and he was ordained with the approval of the Bishops of Caesarea and Jerusalem—but not the approval of the bishop of his home diocese, Alexandria.[9] Eusebius thus sees the reason for opposition to Origen not in his teaching, but because of his imprudent youthful act that took too literally the Savior's words about those who make themselves "eunuchs for the sake of the kingdom of heaven" (Mt 19:12). After much preaching, writing commentaries, teaching students, and assisting bishops, Origen was tortured in the imperial persecution. He had written an *Exhortation to Martyrdom*, and he was prepared to practice what he preached.[10] Everybody, so it seemed, knew that he was willing to die for the faith, and his captors did not want to make him a martyr. They therefore tortured him without killing him. After the persecution lifted, Origen died either in 253 or 254.

Known as the Church's most influential exegete, loved and imitated or hated and excoriated, Origen should be ranked as nothing less than pre-Nicene Christianity's most significant preacher after the apostolic era. While some may regard preaching and teaching as very different exercises, Origen considered himself as a *didaskalos* or teacher in preaching. No term particularly designated the preacher in his day.[11] With an unparalleled knowledge of the Sacred

9 Eusebius, *Ecclesiastical History* 6.8.

10 For a translation of this protreptic, which is meant for all called to pick up their cross and follow Jesus, see *Origen*, translation and introduction by Rowan A. Greer, preface by Hans Urs von Balthasar, CWS (New York: Paulist Press, 1979), 41–79.

11 Pierre Nautin, *Origène: Homélies sur Jérémie*, vol. 1 (Homilies 1–11) SC 232 (Paris: Éditions du Cerf, 1976), 152. Nautin's treatment of "Origène Prédicateur," 100–91, offers an important discussion. Although not using Nautin's work, Werner Schütz also has a useful study of the sermon in Origen's writings. See his *Der christliche Gottesdienst bei Origenes*, CTM (Stuttgart: Calwer Verlag, 1984), 82–119. In this section, Schütz treats four areas: the nature and function of the sermon; scriptural interpretation in the sermon; the role of the listeners in the sermon; and the sermon and rhetoric.

Scriptures, Origen the consummate teacher preached several hundred homilies because of his great desire for what he considered to be the goal of preaching: the edification of the Church. Eusebius reports that only after Origen turned sixty did he feel that his powers were sufficient to allow stenographers to record his talks (*dialexeis*).[12] Therefore, the homilies we have are the fruit of decades of intensive labor over Scripture from this most brilliant mind.

Many specialists on the history of preaching and on Origen offer profuse praise. Thomas Carroll calls Origen "the first and foremost of all Christian homilists."[13] David Dunn-Wilson remarks, "Above all else, Origen is the prince of exegetical preachers."[14] William Rusch regards Origen as certainly "one of the most impressive homilists in the history of the church."[15] Henri de Lubac speaks of Origen the preacher in these terms: "At all times, in all places, he is the Doctor, the man of the Church, attentive to the present situation, concerned about the duties and needs of souls."[16] Others, however, give a more guarded assessment of Origen's preaching. For example, Joseph Trigg notes Origen's complaint that his congregation's members were not listening or not wanting to hear what he had to say.[17] Trigg comments, "Although his thoughtful homilies pointedly address moral and spiritual concerns, Origen evidently

12 Eusebius of Caesarea, *Ecclesiastical History* 6.36.1 (EW 2.2, Schwartz, 590). See Henri Crouzel, *Origen: The Life and Thought of the First Great Theologian*, translated by A. S. Worrall (San Francisco: Harper & Row, 1989), 29, where he discusses interpretations of what this means.

13 Thomas K. Carroll, *Preaching the Word*, Message of the Fathers of the Church 11 (Wilmington, DE, Michael Glazier, Inc., 1984), 42.

14 David Dunn-Wilson, *A Mirror for the Church: Preaching in the First Five Centuries* (Grand Rapids, MI: Eerdmans, 2005), 37.

15 William G. Rusch, "Preaching" in *The Westminster Handbook to Origen*, ed. John Anthony McGuckin (Louisville, KY: Westminster John Knox Press, 2004), 177–78, at 178.

16 Henri de Lubac, SJ, *History and Spirit: The Understanding of Scripture according to Origen*, translated by Anne Englund Nash, with Greek and Latin translation by Juvenal Merriell of the Oratory (San Francisco: Ignatius Press, 2007), 143. De Lubac's appreciative *Histoire et esprit*, published originally in 1950, charted a new course in studies of Origen's scriptural interpretation.

17 Cf. *Homilies on Genesis* 10.1 and *Homilies on Jeremiah* 20.6.

was not a preacher who could (or necessarily wanted to) control a congregation like John Chrysostom or Augustine."[18]

Whether his preaching style was captivating or not, we attend to some records of his preaching. For Origen, the Word was in his flesh, and he wanted the baptized to know that the Word was in their flesh too for their holiness. The rest of this chapter will explore holiness in Origen's preaching: first in his *Homilies on Leviticus* and then in the recently discovered Greek *Homilies on the Psalms*.

Homilies on Leviticus

Origen preached his *Homilies on Leviticus* for the priestly holiness of all the faithful in Caesarea probably between 239 and 242. These homilies offer a wealth of material on many important interrelated topics, such as scriptural interpretation, ecclesiology, and Origen's relationship with Judaism, but our interest is especially on the deified life communicated in what Origen calls "the ministry of God's Word" (*ministerium verbi Dei*).[19] That Origen *preaches* about the priestly role of ministering the Word makes our study now attuned to his self-reflection. But more important than this implicit self-representation in the homiletic act is his overriding concern to actualize Leviticus through his preaching so that God's nation of priests may grow in understanding the Word and holiness in life.

Before we approach this set of homilies, a preliminary caution must first be given. These Greek homilies have been preserved only in a Latin translation in the early fifth century by Rufinus—who

18 Joseph W. Trigg, *Origen*, ECF (London: Routledge, 1998), 40. Origen's preaching does not display the rhetorical flourish expected in the greatest orators. Nautin writes that Origen knows the classical rules of composition and delivery, but he takes with them much freedom. See his introduction in SC 232, 121.

19 E.g. *Homilies on Leviticus* 5.7 (SC 286, 238; Barkley, 103).

thought, ironically, the original too homiletic![20] Rufinus rightly observes that Origen preached "not so much with the intention of explanation as of edification."[21] In looking back on his translation of various homilies, Rufinus says that he especially made changes to the *Homilies on Leviticus*, in which Origen spoke in a hortatory manner. "For this reason I took the trouble to fill in things lacking," Rufinus explains, "lest the striking and unanswered questions, which in the homiletic style of speaking he often had, generate weariness for the Latin reader."[22] This Latin adaptation impedes our ability to receive Origen's preaching in its most authentic form, but it does not wholly prevent us from discovering aspects of Origen's exemplary preaching.[23] Grateful for Rufinus's admission, we should not forget that Origen constantly asked questions. What have we lost when preachers do not question their hearers, themselves, the holy ones depicted in the scriptural narrative, and, above all others, God in their preaching?

Origen as a model preacher can assist now in the need to make the Word of God better understood and bear fruit in the lives of God's priestly people.

20 Rufinus, *Praefatio atque Epilogus in Explanationem Origenis super Epistulam Pauli ad Romanos*, ed. Manlio Simonetti, *Tyrannii Rufini Opera*, CCL 20 (Turnhout: Brepols, 1961), 276–77. Rufinus translated the homilies between 403 and 405. For Barkley's assessment of the significance of these homilies, including Rufinus's translation, see Barkley, *Homilies on Leviticus*, 21–25.

21 Rufinus, *Epilogus* (CCL 20, 276).

22 Rufinus, *Epilogus* (CCL 20, 276).

23 For assessments of the benefit of studying Origen's homilies, recognizing limitations imposed by Rufinus's translation, see Barkley, *Homilies on Leviticus*, 23, where he concurs with Ronald Heine, Annie Jaubert, and Henri de Lubac on the genuineness of Origen's thought in the homilies. Similarly, see Robert J. Daly, SJ, who thinks that the homilies can be used as guides to Origen's thought, in his "Sacrificial Soteriology in Origen's Homilies on Leviticus," in *StPatr* 17 (1979): 872–78, at 871. For Daniélou's reservation on the translated homilies' inaccuracies, see Jean Daniélou, SJ, *Origen*, translated by Walter Mitchell (New York: Sheed and Ward, 1955), x-xii.

Preaching on Leviticus: Letter and Spirit

As Origen's preaching serves and completes his scriptural interpretation, one would not likely accept Origen's theology of preaching if one rejects his treatment of the Bible. R. P. C. Hanson's view epitomizes this critique: "Origen was, generally speaking, not seriously restrained by the Bible; he knew very little about the intellectual discipline demanded for the faithful interpretation of biblical thought; his presuppositions were very little altered by contact with the material in the Bible." Hanson derides Origen: "Where the Bible did not obviously mean what he thought it ought to mean, or even where it obviously did not mean what he thought it ought to mean, he had only to turn the magic ring of allegory, and—Hey Presto!—the desired meaning appeared."[24]

Much of this discussion on Origen's preaching on Leviticus will answer Hanson's objection by considering how biblical images thoroughly inform Origen's ministry of God's Word. The Word in the flesh of Scripture comes to dwell in the flesh of Origen and his hearers, with particularity and concreteness. Yet, it can be conceded to Hanson that Origen does not offer a modern "historical-critical" approach to Leviticus.[25] Rather, Origen accepts the letter as containing something that initially cannot be seen. This approach has currency in contemporary approaches to reading, including the reading of Leviticus. For example, the Jewish scholar Jacob Milgrom begins his commentary on Leviticus:

24 R. P. C. Hanson, *Allegory & Event: A Study of the Sources and Significance of Origen's Interpretation of Scripture*, with an introduction by Joseph W. Trigg (Louisville, KY: Westminster John Knox Press, 2002), 371. Trigg's introduction to this reprint of Hanson's 1959 work provides an update on Origen studies biased toward Hanson's critique against de Lubac. Frances W. Young calls Hanson's portrayal "the standard English account of Origen's exegesis." See her *Biblical Exegesis and the Formation of Christian Culture* (Peabody, MA: Hendrickson Publishers, 2002), 3.

25 John David Dawson considers Hanson's critique to be the fullest elaboration of Erich Auerbach's negative assessment against Origen's allegorical hermeneutic. For Dawson's own response to Auerbach on figural reading and history, see his *Christian Figural Reading and the Fashioning of Identity* (Berkeley: University of California Press, 2002), 83–137, esp. 125–26 concerning Hanson.

> Values are what Leviticus is all about. They pervade every chapter and almost every verse. Many may be surprised to read this, since the dominant view of Leviticus is that it consists only of rituals, such as sacrifices and impurities. This, too, is true: Leviticus *does* discuss rituals. However, underlying the rituals, the careful reader will find an intricate web of values that purports to model how we should relate to God and to one another.[26]

Beyond his own rabbinic and historical-critical training, Milgrom relies in part upon Mary Douglas's anthropology; but more importantly for the present purpose his view expresses a wider phenomenon of seeking textual readings of what underlies the letter.[27]

Milgrom's own teaching at a Protestant seminary in Germany made him think that "Leviticus would be useless to seminary students in preparing their sermons."[28] Indeed, the third book of the Pentateuch poses challenges too often deemed insurmountable for the Christian pulpit.[29] Origen, on the other hand, demonstrates an enthusiastic love for preaching Leviticus and seeks to win his listeners over to the mysteries contained in this book of the Law.[30] He finds that one who is still an infant in spirit gladly hears books such as Esther, Judith, Tobit or the precepts of Wisdom. "But if the book

26 Jacob Milgrom, *Leviticus: A Book of Ritual and Ethics*, A Continental Commentary (Minneapolis, MN: Fortress Press, 2004), 1.

27 For the work of Mary Douglas, see esp. her *Purity and Danger* (London: Routledge, 1966) and *Leviticus as Literature* (Oxford: Oxford University Press, 1999).

28 Milgrom, *Leviticus*, xii.

29 This assessment derives from not merely the anecdotal, but the structural. The Roman Catholic lectionary, proven influential for other Christian lectionaries, has only two truncated readings from Leviticus in its three-year cycle of Sunday readings. Moreover, its appearances on the Sixth Sunday of Year B and the Seventh Sunday of Year A come at a time often passed over in the transition between the Ordinary Time before Lent and the Ordinary Time after the Easter Season.

30 "The chief task of a Christian preacher on Leviticus," comments Robert L. Wilken, "was to ensure that the book was not ignored and continued to be read. This could only be done by making it intelligible and applicable to the lives of Christians. Its language, its images, as well as its ideas, had to find a place in Christian practice and belief." See Wilken's "Origen's *Homilies on Leviticus* and *Vayikra Rabbah*," in *Origeniana Sexta: Origen and the Bible*, Acts from the Sixth Origenian Colloquium, Chantilly, 1993, eds. Gilles Dorival and Alain le Boulluec (Leuven: University Press, 1995), 81–91, at 89.

of Leviticus is read to him," Origen says, "his mind immediately stumbles and he flees from it as from something that is not his own food."[31] Although he acknowledges the common people's lack of attention and refusal to accept the Word in Leviticus, Origen does not discard this book, or even reserve it to some gnostic elite. Rather, the *Homilies on Leviticus* demonstrate Origen's attempt to overcome these obstacles and move his people further into spiritual maturity. He does this first by connecting what his people hear with what is experienced in Christ himself. For Origen's careful listener in the Church, the letter of Leviticus communicates through a spiritual interpretation the Word of God who is none other than Jesus Christ.[32] Origen's allegory to discover the hidden meaning is unabashedly at the service of Christ, and not Christ at the service of allegory.[33] He wants his people to experience the Word in the Bible and in their own lives. Peter Martens writes, for Origen, "the ideal scriptural interpreter was someone who embarked not simply upon a scholarly journey, but, more ambitiously, upon a way of life, indeed a way of salvation, that culminated in the vision of God."[34] Commenting on Origen's preaching on Leviticus, Robert L. Wilken states: "Much to Origen's credit he saw that Leviticus was not irrelevant to Christian life and piety. Embedded in its regulations and prescriptions he discovered a theme that is central to the New Testament, namely 'holiness.' From Leviticus he learned that holiness

31 *Homilies on Numbers* 27.1 (SC 461, 272; Scheck, 168).

32 De Lubac emphasizes that the Word in Scripture and the Word incarnate are not two Words, but the same Word for Origen. See de Lubac, *History and Spirit*, 385. Origen's exegesis of course has been the subject of numerous studies since de Lubac's 1950 classic. For one recent revision of Origen's incarnational reading, see Boersma, *Scripture as Real Presence*, 105–30.

33 Patricia Cox Miller's inverted conclusion makes Origen's Christological reading awaken the mind to the allegory of poetics. See her "Poetic Words, Abysmal Words: Reflections on Origen's Hermeneutics," in *Origen of Alexandria: His World and His Legacy*, eds. Charles Kannengiesser and William L. Petersen, CJA 1 (Notre Dame, IN: University of Notre Dame Press, 1988), 165–78.

34 Peter W. Martens, *Origen and Scripture: The Contours of the Exegetical Life*, OECS (Oxford: Oxford University Press, 2012), 6.

was not first and foremost a moral or ethical category, but a divine quality."[35] We can now trace Origen's divine approach to Leviticus.

In his introduction to the first homily on Leviticus, Origen announces his incarnational interpretation of Scripture and applies it to that biblical book.[36] The preacher begins:

> Just as "in the last days" (Acts 2:17) the Word of God, clothed with flesh from Mary, came into this world and there was one thing which was seen in him and another which was understood—for the appearance of flesh was evident in him to all, but knowledge of his divinity was given only to the few chosen ones—so too when the Word of God is brought forth to humans through the prophets or the lawgiver he is brought forth not without proper clothing.[37]

Both the incarnation and Scripture have veils that cover the Word within them. With regard to Scripture, the veil is the letter whereas the "spiritual sense hiding inside is experienced as divinity."[38] As for Leviticus, Origen summarizes its letter as treating various sacrificial rites, different offerings, and the priestly ministries—an assessment agreeable to historical-critical methods today. Origen then counts blessed those eyes that see the divine spirit, and blessed those clean

35 See Wilken, "Origen's *Homilies on Leviticus* and *Vayikra Rabbah*," 89–90.

36 Cf. de Lubac., chap. 8, "The Incorporations of the Logos," in *History and Spirit*, esp. 388–89.

37 *Homilies on Leviticus* 1.1 (SC 286, 66; Barkley, 29 [alt.]). Origen spends much time preaching on Leviticus's account of proper clothing, such as in Homily 6 on priestly vesture in Leviticus 7. Attention to clothing is a part of the recent "material turn" in the academy, including early Christian studies. For example, see Arthur Urbano's works on clothing that include: "Tailoring Rhetoric: Verbalizing Philosophical Dress in the Second Sophistic," in *"The One Who Sows Bountifully": Essays in Honor of Stanley K. Stowers*, eds. Caroline Johnson Hodge, Saul M. Olyan, Daniel Ullucci, and Emma Wasserman, BJS 356 (Providence, RI: Brown Judaic Studies, 2013), 243–54; "Sizing-Up the Philosopher's Cloak: Christian Verbal and Visual Representations of the Tribon," in *Dressing Judeans and Christians in Antiquity*, eds. Kristi Upson-Saia, Carly Daniel-Hughes, and Alicia J. Batten (Burlington, VT: Ashgate, 2014), 175–94; and "Jesus' Dazzling Garments: Origen's Exegesis of the Transfiguration in the Commentary on Matthew" in *The Garb of Being: Embodiment and the Pursuit of Holiness in Late Ancient Christianity*, eds. Georgia Frank, Susan R. Holman, and Andrew S. Jacobs (New York: Fordham University Press, 2020), 35–56.

38 *Homilies on Leviticus* 1.1 (SC 286, 66; Barkley, 29 [alt.]).

ears of the inner person that hears. For otherwise, Origen says, one will perceive in these words merely the letter that kills (cf. 2 Cor 3:6). Origen intensifies this in a later homily on Leviticus: "For even in the Gospels, it is the letter that kills. Not only in the Old Testament is the killing letter observed. There is even in the New Testament the letter that kills the one who does not spiritually perceive the things said."[39]

This not only summarizes Origen's spiritual interpretation; it also describes the stakes of the preacher's mission. The one who explains the words of Scripture does so as a matter of life and death—*the letter kills*.[40] Origen compares himself with Susanna. If he submits himself to the presbyters who follow the letter of the Law, then in Susanna's words, "It will be death for me" (Dn 13:22). But if he does not, then he would still not escape the wicked presbyters, and it would mean sinning against the Lord. That would be not simply Origen's death, but the death of all those who hear the Word. Origen encourages his listeners to stay faithful to the Lord under this threat of death so that the "Church, having already turned to the Lord, may know the truth of the Word of God enveloped by the covering of the letter."[41]

After praying for the Holy Spirit's removal of every cloud and darkness in order to see the spiritual knowledge of the Law, Origen describes his homiletic purpose. "Therefore, as we are able,

39 *Homilies on Leviticus* 7.5 (SC 286, 338; Barkley, 146 [alt.]). This may, in part, lie behind Augustine's *On the Spirit and the Letter*, which influenced Thomas Aquinas's famous phrase in *Summa Theologiae* II-II, q. 106, a. 2, co.: "Even the letter of the Gospel would kill unless the healing grace of faith were interiorly present." Such a reading points to the relationship between literal and spiritual interpretations with Law and grace, and so Scripture's spiritual interpretation should have great bearing upon the theology of grace today.

40 In his *Homilies on Luke*, Origen says that the devil does not tempt Jesus with anything other than the divine books, and the devil does so by interpreting the Bible literally. Origen speaks to the devil, "You read, not to become better through reading the holy books, but to use the simple letter for killing those who are the friends of the letter." See *Homilies on Luke* 31.2 (SC 87, 378; Lienhard, 126 [alt.]).

41 *Homilies on Leviticus* 1.1 (SC 286, 68; Barkley, 30 [alt.]).

let us relate briefly a few things from many, not striving after the explanation of single words—for this is done in a writer's leisure—but making known things that pertain to the edification of the Church."[42] Origen, later in these homilies, repeats the distinction between edifying the Church and providing a detailed explanation in commentaries.[43] The preacher must know the true meaning of the Scriptures and communicate it to the listeners, viewed as "wise" (cf. Prv 9:9). Precisely because his preaching is the edification of the Church, Origen's homilies bolster the listening Christians to perceive the spiritual meaning of the Scriptures for a greater awareness of God's work in their lives.

The spiritual meaning is conveyed only through the letter. Even if the letter has no "bodily" sense in a particular passage for Origen, the letter still enfleshes what is higher and saving. Our continuing exploration of the *Homilies on Leviticus* demonstrates the seriousness with which Origen accepted the letter in order to derive spiritual meaning for the faithful. In fact, all of his homilies are thoroughly imbued with careful textual links suggesting that the letter, when properly treated, does not kill, but conveys the Spirit's life.[44] Against Hanson's reading of Origen, this study argues that Origen's way of preaching, as communicating the spiritual interpretation, is inseparable from the letter of Leviticus—and it is about the life of

42 *Homilies on Leviticus* 1.1 (SC 286, 70; Barkley, 31 [alt.]).

43 *Homilies on Leviticus* 7.1 (SC 286, 298; Barkley, 129). For some differences between Origen's homilies and commentaries, see Éric Junod, "Wodurch unterscheiden sich die Homilien des Origenes von seinen Kommentaren?" translated from French by Marianne Mühlenberg, in *Predigt in der Alten Kirche*, eds. Ekkehard Mühlenberg and J. van Oort (Kampen, The Netherlands: Kok Pharos Publishing House, 1994), 50–81. See especially his treatment of building up the Church in 62–74.

44 Joseph T. Lienhard, SJ, astutely comments, "It is too often forgotten that spiritual exegesis, Origen's and others', is based on an utterly literal reading of the texts." See his "Origen as Homilist," in *Preaching in the Patristic Age: Studies in Honor of Walter J. Burghardt, SJ*, ed. David G. Hunter (New York: Paulist Press, 1989), 36–52, at 46. For an insightful argument that the literal sense must always be understood as the literal sense *of Scripture*, see John C. Cavadini, "From Letter to Spirit: The Multiple Senses of Scripture," in *The Oxford Handbook of Early Christian Biblical Interpretation*, eds. Blowers and Martens, 126–48.

Christ that Christians are called to share in holiness. Indeed, Origen frequently fills his teaching with biblical images that cannot be removed from the spiritual doctrine and are to be experienced by his people.[45] These images pertaining in their letter to the priestly regulations of ancient Israel spiritually signify Christ and the lives in Christ of his faithful ones, the nation of priests. The selection of terms studied here comes from Leviticus, whose letter for Origen is "as it were, the flesh of the Word of God and the clothing of his divinity."[46] In God's design for our salvation, holiness is clothed in flesh. For our present study, we focus on the sacrificial offerings of animal flesh present in the first five *Homilies on Leviticus.*

Preaching on Leviticus: Sacrificial Offerings

The Book of Leviticus begins with the Lord calling Moses and speaking to him from the tent of meeting about how the people of Israel should make an offering to the Lord. It then takes up the first instruction of a whole burnt offering from the herd (Lv 1:3–9). Again, to orient Origen's preaching for our context today, we can hear first from Jacob Milgrom: "This first chapter of Leviticus ostensibly discusses the burnt offering. However, the current that runs beneath the technical description of the offering reveals much about the emerging Israelites' efforts to distinguish their religion from the pagan religions that existed at the same time."[47] For Origen, to repeat Milgrom, the "current that runs beneath the technical description of the offering reveals much" about Christ and the priestly act of preaching *in the present.* From the very details of Leviticus' narrative, Origen, in the midst of speaking of Christ as the burnt offering, constructs his preaching for the Church gathered around the living

45 For a book running over 800 pages on images in Origen's ecclesiology, see F. Ledegang, *Mysterium Ecclesiae: Images of the Church and Its Members in Origen*, BETL 156, translated by F.A. Valken (Leuven: Leuven University Press, 2001).

46 *Homilies on Leviticus* 1.1 (SC 286, 68; Barkley, 29).

47 Milgrom, *Leviticus*, 21.

Word.[48] Subsequently, Origen gives the moral sense for believers in Christ to offer their own flesh by a reasonable service (cf. Rom 12:1).[49] Origen appropriates the sacrificial language to describe the ministry of God's Word:

> I myself think that the priest who removes the hide *of the calf* offered in a *whole burnt offering* and takes away the skin by which its members were covered is the one who removes the veil of the letter from the Word of God and lays bare its insides, which are the members of spiritual intelligence. He also places these members of the interior word of knowledge not in some base location, but in one high and holy, i.e. he lays them *upon the altar*. He opens the divine mysteries not with unworthy people living a base and earthly life, but with those who are the altar of God, in whom the divine fire always burns and the flesh is always being consumed.[50]

Such a statement can help us understand the sacrificial character of preaching for Origen, a topic that deserves closer attention. For example, Robert J. Daly has studied the *Homilies on Leviticus* for their sacrificial theme. He writes, "In these homilies (once Jewish and pagan priesthood are excluded) Origen, when speaking of priesthood, has in mind either the priesthood of Jesus Christ or the priesthood of every true Christian. There is no mention of the office of a class of specially ordained hierarchical Christian priests."[51] I do

48 For an analysis of the first homily, see Gaetano Lettieri, "Omelia I: Il sacrificio del Logos," in *Omelie sul Levitico: Lettura origeniana*, eds. Mario Maritano and Enrico dal Covolo, Biblioteca di Scienze Religiose 181 (Rome: Libreria Ateneo Salesiano, 2003), 15–47.

49 On Origen's spiritual and moral readings of Lv 1:1–5, see Elizabeth Ann Dively Lauro, *The Soul and Spirit of Scripture within Origen's Exegesis*, BAC vol. 3 (Boston: Brill, 2005), 163–75. Lauro does not treat here *Homilies on Leviticus* 1.4 where Origen discusses the priest's role in preparing the sacrifice of the Word before Origen gives the moral sense in *Homilies on Leviticus* 1.5.

50 *Homilies on Leviticus* 1.4 (SC 286, 78–80; Barkley, 35 [alt.]).

51 Robert J. Daly, SJ, "Sacrificial Soteriology in Origen's Homilies on Leviticus," in *StPatr* 17 (1982): 872–78, at 875. For a more recent study of sacrifice in these homilies, see Samuel Johnson, "The Sacrifice of the Law in Origen's Homilies on Leviticus," in *Origeniana Duodecima: Origen's Legacy in the Holy Land–A Tale of Three Cities: Jerusalem, Caesarea, and Bethlehem*, eds. Brouria Bitton-Ashkelony, Oded Irshai, Aryeh Kofsky, Hillel Newman,

not dispute Daly's recognition of Origen's overwhelming concern for Christ's priesthood and the universal priesthood of the faithful. Yet it is precisely in this concern Origen frequently presents a priestly ministry of God's Word that brings Christ the great priest and the priestly people together. Restriction of priesthood to only the two categories of Christ and every true Christian does not do justice to the rich complexity of Origen's understanding of priesthood, and particularly the priestly sacrifice of teaching Scripture.[52] Origen himself exercises this priestly role by interpreting Leviticus to the Church within a liturgical setting.[53]

Leviticus further specifies in its first chapter that priests should separate the whole burnt offering limb by limb before adding the firewood. Origen explains that this separation occurs when the priest "can explain in order and speak with proper distinction" the Gospel's portrayal of contact with Christ in threefold fashion.[54] The priest must discuss the causes of these things for those beginning, those progressing in the faith, and those already perfect in Christ's knowledge and love. Thus, the animal is separated "limb by limb." The addition of the firewood occurs, for Origen, when the preacher treats not only Christ's bodily virtues but also his divinity. For all should understand that the whole burnt offering of Christ's flesh

---

and Lorenzo Perrone, BETL 302 (Leuven: Peeters, 2019), 603–16. Johnson wants his essay "to recover a sense of the Word of God's preeminence in Origen's teaching on the sacrifices of the Law" (603).

52 Cf. Pamela Bright, "Priesthood," in *The Westminster Handbook to Origen*, ed. John Anthony McGuckin (Louisville, KY: Westminster John Knox Press, 2004), 179–81. Bright recognizes six distinct considerations of priesthood for Origen, not including the ordained priesthood which Bright acknowledges that Origen presumes.

53 Thomas K. Carroll mentions that Origen preached before his ordination, but Carroll confusingly adds a dichotomy: "as preacher he remained more prophet than priest." See his *Preaching the Word*, 42. For Origen, preaching is eminently priestly.

54 *Homilies on Leviticus* 1.4 (SC 286, 80; Barkley, 35). For Origen's Gospel portrait here, see Mt 9:20, Lk 7:44, 7:46, and Jn 13:25, 21:30.

through the wood of the cross unites heaven and earth, the human and the divine.[55]

Origen's third homily treats Leviticus 5. When speaking on the guilt offerings mandated from one who sins against the holy things of the Lord, Origen adopts this as the example of what preaching is and the fact that people sin against what they have heard in preaching. Admitting his sinfulness, Origen says, "Nevertheless, because the dispensation of the Lord's Word has been entrusted to me, I seem to have the holy things of God committed to me."[56] Origen understands these holy things as the money from the Gospel of Matthew's Parable of the Talents (cf. Mt 25:14–30). He dispenses the holy things so that they may multiply in the lives of the people. But when the faithful people sin against the holy things through forgetfulness of what they heard, they return without a multiplication. Origen thus makes clear the productivity that is to occur in the daily Christian life from listening to and enacting the homily. Again, Origen emphasizes the priestly role of the preacher as a steward dispensing God's gifts and expecting a profitable return.

In his fourth homily, when speaking on Lv 6:1–6, Origen finds that it is written about the fire for sacrifice: "the fire will always burn upon the altar and not be extinguished." Origen's preaching actualizes how each believer is called to be a priest, a favorite theme inspired by Is 61:6 and 1 Pt 2:9. "If therefore," Origen preaches, "you want to exercise the priesthood of your soul, let the fire never depart from your altar."[57] In Homily 5, Origen makes known that people not only have the altar's fire in the soul, but also the animals. Origen proclaims that those living reasonably in faith as Abraham's descendants have herds of cattle, sheep, and goats as well as the

55 Another important treatment of the whole burnt offering appears in *Homilies on Leviticus* 9.9.

56 *Homilies on Leviticus* 3.7 (SC 286, 148; Barkley, 64–65 [alt.]).

57 *Homilies on Leviticus* 4.6 (SC 286, 180; Barkley, 78).

birds of the sky within them to offer up as sacrifice. But the faithful have so much more than altar, fire, and animals within them. Origen asks the people, "Do you wish to hear further something about your very self, lest perhaps thinking little and lowly things about yourself you neglect your life as something vile?"[58] He quotes for them the Scripture "Do I not fill heaven and earth says the Lord?" (Jer 23:24). Then he brings home for his people a more intimate presence: "Hear, therefore, what this omnipotent God says about even you, that is what he says about human beings. He says, 'I will live in them and I will walk among them' (cf. 2 Cor 6:16)."[59] He goes on to say that they have the Son of God and the Holy Spirit within them. In short, Origen actualizes the sacrifices of Leviticus within the souls of the Christian faithful so that they can consider the awesome hidden dignity that God has given them in their ability to offer priestly sacrifice.

Also in Homily 5, Origen quotes Lv 7:15: "It will be eaten in the day and nothing should remain from it in the morning." This prompts him to compare this with other injunctions concerning time in the law, such as the command that the Passover sacrifice should be offered in the evening so that nothing should remain from the flesh in the morning (cf. Ex 12:6, 10). Origen links this prohibition to Ezekiel's assertion, "Even yesterday's meat never entered my mouth" (Ez 4:12). From this careful attention to the letter, Origen declares the meaning for a spiritual teaching in the Church:

> Hear this, all you priests of the Lord, and understand more attentively the things said. The flesh, which is set aside from the sacrifices for the priests, is the *Word of God,* which they teach in the Church. For this reason, they are reminded by mystic figures so when they begin to bring forth speaking to the people they may not bring forth something from *yesterday*—that they

58 *Homilies on Leviticus* 5.2 (SC 286, 212; Barkley, 92 [alt.]).
59 *Homilies on Leviticus* 5.2 (SC 286, 212; Barkley, 92 [alt.]).

> should not proclaim old things which are according to the letter—but they should always bring forth new things through the grace of God and always find spiritual things.[60]

Later in this same homily, Origen comments on the instruction of Leviticus 7 concerning the portions of priests from the salutary offering (*salutaris hostia*, which more frequently appears as "peace offering" in translations from the Masoretic text). Again, Origen is explicit about the need to interpret the law for the edification of those hearing it. Otherwise, why would one read it in Church?[61] Applying Leviticus 7 within his ministry of God's Word, Origen offers an important thought: "If, therefore, the priest of the Church, through words, and doctrine, and his great concern and work of vigilance, could convert a sinner and teach that one to follow a better way so as to return to the fear of God," the sinner should bring the priest a "salutary offering" in thanksgiving to God.[62] This does not mean that the converted should pay the preacher! Rather, the salutary offerings are the parts described in Leviticus 7, now parts not of an animal sacrifice but of the faithful themselves who are sacrificed. Their breast and right limb, which the Law commanded to be given to the priest, are offered back to the priest to express how the priest's labor had converted them from evil thoughts so that they may see God.

Before concluding this section, we can hear Jean Laporte's assessment from his study of Philonic models in Origen's teaching on sacrifice. Laporte writes, "For the explanation of Origen's doctrine of sacrifice the best methodology is to recognize his real

60 *Homilies on Leviticus* 5.8 (SC 286, 242; Barkley, 105). For an application of this in twentieth-century theology, see Hans Urs von Balthasar's conclusion to his "Priestly Existence," translated by Brian McNeil, CRV in *Explorations in Theology II: Spouse of the Word* (San Francisco: Ignatius Press, 1991), 373–419. For further analysis in Balthasar's theology of preaching, see Andrew Hofer, OP, "Proclamation in the Theological Aesthetics of Hans Urs von Balthasar," *Worship* 79, no. 1 (2005): 20–37, at 32–33.

61 *Homilies on Leviticus* 5.12 (SC 286, 260).

62 *Homilies on Leviticus* 5.12 (SC 286, 260; Barkley, 113).

models in his sources, i.e., Leviticus as interpreted by Philo. Origen repeats Philo's teachings on sacrifice without much alteration."[63] Yes, Origen is heavily indebted to Philo, as for example we can read in Philo, "the true altar of God is the thankful soul of the wise person."[64] But this comment—"without much alteration"—at the end of Laporte's study seems exaggerated, as Laporte himself draws attention to Origen's constant Christological interpretation.[65] Origen's interpretation differs in important respects from Philo's treatment of the Word. Laporte knows that for Philo the mediation of the Word between God and humans vanishes away, that the Word does not have a distinct individual or "personal" existence for Philo, and that the Word did not become flesh as Jesus Christ with the scriptural and soteriological meaning that Origen understands from the incarnation.[66] Particularly pertinent to the present study, Philo does not develop an understanding of the preacher's sacrificial role within the ministry of God's Word. Philo himself is not preaching to an assembly of common people gathered when he gives his learned study. Moreover, Philo's reliance on Moses the Lawgiver and his emphasis on the interiority of the wise person do not elicit reflection on ministering the Word to the faithful in the same way as is found in Origen's *Homilies on Leviticus*. For Origen, on the other hand, the ministry of God's Word as a priestly role forms an integral part of interpreting the Levitical sacrifices for the Church's benefit. Preaching on Leviticus in the Church's worship

63 Jean Laporte, "Sacrifice in Origen in the Light of Philonic Models," in *Origen of Alexandria: His World and His Legacy*, eds. Charles Kannengiesser and William L. Petersen, Christianity and Judaism in Antiquity, vol. 1 (Notre Dame, IN: University of Notre Dame Press, 1988), 250–76, at 274.

64 Philo, *On the Special Laws* 1.52.287 (LCL 320, 266; Colson, 267 [alt.]). Cf. Origen, *Homilies on Leviticus* 1.4 treated above.

65 Cf. Frances M. Young's study of Origen's similarities with and differences from Philo in her *The Use of Sacrificial Ideas in Greek Christian Writers from the New Testament to John Chrysostom*, PMS 5 (Cambridge, MA: The Philadelphia Patristic Foundation, Ltd., 1979), 120–26. Most importantly, Young writes, "But Origen's scheme is quite different because all sacrifices are regarded as types of the sacrifice of Christ" (123).

66 Cf. Laporte, "Sacrifice in Origen," 260.

makes present the Word given and sacrificed in the church building and in the lives of the faithful.

Homilies on the Psalms

While explaining the verse, "I have not seen a just person forsaken or his seed seeking bread" (Ps 36:25), Origen elucidates the mystery in this way. "If you pray for me, so that I become just and that I receive more grace, word, and wisdom daily and a word of knowledge," he continues, "so, would that the word, as a seed entering the souls of you hearers, form you when Christ is formed in you."[67] By the prayers of his people, Origen can become that just person, and his seed, that is his people, may never lack what they need as they receive salvation through Origen's preaching of the Word. Origen's audible voice is purely at the service of the Word within us.

In another homily on the Psalms, Origen asks for his people's prayers by reflecting on the phrase "my glory has exulted" (Ps 15:9). What is Origen's glory? He explains that for an athlete it is his excellent body, for a physician it is medicine, for an artisan it is hands. "The glory of a wise person," Origen continues, "when he is saying divine and holy things, is his tongue. . . . Pray for me, even if I am unworthy, that, out of his love and yours, God may give me tongue and glory, so that my tongue may be glorified by God and by human beings. For my tongue will be my glory, if you have been heard."[68]

These examples of Origen's expressed dependence on his people for their mutual salvation, priest and priestly people together, come from the twenty-nine recently discovered Greek sermons on the Psalms, a veritable treasure of patristic preaching. In 2012,

67 *Homily 4 on Psalm 36.3* (OW 13, 169; Trigg, 133 [alt.]). For an insightful study, see Daniel Sheerin, "The Role of Prayer in Origen's Homilies," in *Origen of Alexandria: His World and His Legacy*, eds. Charles Kannengiesser and William L. Petersen, CJA 1 (Notre Dame, IN: University of Notre Dame Press, 1988), 200–14.

68 *Homily 2 on Psalm 15.7* (OW 13, 104; Trigg, 70).

Marina Molin Pradel was cataloguing manuscripts in the Bavarian State Library. She noticed several features of an ignored set of Greek homilies that resembled what she already knew of Origen's preaching on the Psalms, as a few sermons had been preserved by Rufinus in Latin. Lorenzo Perrone confirmed her discovery of these authentic works of Origen, and made the critical edition with her assistance and that of others.[69] Joseph Trigg has now translated the *Homilies on the Psalms* into English.[70] This is the most significant discovery of early Christian preaching in decades.[71] Before this discovery, 279 of Origen's homilies were known, but with the exception of Origen's preaching on the witch of Endor and twenty of the twenty-two extant homilies on Jeremiah and other homiletic fragments in Greek, all had been preserved only in translation.[72] As a point of perspective on the first centuries of Christian preaching, very few homilies have survived from the time before Origen.[73] Perrone dates the Psalm homilies to 248–49, a few years before Origen's torture and eventual death. This sermon collection can be called the Church's most complete transcript of speaking before the fourth century.

69 *Die neuen Psalmenhomilien: Eine kritische Edition des Codex Monacensis Graecus 314*, ed. Lorenzo Perrone, together with Marian Molin Pradel, Emanuela Prinzivalli, and Antonio Cacciari, GCS, new series 19; OW 13 (Berlin: De Gruyter, 2015).

70 I am grateful to Trigg for giving me an advance copy before publication. See *Origen, Homilies on the Psalms: Codex Monacensis Graecus 314*, translated by Joseph W. Trigg, FC 141 (Washington, DC: The Catholic University of America, 2020).

71 Reviewing the critical edition, Peter Martens writes, "For a discovery of similar magnitude for the study of Greek early Christianity we are required to look back over seventy years to the Tura papyrus find, where a number of Origen and Didymus's previously lost works were uncovered." See the review of Peter W. Martens in *JECS* 24, no. 4 (2016): 628–30, at 629.

72 For an English translation of the Greek homilies known before 2012, see *Origen: Homilies on Jeremiah and 1 Kings 28*, translated by John Clark Smith, FC 97 (Washington, DC: The Catholic University of America Press, 1998). Smith aptly writes, "Of all his [Origen's] works, the most accessible and yet immensely interesting are the homilies" (xv).

73 Henri Crouzel, SJ, lists as extant from the time before Origen only the homily called 2 Clement, *On Pascha* by Melito of Sardis, Clement of Alexandria's *Quis dives salvetur*, the *De Antichristo*, and some fragments of Hippolytus. See Crouzel, *Origen*, 29.

Recall that in our study of the *Homilies on Leviticus* we saw that Rufinus smoothed over the many striking and unanswered questions in Origen's preaching when rendering it in Latin. While we are still able to learn from Origen through Rufinus's translation, we miss a crucial aspect of his preaching. Lorenzo Perrone writes, "Not only in his commentaries and treatises, but also in his homilies, Origen frequently applied the technique of *quaestiones et responsiones*, which he appropriated both from a philological-rhetorical and a philosophical tradition."[74] The technique of "questions and answers," or "problems and solutions," was its own literary genre, but it also appears in other genres, including preaching. This is exactly what we find in Origen's preaching on the Psalms, which Margaret Mitchell expertly develops, following Perrone, in a study on *Homily 1 on Psalm 77*.[75] Moreover, this emphasis on questioning and answering is complementary to Karen Jo Torjesen's argument for Origen's hermeneutics and Mark Randall James's own study of the Greek *Homilies on the Psalms*.

Torjesen has argued that, for Origen, the Christian life proceeds with the perfect goal of communion with God. And so his preaching is especially concerned about the "journey of the soul."[76] Torjesen came to that position from working on Origen's preaching, especially on the Psalm homilies in Rufinus's Latin translation. Supporting her work, Joseph Trigg writes that Torjesen "settled on Origen's homilies on Psalm 36, in Rufinus's translation, as the best texts from Origen's corpus to illustrate how his exegetical procedure was intended to further the transforming activity of Christ in

74 Perrone, "Codex Monacensis Graecus 314:29 Psalmhomilien des Origenes," in OW 13, 9–10 (my translation). Perrone discusses this within his argument from internal evidence that Origen is indeed the author of these homilies on the Psalms.

75 Margaret M. Mitchell, "'Problems and Solutions' in Early Christian Biblical Interpretation: A Telling Case from Origen's Newly Discovered Greek Homilies on the Psalms (*Codex Monacensis Graecus* 314)," *Adamantius* 22 (2016): 40–55.

76 Karen Jo Torjesen, *Hermeneutical Procedure and Theological Method in Origen's Exegesis*, PTS 28 (Berlin: De Gruyter, 1985), 29–34.

the human soul. The newly discovered Psalm homilies vindicate her intuition."[77]

Torjesen identifies a four-step method in Origen's preaching on the Psalms:

> The four steps link together in a natural movement, the first step giving the actual words of the prayer, the second step describing the attitude of the one praying, the third step translating this attitude into the form of a first person confession, and the fourth step tying this confession back into the words of the Psalm as the hearer's own, and as the opening step for the exegesis of the next verse.[78]

Certainly, Torjesen has detected a process that shows not only Origen the exegete, but even more so Origen the preacher. He includes his audience and blends him and them together to pray the Psalm with understanding, step-by-step, verse-by-verse in a manner of searching and questioning.

For Mark Randall James, Origen's Greek *Homilies on the Psalms* communicate a way for his audience to learn a linguistic competence to rise from *lexis* to *logos*, from the words of Scripture to the Word.[79] I agree. James also argues that "a contemporary Origenism should be a form of scriptural pragmatism that puts the formation of wise Christian linguistic competence logically prior to doctrinal formulations and theological constructions."[80] Therein lies a danger.

77 Joseph Trigg, "Being and Becoming God in Origen's *Homilies on the Psalms*," presentation to the North American Patristics Society, 2016. Unpublished manuscript. Trigg cites in particular Torjesen, *Hermeneutical Procedure and Theological Method in Origen's Exegesis*, 22–29.

78 Torjesen, *Hermeneutical Procedure and Theological Method in Origen's Exegesis*, 28.

79 Mark Randall James, *Learning the Language of Scripture: Origen, Wisdom, and the Logic of Interpretation*, STT 24 (Leiden: Brill, 2021). Cf. John Solheid application of Brian Stock's term of "textual communities" to Origen's Psalm preaching. See John Solheid, "Scripture and Christian Formation in Origen's *Fourth Homily on Psalm 77(78)*," *JECS* 27, no. 3 (2019): 417–42. For Stock's work, see Brian Stock, *Listening for the Text: On the Uses of the Past* (Baltimore: Johns Hopkins Press, 1990).

80 James, *Learning the Language of Scripture*, 25.

How would our scriptural reading and preaching be guided by the apostolic preaching's rule of faith, which underpins Origen's entire thinking, with the goal of deified union with God? Such a rule of faith, rather than merely a philological or philosophical rule, saved Origen from the arbitrariness that James seeks to clear him of in modern misunderstandings. According to Peter Martens, Origen understands the rule of faith to be "a précis of the *entire* scriptural message as seen through the eyes of the apostles."[81] Although Origen does not explicitly mention the rule of faith in his Greek *Homilies on the Psalms*, he most certainly takes as a first principle what the entirety of Scripture means for the apostles. About another Psalm homily, Margaret Mitchell accurately observes, "Origen regards the evangelist Matthew as providing the Christian reader with the key to the meaning of Ps 77:1–2."[82] The Word incarnate makes clear the meaning of that passage, and it is the same Word of God speaking in the Psalm and in Origen's interpretation of the Psalm.

By attending to this newly discovered preaching, we have Origen's remarkable testimony to holiness within the dynamic homiletic act of seeking and finding Christ the Word at work in Scripture, preacher, and people. In reviewing these recently discovered homilies, we will first consider how deification changes a sinner to be holy—spirit, soul, and body (cf. 1 Thes 5:23) with focus on what Origen preaches and how he preaches in *Homily on Psalm 81*. Then we will review how Christ not only lives in his holy ones, but also speaks in them, as preached elsewhere in this set of Greek sermons.

The Holiness of Deification in the *Homily on Psalm 81*

Before the twenty-nine Greek homilies on the Psalms were discovered, Norman Russell could say, "Considering the bulk of his

81 Martens, *Origen and Scripture*, 210 (original emphasis).

82 Margaret M. Mitchell, "Origen and the Text-Critical Dilemma: An Illustration from One of His Newly Discovered Greek Homilies on the Psalms," *BR* 62 (2017): 61–82, at 68.

writings, his [Origen's] references to deification are relatively few."[83] This discovery of homilies certainly adds to our understanding of Origen's theology of deification, as the theme appears in varied ways throughout this homiletic corpus.[84] Of all the recently discovered Greek homilies, the last one, on Psalm 81, offers the fullest account of deification.[85] This Psalm has the verse, "You are gods and sons of the Most High," (Ps 81:6), quoted by Jesus when defending his title of Son of God: "Is it not written in your law, 'I said, "You are gods"'?" (Jn 10:34).[86] Origen takes the opportunity through sustained attention to that Psalm to preach at length on what deification means. That this is the last extant sermon before he was tortured for his faith makes it even more a poignant witness to holiness in the flesh.

Origen begins, "The goal (*skopos*) for a disciple is to become like the teacher, and the ideal (*telos*) of a slave is to become like the lord," and proceeds to quote Mt 10:25. That verse serves as the basis for Origen's variation that interjects the language of *skopos* and *telos*.[87] Not only is this what a disciple or slave aims at, it is what a good teacher and lord wants. Christ is precisely that Teacher and Lord (cf. Jn 13:13), "for everything at all that the Savior is, he calls also his disciples to be."[88] In proof of this, Origen quotes, "You are the light

83 Russell, *Doctrine of Deification in the Greek Patristic Tradition*, 140.

84 Trigg calls the deification of humanity "a pervasive subject throughout the homilies" on the Psalms. See Trigg, *Homilies on the Psalms*, 6. For an excellent survey of Origen on deification with close attention to the Greek *Homilies on the Psalms*, see Lorenzo Perrone, "'Et l'homme tout entier devient dieu': La déification selon Origène à la lumière des nouvelles *Homélies sur les Psaumes*," *TV* 58, no. 2 (2017): 187–220.

85 The Septuagintal numbering of the Psalms is used here and when citing directly other patristic quotations of the Psalms. Here is the correlation between Greek Septuagintal numbering (also found in the Latin Vulgate) with the Hebrew Masoretic numbering of the Psalms, found in most Bibles today: Psalms 1–8 the same; 9 Greek = 9–10 Hebrew; 10–112 Greek = 11–113 Hebrew; 113 Greek = 114–115 Hebrew; 114–115 Greek = 116 Hebrew; 116–145 Greek = 117–146 Hebrew; 146–147 Greek = 147 Hebrew; 148–150 the same.

86 For an insightful study of this Psalm's prominence for the earliest Christian accounts of deification, see Carl Mosser, "The Earliest Patristic Interpretations of Psalm 82, Jewish Antecedents, and the Origin of Christian Deification," *JTS* 56, no. 1 (2005): 30–74.

87 *Homily on Psalm 81*.1 (OW 13, 509; Trigg, 439).

88 *Homily on Psalm 81*.1 (OW 13, 509; Trigg, 439).

of the world" (Mt 5:14), and shows that Christ says this because he also says, "I am the light of the world" (Jn 8:12). Moreover, Origen understands that Christ himself speaks through the Psalmist, being himself a christ, an anointed one, speaking in the *persona* of Christ: "Do not touch my christ, and among my prophets do not do evil" (Ps 104:15). Therefore, before Origen quotes the Psalm, he has announced its meaning. It is, in a sense, a first principle or rule that guides his entire reading of the Psalm.

Before Origen quotes a verse, he often provides the scriptural meaning of a term found in the verse. After the homily's introduction, he attends to "gathering," a key word in the first verse of the Psalm. But before he quotes the Psalm, he explains what a "gathering" is, and that if we do not do the works of the flesh, "it is not a gathering of human beings, but a gathering of gods."[89] In such a gathering where there are the fruits of the spirit rather than the works of the flesh, the devil can do nothing. Origen continues, "God visits, and he visits standing in the midst of the gathering of gods."[90] Only after that does Origen quote the Psalm. "Therefore," Origen preaches, "it is said, 'God stood in the gathering of gods.' He asks, "But what makes us human beings, so that, having fallen from divinity, we might destroy the legacy calling us to become gods?"[91]

Origen answers the startling question, which gives a disjunction between humans and gods, through recourse to another divine voice outside the Psalm itself. Here Origen makes a Pauline argument that we are mere human beings, merely fleshly, when we sin. Paul takes note of the jealousy and strife among the Corinthians and asks, "Are you not human beings?" (1 Cor 3:4). Origen understands Paul to mean that we are called to a higher dignity. But we should not lose sight that Origen makes a startling determination

89 *Homily on Psalm 81*.1 (OW 13, 510; Trigg, 440).
90 *Homily on Psalm 81*.1 (OW 13, 510; Trigg, 440).
91 *Homily on Psalm 81*.1 (OW 13, 511; Trigg, 440).

that being "human" means to be sinful. While he certainly does not think that even the human body is annihilated in deification, as we will see, we must pay attention to his way of presenting the Scriptures on being human. Here, it is the opposite of being deified. While Origen does not adduce this comparison, the Pauline question could be matched with Christ's reproach to Simon Peter, "You are not thinking the things of God, but the things of human beings" (Mt 16:23). It is because we practice things not worthy of divinity, things only of the flesh that we die as human beings. We need to put to death the deeds of the flesh: "For when the deeds of the body are put to death, so that there are no longer deeds of the body in us, then we have been made gods."[92]

Origen then proclaims, "God the Word, if produced in the soul, makes the soul that receives it a god. For if a small leaven leavens the whole lump, what is to be said, not concerning a small and insignificant leaven, but about the god-making Word, but that he, having come to be in the soul, leavens the whole lump of a human being into godhood and the whole human being becomes a god?"[93] Origen recalls the Lord's parable of the woman who took yeast and hid it in three measures of wheat flower until the whole batch was leavened (cf. Mt 13:33). For Origen, the woman represents the Church, who has received Christ, and the yeast itself is precisely preaching to the three measures: the spirit, soul, and body of the human being, which is the tripartite anthropology described when the Apostle Paul asks that the God of peace may make his listeners perfect in holiness (cf. 1 Thes 5:23). The whole human being then becomes a god. Origen explains this total deification in the following way.

He begins with the spirit, that highest and most noble aspect of the human being, already in kinship with the incorruptible Spirit. It is not marvelous that our spirit would be divinized, but it would be

92 *Homily on Psalm 81*.1 (OW 13, 512; Trigg, 441).
93 *Homily on Psalm 81*.1 (OW 13, 512; Trigg, 441).

marvelous for our soul to be divinized. What would the divinization of the soul mean? The soul would no longer sin or be mortal. Origen continues:

> But what is more marvelous than all of these is that the body has been divinized, so that it is no longer flesh and blood, but it becomes conformed to Christ Jesus' body of glory; and, having been divinized, it is received into heaven according to the saying, "We shall be taken in the clouds to meet the Lord in the air, and thus we shall forever be with the Lord" (1 Thes 4:17), having become gods.[94]

The divinization of the body manifests the final eschatological realization of the saints.[95] He continues to interpret the Psalm with attention to the words that God "distinguishes gods" (Ps 81:1). What does that mean? God distinguishes the gods by rewarding them in their transformation to be like the sun, the moon, and the array of stars (cf. 1 Cor 15:41).[96] Therefore, some bodily divinization will occur.

Origen says that God judges those who are outside, but for those inside he does something better. He asks, "What is that better thing? Hear the prophet say, 'God stood in the gathering of gods; in the midst he distinguishes gods.'"[97] He imagines an emperor on a glad day speaking of who is more worthy and less worthy of him. Origen then translates that to be precisely what God does on the

94 *Homily on Psalm 81*.1 (OW 13, 512–13; Trigg, 442 [alt.]). The final sentence continues in Trigg's translation "with a god standing in the middle of our gathering, Jesus Christ." Trigg translates *theos* as "a god" and *ho theos* as "God." Origen invests the absence of the article to distinguish *ho theos* and *theos*, as we find in John 1:1, and one who belongs to Christ is called *theos* without the article, as Jesus himself is called. For his discussion in this set of Psalm homilies, see *Homily 1 on Psalm 67*.5. Origen understands the Word, the Son, to be the eternal *theos logos* who has taken upon himself our human nature for our salvation.

95 Lorenzo Perrone calls the divinization of the body somewhat surprising, but also shows its consistency with Origen's eschatology. See Perrone, "Et l'homme tout entier devient dieu," 209.

96 Cf. *Homily 2 on Psalm 76*.5.

97 *Homily on Psalm 81*.2 (OW 13, 513; Trigg, 442).

last day, likening it to the gradated glories of sun, moon, and stars as described in 1 Cor 15:41. Explaining the different glories of those worthy of the resurrection, Origen says, "When that occurs, God stood in the gathering of gods; in the midst he distinguishes gods."[98]

This follows from the verse: "How long will you judge unjustly and receive the *personae* of sinners?" (Ps 81:2). Origen says that the sin of preferring the wealthy is "frequent among us wretched human beings." He continues, "It has become our custom to give preference to those who are exceptional, not according to God, but according to the world, and to exclude and despise those who are exceptional according to God."[99] Origen attends to this term *personae*, and recognizes that actors take upon themselves various *personae*, or characters, in their stage performances. Something like that occurs on the stage of the world. We can take the *persona* of God, of Christ, of the Spirit, or of an angel. We can also take the *persona* of the devil, of the antichrist, of a demon. In each sin, we take the *persona* of that sin, such as the spirit of sexual immorality. Origen urges his people to receive the *persona* of Christ himself. He bids them, "Say, 'Or do you seek proof of Christ speaking in me?'"[100]

Later in this homily, Origen explicitly wants all the faithful to be gods—and knows how they may fall. In taking a *persona* in his preaching, he speaks in the divine voice, "I did not call some of you to be gods without calling others." He mentions bishops, presbyters, and deacons belonging to God, yet that is not enough: "I want you from the people to be gods."[101] Continuing in that same *persona*, Origen continues by explaining that is "not some of you to the exclusion

98 *Homily on Psalm 81*.2 (OW 13, 514; Trigg, 443).

99 *Homily on Psalm 81*.3 (OW 13, 514; Trigg, 443 [alt.]).

100 *Homily on Psalm 81*.3 (OW 13, 516; Trigg, 445).

101 *Homily on Psalm 81*.7 (OW 13, 519; Trigg, 448). Trigg notes "*Ek tou laou*, 'from the people,' is an early use of 'people' to distinguish Christians who do not belong to the three orders of clergy" (448n67).

of others—but *all*."[102] And yet when people sin "you die as human beings" (Ps 81:7). Just as Satan fell from heaven "like lightning" (Lk 10:18), so too sinners fall. Origen underscores, "you are in heaven when you believe in Christ, and in heaven when you recognize God; you are in heaven when you receive the Holy Spirit."[103] Our citizenship is in heaven (cf. Phil 3:20), but when we sin we fall in imitation of Satan, ruler of this world. Origen gives hope for us all in Christ who came to save those who have fallen—or who have even died in sin: "Therefore, let us also beseech God, let us say if we also fall, let us say even if we have died, '*Arise, God, judge the earth, because you will make a bequest in all the gentiles*,' through Jesus Christ, to whom is the glory and might to the ages of ages. Amen."

Do You Seek Proof of Christ Speaking in Me?

As we have just seen, Origen bids his people to repeat what Paul says, "Do you seek proof of Christ speaking in me?" (2 Cor 13:3). Origen cites this verse no less than six times in five Psalm homilies.[104] Some may take the Apostle's question to be indicating his unique status as the inspired vessel of election. Rather than being unique in this case, Paul is a model of conformity to Christ because he is in Christ and Christ is in him. We are, after all, bidden to imitate Paul as he imitates Christ. Origen preaches, "Become his [the Lord's] imitator like Paul, and you will find that the Lord is always in you. For you also will say, 'It is no longer I that live, but Christ lives in me.'"[105] That living is made known in an eminent way through our own speech, "for you also will *say*." Those speaking the words of

102 *Homily on Psalm 81.7* (OW 13, 519–20; Trigg, 448).

103 *Homily on Psalm 81.7* (OW 13, 522; Trigg, 449–50).

104 *Homily 2 on Psalm 15.1*; *Homily 3 on Psalm 36.11*; *Homily 1 on Psalm 67.1* and 2; *Homily 2 on Psalm 80.3*; *Homily on Psalm 81.3*. Lorenzo Perrone writes of what he calls christification in these sermons: "the saint or the perfect one becomes then an *alter Christus* [another Christ]. In this regard, Origen very frequently resorts to 2 Cor 13:3" (my translation). See Perrone, "Et l'homme tout entier devient dieu," 205.

105 *Homily 2 on Psalm 15.5* (OW 13, 102; Trigg, 67).

God have the Word within them. On his reading of Origen's Greek *Homilies on the Psalms,* Mark Randall James writes, "The goal of interpretation is to acquire the capacity to speak according to the example of the scriptures, which I refer to as 'learning the language of scripture.'"[106] Much later in his learned study, James writes "Origen himself frequently identifies the words of deified Christians with those of the Logos, often using for this purpose Paul's words in 2 Cor 13:3."[107] We now explore the Apostle's question, "Do you seek proof of Christ speaking in me?" in Origen's other Psalm homilies.

In *Homily 2 on Psalm 15,* Origen relates the account of Peter's preaching on this Psalm from the Acts of the Apostles. Peter is said to have "stood up with the Eleven" to preach. Origen takes this to mean that the apostles collectively bear witness that Jesus fulfills this Psalm's words:

> I have foreseen the Lord face to face through everything, because he is at my right hand, so that I will not be shaken. Therefore, my heart has rejoiced and my tongue has exulted, and my flesh will still set up a tent in hope, because you will not abandon my soul in hell nor will you allow your devout one to see corruption.

Clearly, the words are not the words of David, as the apostolic preaching in Acts makes evident, but they are the words of Christ.

Moreover, Christ speaks not only the Psalm itself, he speaks also the homily *about* the Psalm. "Or do you seek proof of Christ speaking in me?" (2 Cor 13:3), Origen quotes Paul. So wonderful is this act of Christ's assistance that Origen calls upon his people to pray for him:

> Just as, on other occasions, your prayers and requests for good things from God have helped us make Scripture clear, let them

106 James, *Learning the Language of Scripture,* 22.
107 James, *Learning the Language of Scripture,* 209.

> also come to our assistance now, that God may furnish a word to us who thirst and ask for enlightenment on matters that need clarity, and that we, through your prayers, even if at first we do not fully understand, may now, enlightened by the Word, present what must be explained in the Psalm with understanding.[108]

Origen does not mean that Christ is a ventriloquist, for he says that we are to hear both Jesus and Paul, for Paul says, "Be imitators of me, as I also am of Christ" (1 Cor 11:1). This imitation of Christ reaches even to the depths of divinity. By God's grace, we are called to "become perfect, as your Father in heaven is perfect" (Mt 5:48) and "Be holy, because I am holy, the Lord your God" (Lv 11:45; cf. 1 Pt 1:16) and again "be perfect before the Lord your God" (Dt 18:13).[109] As a preacher, Origen's primary concern is his people's growth in the mystery of Christ. Commenting on the words, "I have foreseen the Lord face to face through everything," Origen says: "For the Lord also dwells in you, if you wish, 'through everything.' Become his imitator like Paul and you will find that the Lord is always in you. For you also will say: 'It is no longer I that live, but Christ lives in me'" (Gal 2:20).[110]

Origen takes Paul again as his example in *Homily 3 on Psalm 36* when he preaches on the verse "The sinner borrows and will not pay back, but a just person is merciful and would give" (Ps 36:21). If taken literally, Origen argues, that does not make sense, because many sinners borrow money and pay back with interest. Surely, another meaning must be understood. Who is lending and who is borrowing? Origen takes the example of Paul lending and his listeners borrowing the approved silver in Paul's mouth. If the one borrowing is just, "he will give back with interest and say, 'You have

108 *Homily 2 on Psalm 15*.1 (OW 13, 92; Trigg, 59 [alt.]).
109 *Homily 2 on Psalm 15*.4 (OW 13, 100; Trigg, 65).
110 *Homily 2 on Psalm 15*.5 (OW 13, 102; Trigg, 67).

given me one sum. See, I have made ten sums.'"[111] Origen uses the Parable of the Talents in Mt 25:14–30 to show how the just return with interest what they have received from preaching, while the sinner "squanders everything that he borrowed."[112]

Origen then vividly turns to his people listening to him. "All of you are borrowing now. These are the loans; these words are the silver."[113] Origen recalls the Psalm verse "The oracles of the Lord are pure, refined silver, proven, cleansed for earth seven times." If Origen teaches badly, his silver is unproven. But if he teaches well, his silver, which is in fact the Lord's, is proven. "I am allowed to lend the Lord's silver, but I am not allowed to lend my own," he proclaims.[114] Valentinus, Basilides, and Marcion, infamous heretics of the previous century, gave only what was from themselves, not from the Lord. "But if you see someone speaking, not what is his own, but what is God's," Origen says, "and daring to say truly, 'Or do you seek proof of Christ speaking in me?" know that such a person lends, not what belongs to him, but what is the Lord's."[115] Origen humbly submits that he desires to give not from himself, but what he finds in the Gospels and the apostles, so that, as he says, "I should not be a sinner, so that I may not be punished, but as a just person I can return with interest from my conduct the capital of the words I have heard."[116]

Origen begins *Homily 1 on Psalm 67* by focusing on his Savior's words, "Learn from me, because I am gentle and lowly in heart" (Mt 11:29). He is persuaded that every word "without Christ's presence in the speaker is empty and from earth" (cf. 1 Cor 15:47; 1 Sam 3:19).[117]

111 *Homily 3 on Psalm 36*.11 (OW 13, 154; Trigg, 117).
112 *Homily 3 on Psalm 36*.11 (OW 13, 154; Trigg, 117).
113 *Homily 3 on Psalm 36*.11 (OW 13, 154; Trigg, 117).
114 *Homily 3 on Psalm 36*.11 (OW 13, 154; Trigg, 117).
115 *Homily 3 on Psalm 36*.11 (OW 13, 154; Trigg, 117).
116 *Homily 3 on Psalm 36*.11 (OW 13, 155; Trigg, 118 [alt.]).
117 *Homily 1 on Psalm 67*.1 (OW 13, 173; Trigg, 138).

He asks his people to pray with him the Psalmist's words "God, come to my assistance. Lord, hasten to assist me" (Ps 69:2). He wants a word to be given from God the Father so that he may give that word to his people, who can then rejoice. "I would therefore say; 'May they be delighted and gladdened' on your behalf today through 'Christ speaking in me.'"[118] He professes his own destitution and poverty, but he knows that God can gladden his people through his preaching. In this way will the Psalm's words be fulfilled, "Let God rise up, and let his enemies be scattered . . . and let the just rejoice, let them be glad before God, let them be delighted for joy." The entire homily is taken up with an interpretation of that passage, and we can focus with Origen on the command to tell God what to do: "Let God rise up."

Origen affirms that no one may give orders to God, and yet it seems God wants us to do just that in speaking to him. "For if masters have received a command from Christ speaking in Paul," Origen says alluding to 2 Cor 13:3, "'to allow yourselves fairness and equality towards slaves' (Col 4:1), why is it inappropriate for someone who has been ordered by God, and has received orders, to be confident about observing those orders with a certain freedom of speech, by giving an order reciprocally when praying to God?"[119] In short, God commands things of us, and he wants us to command things of him. "For commanding God is not a greater thing than becoming his heir. Commanding God is not a greater thing than becoming a joint heir with Christ himself," Origen boldly proclaims.[120] After all, he says, Christ came in the midst of human beings as one who serves. It is not because we are worthy to give orders to God, but it is on account of God's charity and indulgence

118 *Homily 1 on Psalm 67*.1 (OW 13, 174; Trigg, 139).
119 *Homily 1 on Psalm 67*.2 (OW 13, 175–76; Trigg, 141).
120 *Homily 1 on Psalm 67*.2 (OW 13, 177; Trigg, 142).

toward us. Not only does Christ speak in us, we are to have his freedom of speech towards God his Father.

Meditating on "I will remember your marvels from the beginning, and I will study all your works. And in your pursuits I will be talkative" (Ps 76:12–13), Origen returns to 2 Cor 13:3 in his *Homily 2 on Psalm 76*. He is helped by Pauline exegesis of Genesis. Referring to Eph 5:32, he accepts the great mystery of Christ and his Church in Gn 2:24, which speaks of man becoming one flesh with his wife. Referring to Gal 4:24, he accepts that Sarah and Hagar allegorically represent two covenants found in Gn 16:15. This mode of interpretation allows him to remember all of God's works from the beginning, from Genesis. What are God's works? All that turns out well, just as all good words are from God. Origen then refers to himself. As for all the words that proceed from his mouth, "those that are unassailable and divine are not mine but God's, so that I say confidently: "or do you seek proof of Christ who speaks in me?"[121] Those with lives filled with the gifts of God in grace may speak of the Scriptures not in worldly terms, but in godly terms. They speak the Word of God. How? Jesus says, "I am the way, and the truth, and the life" (Jn 14:6). Where is God's way? Origen answers, "In the holy one, if you are holy, keeping the command, 'You shall be holy, because I the Lord your God am holy'" (Lv 11:45).[122] Thus, Origen continues to interpret the next line of the Psalm, "O God, your way is in the holy one" (Ps 76:14).

We are like instruments of God, Origen maintains in *Homily 2 on Psalm 80*, who "seeks a lyre musically in tune, a harp well-tuned, a psaltery on which the strings have been tightened as they need to be."[123] Why does the Psalm mention these details of instrument? Origen's question is answered. God can play heavenly music

121 *Homily 2 on Psalm 76.4* (OW 13, 318; Trigg, 258).
122 *Homily 2 on Psalm 76.5* (OW 13, 320; Trigg, 259).
123 *Homily 2 on Psalm 80.1* (OW 13, 496; Trigg, 425).

with human beings as his instruments, if they are not silent. Origen preaches, "It is even possible for God to use the tongue of a just person as his own tongue and for God to use the mouth of a holy person, so that it is possible to say, 'The mouth of the Lord has spoken these things' (Is 40:5)"[124] Ultimately, it is a matter of a completeness of life: "Blessed is that person, who entirely becomes, in all the parts of the body, through the entire faculty of sensation, an instrument of Christ, an instrument of God's Word in such a way as to say: 'I no longer live, but Christ lives in me.'"[125]

Later in *Homily 2 on Psalm 80*, Origen interprets the verse "If you will hear me, there will not be in you a recent god" (Ps 80:9b-10a). Origen makes bold to say "that all human beings have in them either the genuine God or a recent, alien god."[126] He reads in the Psalms that "all the gods of the nations are demons" (Ps 95:50), and these "so-called but non-existent gods are in those who are enslaved to sins."[127] Origen gives as an immediate example the sin of covetousness: "Whenever they deify and lift up money as a god, there is in them a demonic object of idolatry."[128] Likewise, one overcome by sexual sin has become a temple not of the Holy Spirit, but of the spirit of sexual immorality. But the holy person says, "Or do you seek the proof of Christ speaking in me?" How different that is from sinners through whom we can hear the voices of demons. "When we are angered," continues Origen, "the spirit of anger employing us as prophets speaks what it has to say. Whenever we calm down, so that we become different from what we had been, we no longer say these things, for the spirit activating us has departed."[129] In this way, Origen tells his audience to heed the Proverb of "keep your

124 *Homily 2 on Psalm 80*.1 (OW 13, 497; Trigg, 426).
125 *Homily 2 on Psalm 80*.1 (OW 13, 497; Trigg, 427 [alt.]).
126 *Homily 2 on Psalm 80*.3 (OW 13, 499; Trigg, 429).
127 *Homily 2 on Psalm 80*.3 (OW 13, 499–500; Trigg, 429).
128 *Homily 2 on Psalm 80*.3 (OW 13, 500; Trigg, 429).
129 *Homily 2 on Psalm 80*.3 (OW 13, 500–501; Trigg, 430).

heart guarded with care" (Prv 4:23) and so "there will not be in you a recent god."[130]

As we see in his use of Paul's question in 2 Cor 13:3, Origen repeatedly interprets the Psalms, these divinely inspired prayers, to pertain to himself and his people so that they may avoid sin and experience the holiness that is deification, with the divine at work within their very being. Origen seeks to show how they can live out what the Apostle Paul himself experienced. It is a process of deification, which is complete only at the end of time. Every scriptural detail is fulfilled in Origen's preaching for the people's holiness, as the Word is given for our salvation.

Conclusion

Origen did not win everyone over to his understanding of preaching the Scriptures, either in his own time or in ours. R. P. C. Hanson was certainly not convinced that Origen understood the Bible or taught what the Bible says. Even Mark Randall James, deeply sympathetic to Origen's exegetical project, does not support Origen's practice of allegory for today. "To be frank," James admits, "I do not believe allegory remains viable in anything like the general way Origen used it. If there are good reasons to use allegory, there are often better reasons not to do so."[131]

Many people through the ages, however, appreciate the allegories taught in Origen's ministry of God's Word. Origen preached so that the Church may be built up. He labored over the letter so that the priestly people may advance from the letter to spiritual understanding, without abandoning the letter. He wanted his people to be deified. As I have argued, Origen exemplifies Benedict XVI's exhortation that the liturgical homily should "foster a

130 *Homily 2 on Psalm 80*.3 (OW 13, 501; Trigg, 430).
131 James, *Interpreting the Language of Scripture*, 23–24.

deeper understanding of the word of God, so that it can bear fruit in the lives of the faithful."[132] By studying Origen on holiness in his preaching on Leviticus and on the Psalms, we can accept a model for preaching: namely, communicating how the baptized come to know the Word in their own lives. Holiness is a process in which we ask, seek, and knock (cf. Mt 7:7), one of Origen's favorite scriptural motifs.[133] By his preaching, and its questioning, Origen sets the tone for the history of preaching as a record of a quest for life's conformity with the Word, found in Scripture and celebrated in the Church's liturgy.

Pope Benedict gives this expressed wish for those who hear about Origen: "I invite you—and so I conclude—to welcome into your hearts the teaching of this great master of faith. He reminds us with deep delight that in the prayerful reading of Scripture and in consistent commitment to life, the Church is ever renewed and rejuvenated."[134] In the desire to see the Church edified, "this great master of faith" concludes his homilies with a doxology. Almost always it is an explicitly Christological doxology, such as what we find at the end of 1 Pt 4:11:

> Whoever preaches, let it be with the words of God; whoever serves, let it be with the strength that God supplies, so that in all things God may be glorified through Jesus Christ, to whom belong glory and dominion forever and ever. Amen.[135]

Following the Petrine example, Origen thus directs the people's attention away from himself—and away from themselves—to the Word in praise. It is an act of humility in praise.

132 *Sacramentum Caritatis*, no. 46.

133 For examples, see Origen's counsel to interpret Scripture in the conclusion to his brief *Letter to Gregory, On First Principles* 2.9.4, and *Homily 2 on Psalm 67*.1.

134 Pope Benedict XVI, general audience, April 25, 2007.

135 For a study of Origen's conclusion to the homily, which is almost always explicitly Christological in its doxology, see Nautin, *Origène: Homélies sur Jérémie*, vol. 1, 129–31.

Following this focus in Origen on holiness, the goal of the virtuous life, for him and the people gathered before him to worship God together, we will see in the next chapter's attention to Ephrem the Syrian how the Word humbles himself for our repentance in humility, the ground of the virtuous life.

CHAPTER 2

EPHREM THE SYRIAN

The Word in Our Flesh for the Humility of Repentance

Of all the sins that early Christians recognize as antithetical to living a holy life in the Word, pride has the most inglorious place. As a response, preachers often turn in repentance to the Word's own humility. For example, the Apostle Paul, who wanted his listeners to have the same mind as that which was in Christ Jesus, observes that Christ "emptied himself, taking the form of a slave, coming in human likeness, and found human in appearance, he humbled himself, becoming obedient to death, even death on a cross" (Phil 2:7–8). Christ himself preaches, "Come to me, all you who labor and are burdened, and I will give you rest. Take my yoke upon you and learn from me, for I am meek and humble of heart; and you will find rest for yourselves" (Mt 11:28–29). Knowing our need for holiness, Christ humbled himself to be in our condition of servitude so that way we might learn humility from him and, by his grace, be freed to make his humility manifest. Preachers conformed to the Word enfleshed can show his humility by their own humble words and deeds.

Ignatius Zakka I Iwas, Syrian Orthodox Patriarch of Antioch and all the East from 1980 to 2014, explains: "Humility is the foundation and the culmination of all Christian virtues. Moreover, meekness is the ripe fruit of humility, and its companion in the spiritual struggle." The Patriarch continues:

> The virtue of humility, when established in the heart and mind of a person, becoming a part of him, directs his behavior and others see it in him through his behavior. As that person acquires meekness, he is given enough spiritual courage to wrestle the cursed devil and overcome hard temptations.

The Patriarch teaches about the humble one:

> God grants him sufficient strength for self-control to overcome raging anger, limit evil thoughts and keep away from hatred, jealousy and enmity, thereby obeying God's commandments: "Do not resist an evil person. But whoever slaps you on your right cheek, turn the other to him also. If anyone wants to sue you and take away your tunic, let him have your cloak also" (St. Matthew 5:39–40).[1]

From this Syrian Orthodox Patriarch's reflection, we now turn in our study of incarnation, deification, and proclamation to an early Christian saint who preaches melodiously about the Lord's humility as a basis for ours: Ephrem the Syrian (d. 373).

The Word in Ephrem's Flesh for Us

"Goodness encountered slandering mouths and made them praising harps; this is why all mouths should give praise to the one who removed slanderous speech from them." This is how Ephrem's

1 His Holiness Moran Mor Ignatius Zakka I Iwas, "Meekness and Humility," Message of January 20, 2007. https://www.malankara.com/node/2846 accessed on April 25, 2020.

Homily on Our Lord begins.[2] Ephrem is the greatest teacher of the Syriac Christian tradition.[3] In this beautiful sermon, he meditates on how the goodness of the Lord's humble speech wins over enemies to repentance and the praise of God.[4] Victory through humble speech is not an isolated aspect of his understanding of Christ in this particular prose work, but characterizes his entire theological project. For Ephrem, the all-powerful and infinitely majestic Lord seeks human conversion through the revelation of the incarnation's divine humbling. Ephrem deftly lays out this understanding for his hearers so that they may be touched by the Lord's humility and turn back to the Lord. Ephrem's praise of humility has much to offer today, especially to those Christians dedicated to evangelization.

Ephrem holds a unique position among Christian preachers and teachers.[5] For example, among Doctors of the universal Church recognized by Rome from the first eight Christian centuries, only

2 *Homily on Our Lord* 1, 1 in Edward G. Mathews, Jr. and Joseph P. Amar, *St. Ephrem the Syrian: Selected Prose Works; Commentary on Genesis, Commentary on Exodus, Homily on Our Lord, Letter to Publius*, ed. Kathleen McVey, *The Fathers of the Church* vol. 91 (Washington, DC: The Catholic University of America Press, 1994), p. 273.

3 Perhaps the best book in English for introducing the Syriac Christian tradition is *The Syriac Fathers on Prayer and the Spiritual Life*, translated by Sebastian Brock (Kalamazoo, MI: Cistercian Publications Inc., 1987). In this work, the Oxford University Syriac specialist Sebastian Brock says, "As both poet and theologian St Ephrem is unsurpassed among Syriac writers" (p. 30).

4 This twin emphasis of repentance and praise in Christ has the greatest importance for salvation. Khaled Anatolios argues: (1) that Christ saves us by fulfilling our original vocation to participate in the mutual glorification of the three persons of the Trinity; and (2) that Christ saves us by vicariously repenting for our rejection of this doxological vocation. For this argument of "doxological contrition," see Khaled Anatolios, *Deification through the Cross: An Eastern Christian Theology of Salvation* (Grand Rapids, MI: Eerdmans, 2020).

5 For an overview of Ephrem in English, see esp. Mathews and Amar, *Selected Prose Works*, 3–56; Paul S. Russell, "St. Ephraem, the Syrian Theologian," *ProE* 7, no. 1 (1998), pp. 79–90; Sidney H. Griffith, "A Spiritual Father for the Whole Church: the Universal Appeal of St. Ephraem the Syrian," *Hugoye* 1, no. 2 (1998 [2010]): 197–220, and Sebastian Brock, *The Luminous Eye: The Spiritual World Vision of Saint Ephrem the Syrian*, CSS no. 124 (Kalamazoo, MI: Cistercian Publications, 1985) and *Singer of the Word of God: Ephrem the Syrian and his Significance in Late Antiquity*, Sebastianyotho 1 (Piscataway, NJ: Gorgias Press, 2020). For a pioneering assessment that now has rather dated critical analysis, see Arthur Vööbus, *Literary, Critical, and Historical Studies in Ephrem the Syrian*, Papers of the Estonian Theological Society in Exile, vol. 10 (Stockholm: ETSE, 1958).

Ephrem wrote in a language that was neither Latin nor Greek.[6] Little is known about this Syriac Father's life beyond what he himself shares, and that in itself is open to interpretation on account of his poetic expression and doubts about the authenticity of the text.[7] He was born in the first decade of the fourth century in the Syriac-speaking city of Nisibis, a Roman stronghold on the frontier against the Persians. It is near the present-day border of Turkey and Syria. "Ephrem was a voluminous author," says Jeffrey Wickes, "but we do not know exactly where or how he was educated. Besides the Bible, we do not know what he read. Even with the Bible, we do not know precisely how he learned to read it."[8] Ephrem uses the word *'allānâ* to designate his office, a term interpreted to mean that he was a deacon.[9] As such, he served the successive bishops of Nisibis through a vigorous defense of the faith in his prolific preaching and writing. At some point in connection to the Roman Empire's ceding of Nisibis to Persia in 363, Ephrem moved to the cosmopolitan center of learning of Edessa within the Roman Empire where he continued to write. According to tradition, his death occurred on June 9, 373.[10]

Because he is known primarily for his verse, some may object to the presentation of Ephrem as an example of "preaching." But

6 See the encyclical *Principi Apostolorum Petro* of Pope Benedict XV, October 5, 1920, in Claudia Carlen, *The Papal Encyclicals 1903–1939* (Raleigh, NC: McGrath Publishing Company, 1981), pp. 195–201. Pope Benedict XV noted Ephrem's own humility in extolling him: "Therefore, God, who has 'exalted the humble,' bestows great glory on blessed Ephrem and proposes him to this age as a doctor of heavenly wisdom and an example of the choicest virtues" (no. 15 on p. 198).

7 For a call to reassess the corpus of Ephrem's writings, see Blake Hartung, "The Authorship and Dating of the Syriac Corpus attributed to Ephrem of Nisibis: A Reassessment," *ZAC* 22, no. 2 (2018): 296–321. Some of what Edmund Beck judged to be spurious collections may in fact contain smaller authentic writings.

8 Jeffrey Wickes, *Bible and Poetry in Late Antique Mesopotamia: Ephrem's Hymns on Faith*, CLA 5 (Oakland, CA: University of California Press, 2019), 1.

9 *Hymns against Heresies* 56.10 in Mathews and Amar, *Selected Prose Works*, 29. The term is not the usual Syriac word for deacon, but Amar and Mathews write, "there is little reason to doubt this tradition" (29).

10 The year seems nearly certain, while the less certain sixth-century Chronicle of Edessa provides the date of June 9.

we must accept that preaching has had many senses in Christian history, and a case can be made to include Ephrem as one of the greatest early preachers. He wrote both poetry and prose to praise God and teach the people. More famous for his poetry than his prose, Ephrem wrote in two poetic genres, *madrāšê* (teaching songs or hymns) and *mêmrê* (metrical homilies).[11] According to Sidney Griffith, the former, with its unique complexity, was Ephrem's "signature literary form," and the subsequent Syriac liturgical composers Jacob of Serūg (ca. 451–521) and Narsai of Nisibis (d. ca. 501) preferred to compose in the latter's simpler form, which Ephrem also pioneered.[12]

Ephrem's prose is likewise subdivided into two groups, expository prose and rhetorical prose. His writings demonstrate a love of symbolism in a scripturally-based theological method.[13] Sacred

11 Sidney Griffith opts for Andrew Palmer's phrase of "teaching songs" over "hymns" in translating *madrāšê*. See Sidney Griffith, "'Spirit in the Bread; Fire in the Wine': The Eucharist as 'Living Medicine' in the Thought of Ephraem the Syrian," *MoTh* 15, no. 2 (1999): 225–46 at 227. Griffith is following Andrew Palmer, "A Lyre without a Voice, the Poetics and the Politics of Ephrem the Syrian," *ARAM* 5 (1993): 371–99. Wickes writes that Ephrem's "*madrāšê* were not sermons; they were metered, philosophically and theologically subtle songs." See Jeffrey Wickes, "Between Liturgy and School: Reassessing the Performative Context of Ephrem's *Madrāšê*," *JECS* 26, no. 1 (2018): 25–51, at 37. But as for the verse homilies in the Syriac tradition, these "would have been chanted by the male preacher." See Susan A. Harvey, "Revisiting the Daughters of the Covenant: Women's Choirs and Sacred Song in Ancient Syriac Christianity," *Hugoye* 8, no. 2 (2005[2009]): 125–49, at 137.

12 Sidney H. Griffith, "'Denominationalism' in Fourth-Century Syria: Readings in Saint Ephraem's *Hymns against Heresies, Madrāshê* 22–24," in *The Garb of Being: Embodiment and the Pursuit of Holiness in Late Ancient Christianity*, eds. Georgia Frank, Susan R. Holman, and Andrew S. Jacobs, OCCT (New York: Fordham University Press, 2020), 79–100, at 82. Sebastian Brock writes, "The basic organizing principle of Syriac poetry is syllable (*hegyānā*) count. Although it has sometimes been claimed that stress patterns also played a role, this has never been satisfactorily substantiated. Rhyme is occasionally found in early poetry, but it is only used for special effect. The regular use of rhyme becomes a common feature from about the 9th cent. onwards, due to the influence of Arabic poetry." See Sebastian P. Brock, "Poetry," in *Gorgias Encyclopedic Dictionary of the Syriac Heritage*, eds. Sebastian P. Brock, Aaron M. Butts, George A, Kiraz, and Lucas Van Rompay (Gorgias Press, 2011; online ed. Beth Mardutho, 2018), https://gedsh.bethmardutho.org/Poetry.

13 See Tanios Bou Mansour, *La Pensée Symbolique de Saint Ephrem le Syrien*, Bibliothèque de l'Université Saint-Esprit 16 (Kaslik, Lebanon: Bibliothèque de l'Université Saint-Esprit 1988). For an extended argument against claims that Ephrem was ignorant of Greek philosophy, see Ute Possekel, *Evidence of Greek Philosophical Concepts in the Writings of Ephrem the Syrian*, *CSCO* vol. 580; *Subsidia* tom. 102 (Leuven: Peeters, 1999). More

poetry and preaching arguably have much in common. For instance, in the Syriac tradition, the women in the choirs that Ephrem established are called *malphānyāthâ*, "teachers" in the feminine form, "a weighty term in Syriac, connoting learning, authority, and wisdom."[14] Cannot Ephrem himself be considered their preacher and ours? Writing less than 15 years after Ephrem's death, Jerome gives this entry for him in his *On Illustrious Men*, which indicates that his writing was used for liturgical preaching:

> Ephrem, deacon of the church at Edessa, composed many works in Syriac (*multa Syro sermone*), and came to enjoy such prestige that his works are read publicly after the Scripture readings in some churches. I once read in Greek his work, *On the Holy Spirit*, which someone had translated from the Syriac language, and even in translation, I could recognize the acuteness of lofty genius. He died in the reign of the emperor Valens.[15]

That work on the Holy Spirit praised by Jerome is not extant and seems otherwise unknown.[16]

---

recently, Lewis Ayres has written, "When we read Ephrem against the background of his pro-Nicene contemporaries we need to move beyond assuming that his love of imagery and paradox is what marks his theology as essentially Syriac and un-Hellenic.... Whereas previous study has frequently assumed that the presence or not of discernable equivalents to Greek philosophical terminology is the point of reference for indicating depth of contact with the Greek world, this book's account of pro-Nicene theology should suggest alternative routes for investigation." See his *Nicaea and its Legacy: An Approach to Fourth-Century Trinitarian Theology* (Oxford: Oxford University Press, 2004), 235. One general point lost on some readers is that the Fathers of the Church of various languages, including Greek writers, denounced the wisdom of the "Greeks" as foolishness, following Paul writing in Greek to the Greeks of Corinth (cf. 1 Cor 1:18–25); but this hardly means that they shunned the language and culture of the Greek world. For a brief overview of Ephrem's Greco-Roman context, see Wickes, *Bible and Poetry in Late Antique Mesopotamia*, 12–14.

14 Susan Ashbrook Harvey, "Patristic Worlds," in *Patristic Studies in the Twenty-First Century*, eds. Brouria Bitton-Ashkelony, Theodore de Bruyn, and Carol Harrison (Tournhout: Brepols, 2015), 25–53, at 33. Among her sources, Harvey notes the Syriac vita of Ephrem, chap. 31 (*The Syriac* Vita *Tradition of Ephrem the Syrian*, edited and translated by Joseph P. Amar [CSCO, 629–30], 71) and Jacob of Serug's *Homily on Ephrem*, vv. 41–42 (*A Metrical Homily on Holy Mar Ephrem by Mar Jacob of Serug*, ed. and tr. Joseph P. Amar [PO, 47], 35). Also, see Harvey, "Revisiting the Daughters of the Covenant: Women's Choirs and Sacred Song in Ancient Syriac Christianity."

15 Jerome, *On Illustrious Men*, chap. 115 (TU 14, 51; Halton, 149 [alt.]).

16 For a recent argument for Ephrem's high pneumatology within the pro-Nicene movement, see David Wesley Kiger, "Fire in the Bread, Life in the Body: The Pneumatology of Ephrem the Syrian," Ph.D. diss., Marquette University, 2020.

Indeed, the legacy of Ephrem is a mixed story of both great fame and obscurity. Ephrem quickly became renowned throughout the Christian world.[17] His original writings were translated into such languages as Greek, Armenian, Latin, Coptic, Ethiopic, Georgian, and Slavonic.[18] Yet his popularity undermined his own work soon after his death.[19] For not only were his original writings translated; soon other writings with claims to being Ephrem's sprang up. Patristic scholars introduced the term "Ephrem Graecus" to name the author of any Greek writing claimed to be Ephrem's. Edward G. Mathews and Joseph P. Amar judge that "the Greek words attributed to Ephrem are so numerous that even in the native Greek patristic tradition only the works of John Chrysostom exceed them."[20] Today, Syriac studies are retrieving the authentic Ephrem and making him more accessible to a general readership.[21] The spectacular results show that Ephrem deserves a prominent place in the study of early Christian preaching.

Ephrem is a model of communicating the faith through scriptural imagery.[22] As spiritual exercises, Ephrem's teachings allow believers to consider and reconsider from various angles how biblical symbols inform the profession of faith for their growth in

17 All of the various Churches whose divisions resulted from the Christological controversies of the fifth century claim the fourth-century Ephrem as an eminent authority.

18 One scholar of patristic preaching surmises that "no other poet-preacher in Christian antiquity rose to the level of fame as Ephrem;" the Syriac doctor displayed excellence in both theology and poetry. Jonathan Armstrong, "Ephrem the Syrian: Preaching Christ through Poetry and Paradox," in *A Legacy of Preaching*, vol. 1, *Apostles to the Revivalists*, foreword by Timothy George, edited by Benjamin K. Forrest, et al. (Grand Rapids, MI: Zondervan Academic, 2018), 95–110, at 106.

19 This obscuring of the authentic Ephrem occurred most notably among his own Syriac Christians, who relied upon Greek hagiographical models of monasticism to reconfigure the story of Ephrem's life. See *The Syriac* Vita *Tradition of Ephrem the Syrian*, edited and translated by Joseph P. Amar, CSCO 629–30 (Leuven: Peeters, 2011).

20 Mathews and Amar, *Selected Prose Works*, 39.

21 Particularly outstanding in his work for critical editions and German translations of Ephrem was Edmund Beck, a Benedictine monk of Metten Abbey, in the *CSCO*.

22 For the meaning of faith and how to express it, see Sidney H. Griffith, "'Faith Seeking Understanding' in the Thought of St. Ephraem the Syrian," in George C. Berthold, ed. *Faith Seeking Understanding: Learning and the Catholic Tradition*, Selected papers from the Symposium and Convocation celebrating the Saint Anselm College Centennial (Manchester, New Hampshire: Saint Anselm College Press, 1991), 35–55.

discipleship, beginning from where they are and ending only in the praise of the ineffable.[23] Jeffrey Wickes argues that "the meanings Ephrem drew from the Bible were irrevocably entangled with the poetic self he presented, the audience for whom he presented them, and the divine Christ about whom he sang."[24] His style lends itself to meditating upon biblical passages for their cumulative impression upon the believer. Preachers would therefore do well to follow Ephrem in not only communicating correct information, but doing so in the radiance of beauty so as to let the Word of God attract those who hear the Christian message on their level.[25] In a particularly compelling way, Ephrem's emphasis on the Lord's humility can serve to demonstrate his homiletic and didactic power. Wickes says that Ephrem "presented himself as reticent in his speech and as an instrument of the divine—an instrument anchored in the biblical text. At the same time, he presented his poetic self through the lens of sinful or marginal biblical characters to craft a rhetoric of humility."[26]

What exactly does "humility" mean and how does it function within Ephrem's teaching? Because of the varieties of languages, cultures, and theological expressions in the early Church, its historical use should first be established. For example, Augustine frequently uses the Latin *humilitas* and related words to speak of the mystery of the incarnation, the Christian life lived in charity, and the exercise of ministry.[27] John Chrysostom, on the other hand, is famous for speaking of "humility" as the condescension expressed

23 For comparing speech with silence in Ephrem, see Paul S. Russell, "Ephrem the Syrian on the Utility of Language and the Place of Silence," *JECS* 8, no. 1 (2000): 21–37.

24 Wickes, *Bible and Poetry in Late Antique Mesopotamia*, 1.

25 Narsai in the fifth century and Jacob of Serug at the end of the fifth century and beginning of the sixth, are witnesses of Ephrem's influence in the Syriac tradition. Romanos the Melodist, a sixth-century Syrian who wrote in Greek, could also be seen in this tradition.

26 Wickes, *Bible and Poetry in Late Antique Mesopotamia*, 6.

27 See Deborah Wallace Ruddy, "A Christological Approach to Virtue: Augustine and Humility," Ph.D. diss., Boston College, 2001.

in the Greek *synkatabasis*. Here it shows God's adaptation to our creaturely needs and provides the model for a preacher's own adaptation to audiences.[28] Going farther east (and still earlier) we find that Syriac writers such as Ephrem use words related to humility in the nominal, adjectival, and verbal parts of speech from the root *m-k-k*.[29] On the most basic level, *m-k-k* implies a spatial meaning of low, short, deflated, prostrate, flattened, and beneath everything. *M-k-k* is found in the Syriac Bible in such places as the title of Psalm 130 [131], the meekness described in Mt 5:5, 11:29, and 21:5, and Paul's levelling of pride in 2 Cor 10:4. Ephrem's special use of *m-k-k* is significant, because he meditates on biblical passages that do not literally have this word but are interpreted through the paradox of divine humility.

Also, Ephrem offers a humility to counter his theological opponents' pride in their unlawful investigation of divine matters. As Wickes shows, Ephrem uses the verbs *bṣâ* and *b'â* in different ways to speak of searching or requesting.[30] Often, in Ephrem's understanding, this is not acceptable, because such investigation does not proceed from a humble faith in what God has revealed to us. Ephrem's frequent denunciation of his opponents' pride in divine matters should therefore not be interpreted as anti-intellectualism, but rather as a lived humility made manifest in speech. The following will illustrate Ephrem's keen attention to humility as a way of unlocking the meaning of God's revelation for human conversion, by grasping terms that God wants us to know and accept.

Axiomatic for Ephrem is that all theological reasoning and speaking begins with listening to God, who gives us the witnesses of creation and Scripture. Moreover, he understands that God is

28 See Rylaarsdam, *John Chrysostom on Divine Pedagogy*.

29 Of related interest is the root *srq* concerning emptying, used to translate Phil 2:7.

30 Wickes also relates other key terms, such as for debating and disputing, that Ephrem uses against his theological opponents. See Wickes, *Hymns on Faith*, 43–52.

revealed in scriptural terms in different ways. For example, when Ephrem speaks of God's revelation in the Bible, he says frequently that God "puts on names."[31] These names, or metaphors, show the greatness of the divine condescension, whereby God deigns to speak to us on our level, in our feeble terms.[32] Metaphors do not tell us fully who God is, but do reveal God's gracious act of lowering himself. God wants to communicate to us on our own level. Ephrem expresses this so beautifully. After citing the case of condescension in teaching speech to a bird, Ephrem writes:

> The Essence, exalted above all in all,
> Bent down his height lovingly and acquired our habit.
> He labored in every way to turn all to himself.[33]

Ephrem does not want his listeners, however, to confuse the Lord's loving kindness in this condescension with their own mundane experiences and way of speech. Believers need *pûršānâ*, the discernment and discretion to appreciate what God is saying to us. This requires knowing that God's humility in revelation expresses the Almighty's merciful goodness for us who are lowly creatures, very much bound by limitations. For example, Ephrem says,

> If someone concentrates his attention solely
> on the metaphors used of God's majesty,
> he abuses and misrepresents that majesty
> and thus errs

31 Brock, *The Luminous Eye*, 42 and 60–66.

32 Ephrem certainly does not view all of God's revelation as metaphorical. For example, he says,

> He has names perfect and accurate,
> And he has names borrowed and transient.
> He has quickly put them on and quickly taken them off.

See *On Faith* 44.2 (Wickes, *Hymns on Faith*, 241; cf. discussion of Brock, *The Luminous Eye*, pp. 60–66). Father, Son, and Holy Spirit are examples of "perfect" names. See also *On Faith* 46.12.

33 *On Faith* 31.7 (Wickes, *Hymns on Faith*, 194; cf. Brock, *The Luminous Eye*, 62).

> by means of those metaphors
> with which God clothed himself for his benefit,
> and he is ungrateful to that Grace
> which stooped low
> to the level of his childishness;
> although it has nothing in common with him,
> yet Grace clothed itself in his likeness
> in order to bring him to the likeness of itself.[34]

This is a remarkable passage that illustrates not only Ephrem's understanding of revelation, but his view of divine humility in general. The lowliness to which God stoops shows his mercy to us who should taste his sweetness and give praise.[35] If we see divine lowliness as only lowliness, we would miss the great revelation that the glorious and ineffable divinity has been humbled in order to bring us "to the likeness of itself." Its very purpose is conversion and elevation.

For this reason, Ephrem knows that if we do not think rightly in faith, we will be confused about who Christ is and who we are to become through Christ. He begins *Hymn 29 on Faith* in this way that puts deification in the foreground:

> God, in his mercy, called
> Mortals gods, by grace.[36]

Ephrem then shows how the One who is above cherubim, seraphim, and all the heavenly watchers is born in the flesh—for our salvation:

34 *Hymns on Paradise* 11.6 in *Saint Ephrem: Hymns on Paradise*, translated by Sebastian Brock, PPS (Crestwood, New York: St. Vladimir's Seminary Press, 1990), 156.

35 See *On Faith* 63.11 (Wickes, *Hymns on Faith*, 320; cf. Brock, *The Luminous Eye*, 64–65).

36 *On Faith* 29.1 (Wickes, *Hymns on Faith*, 186).

> The weak body which he came down and put on,
> His names and his actions are like it.
> And just as it was necessary for him to be hungry,
> And it was necessary for him to pray.
> And just as all his hunger was of the body.
> All his want was of the body.
> Do not die because of the names
> That Life put on to make all live.
> The Great One has put on
> Needy names out of love for you, because of the body.[37]

In his experience of the Word in his life, Ephrem develops what we can call a "soteriology of humility." We can see that both in his reading of God's humble Word in Scripture and in his understanding of that same Word in the humility of our lives.

God's Word of Humility in Scripture

Humility in the Beginning: *Commentary on Genesis*

For a clarifying insight into divine humility in the language of revelation, let us listen to Ephrem's comments on the story of Gn 6:5–8. This passage narrates from God's perspective the sinfulness of the human race during the time of Noah. About God's being sorry from having made creation, Ephrem writes:

> God *was sorry* does not mean that God did not know that they would come to this, but rather that He wished to make their great wickedness manifest before the generations to come, that they had committed such wantonness that they even brought to remorse God, who does not feel remorse. In addition, God defended his justice; He did not drown them in the

37 *On Faith* 29.2–3 (Wickes, *Hymns on Faith*, 186).

> flood without reason. That Nature that does not feel remorse humbled itself to say, 'I am sorry,' so that that rebellious generation might hear and quake in fear, and so that remorse might be sown in those whose heart rebelled against remorse.[38]

This illustrates how Ephrem often pairs acts of divine lowliness with the appropriate response of human repentance of sinful pride. In this case, the pairing instructs those later generations that will hear the story as well as the generation in the story. God's revelation is understood both in its original context and in its application to subsequent ages. Ephrem frequently unveils the opportunity for a human response in repentance within the scene being narrated. This literary device engages the reader, who overhears Ephrem's comments directed to individuals mentioned in the Scriptures. The following two stories from the *Commentary on Genesis* display this literary device in Ephrem's exegesis.

First, Ephrem understands that if Adam and Eve had repented of their sin of transgressing God's commandment, they would have escaped the curses decreed. Therefore, God gave them various opportunities, through his divine condescension, to do so. For example, God waits before coming down—so that Adam and Eve could admonish themselves. Then, God makes sound come from his feet so that Adam and Eve could hear him approach and thus offer words of repentance. Finally, God—who is all-knowing—asks, "Where are you, Adam?" Ephrem interjects his own words to Adam: "Speak to God now, before he asks you about the coming of the serpent and about the transgression that you and Eve committed."[39] But Adam instead blames Eve. After God "came down to question

38 *Commentary on Genesis* 6.7 (Mathews and Amar, *Selected Prose Works*, 137). Ephrem argues against a Marcionite interpretation of anthropomorphism in the Scriptures. In *Hymns on Virginity and the Symbols of the Lord* 29.6, Ephrem says, "The children of the left hand heard this and were perplexed. They held that his nature was susceptible to regret" in Kathleen McVey, *Ephrem the Syrian: Hymns*, CWS (New York and Mahwah, NJ: Paulist Press, 1989), 392.

39 *Commentary on Genesis* 2.25 (Mathews and Amar, *Selected Prose Works*, 116).

Eve," Eve in turn blames the serpent. The final extent of the divine condescension is then reached, for neither Adam nor Eve gives a sign of repentance, and the serpent is incapable of repentance. God never speaks humble words to the serpent. Why? Ephrem explains, "For where there is opportunity for repentance, it would be right to inquire, but to one who is a stranger to repentance judgment is fitting."[40] For Ephrem, God judged the serpent first so that Eve and Adam would still have time to repent upon hearing its punishment. Since Adam would not repent even after hearing Eve's punishment, Ephrem comments thus on the punishment given to Adam: "Because 'you are from the dust,' and have forgotten yourself, 'you shall return to your dust,' so that, through your state of humiliation, you shall come to know your true essence."[41]

Second, Ephrem considers how God interacts with Cain, who together with Abel prepared offerings for God. Rather than being filled with gloomy tears that God did not accept his sacrifice, Cain is enraged. Ephrem comments that Cain's sacrifice was "not accepted because of his spitefulness and his lack of virtue."[42] After Cain murdered his brother Abel and lied to his parents, claiming that Abel had entered Paradise,[43] God appears to Cain and asks, "Where is Abel your brother?" Again, Ephrem emphasizes how the Lord stoops to ask what he already knows. Ephrem teaches, "God appeared to Cain with kindness so that if he repented, the sin of murder that his fingers had committed might be effaced by the compunction on his lips. . . . To him who knows all, who asked him about his brother in order to win him back, [Cain] retorted

40 *Commentary on Genesis* 2.29 (Mathews and Amar, *Selected Prose Works*, 118).

41 *Commentary on Genesis* 2.31 (Mathews and Amar, *Selected Prose Works*, 120), cf. Gn 3:19.

42 *Commentary on Genesis* 3.4 (Mathews and Amar, *Selected Prose Works*, 126).

43 Ephrem explains that Cain spoke this lie to Adam and Eve so that no one would seek vengeance for Abel; cf. *Commentary on Genesis* 3.5 (Mathews and Amar, *Selected Prose Works*, 126–27).

angrily and said, 'I do not know, am I my brother's keeper?'"[44] As in his earlier direct address to Adam, Ephrem now speaks to Cain and gives the reason for the punishment of wandering about on the earth in fear: "because you have walked on it in arrogance and in haughtiness."[45] Cain is thus humiliated, and God ensures that Cain lives in a lowly state but without himself being murdered. Ephrem says that "because Cain sought death so that no one would mock his lowly state, seven generations would come and see his lowly state and then he would die."[46] Like his parents' offense, Cain's sin of pride and obstinate refusal to repent after divine condescension result in a forced humiliation.

Ephrem does not understand forced humiliation to be the last word in the relationship between God and the human race. God continues to attract proud humans to humility through examples of humility, such as the humility of Moses, the meekest man in the world (cf. Nm 12:30). For instance, God uses Moses' humility to preserve Israel after their sin of worshiping the golden calf. God asks for Moses' permission to annihilate Israel in order to elicit Moses' humble prayer. Ephrem explains, "Therefore, by revealing this to [Moses], it is clear that he was not going to do the people harm; he was prepared to forgive."[47] In another place, Ephrem returns to the story of the humble Moses amidst the proud people of Israel at the time of the Exodus. Ephrem says, "God, who needed nothing to save his people, later found himself in need of the humility of Moses just to abide the grumbling and complaining of (his) critics."[48] But the humility manifested on Mount Sinai after the people's idolatry is a preparation for the greatest act of humility. For Ephrem, the

44 *Commentary on Genesis* 3.6 (Mathews and Amar, *Selected Prose Works*, 127).

45 *Commentary on Genesis* 3.8 (Mathews and Amar, *Selected Prose Works*, 128).

46 *Commentary on Genesis* 3.8 (Mathews and Amar, *Selected Prose Works*, 128–29).

47 *Commentary on Exodus* 32.6 (Mathews and Amar, *Selected Prose Works*, 264).

48 *Homily on Our Lord* 41.1 (Mathews and Amar, *Selected Prose Works*, 315).

humility of Moses is a mere "shadow of the humility of our Lord."[49] Indeed, the all-merciful God who was clothed in humble, human words will be clothed in a humble, human body so that creatures can learn humility and be converted.

Humility in the Incarnation: *The Homily on Our Lord*

Ephrem is in his finest poetic form when he speaks about the incarnation of Christ, the infinite one who becomes finite for our salvation. Ephrem expresses the Christian faith in this mystery as a paradox that we can only look at with ceaseless awe. God puts on a body like clothes, with all the lowliness of the human condition, and yet remains the incomprehensible One who contains everything.[50] In exposing this paradox, Ephrem emphasizes that the humble condition demonstrates the loving kindness of God for creatures. For example, Ephrem alludes to Mary's hymn of the Magnificat, but applies the great reversal not to the world's rich and the poor, as Mary did, but to the divine and the human. Here, God's putting on a body means that the Rich One clothes us through his being stripped:

> The womb of your mother overthrew the orders:
> The Establisher of all entered a Rich One;
> He emerged poor. He entered her a Lofty One;
> He emerged humble. He entered her a Radiant One,
> and he put on a despised hue and emerged.
> He entered a mighty warrior, and put on fear
> inside her womb. He entered, Nourisher of all,
> and he acquired hunger. He entered, the One who gives drink
> to all,

49 *Homily on Our Lord* 41.1 (Mathews and Amar, *Selected Prose Works*, 315).

50 For this emphasis in Ephrem and the Syriac tradition, see Chapter 10, "'Clothed in the Body' as a Metaphor for Incarnation," in Hannah Hunt, *Clothed in the Body: Asceticism, the Body and the Spiritual in the Late Antique Era*, Ashgate Studies in Philosophy & Theology in Late Antiquity (London: Routledge, 2016), 137–57.

and he acquired thirst. Stripped and laid bare,
He emerged from [her womb], the One who clothes all.[51]

When considering the deeds of Christ, Ephrem continues this paradoxical meditation on such awe-inspiring mysteries as the baptism in the Jordan, the fast in the desert, the dispute with Satan, the passion, and the descent to the dead. Of these, the dispute with Satan can serve to introduce Ephrem's predilection for divine humility in the actions of Christ. In a hymn from *On Virginity and the Symbols of the Lord*, Ephrem teaches that Christ conquered Satan by putting on the simplicity of the Scriptures:

He merely quoted again and again, and the evil one wailed
to see that he took refuge in simplicity.

Ephrem is quick here to draw an unfavorable comparison to himself and his listeners. He laments:

Our pride is not able to put on
the armor of your humility.[52]

Because of the vastness of this topic, we limit the study of Christ's humble words to Ephrem's *Homily on Our Lord*.[53] In this work, Ephrem preaches with great appreciation for the power of

51 *Hymns on the Nativity* 11.7–8 (McVey, *Hymns*, 132).

52 *Hymns on Virginity and on the Symbols of the Lord* 14.5 (McVey, *Hymns*, 321).

53 The German Benedictine editor of Ephrem's corpus, Edmund Beck, judged Sections 34 and 35 of the *Homily on Our Lord* to be later insertions. See Amar's comments in *Selected Prose Works*, 310, n. 192 and Beck, *Sermo de Domino nostro, CSCO* 271, i. Nothing from these sections appears in my treatment. The interpolation construes from the humility of the Lord that Christ has two natures, the lofty divine nature and the humble human nature. While the attention to two natures is a sign that these words post-date the fourth-century Ephrem, it should be recalled that the divine nature expresses itself in humility for Ephrem. For a study on select areas of this work, see Angela Y. Kim, "Signs of Ephrem's Exegetical Techniques in his *Homily on Our Lord*," *Hugoye* 3, no. 1 (2000 [2010]): 55–70. Kim writes, "Ephrem's exaltation of humility in the face of bold questioning probably is generated by

words, a power that most specifically characterizes humans among all creatures. Commenting upon the healing of deaf-mutes worked by Jesus, Ephrem says, "If it is by reason of speech that we surpass all creatures, then its deficiency is the greatest of all deficiencies."[54] It follows that Ephrem's soteriology of humility is emphatic about the Lord's healing of our speech, especially for singing praise to God.

With this careful attention to the power of the spoken word, Ephrem realizes that humble words help others, especially fierce opponents, to accept the truth. He writes, "Since all assistance accompanies humble speech, he who came to give assistance used (humble speech)."[55] Ephrem then attends to how Jesus Christ demonstrates the power of humble speech with two opponents. The first is with Simon the Pharisee at his home; the second is with Saul the Pharisee on his way to Damascus. Both encounters can remind Ephrem's reader of his treatments of how God comes, first to Adam and Eve and then to Cain, in order to convince the proud of heart through humble words to repent. In both encounters, Ephrem understands Jesus to be victorious through humility where both sons of Israel are overpowered by the humble words of Christ.

In the first of these encounters, Ephrem interprets the Gospel scene where Jesus is dining in the home of Simon the Pharisee (cf. Lk 7:36–50). During the meal, a woman who is known to be a sinner approaches Jesus. She bathes Jesus' feet with her tears and dries them with her hair, kissing his feet and anointing them with ointment. Simon the Pharisee thought to himself, "If this man were a prophet, he would know that this woman is a sinner."[56] Jesus then

---

2 Cor 10–13 and Paul's words that 'power is made perfect in weakness' (2 Cor 12:9)" (66, n. 18).

54 *Homily on Our Lord* 11.1 (Mathews and Amar, *Selected Prose Works*, 278).

55 *Homily on Our Lord* 23.1 (Mathews and Amar, *Selected Prose Works*, 299).

56 *Homily on Our Lord* 21.1 (Mathews and Amar, *Selected Prose Works*, 295). This is a short form of Lk 7:39.

proceeds to tell the parable of a creditor and two debtors in order to win Simon the Pharisee back through humility.

Ephrem explores this scene repeatedly by examining details in order to emphasize humility, especially how Christ exploits humility to win over enemies. Ephrem asks, "Now why did our Lord offer that Pharisee a persuasive parable rather than a stiff reprimand? He offered that crafty fellow a parable to lure him, without his even being aware, to straighten out his crooked ways."[57] In the Syriac tradition of Christ as the treasurer, Ephrem says that Christ placed within the Pharisee's reach the "treasury of humility."[58] For Ephrem, the treasurer offered humility to everyone, and thus showed how his treasury was free of the symptoms of pride.[59]

Moreover, Ephrem remarks that this humility of Christ in his first coming is particularly appropriate, because his next coming will be in retribution.[60] The earlier coming is a mission of salvation, whereas the next is a rendering of judgment. Therefore, Christ humbly admonishes the Pharisee rather than giving a stern rebuke. Ephrem writes, "Our Lord gave most of his assistance with persuasion rather than with admonition. Gentle showers soften the earth and thoroughly penetrate it, but a beating rain hardens and compresses the surface of the earth so that it will not be absorbed."[61] Ephrem thus considers humble speech to be saving not only in Christ's earthly ministry, but also in those who imitate him. Ephrem often adds remarks that indicate the universal appeal of Christ's pattern of speech. For instance, Ephrem exhorts his readers to

57 *Homily on Our Lord* 22.1 (Mathews and Amar, *Selected Prose Works*, 298).

58 *Homily on Our Lord* 22.2 (Mathews and Amar, *Selected Prose Works*, 298) and cf. *Homily on Our Lord* 9.3 (Mathews and Amar, *Selected Prose Works*, 285, n. 74) and Robert Murray, *Symbols of Church and Kingdom: A Study in Early Syriac Tradition* (Cambridge: Cambridge University Press, 1975), 193–95.

59 *Homily on Our Lord* 22.2 (Mathews and Amar, *Selected Prose Works*, 298).

60 *Homily on Our Lord* 22.3 (Mathews and Amar, *Selected Prose Works*, 298).

61 *Homily on Our Lord* 22.3 (Mathews and Amar, *Selected Prose Works*, 298).

"consider the power of humble speech: it suppresses fierce rage and it calms the waves of a tempestuous mind."[62]

Ephrem displays fondness for the paradox of humility's gentle violence in analyzing Christ's words to Simon. He considers the Lord's words to be like an arrow, tipped with conciliation and anointed with love. With the humble statement, "Simon, I have something to say to you," Jesus shoots the arrow and elicits humble words of the Pharisee's faith in return: "Speak, my Lord." Indeed, Ephrem judges that the Lord subdued Simon the Pharisee:

> A sweet utterance penetrated a bitter mind and brought forth fragrant fruit. He who had been a secret detractor before the utterance gave public praise after the utterance. With a sweet tongue, humility subdues even its enemies to do it honor. For it is not among its friends that humility puts its power to the test, but among those who hate it that it displays its trophies.[63]

Another great trophy of Christ's humility comes next in Ephrem's homily. The Syriac saint likens the words of Jesus in the home of Simon to the words spoken to Paul on his way to Damascus. Rather than condemning Paul, the risen Lord Jesus says in a humble voice, "Saul, Saul, why do you persecute me?" (Acts 9:4). Ephrem describes this in terms of a battle in humility that Christ wins against Paul, and that Paul himself will win against those who listen to him:

> The King of heaven armed himself with the weapon of humility and conquered an obstinate man, eliciting a good response from him as proof! Of this weapon Paul says: *With it we lay low the pride which rears itself against the knowledge of God.* Paul based this on his own experience. For just as he had battled proudly but was humbly defeated, so is every pride defeated that rears itself against this humility. The Saul who had set out

62 *Homily on Our Lord* 23.1 (Mathews and Amar, *Selected Prose Works*, 299).

63 *Homily on Our Lord* 24.2 (Mathews and Amar, *Selected Prose Works*, 299–300).

> with harsh words to subdue the disciples was subdued by the Lord of those disciples with a humble word. The One for whom everything is possible forsook everything and appeared and spoke to him in humility alone, to teach us that nothing is better suited to harsh minds than a humble tongue.[64]

Ephrem advances this image of humble, non-violent victory as the only way to conquer those who war against God and his holy ones. He shows that this victory is the cruciform pattern of the Christian life: Saul "was subdued by the cross, silencer of evil voices; none who are nailed to it can do harm or strike a blow."[65]

But one could object that Christ was not humble toward Saul. After all, the light of the risen Lord blinded Saul. Ephrem anticipates this objection and argues that the impairment did not result from "our compassionate Lord, who spoke humbly there."[66] He observes that heaven's brilliant light is pleasing to eyes of fire and spirit above in paradise. On earth, though, it is true that such light is found to be harsh to physical eyes.[67] Balancing both humility and majesty, Ephrem in the end sides more with the power of divine humility over majesty for conversion:

> This is amazing. Until our Lord humbled his voice, Paul did not humble his actions. Although our Lord was in splendor with his Father before he came down to put on a body, people did not learn of his humility from his splendor. But when he humbled himself and came down from his splendor, then in his humiliation his humility took root among people. When he was raised and ascended, again he was in glory at the right (hand) of his Father. But Paul did not learn his humility from this splendor. This is why the One who was exalted and sat at the right (hand) of his Father forsook glorious and exalted sounds, and

64 *Homily on Our Lord* 25.1 (Mathews and Amar, *Selected Prose Works*, 300). Cf. 2 Cor 10:4–5.

65 *Homily on Our Lord* 25.3 (Mathews and Amar, *Selected Prose Works*, 300–301).

66 *Homily on Our Lord* 26.2 (Mathews and Amar, *Selected Prose Works*, 301).

67 *Homily on Our Lord* 26.2 (Mathews and Amar, *Selected Prose Works*, 301–2).

> in feeble, humble tones, like someone oppressed and wronged, cried out and said: 'Saul, Saul, why do you persecute me?'[68]

Ephrem maintains that this divine humility was the best bridle for Paul, as "humble whispers overcame harsh bridles, for with humble whispers as bridles, the One who was persecuted led his persecutor from the wide road of persecutors to the narrow road of the persecuted."[69] Humility is thus far more powerful than signs in effecting conversion in Ephrem's estimation. He notes, "When all the signs that took place in the name of our Lord failed to convince Paul who was hurrying down to Damascus with arrogant haste, our Lord rushed to refute him humbly."[70] Ephrem likewise states that Simon the Pharisee was not convinced by the wondrous signs that he had seen: the dead raised, lepers cleansed, and the blind made able to see. Simon furthermore did not come to belief through the "even greater signs" worked within the Pharisee's own house of the sinful woman's return to the Lord.[71] Indeed, Simon the Pharisee imitated the folly of Israel in the Exodus by attributing weakness to God, whose power had already been made manifest in signs, rather than to himself. Therefore, observes Ephrem, in an act of humility toward the Pharisee, Jesus "quickly came up with a simple statement suited to an infant growing up on milk but incapable of solid food."[72] Humble words, not glorious signs, caused the conversion.

Ephrem thus connects the case of Paul on the way to Damascus with Simon the Pharisee through the link of the Lord's humility. In fact, Jesus is said to have used "the same humble words" with Simon the Pharisee as with Paul. Ephrem then makes another summary observation about the ways of God: "Humility is so powerful

68 *Homily on Our Lord* 40 (Mathews and Amar, *Selected Prose Works*, 314–15).

69 *Homily on Our Lord* 40 (Mathews and Amar, *Selected Prose Works*, 315).

70 *Homily on Our Lord* 40 (Mathews and Amar, *Selected Prose Works*, 315).

71 *Homily on Our Lord* 42.2 (Mathews and Amar, *Selected Prose Works*, 317).

72 *Homily on Our Lord* 42.3 (Mathews and Amar, *Selected Prose Works*, 317).

that even the all-conquering God did not conquer without it."[73] The stories of Saul and Simon the Pharisee therefore serve as examples of how the Lord converts opponents and relate the fulfillment of Ephrem's opening in the *Homily on Our Lord*: "Goodness encountered slandering mouths and made them praising harps."[74]

Humility in Our Life and Speech

Imitating the Lord's Humility

From the treatments above, we see that Ephrem stressed the Lord's humility within a soteriology that meets our need for the Lord to come to us where we are. God stoops down to speak on our level so that we may be saved. By this divine condescension, God heals sinners from their spiritual illnesses, such as anger and pride.[75] In this saving process, as Ephrem knows, Christians themselves are transformed into humble speakers in imitation of the Lord. This humility recognizes the greatness of who God is and the smallness of who humans are. By holding these together Christians can then praise God, using their gift of speech according to the primary purpose for which God had bestowed it upon humanity. We now consider the Christian imitation of the Lord's humility.

Ephrem adduces Christ as a life-giving model of humility for all, but especially for leaders. For example, when praising the wondrous nativity of Christ, he has this instruction:

73 *Homily on Our Lord* 41.1 (Mathews and Amar, *Selected Prose Works*, 315).

74 *Homily on Our Lord* 1.1 (Mathews and Amar, *Selected Prose Works*, 273).

75 For humility as the remedy for wrath/anger and pride/haughtiness, see Aho Shemunkasho, *Healing in the Theology of Saint Ephrem*, Gorgias Dissertations Near Eastern Studies 1 (Piscataway, NJ: Gorgias Press, 2002), 322–25.

On this day on which God came into the presence of sinners, let
not the just man exalt himself in his mind over the sinner.
On this day on which the Lord of all came among servants,
let the lords also bow down to their servants lovingly.
On this day when the Rich One was made poor for our sake,
let the rich man also make the poor man a sharer at his table.[76]

This attitude is reflected as well in his focus on humble words. In a pointed remark for the Christian community, Ephrem writes concerning the encounter with Saul: "Our Lord spoke humbly from above so that the leaders of his church would speak humbly."[77]

Inspired by the example of Christ, all Christians can keep silence when necessary and also speak well when necessary. Humble speech is itself a wondrous gift for believers in Christ that makes them great in conveying the truth of the Gospel. Ephrem understands the woman at the well to be a model disciple of Jesus. He likens this woman to the mother of Jesus because of her speech:

O, to you, woman in whom I see
a wonder as great as in Mary!
For she from within her womb
in Bethlehem brought forth his body as a child,
but you by your mouth made him manifest
as an adult in Shechem, the town of his father's household.
Blessed are you, woman, who brought forth by your mouth
light for those in darkness.[78]

76 *Hymns on the Nativity* 1.92–94 (McVey, *Hymns*, 73–74).

77 *Homily on Our Lord* 26.1 (Mathews and Amar, *Selected Prose Works*, 301).

78 *Hymns on Virginity and the Symbols of the Lord*, 23.4. The previous hymn, which also concerns the woman at the well, has as its refrain, "Praises to your humility!" while Hymn 23 has for its refrain what can be translated as "Glory to the Discoverer of all!" or "Glory to the Omnipotent One!" (McVey, *Hymns*, 355 and 361). Within this hymn, Ephrem uses one of his many beatitudes "Blessed are you, woman...." For a study with a complete reference

Ephrem wants all Christians to imitate the Samaritan woman's speech. As praising God is the fruit of humble speech, Ephrem considers the greatest offense against the humility of speech to be the lack of discretion that some have in speaking about God. Renowned for opposing various heretics such as Marcion, Bardaisan, Mani, and Arius, Ephrem finds that they have in common, speech that violates *pûršānâ,* that Syriac word encountered earlier for discernment or discretion, about things that they do not know. In this, they have transgressed the proper limits of human speech. Opposing the heretical limiting of the generation of the Son from the Father, Ephrem cries out:

> The one who is able to investigate
> Set limits upon it.
> A knowledge that can
> Limit the Knower-of-all
> Is greater than he, for it can
> Measure all of him.
> Whoever has investigated the Father and the Son
> Is greater than both.
> God forbid that
> The Father and the Son would be investigated
> And dust and ash would be exalted.[79]

Of course, Ephrem knows that those who are still within the truth of the Church could fall into boastful speech in divine matters. Specifically, Ephrem argues against those who assert that God should have done something that in his providence he did not do. In no uncertain terms, Ephrem says:

---

list of beatitudes in the extant *madrāšê,* see Andrew Hayes, "Ephrem the Syrian's Use of Beatitudes," *ZAC* 24, no. 3 (2020): 509–48.

79 *On Faith* 9.16 (Wickes, *Hymns on Faith,* 120; cf. Brock, *The Luminous Eye,* 27).

> The first requirement of all is this: man does not teach God what he should do. It is not man who should be God's teacher. It is the greatest insult that we should become masters of the one by whose exquisite creation these created mouths of ours are able to speak. It is an unpardonable offense that an audacious mouth should teach God, who in his goodness taught it how to speak, what (God) should do.[80]

Ephrem is so vociferous in his denunciation of those who claim that "God should have done this" that he is tempted to say, "God should have denied humanity the freedom that it uses to find fault with the One who is faultless."[81] And yet, Ephrem knows that he cannot say that, because that would be to fall into the same arrogance as his opponents in saying what God should have done. Rather, Ephrem concludes that the Just One in goodness gives freedom even to slanderers so that God "could not justly find fault with himself."[82]

As just seen, Ephrem occasionally makes autobiographical references to humility. While the *Vita* tradition gives rather exaggerated accounts of his humility and other virtues, Ephrem's authentic writings do portray someone who himself practiced humility in speech and life.[83] It is not uncommon to find self-referential statements in Ephrem's writings about how the majesty of the Lord overawes him. These statements, in a sense, enfold those who repeat his words, as well as those who listen to them, to be within that frame of mind. For a concrete example that Ephrem offered to his readers, we can turn to his *Letter to Publius*, which he concludes with an account of his own repentance. After stating that he had received visions in

80 *Homily on Our Lord* 30.1 (Mathews and Amar, *Selected Prose Works*, 305).

81 *Homily on Our Lord* 30.2 (Mathews and Amar, *Selected Prose Works*, 306).

82 *Homily on Our Lord* 30.2 (Mathews and Amar, *Selected Prose Works*, 306). Ephrem places great emphasis on the human free will.

83 Again, for the stereotypical monastic traditions of describing the life of Ephrem, see Amar, *The Syriac* Vita *Tradition of Ephrem the Syrian.*

the bright mirror of the Gospel concerning all human deeds from Adam unto the end of the world, Ephrem writes:

> I took refuge in repentance and I hid myself beneath the wings of compunction. I sought refuge in the shade of humility and I said, 'What more than these am I required to offer to Him who has no need of sacrifices and burnt offerings?' Rather, *a humble spirit*, which is the perfect sacrifice that is able to make propitiation for defects, *a broken heart* in the place of burnt offerings, and tears of propitiation in the place of a libation of wine are things which God will not reject.[84]

For Ephrem, once he has in humility turned back to God, God in divine condescension accepts human repentance, thanksgiving, and praise. Ephrem elsewhere sings out:

> Glory to the One who saw that we had been pleased
> to resemble the animals in our rage and greed,
> and [so] he descended and became one of us that we might become heavenly.
> Glory to him who never needs us to thank him.
> Yet he [became] needy for he loves us, and he thirsted for he cherishes us.
> And he asks us to give to him so that he may give us even more.[85]

Ephrem experienced God's own gracious humility in his life, imitated it, and thus himself became the "Harp of the Spirit" to praise God.[86]

84 *Letter to Publius*, 24 (Mathews and Amar, *Selected Prose Works*, 355; cf. Brock, *Singer of the Word of God*, 192).

85 *Hymns on the Nativity* 3.16–17 (McVey, *Hymns*, 86–87).

86 "Harp of the Spirit" is one of the most beloved titles for Ephrem in the Syriac tradition.

Humility and preaching against theological opponents?

Before concluding this chapter on humility, it would be good to turn Ephrem's own principles more sharply back upon himself. Put bluntly, does Ephrem practice what he preaches about humility when he speaks about the Jewish people and those whom he considers heretical? This is a delicate question, but those who take Ephrem as not just an interesting historical figure, but as a model preacher should ask it today.

As we have seen, Ephrem faults the various heretics for not observing humble speech. Ephrem himself, however, does not always use humility to win heretics back to the truth. In his study of Ephrem's *Hymns against Heresies,* Sidney Griffith elucidates Ephrem's distinction between those heretics he considered "outsiders" and those he consider "insiders."[87] The "insiders" include the followers of Arius, who still have much of the true Church's sacramental and pastoral practices, about whom Ephrem prays that "the Good [Shepherd] might bring them back to his fold."[88] The outsiders, on the other hand, are the followers of such heretics as Marcion, Bardaisan, and Mani, whom Ephrem calls the "weeds" referenced at Mt 13:24–30, 36–43. Ephrem says that Christ "has thrown them out of his house."[89] Elsewhere, Ephrem interprets the parable of the weeds as reason for the Church's present action of uprooting. Ephrem encourages Bishop Abraham of Nisibis to fight the heretics of his area in these words: "Be zealous, O farmer, against the weeds that have sprung up and assailed among the wheat. The thicket is (to be) cut off to the root, for its growth is from negligence."[90] Regarding

87 Sidney H. Griffith, "Setting Right the Church of Syria: Saint Ephraem's *Hymns against Heresies,*" in *The Limits of Ancient Christianity: Essays on Late Antique Thought and Culture in Honor of R. A. Markus*, eds. William E. Klingshirn and Mark Vessey (Ann Arbor, MI: The University of Michigan Press, 1999), 97–114.

88 *Hymns against Heresies* 22.4 (Griffith, "Setting Right the Church of Syria," 102).

89 *Hymns against Heresies* 22.2 and 3 (Griffith, "Setting Right the Church of Syria," 102).

90 *Nisibene Hymns* 22.2 in Kuriakose Antony Valavanolickal, *The Use of the Gospel Parables in the Writings of Aphrahat and Ephrem*, Studies in the Religion and History of Early

efforts to bring the outsiders back to the truth, Ephrem writes in *Hymns against Heresies*:

> When rebels do not come to the Way with gentleness,
> With bridle and yoke will stubbornness be persuaded
> To come to the right way. If they rebel, it will be for torture;
> If they go aright it will be for ease. If they are hardened
> Their leader is the rod; if they are obedient, love is their guide.[91]

Ephrem describes this approach with a pithy statement that qualifies his stress on humility in the *Homily on Our Lord*: "When hard elements are to be worked, hard tools come to the job."[92] Coercion rather than humble speech seems to be Ephrem's response in this case.

Even more notorious is Ephrem's rhetoric against the Jews.[93] For example, while Ephrem regards Pilate and his wife favorably as representing the nations, he imputes the guilt of Christ's crucifixion entirely to the Jews:

> The Gentiles were gleaming and purified and cleansed,
> but the [Jewish] people were blackened and defiled by that blood.[94]

In blaming Christ's death on the Jewish people, Ephrem has these words coming from personified Death: "How hateful then the

Christianity, no. 2 (Frankfurt am Main: Peter Lang, 1996), 66. For Ephrem's anti-Judaic polemic in parable interpretation that exceeds the criticism leveled against the Jews by Aphrahat, see Valavanolickal, 333–35.

91 *Hymns against Heresies* 24.2 (Griffith, "Setting Right the Church of Syria," 109).

92 *Hymns against Heresies* 24.1 (Griffith, "Setting Right the Church of Syria," 109).

93 This is widely recognized by scholars working on Ephrem's writings. For example, Robert Murray writes, "it must be confessed with sorrow that Ephrem hated the Jews." See his chapter 10, "The Nation and the Nations," in *Symbols of Church and Kingdom*, 41–68, at 68.

94 *Hymns on Virginity and the Symbols of the Lord*, 26.15 (McVey, *Hymns*, 381).

People, that are yet more hateful than I!"[95] Scholars have suggested a variety of reasons for Ephrem's bitter attack on the Jews: Ephrem is reacting against Judaism's continuing attraction of Christians; he uses anti-Judaism as a rhetorical device in the campaign against Arian Christians; and he has a fiery temperament against those who oppose his Christian faith.[96] In the end, no reason may fully explain Ephrem's virulent speech against the Jewish people and other adversaries. Whatever the case, we may recognize Ephrem's limits to his humility in speech.[97]

Conclusion

These last considerations show that we must exercise discretion in appropriating Ephrem's preaching on humble speech. We must show humility even toward our enemies. Patriarch Ignatius Zakka I Iwas tells us:

> Also, "love your enemies, bless those who curse you, do good to those who hate you, and pray for those who spitefully use you and persecute you" (St. Matthew 5:44). Only in this manner, meekness becomes our second nature by which we deal with others in kindness and charity. This is how we may imitate Christ, our Lord, who bids us to learn from him, for he is meek and humble of heart.[98]

95 *Nisibene Hymns* 67.3 (NPNF 2.13, Stopford, 218).

96 The body of literature on this continues to grow. For the first thesis, see Stanley Kazan, "Isaac of Antioch's Homily against the Jews," *OChr* 45 (1961): 30–53; 46 (1962): 87–98; 47 (1963): 89–97; 49 (1965): 57–78. In exposing Isaac's attitude toward the Jews, Kazan gives special attention to Ephrem. For the second position, see Christine Shepardson, "Anti-Jewish Rhetoric and Intra-Christian Conflict in the Sermons of Ephrem Syrus," in *StPatr* 35 (2001): 502–7. For the third, see A. P. Hayman, "The Image of the Jew in the Syriac Anti-Jewish Polemical Literature," in *"To See Ourselves as Others See Us:" Christians, Jews, and "Others" in Late Antiquity*, eds. Jacob Neusner and Ernest S. Frerichs (Chico, CA: Scholars Press, 1985), 423–41, esp. pp. 429 and 433.

97 On a different note, for Ephrem's understanding of the Lord's limits in speaking humbly, see *Commentary on Genesis* 2.29 (Mathews and Amar, *Selected Prose Works*, 118) and *Homily on Our Lord* 22.3 (Mathews and Amar, *Selected Prose Works*, 298) analyzed separately above.

98 His Holiness Moran Mor Ignatius Zakka I Iwas, "Meekness and Humility," Message of January 20, 2007.

The importance of Ephrem's main insight remains: the goodness of humble speech puts a bridle on listeners' mouths in order that the proud may repent and praise God. Fundamentally, this work of humble speech is what God shares in his revelation, through his adaptation to our lowliness, but it also includes our response of praising without arrogantly prying into divine mysteries.

By returning to Ephrem, we find a patristic emphasis on the necessity of humility for our initial repentance and a continual repentance in life, because God humbled himself for our salvation. It is in Christ, meek and humble of heart, that we find what humility most purely means. From the beginning of revelation, God lowered himself for human conversion—even stooping to common metaphors so that humans may understand and repent. God was not satisfied in putting on words, however, so great was the divine love. Rather, the Lord reached down to our level even more completely by putting on a humble body.

To celebrate the sixth Sunday of the year, the Roman liturgy's Office of Readings provides an excerpt from the *Commentary on the Diatesseron* by Ephrem (or perhaps a Pseudo-Ephrem).[99] The selection begins, "Lord, who can comprehend even one of your words?"[100] Those familiar with this reading may recall Ephrem's image of God's speech as an inexhaustible spring: "do not foolishly

99 According to a traditional interpretation dependent on Eusebius of Caesarea, the *Diatesseron* offers a harmony of the four (Greek: *tessera*) Gospel accounts made by Justin Martyr's student Tatian in the second century, but the *Diatesseron* could be, more simply, Tatian's edition of the Gospel. See Matthew R. Crawford, "Diatesseron, a Misnomer? The Evidence from Ephrem's Commentary," *EChr* 4, no. 3 (2013): 362–85. The *Diatesseron* is the textual Gospel as understood in Ephrem's church. For an English translation of the Syriac original and Armenian fragments of this work not extant in its entirety, see Carmel McCarthy, *Saint Ephrem's Commentary on Tatian's Diatessaron, An English Translation of* Chester Beatty *Syriac MS 709 with Introduction and Notes*, JSSS 2 (Oxford University Press, 1993 [2000 reprint]). Questions of interpolations arise in addition to the more basic question of Ephrem's authorship of this Gospel commentary. For Matthew Crawford's argument that the commentary's author knows a text by Eusebius, see his "Resolving Genealogical Ambiguity: Eusebius and (ps-)Ephrem on Luke 1.36," *ArSt* 14 (2016): 83–97.

100 *The Liturgy of the Hours according to the Roman Rite*, vol. III, Ordinary Time Weeks 1–17, ICEL (New York: Catholic Book Publishing Co., 1975), 199–200, at 199. The reading is taken from the *Commentary on the Diatesseron* I.18–19 (SCh 121, 52–53).

try to drain in one draught what cannot be consumed all at once."[101] What many may not realize is that the context of the selection is a commentary on Zechariah's being struck mute for misspeaking in unbelief. Zechariah was given the good news that he and his wife, both advanced in years, would have a son named John, the Lord's forerunner (Lk 1:5–25). Ephrem's comments taken up into the Roman liturgy appear in a scene especially instructive of humble speech. Some lines before the question, "Lord who can comprehend even one of your words?" we read: "Because he [Zechariah] did not believe in the living mouth, his mouth became dead to the word. And because he believed in a barren womb more than in the angel, his lips became sterile, without words."[102] Zechariah, in a sense, is like Simon the Pharisee and Saul the Pharisee as Ephrem presents them in his *Homily on Our Lord*. Ephrem comments, "Only when his lips were unable to give birth to speech [did he believe that] his old age would be able to procreate a son."[103] After the birth of John the Baptist, Zechariah sings out his praise in the Benedictus, "Blessed be the Lord, the God of Israel" (Lk 1:68). We should recall that Ephrem preaches at the beginning of the *Homily on Our Lord*: "Goodness encountered slandering mouths and made them praising harps; this is why all mouths should give praise to the one who removed slanderous speech from them."[104] We cannot totally understand anything that God says to us, and knowing that allows us to be converted to his goodness that far surpasses our understanding. The goodness of God stoops to the level of the proud, stops them silent, and brings them to give praise in humility for the Word made flesh. Preaching sings out God's glory on the face of Christ!

101 *Commentary on the Diatesseron*, I.17 (McCarthy, 17).
102 *Commentary on the Diatesseron* I.17 (McCarthy, 49).
103 *Commentary on the Diatesseron* I.21 (McCarthy, 51).
104 See reference at the beginning of this chapter's "The Word in Ephrem's Flesh for Us."

Christian preachers, therefore, do well to learn from Ephrem's soteriology of humility. All of us committed to speaking the Word of God can be mindful of our own sinful pride. We can speak humbly to the Lord and make Ephrem's awe-inspired prayer our own: "Make me worthy, even me, to offer praise to you."[105]

In our next chapter, featuring Gregory of Nazianzus, we will see that in humility the Lord addresses our minds to purify us. Here we begin our series of chapters on the theological virtues of faith, hope, and love. In Gregory's preaching, the Word comes so that we, by purification, can be raised to have faith in the Trinity and live a godly life.

105 *Hymns on the Nativity* 2, from the refrain (McVey, *Hymns*, 76).

CHAPTER 3

GREGORY OF NAZIANZUS

The Word in Our Flesh for Purification and Faith

Purification accompanies belief in Christ, as we see in the following Petrine examples from the New Testament. According to the Acts of the Apostles, St. Peter preached about God's gift of conversion to the Gentiles, allowing them to be baptized: "He made no distinction between us and them, for by faith he purified their hearts" (Acts 15:9).[1] In the First Letter of Peter's exhortation on the baptismal life, we read "you have purified yourselves by obedience to the truth" (1 Pt 1:22). By faith in Christ we have newness of life, a rebirth for an abundance of life: "You have been born anew, not from perishable but from imperishable seed, through the living and abiding word of God" (1 Pt 1:23). And yet we know that the newness of life is under attack. Peter exhorts: "Rid yourselves of all malice and deceit, insincerity, envy, and all slander; like newborn infants, long for pure spiritual milk, so that through it you may grow into salvation, for you have tasted that the Lord is

1 "The Holy Spirit had descended on the Gentiles of Cornelius and his household while Peter was speaking to them" (Acts 10:44).

good" (1 Pt 2:1–2). Purification has not been completed solely by receiving faith, but rather the life of faith is a life of purification so as to be ready for everlasting life with the risen Lord.

On this Paschal faith and its purifying effect on us, Patriarch Bartholomew (Ecumenical Patriarch of Constantinople since 1991) expounds the "life in abundance" (Jn 10:10) that Christ brings—and the opposition within us:

> The devil assaults Life by means of the sinful tendency that exists within us like "old rust," using this to entrap us either into tangible sin or delusional belief. Hubris [Pride] is the offspring of that "rust," while both comprise the sinister couple responsible for disrupting relationships within ourselves, with others, as well as with God and the whole creation.

The Patriarch then continues:

> Accordingly, it is imperative that we purify ourselves of this rust with great attentiveness and carefulness in order that the profuse life-giving light of the Risen Christ may shine in our mind, soul and body, so that it may in turn dispel the darkness of hubris and pour the "abundance" of life to all the world. This cannot be achieved by philosophy, science, technology, art, or any ideology; it can only be achieved through faith in what God has condescended for us human beings through his Passion, Crucifixion and Burial, descending to the depths of hades and rising from the dead as the divine-human Jesus Christ.[2]

With the Patriarch's emphasis on purification and faith in view, we now turn to Gregory of Nazianzus for our consideration of incarnation, deification, and proclamation. Gregory is honored as Bartholomew's saintly predecessor in Constantinople leading up

2 Patriarch Bartholomew, "Participants of Abundant Life," Holy Pascha, 2010, in *Speaking the Truth in Love: Theological and Spiritual Exhortations of Ecumenical Patriarch Bartholomew*, ed. with introduction by John Chryssavgis (New York: Fordham University Press, 2011), 47–49, at 48.

to the second ecumenical council of the Church, Constantinople I (381).

The Word in Gregory's Flesh for Us

We are largely dependent on Gregory's own ample writing for details of his life.[3] He appears as the Greek Father most attentive to detailing his life in the Word—and the Word in his life—through his preaching and writing.[4] In one oration, when applying his observation of the choppy waves of the sea to his life, he confesses being "the kind of person who relates everything to myself."[5] He did apply everything, especially the Word, to himself. Gregory describes his inseparability from the Word in this way:

> I cling to the Word alone, as servant of the Word, and would never willingly neglect this possession, but on the contrary honor him and embrace him and take more pleasure in him than in all other things combined that delight the multitude; and I make him the partner of my whole life.[6]

3 Jerome is an example of an external contemporary witness to Gregory's life. He calls Gregory a most eloquent man and his teacher who explained the Scriptures to him. See Jerome, *On Illustrious Men,* chap. 117 (TU 14, 51–52).

4 For overviews of Gregory's life, see John A. McGuckin, *St. Gregory of Nazianzus: An Intellectual Biography* (Crestwood, NY: St. Vladimir's Seminary Press, 2004) and the Introduction in Brian E. Daley, SJ, *Gregory of Nazianzus,* ECF (London: Routledge, 2006), 1–61. For a consideration of Gregory's Trinitarian theology, see Christopher A. Beeley, *Gregory of Nazianzus on the Trinity and the Knowledge of God: In Your Light We See Light,* OSHT (New York: Oxford University Press, 2008). For an argument that Gregory gives voice to the blending of Christ's life with his own, see Andrew Hofer, OP, *Christ in the Life and Teaching of Gregory of Nazianzus,* OECS (Oxford: Oxford University Press, 2013).

5 *Or.* 26.9 (SC 284, 244; Daley, 110).

6 *Or.* 6.5 (SC 405, 132–34; Vinson, 7 [alt.]). I follow the capitalization of PG 35:728, which has both uses of *logos* capitalized. Vinson's translation reverses the capitalization in the SC text so that Gregory clings to the Word alone as a servant of the word. For an interpretation similar to Vinson's, which contrasts *or.* 6.5 with the *logoi* of *or.* 4.100 (SC 309, 248), see Neil McLynn, "Among the Hellenists: Gregory and the Sophists" in *Gregory of Nazianzus: Images and Reflections,* ed. Jostein Børtnes and Tomas Hägg (Copenhagen: Museum Tusculanum Press, 2006), 213–38, at 226.

This great theologian who speaks so eloquently about God does so from his life's experience. Distrusting Gregory's reliability in providing accurate information about his life, one scholar recently opined that we should resist Gregory's "autohagiobiography."[7] Christian traditions, however, lavish praise on him and rank him as one of the foremost saintly authorities in history. He who spoke so lovingly of "my Jesus" and "my Christ," has been regarded as representing Christ himself. For example, Cosmas of Jerusalem, writing in the eighth century, communicates this counsel: "'Be like my Gregory,' Christ says. . . . 'For he was not the speaker. I was.'"[8]

Gregory was born around the year 329 to Nonna, who came from a Christian family and whose prayer guided Gregory from the beginning. Gregory's father was also known as Gregory of Nazianzus, a convert from a sect called the Hypsistarians who became the Bishop of Nazianzus. Our Gregory had one older sister, Gorgonia, and one younger brother, Caesarius. Gregory wrote extensively about his immediate family, and they are all considered saints.[9]

He grew up in the province of Cappadocia in modern-day Turkey, where he received the first of his many years of education. In pursuit of the finest learning possible, he studied in Caesarea in Palestine and in Alexandria in Egypt, the two principal places where Origen taught. In his voyage from Alexandria to study in Athens,

7 Bradley K. Storin, "Autohagiobiography: Gregory of Nazianzus among His Biographers," *SLA* 1, no. 3 (2017): 254–81. Storin claims, "His authorial interests and rhetorical aims so pervade his autobiographical texts as to make any glimpse of his authentic personality impossible" (280). Arguably, because we detect his authorial interests and rhetorical aims, we can know something of who he is and how he wants his listeners to experience the Word through him.

8 Cosmas of Jerusalem (also known as Cosmas the Hymnographer, Bishop of Maiuma), *Commentary on the Poems of Gregory of Nazianzus*, proemium, lines 88–90 in G. Lozza, *Cosma di Gerusalemme. Commentario ai Carmi di Gregorio Nazianzeno*, ST 12 (Naples, M. D'Auria, 2000); cf. Raymond Van Dam, *Kingdom of Snow: Roman Rule and Greek Culture in Cappadocia* (Philadelphia: University of Pennsylvania Press, 2002), 201 and 248n21.

9 For Gregory's funeral orations of his brother, sister, and father, see respectively *Orations* 7, 8, and 18. Gregory speaks of his family in many other places. For example, he composed 37 epigraphs for his mother alone (*Carm.* 2.2.66–102).

the classical center of education, Gregory's ship was threatened by a long and violent storm. He recounts in tragedy's iambic trimeter: "Those murderous waters were keeping me away from the purifying waters which divinize us."[10] He promised to be baptized, and Christ preserved him and his shipmates. After Gregory arrived at Athens, Basil went there; the two of them, as later recounted by Gregory, dedicated themselves completely to Christ.[11]

Coming back to what is now called Turkey, he undertook an ascetic life, at times in association with the great Basil. Perhaps the two of them edited selections from Origen during one of their times together, as Gregory later sends the *Philokalia* (love of beauty), an anthology of Origen's writings on topics such as scriptural interpretation, to Theodore of Tyana as a reminder of both Basil and himself.[12] Gregory was ordained a priest by his father around the turn of 361/62, and then fled the responsibility of taking up the ministry. After making a retreat with Basil, Gregory returned to Nazianzus by Easter 362 to begin his priestly ministry alongside his father. His *or.* 1, *On Pascha*, communicates his resounding earliest preaching, which announces our deified union with Christ:

> Let us become like Christ, since Christ also became like us; let us become gods because of him, since he also because of us became human. He assumed what is worse that he might give what is better. He became poor that we through his poverty might become rich. He took the form of a slave, that we might regain freedom. He descended that we might be lifted up, he

10 Gregory of Nazianzus, *On his own life*, *Carm.* 2.1.11.163–65 (PG 37:1041; Meehan, 81–82).

11 See especially Gregory's *or.* 43, *In Praise of the Great Basil.*

12 *Ep.* 115, Storin, 97. This *Philokalia* of Origen should not be confused with the multi-volume *Philokalia* of Eastern Christian writings compiled in the 18th century by Nicodemus of the Holy Mountain and Macarius of Corinth. For the former, see SC 302 and *The Philocalia of Origen*, translated by George Lewis (Edinburgh: T & T Clark, 1911). McGuckin counters Marguerite Harl's arguments calling into question Gregory's involvement in editing the *Philokalia*, advanced in her critical edition, the *Philocalie d'Origène*, SC 302, 1–20. See McGuckin, *Saint Gregory of Nazianzus*, 102–4.

> was tempted that we might be victorious, he was dishonored to glorify us, he died to save us, he ascended to draw to himself us who lay below in the Fall of sin.[13]

In 372, after Basil became the metropolitan archbishop of Caesarea in Cappadocia and amidst a restructuring of dioceses, Gregory was made Bishop of Sasima, a town that held strategic importance for Basil's metropolitan oversight, but little else of significance. Gregory resented Basil's political maneuvering. We know that Gregory served as a kind of auxiliary bishop to his father in Nazianzus for a time after 372. Gregory's brother and sister as well as their long-lived father and mother were all dead before the year 375, when he undertook an extended monastic retreat, one of several in his life. After attending a synod in Antioch, he accepted a call to go to Constantinople in 379 to minister to the Nicene minority in the capital city.

Gregory achieved considerable fame for his preaching there, such as delivering the five *Theological Orations*.[14] These orations have as their primary targets the followers of Eunomius of Cyzicus. Eunomius taught that the Son's substance was different from the Father's substance. Moreover, he had a reputation for misusing logic to claim to know God as God knows himself, distorting both what to believe and how to believe.[15] The first *Theological Oration* calls for people to be purified in order to speak theologically. Gregory maintains the absolute importance of thinking about God. He proclaims, "It is more important that we should remember God

13 *Or.* 1.5 (SC 247, 78; Harrison, 59).

14 For an overview of how rhetorical delivery shapes orthodoxy in the fourth century, see Alberto J. Quiroga Puertas, "Preaching and Mesmerizing: The Resolution of Religious Conflicts in Late Antiquity," chap. 10 of *The Role of the Bishop in Late Antiquity: Conflict and Compromise*, eds. Andrew Fear, José Fernández Ubiña and Mar Marcos (London: Bloomsbury Academic 2013), 189–208.

15 For a sympathetic treatment of Eunomius, see Richard Paul Vaggione, *Eunomius of Cyzicus and the Nicene Revolution*, OECS (Oxford: Oxford University Press, 2000).

than that we should breathe."[16] But theology can only be done in the company of purity. Synthesizing a Platonic tradition of purification with the Gospel, Gregory instructs about theology:

> It is not for all people, but only for those who have been tested and have found a sound footing in study, and, more importantly, have undergone, or at the very least are undergoing, purification of body and soul. For one who is not pure to lay hold of pure things is dangerous, just as it is for weak eyes to look at the sun's brightness.[17]

The harm of the sun's brightness to weak eyes recalls *The Republic*, Book 7, where Plato presents the allegory of the cave. Those in the cave cannot bear the sun's brightness, but need training in their ascent to behold that light. Gregory relies on this tradition to extol the Gospel's purification and to show that his Eunomian opponents, heretical in their faith, lacked what is needed.

By his preaching, Gregory follows Christ's own emphasis on purifying listeners through speech: "You are already pure on account of the word that I have spoken to you" (Jn 15:3).[18] In this same *or.* 27, Gregory similarly preaches: "Once we have removed from our discussions all alien elements, and dispatched the great legion into the heard of swine to rush down into the abyss (cf. Mk 5:9–13), the next step is to look at ourselves and to smooth the theologian in us, like a statue, into beauty."[19] One can compare this with

16 *Or.* 27.4 (SC 250, 78; Williams and Wickham, 27–28).

17 Or. 27.3 (SC 250, 76; Williams and Wickham, 27).

18 For attention to this verse's importance in Gregory's orations, relevant to Maximus the Confessor, see Luke Steven, *Imitation, Knowledge, and the Task of Christology in Maximus the Confessor* (Eugene, OR: Wipf and Stock, 2020), 114, which has influenced my interpretation of Gregory's *or.* 27.7.

19 *Or.* 27.7 (SC 250, 86; Williams and Wickham, 30). Gregory then gives a series of questions like an examination of conscience, probing why we are prone to garrulity. In addition, he asks if we are engaging in practices that would enable us to speak rightly, e.g., "Do we commend hospitality? Do we admire brotherly love, wifely affection, virginity, feeding the poor, singing psalms, nightlong vigils, penitence?" (SC 250, 86; Williams and Wickham, 30).

Plotinus, hailed in modern times as the founder of Neoplatonism. Plotinus teaches:

> Go back into yourself and look; and if you do not yet see yourself beautiful, then, just as someone making a statue which has to be beautiful cuts away here and polishes there and makes one part smooth and clears another till he has given his statue a beautiful face, so you must cut away excess and straighten the crooked and clear the dark and make it bright, and never stop "working on your statue" (Plato, *Phaedrus* 252d) till the divine glory of virtue shines out on you, till you see "self-mastery enthroned upon its holy seat" (Plato, *Phaedrus* 254b).[20]

While Gregory explicitly employs the Platonic image of the statue, he does so reminiscent of Christ's "I am the Vine" speech in John 15 with its language of pruning and purification. For Gregory, the call to purification in the orthodox Christian faith continues the best of philosophical counsels to be purified to think rightly.

Gregory's opponents included many more than the Eunomians; he suffered at the hands of his own faith's fellow leaders, whom he deemed to be unpurified, inept in faith's mysteries, and unworthy of ministry. After hailing one man as a model philosopher, that one betrayed him and tried to remove him as Bishop of Constantinople.[21] Gregory came to find that many bishops opposed him. The new orthodox emperor, Theodosius I, had recognized Gregory as Constantinople's authoritative bishop. When Theodosius called for the second ecumenical council, taking place in 381, Gregory served as host. After the death of the council's president, Meletius of Antioch, Gregory assumed the presidency. Bishops there charged that Gregory was not the legitimate authority in Constantinople,

20 Plotinus, *Enneads* 1.6.9 (LCL Plotinus 1.258; Armstrong, 1.259). For context, see Pierre Hadot, *Plotinus or the Simplicity of Vision*, translated by Michael Chase, intro. Arnold I. Davidson (Chicago: University of Chicago Press, 1993), 17–22.

21 See *or.* 25, *In Praise of Hero [Maximus] the Philosopher*. After Maximus's departure, see *or.* 26, *About Himself, On His Return from the Country.*

as he had been consecrated the Bishop of Sasima. The Council of Nicaea (325) in canon 15 had disallowed the transfer of clergy, so that a bishop who left his see to occupy another see should instead be restored to his original see; and his actions in the second see should be considered to be void. Having had enough of the Council of Constantinople, Gregory left the council and eventually the city; he never returned, saying in his farewell oration: "They are not seeking priests, but rhetors; not pure hands to offer sacrifice, but strong hands to hold the reins."[22] The one chosen to succeed Gregory as Bishop of Constantinople, Nectarius, was still only a catechumen, with little knowledge of the faith. One year after the council, when invited back to a synod for further business, Gregory wrote, "This is how things are going with me, if I must write the truth. I want to flee from every gathering of bishops because I have seen a benefit in no synod, not a solving of evils but rather a holding and increase of them."[23]

At this time after the council, Gregory engaged in what is known as the Apollinarian controversy. Apollinarius of Laodicea, who had been a friend of Athanasius, subscribed to the Nicene faith, but said that the Word took the place of the rational soul. Christ would thus have no human mind, the very thought of which was repugnant to Gregory. He thundered in his *ep.* 101, "For that which is not assumed is not healed."[24] In this letter, one of the most important texts for Christology, Gregory lets loose ten anathemas that condemn errors. This includes the heresy that Apollinarius himself so vehemently opposed, namely, that there are "two Sons," two separate Sons of God and Man, instead of the one Lord Jesus Christ,

22 *Or.* 42.24 (PG 36:487; Daley, 152–53). For this address as a retrospective certificate of discharge, see Susanna Elm, "Inventing the 'Father of the Church': Gregory of Nazianzus' 'Farewell to the Bishops' (*Or.* 42) in its Historical Context," in *Vita Religiosa im Mittelalter: Festschrift für Kaspar Elm zum 70. Geburtstag*, eds. Franz J. Felten and Nikolas Jaspert (Berlin: Duncker & Humblot, 1999), 3–20.

23 *Ep.* 130.1 (my translation).

24 *Ep.* 101.5(32) (SC 208, 50; my translation).

whose incarnation is a union or mixture of divinity and humanity.[25] Gregory's own subtle account of the incarnation (in which he uses "mixture" terminology) resists easy classification. Yet it was repeatedly claimed by vying theologians in subsequent debates and was enshrined among the patristic quotations appended to the Council of Chalcedon's Address to the Emperor Marcian, where we first encounter Gregory called "the Theologian."[26]

After again caring for the church of Nazianzus, Gregory "retired" to be of service according to a wider vision. His main work after retirement was writing, editing, and arranging for publication his works in three genres for a perpetual theological legacy. John McGuckin judges that Gregory polished his literary works so that they could "enjoy the largest and most 'exemplary' circulation possible. He would transform them into a veritable compendium of writings and sermons needed in any future bishop's cabinet."[27] We have extant 44 orations,[28] 245 letters (including *Theological Epistles* 101, 102, and 202, transmitted separately from the other

25 For my study of this letter, see Hofer, *Christ in the Life and Teaching of Gregory of Nazianzus*, 123–51.

26 See Oliver B. Langworthy, "Theodoret's Theologian: Assessing the Origin and Significance of Gregory of Nazianzus' Title," *JEH* 70, no. 3 (2019): 455–71.

27 McGuckin, *Saint Gregory of Nazianzus*, 369.

28 45 orations, if *or.* 35 is counted, but it is considered inauthentic. McGuckin says that Gregory's orations remain "the most copied genre of all Byzantine manuscripts after the Bible." See McGuckin, *Saint Gregory of Nazianzus*, 402. Sixteen of Gregory's orations have been read in the Byzantine liturgy annually since the ninth century: *or.* 1, Pascha; *or.* 45, Monday of Bright Week; *or.* 44, First Sunday after Pascha; *or.* 41, Pentecost; *or.* 15, Feast of the Maccabees, August 1; *or.* 24, Feast of St. Cyprian, October 2; *or.* 19, on December 21, when Mt 18:21–36 is read; *or.* 38 on the Nativity of Christ, December 25; *or.* 43, Feast of St. Basil the Great, January 1; *or.* 39, Epiphany, January 6; *or.* 40, Feast of St. John the Baptist, January 7; *or.* 11, Feast of St. Gregory of Nyssa, January 10; *or.* 21, Feast of St. Athanasius, January 18; *or.* 42, Feast of St. Gregory the Theologian, January 25; *or.* 14, Sunday of the Last Judgment; *or.* 16; Forgiveness Sunday. Gregory's preaching echoes through the ages. See Harrison, *Festal Orations*, 191–92.

letters),[29] and over 17,000 lines of poetry.[30] We also have from him the first extant full legal will in the history of the Roman Empire.[31] The literature shows such extensive engagement with the classical models and styles available that arguably no other Father of the Church excels Gregory's broad erudition in Greek literature.[32] Among classical literary and philosophical genres, the tragic—with its catharsis—holds special power in Gregory's writing.[33] Seemingly

29 Not counting *epp.* 88, 241, 243, and 249 (considered inauthentic) or the three *Theological Epistles*, Storin numbers 242 letters. Gregory is the first Greek author known to have formed an anthology of letters. See Neil B. McLynn, "Gregory Nazianzen's Basil: The Literary Construction of a Christian Friendship," *StPatr* 37 (2001): 178–93, at 184. See Storin's focus on Gregory's self-presentation by assembling his own collection of letters for the purposes of philosophy, eloquence, and friendship with Basil in Bradley K. Storin, *Self-Portrait in Three Colors: Gregory of Nazianzus's Epistolary Autobiography*, CLA 6 (Oakland, CA: University of California Press, 2019).

30 Until the last few decades, little of Gregory's poetry was available in English; the nineteenth-century series of Nicene and Post-Nicene Fathers did not include any poetry. For some published translations, see Brian Dunkle, SJ, *Poems on Scripture: Saint Gregory of Nazianzus*, PPS 46 (Crestwood, NY: St. Vladimir's Seminary Press, 2012), Peter Gilbert, *On God and Man: The Theological Poetry of St. Gregory of Nazianzus*, PPS 21 (Crestwood, NY: St. Vladimir's Seminary Press, 2001), Denis Meehan, OSB, *Saint Gregory of Nazianzus: Three Poems; Concerning His Own Affairs, Concerning Himself and the Bishops, Concerning His Own Life*, FC 75 (Washington, DC: The Catholic University of America Press, 1987); Book VIII in *The Greek Anthology*, vol. 2, translated by W. R. Paton. LCL (Cambridge, MA: Harvard University Press, 1970), 399–505; John A. McGuckin, *Saint Gregory Nazianzen: Selected Poems* (Oxford: SLG Press, 1986), and Daley, *Gregory of Nazianzus*, 162–71. Interestingly, Andrew Louth comments on Byzantine hymnography's adaptation of Gregory's writing: "This hymnic use of passages from Gregory's homilies was pursued with enthusiasm by later Byzantine hymnographers. It is striking to note in passing, that it was Gregory's prose that was turned into verse, not the extensive verse with which he occupied his declining years." See Andrew Louth, "St. Gregory the Theologian and Byzantine Theology," in *Re-Reading Gregory of Nazianzus: Essays on History, Theology, and Culture*, ed. Christopher A. Beeley, SEC (Washington, DC: The Catholic University of America Press, 2012), 252–66, at 265.

31 For brief overview and translation of the will, see Daley, *Gregory of Nazianzus*, 184–89.

32 George Kennedy calls Gregory "the most important figure in the synthesis of classical rhetoric and Christianity." See Kennedy, *Greek Rhetoric under Christian Emperors* (Princeton: Princeton University Press, 1983), 215; cf. Neil McLynn, "Among the Hellenists: Gregory and the Sophists," in *Gregory of Nazianzus: Images and Reflections*, eds. Jostein Børtnes and Tomas Hägg, 213–38. For an example of a recent analysis of one poem within the Homeric tradition, see Peter A. O'Connell, "Homer and His Legacy in Gregory of Nazianzus' 'On His Own Affairs,'" *JHS* 139 (2019): 147–71. For my Christological analysis of that Poem 2.1.1, see *Christ in the Life and Teaching of Gregory of Nazianzus*, 77–82.

33 Commenting on *Poem* 1.1.1, Paul Blowers writes, "Gregory is surely speaking of all of his verse when he pleads that his readers be pure or at least in the process of being purged (*καθαιρομένοι*). Foremost he has in mind an ascetical and contemplative cleansing, no doubt, but he is also supposing a deep emotional catharsis as well, insofar as his readers

the most frequently cited authority after Scripture in Byzantine ecclesiastical literature, Gregory bore an influence in the East that can be compared to Augustine's influence in the West.[34]

The theme of purification holds great importance in Gregory's life and his preaching of the faith—a fact too little appreciated today for understanding Gregory and, more significantly, communicating the faith. According to one reckoning, Gregory discusses purification 632 times, of which 392 times appear in his orations.[35] The breadth of purification language covers the practices of one being purified (such as asceticism, works of mercy, and baptism), the benefits of purification (such as contemplation of God, deification, and heaven), and the roles of others in purification (such as by Jesus, his Holy Spirit, or the priest).[36] What underlies all of these varied discussions of purification is Gregory's faith. Even when he borrows from non-Christian philosophical practices of purification, Gregory employs the terms and images from the standpoint of his belief in the Trinity and of the Trinitarian economy of salvation, especially living by the Spirit according to the life of Christ. Purification leads to and accompanies a life of faith that prepares one to see the most pure Trinity in heaven.

From this faith perspective on purification, Gregory so deeply engages with the literary treasures of Greek culture that he seems to be a preacher not only interested in purifying and baptizing the few in church with him, but also in purifying and baptizing a culture

are to be lifted to a uniquely Christian tragical vision of human existence, in which fear and pity are not the only powerful emotions in play." See Paul M. Blowers, *Visions and Faces of the Tragic: The Mimesis of Tragedy and the Folly of Salvation in Early Christian Literature*, OECS (Oxford: Oxford University Press, 2020), 114.

34 Jacques Noret, "Grégoire de Nazianze, l'auteur le plus cité après la Bible, dans la littérature ecclésiastique byzantine," in *II. Symposium Nazianzenum (Louvain-la-Neuve, 25–28 août, 1981): Actes du Colloque International*, ed. Justin Mossay, SGKA, Neue Folge 2, Forschungen zu Gregor von Nazianz (Paderborn: Schöningh, 1983), 259–66.

35 Brian J. Matz, *Gregory of Nazianzus*, FTECS (Grand Rapids, MI: Baker Academic, 2016), 37.

36 For a helpful categorization, see Matz, Gregory of Nazianzus, 37–52.

that was for him the whole inhabited world. Gregory thus follows a Pauline teaching of becoming "all things to all" (1 Cor 9:22), which, he finds, points to Christ himself. Gregory says in *or.* 37 that Christ became "all things to all so that he might gain *all*." He continues, "For he became not only a Jew, but also received upon himself not only so many of the names of things absurd and miserable, but even what is most absurd of all, even being 'sin' itself and a 'curse' itself" (2 Cor 5:21 and Gal 3:13).[37] By allowing himself to be called such things, Christ shows the depth of humility and shapes us in the humility that raises us up.

For Gregory, the Word came to permeate and transform the whole world not just when the enfleshed Word moved on the face of the earth, but also through the Church by the outpouring of the Holy Spirit. Preaching holds a prominent place in this ongoing activity of the Word. "That manifold and patient and formless and bodiless Nature will bear this," Gregory specifies, "namely, my words as if of a body, and weaker than the truth. For if he received flesh, may he also bear such an oration."[38] The Word that became flesh comes in Gregory's preaching to feed the multitudes. Gregory's words, offered as the spiritual bread that the Lord multiplies to feed the hungry, bring his listeners into contact with "the true bread and the source of true life."[39]

37 *Or.* 37.1 (SC 318, 271–72; my translation). While it may be common to call Jesus "a Jew" or "Jewish" today, the Fathers of the Church usually avoided identifying him that way. For a study on early Christian identifications of Jesus's Jewishness, see Andrew S. Jacobs, *Christ Circumcised: A Study in Early Christian History and Difference*, DRLAR (Philadelphia, University of Pennsylvania Press, 2012).

38 *Or.* 37.2 (SC 318, 274; Browne and Swallow, 338 [alt.]).

39 *Or.* 14.1 (PG 35:859; Daley, 76). For a recent overview of this work, *On the Love of the Poor*, with analysis of Gregory's use of Scripture, see Matz, *Gregory of Nazianzus*, 113–26. Matz writes, "Rather than using biblical material to support or to reinforce an argument he has already made with his own words, Gregory uses biblical words to make the arguments themselves" (126). For its Cappadocian context, see Brian E. Daley, SJ, "Building a New City: The Cappadocian Fathers and the Rhetoric of Philanthropy," *JECS* 7, no. 3 (1999): 431–61, and Susan R. Holman, *The Hungry Are Dying: Beggars and Bishops in Roman Cappadocia*, OSHT (New York: Oxford University Press, 2001). For my overview regarding

Gregory's preaching on purification for right faith is intimately bound to the sacrifice of Christ offered on the altar. The liturgical offering unites Christ's sacrificial life with the lives of those who participate in the liturgy. Consider his poetic reflection on this purification:

> The Temple is that sacred place that makes us holy;
> Our gift to God, all-purifying sacrifice;
> The place for offering our gifts, the holy table
> Where God comes down; our priesthood purifies the mind,
> Brings us to God as reconciled, and God to us:
> The Mystery is what we seek in wordless awe.[40]

Moreover, every priest is to minister the purifying Word. In one of his autobiographical poems Gregory writes:

> A priest should have one duty and only one:
> To purify souls both by life and word.[41]

We will now focus on this purifying faith in detail, first in Gregory's *or.* 2, the apology for his flight after ordination that articulates his understanding of priestly ministry, and then his set of Christmastime orations, *ors.* 38–40.

Purification and Faith in *Or. 2, On His Flight*

After Gregory returned to Nazianzus in time for Easter in 362, besides preaching his first oration, *On Pascha,* he also delivered

---

Christ in Gregory's ministry to the poor and rich, see *Christ in the Life and Teaching of Gregory of Nazianzus,* 220–24.

40 Poem 1.2.34.224–29 (PG 37:961–62; Daley, 52).

41 Poem 2.1.12.751–52 (PG 37:1221; Meehan, 72 [alt]).

a defense of his flight following his ordination. This *or.* 2, *On His Flight* or *Apology*, has been taken to be the first treatise on the ministerial priesthood in the history of Christianity.[42] His flight after ordination recalls not only Christian humility, but also the Platonic *topos* of the reluctant ruler. A good ruler should be begged to rule, not beg others to have him rule.[43]

Susanna Elm has placed this magnificent oration within the common setting that Gregory shares with his rival the Emperor Julian, known by Christians as the Apostate.[44] Her thesis is that both men are doing philosophy within the Empire according to competing visions of leading the people. If readers expect a simple discussion of the priesthood in Gregory's *or.* 2, they will be surprised. Let us consider a case that illustrates Elm's thesis but that she does not explore in her book.

Stressing how priestly ministry exceeds the worthiness of even those who are free from vice and at the height of virtue, Gregory famously writes: "To guide the human being, the most variable and manifold of living things, seems to me indeed to be the art of arts and science of sciences."[45] The priest, for Gregory, is the physician of souls and exercises an art of far greater importance than merely healing the body. Gregory the Great would take up again the phrase

42 Brian E. Daley, SJ, writes that *or.* 2 "is the earliest extended work we have in Greek on the responsibilities and the spiritual and personal challenges of Christian ministry." See Daley, *Gregory of Nazianzus*, 51. For a recent French translation of *or.* 2 with introduction and notes, see Philippe Molac, *Discours sur le sacerdoce de Grégoire de Naziance. La dignité du prêtre selon S. Grégoire de Nazianze* (Paris: Artège Lethielleux, 2018).

43 Plato, *The Republic* 6.489: "The true nature of things is that whether the sick man be rich or poor he must needs to go to the door of the physician, and everyone who needs to be governed to the door of the man who knows how to govern, not that the ruler should implore his nature subjects to let themselves be ruled, if he is really good for anything" (LCL *The Republic* 1.24; Shorey, 25). For analysis, see Susanna Elm, "The Diagnostic Gaze: Gregory of Nazianzus' Theory of the Ideal Priest in His Orations 6 (*De Pace*) and 2 (*Apologia de Fuga Sua*)," in *Orthodoxie, Christianisme, Histoire*, eds. Susanna Elm, Éric Rebillard, and Antonella Romano (Rome: École française de Rome, 2000), 83–100, at 92–93.

44 Susanna Elm, *Sons of Hellenism, Fathers of the Church: Emperor Julian, Gregory of Nazianzus, and the Vision of Rome*, TCH 49 (Berkeley and Los Angeles: University of California Press, 2012).

45 *Or.* 2.16 (SC 247, 110; Browne and Swallow, 208 [alt.]).

"art of arts" from *or.* 2 in his *Book of Pastoral Rule,* as we will see in Chapter 7, but the phrase should be seen within a long tradition. The use of the phrase embraces earlier thinkers such as Origen of Alexandria well over a century earlier, Maximus of Tyre a few decades before Origen, and the highly influential early first-century Jewish scholar of Alexandria, Philo.[46]

When Emperor Julian writes to the uneducated Cynics he gives three possibilities for the meaning of philosophy: "[1] the art of arts and the science of sciences, or [2] an effort to become like God, as far as one may, or [3] as the Pythian oracle said, 'Know yourself.'"[47] He then states that the three definitions closely relate to one another. That same threefold philosophical agenda can be seen in Gregory's works.[48] But whereas Julian uses this idea for pagan worship, Gregory does so to assist worship of the Trinity.

Gregory deployed many strands of literary and philosophical treasures of Greek culture in service of biblical faith in the Father, Son, and Holy Spirt; that biblical faith is the controlling factor of his thinking. Brian Matz shows that *or.* 2 contains 508 citations of Scripture and calls it "a masterpiece of Gregory's biblical thinking."[49] Consider this famous passage that blends the classics with Scripture to shape priestly ministry:

> The goal is to provide the soul with wings (cf. Plato, *Phaedrus* 246), to rescue it from the world and give it to God, and to watch over that which is his image (cf. Gn 1:26), if it abides, to

46 For a study on several uses of the phrase, see Andrew Hofer, OP, and Alan Piper, OP, "Retracing the 'Art of Arts and Science of Sciences' from Gregory the Great to Philo of Alexandria," *JHI* 79, no. 4 (2018): 507–26.

47 Julian, *To the Uneducated Cynics, or.* 6 (LCL *Works of the Emperor Julian* 2.10; Wright, 11 [alt.]).

48 See Hofer, *Christ in the Life and Teaching of Gregory of Nazianzus,* 61–63. For a fascinating use of Julian by a pioneer of Catholic modern biblical exegesis, see Marie-Joseph Lagrange, "Julian the Apostate: Priestly Retreat Master," translation by Philip Neri Reese, OP, *Dominicana* (Summer 2014): 78–85. Translation of Lagrange, "Julien l'Apostat prédicateur de retraites sacerdotales," *La Vie Spirituelle, supplément* 17 (1928): 242–48.

49 Matz, *Gregory of Nazianzus,* 54.

> take it by the hand if it is in danger, or restore it, if ruined, *to make Christ to dwell in hearts* (Eph 3:17) by the Spirit: and, in short, to make a god, and bestow blessedness from above upon one conformed to that above.[50]

"To bring Christ home into the human heart, to affiliate man with God," Susanna Elm comments, "that is the *telos* [the end or goal] of Gregory's divine mandate as philosopher and physician of the soul."[51] The Word is meant to be *inside* us. Moreover, in *or*. 2, we find not only a defense of his flight from priestly ministry and his return to take up the priestly duties in earnest, but the personal appeal of a prophetic model for others to follow. Brian Daley writes:

> The portrait of ministry that emerges [in *or*. 2] is clearly a prophetic, rather than a predominately institutional or clerical one. Identifying his own concerns with those of the prophets and Paul, Gregory suggests that the minister must be consumed by the word he proclaims, become personally an embodiment of his own message, if his work of mediation is to be fully authentic.[52]

Combining the image of a physician of souls with spiritual combat, Gregory preaches that priests attend to the "hidden human of the heart" (1 Pt 3:4) by healing the wounds of sin and doing combat with the evil forces within. In opposition to those interior foes, "we are in need of great and perfect faith, and of still greater cooperation on the part of God." Our opposition to evil, Gregory continues, "must manifest itself both in word and deed, if we ourselves, the

50 *Or*. 2.22 (SC 247, 118–19; Browne and Swallow, 209 [alt.]).

51 Elm, *Sons of Hellenism, Fathers of the Church*, 176.

52 Daley, *Gregory of Nazianzus*, 56. See also the following works by Brian E. Daley, SJ: "Walking through the Word of God: Gregory of Nazianzus as a Biblical Interpreter," in *The Word Leaps the Gap: Essays on Scripture and Theology in Honor of Richard B. Hays*, eds. J. Ross Wagner, C. Kavin Rowe, and A. Katherine Grieb (Grand Rapids, MI: Eerdmans, 2008), 514–31, and "Saint Gregory of Nazianzus as Pastor and Theologian." in *Loving God with our Minds: Essays in honor of Wallace M. Alston*, eds. Michael Welker and Cynthia A. Jarvis (Grand Rapids, MI: Eerdmans, 2004), 106–19.

most precious possession we have, are to be duly tended and cleansed and made as deserving as possible."[53]

Gregory does not relax the primary emphasis on the priest's own purification for priestly ministry in the faith. He proclaims, "A man must first himself be cleansed, before cleansing others; himself become wise, that he may make others wise; become light, and then give light: draw near to God, and so bring others near; be sanctified, then sanctify; be guided by the hand to lead others by the hand and to give counsel with understanding."[54] Without this purification, it is not safe for one to undertake priestly ministry.[55]

For Gregory, to cleanse people of their errors is at times like sowing seed upon rocks or speaking to the deaf; the task is so momentous that a Peter or a Paul is needed, and Gregory explores at length how Paul models priestly ministry.[56] "Who can test himself by the rules and standards that Paul laid down for bishops and presbyters, that they are to be temperate, sober-minded, not given to wine, not violent, apt to teach, blameless in all things and beyond the reach of the wicked, without finding considerable deflection from the straight line of the rules?" Gregory asks. He adds, "What of the regulations of Jesus for his disciples, when he sends them to preach?" Gregory then answers, "The main object of these is—not to enter into particulars—that they should be of such virtue, so simple and modest, and to speak concisely, so heavenly, that the Gospel should make its way no less by their manner than by their preaching."[57]

53 *Or*. 2.21 (SC 247, 118; Browne and Swallow, 209).

54 *Or*. 2.71 (SC 247, 184; Browne and Swallow, 219 [alt.])

55 *Or*. 2.91.

56 *Or*. 2.50–56. For the Fathers and Paul generally with mention of Gregory, see Brian E. Daley, SJ, "Saint Paul and the Fourth-Century Fathers: Portraits of Christian Life." *ProE* 18, no. 3 (2009): 299–317, at 301–3.

57 *Or*. 2.69 (SC 247, 182; Browne and Swallow, 219 [alt.]).

To conclude this overview of purification and faith in *or.* 2, we focus on what Gregory calls the first duty of the priest: the distribution of the Word, "that divine and exalted Word."[58] And within that distribution, at the peak of faith is preaching the Trinity. "Now this involves a very great risk to those who are charged with the illumination of others," Gregory warns.[59] He attacks the modalism of Sabellius as tantamount to atheism. Things that pass into one another cease to be, according to Gregory. In other words, if the Father passes into the Son and the Son passes into the Holy Spirit, we can expect that there is no eternal God. He despises the subordinationism of Arius as a form of Judaism, for the Arian denial of the Son's equality to the Father denies the Trinity. He also gives a third possibility of the Father, Son, and Holy Spirit as three separate principles, whether they be in opposition or alliance, as pagan polytheism. Gregory summarizes, "For both the one God must be preserved, and the three hypostases confessed, each with his own property."[60] Gregory thus presents to the people his humble confession:

> A suitable and worthy comprehension and exposition of this subject demands a discussion of greater length than the present occasion or even our life, I suppose, allows, and, what is more, both now and at all times, the aid of the Spirit, by whom alone we are able to perceive, to expound, or to embrace the truth in regard to God. For the pure alone can grasp him who is pure and of the same disposition as himself.[61]

What we see from this reflection on purification and faith at the beginning of his priesthood we find enacted during his preaching ministry.

58 *Or.* 2.35 (SC 247, 133–34).

59 *Or.* 2.36 (SC 247, 136; Browne and Swallow, 212).

60 *Or.* 2.38 (SC 247, 140; Browne and Swallow, 212 [alt.]).

61 *Or.* 2.39 (SC 247, 140; Browne and Swallow, 213).

Purification and Faith in *Ors.* 38–40

While ministering in Constantinople, Gregory preached an Epiphany cycle of *Orations* 38–40.[62] Scholars today more often study his cycle of five *Theological Orations* (*or.* 27–31) also preached in Constantinople during his ministry there (379–81).[63] Yet this set of three orations deserves much more attention than it currently enjoys. The three are *or.* 38, *On the Theophany* or *Nativity of the Savior*, *or.* 39, *On the Lights* (Epiphany, celebrating Christ's baptism), and *or.* 40, *On Baptism*. Gregory announces in *or.* 38 that his intention, when reviewing basic faith in God, is not theology (*theologia*), but economy (*oikonomia*).[64] That is, Gregory does not want to concentrate on God in himself, but on what God has done for us in his saving plan, especially in the incarnation. And who is God? Immediately after indicating this intention to treat the economy of salvation, Gregory underscores that God is Father, Son, and Holy Spirit. Against a Jewish way of thinking, Gregory praises the three, a multiplicity signified by the triple "Holy" of the seraphim (cf. Is 6:3). Against a pagan way of thinking, Gregory extols the single lordship and divinity of the three. Throughout these three *Epiphany Orations*, Gregory wants his listeners to experience God's saving plan through his own ministry. The culmination occurs in *or.* 40, an extended protreptic that exhorts people to be baptized. The two previous orations prepare for the goal of baptism proclaimed in *or.* 40. By focusing on purification and faith in the first

62 Scholars debate the timing, such as whether this is December 379–January 380 or December 380–January 381. I incline toward the latter. See Gallay, *Discours 38–41*, 16–22, and Daley, *Gregory of Nazianzus*, 117. In his extensive research on fourth-century evidence, Hans Förster shows that Gregory's *or.* 38 is the earliest extant example of preaching in the eastern half of the Empire on December 25 celebrated as Christ's birth. See Hans Förster, *Die Anfänge von Weihnachten und Epiphanias: Eine Anfrage an die Entstehungshypothesen*, STAC 46 (Tübingen: Mohr Siebeck, 2007), 180–97.

63 For an important analysis, see Frederick W. Norris, *Faith Gives Fullness to Reasoning: The Five Theological Orations of Gregory Nazianzen*, texts translated by Lionel Wickham and Frederick Williams, SuppVC 13 (Leiden: E.J. Brill, 1991).

64 *Or.* 38.8 (SC 358, 118; my translation).

two *Epiphany Orations*, we will be in a better position to see how Gregory's preaching on the incarnation, with necessary purification of his listeners' minds, prepares for baptismal life. Moreover, we will see how Gregory, as a model preacher, refers to his own purification and purifying role.

Oration 38, On the Theophany or Nativity of the Savior

Or. 38 begins jubilantly: "Christ is born—give praise! Christ comes from heaven—rise up to meet him! Christ is on the earth—be lifted up!"[65] Gregory breathlessly cites scriptural passage after scriptural passage showing the significance of the celebration. After he quotes John the Baptist, "Prepare the way of the Lord" (Mt 3:3; cf. Is 40:3), Gregory exclaims, "I shall cry out the power of this day. The fleshless one is made flesh, the Word becomes corporeal, the invisible is seen, the intangible is touched, the timeless has a beginning, the Son of God becomes Son of Man—'Jesus Christ, yesterday and today, the same also for all ages!'"[66] He celebrates this mystery of salvation as signifying the truth that God who gave "being" now gives "well-being." For although we had fallen from "well-being" through wickedness, "he might lead us back to himself again by becoming flesh."[67] It should be kept in mind that this feast celebrates the entirety of a dynamic faith in Christ through the living out of his mysteries. Gregory wants his listeners to be born with Christ, be crucified with him, be buried with him, and be raised with him.

65 *Or.* 38.1 (SC 358, 104; Daley, 117). Treatments of this oration include: Ben Fulford, "Gregory of Nazianzus and Biblical Interpretation," in *Re-Reading Gregory of Nazianzus*, ed. Beeley, 31–48, at 41–47; Norbert Widok, "Die kerygmatische Dimension der Lehre von der Menschwerdung in der *Rede 38* des Gregor von Nazianz." *ZAC* 11, no. 2 (2007): 335–47; and Hofer, *Christ in the Life and Teaching of Gregory of Nazianzus*, 163–66. For a study of *or.* 38–40, see Susanna Elm, "'O Paradoxical Fusion:' Gregory of Nazianzus on Baptism and Cosmology (*Or.* 38–40)," in *Heavenly Realms and Earthly Realities in Late Antique Religions*, eds. Ra'anan S. Boustand and Annette Yoshiko Reed (New York: Cambridge University Press, 2004), 296–315.

66 *Or.* 38.2 (SC 358, 106; Daley, 118 [alt.]).

67 *Or.* 38.3 (SC 358, 108; Daley, 118).

Rather than celebrating as do the Greek pagans with fancy decorations, dances, feasts, perfumes, and clothes, Gregory celebrates by putting his words at the service of the Word. He announces where he should begin in preaching to those used to luxuries: "purify, for me, your mind and hearing and thinking."[68] This discourse is about God and is itself divine, as Gregory prepares his people to listen to a catechetical review of the faith. "God always was, is, and will be," Gregory explains, "or better, God always is." Gregory then develops an image for God's existence that would have great influence subsequently: God "contains the whole of being in himself, without beginning or end, like an endless boundless ocean of reality."[69] So how can we know him? He can be known only indirectly, as the truth flees before it is grasped. Even that can occur only if we have been purified. Because God is incomprehensible, our wonder might be stirred up, "and through that wonder God might be yearned for all the more, and through our yearning God might purify us, and in purifying us God might make us like God."[70] Through this purification, ventures Gregory in a self-professed daring manner, God might come to us as his friends, "uniting himself with us, making himself known to us as God to gods."[71] He then steers between two errors: the mistakes of thinking either that God is "completely incomprehensible or perfectly comprehensible."[72]

In his catechetical review, Gregory preaches about God, the creation of angels and the visible cosmos, the creation of the human being, and the tree of knowledge of good and evil. That tree, Gregory is at pains to stress, was a good thing—it was contemplation

68 *Or*. 38.6 (SC 358, 114; Daley, 119 [alt.]).

69 *Or*. 38.7 (SC 358, 114; Daley, 120). See John of Damascus, *On the Orthodox Faith*, chap. 9 (1.9 in Western enumerations). For one Western adaptation, see Thomas Aquinas, *Summa Theologiae* I, q. 13, a. 11.

70 *Or*. 38.7 (SC 358, 116; Daley, 120 [alt.]).

71 *Or*. 38.7 (SC 358, 116; Daley, 120).

72 *Or*. 38.7 (SC 358, 116; Daley, 120).

(*theōria*)—but needed to be approached at the right time. Gregory calls contemplation "something which may only safely be attempted by those who have reached perfection in an orderly way."[73] It is not for the spiritually immature, just as tough food is not for infants, who need milk. But because of the envy of the devil and the insult of his wife, the man partook of the forbidden food, and was banished from the tree of life and paradise. The first thing he came to know, after eating of the tree of knowledge of good and evil, was his shame. With that knowledge, he hid himself from God.

God always cared for human beings who sinned, imposing various disciplines on them in loving kindness, but stronger medicine was needed. It came in the incarnation. Here is where purification most especially occurs: "He came to his own proper image and bore flesh for the sake of flesh, and mingled with a rational soul for my soul's sake, wholly cleansing like by like."[74] Whereas Gregory's rival Apollinarius of Laodicea understands Christ to save us by being unlike us, even saying at times that Christ is not a human or is a human equivocally speaking, Gregory rejoices that Christ saved him by being just like him—except for sin.[75] This difference with Apollinarius, who also used abundant mixture language for the incarnation, is not minor. Our salvation is at stake in this difference,

73 *Or.* 38.12 (SC 358, 128; Daley, 123).

74 *Or.* 38.13 (SC 358, 132; Daley, 123). For Gregory's understanding of "image," see Gabrielle Thomas, *The Image of God in the Theology of Gregory of Nazianzus* (Cambridge: Cambridge University Press, 2019).

75 For Apollinarius's claim that Christ is not a human, see frag. 45 (Lietzmann, 214.28–29). In *Anacephalaeosis* 16 (Lietzmann, 244.2–5), Apollinarius says: "God dwelling in a human is not a human. A human is a spirit united to flesh. Christ is 'a human,' as is said, equivocally; thus he is divine spirit united to flesh." Cf. Charles E. Raven, *Apollinarianism: An Essay on the Christology of the Early Church* (Cambridge: Cambridge University Press, 1923), 188, and Hofer, *Christ in the Life and Teaching of Gregory of Nazianzus*, 132. For an emphasis on the contrast between soteriologies of Christ's likeness versus unlikeness to us, see Brian E. Daley, SJ, "'Heavenly Man' and 'Eternal Christ': Apollinarius and Gregory of Nyssa on the Personal Identity of Christ," *JECS* 10, no. 4 (2002): 469–88. Daley writes, "For Apollinarius, Christ's role as savior rests primarily on the fact that he is unlike us" (478).

as Christ saves us by having a rational soul like ours. About the union of divinity and humanity, Gregory exclaims:

> O new mixture! O unexpected blending! *He who is* (Ex 3:14) has come to be, the uncreated one is created, the uncontained is contained, through the mediation of a rational soul standing between divinity and the coarseness of flesh. The rich one begs—for he begs in my flesh, that I might become rich with his divinity. And the full one has emptied himself—for he emptied himself of his own glory for a while, that I might have a share of his fullness.[76]

Gregory then asks a barrage of questions to those who think little of Christ because of the humility of the incarnation: "Do you decry God for his benefaction? Is he any the less, because he humbled himself for your sake?"[77] The series of questions exposes the errors of heretics who do not have the faith that purifies minds to grasp who Christ is and what Christ has done. The one Christ is "twofold," a mixture and blending that shows him to be singularly both God and man. One without the other would not give us the mystery of our salvation in the one Christ.[78]

Although Gregory has much to say about purification of bodily works in the moral sphere, even more fundamental is the purification of the mind by right faith. For example, if heretics do not recognize the divinity of Jesus, they are worse than the demons, as even demons do that. Gregory reminds us that Jesus came to heal our souls. He was baptized to cleanse our waters for our baptizing,

76 *Or*. 38.13 (SC 358, 134; Daley, 123–24 [alt.]).

77 *Or*. 38.14 (SC 358, 134–36; Daley, 124 [alt.]).

78 Labelling Gregory's Christology as "unitive," without qualification, as the alternative to "dualist," would make his "double" or "twofold" language inconsistent with his own thinking. If we appreciate more the consistency and variety of Gregory's mixture language for the incarnation, we can see why he admits at times a twoness within the one Christ, God blended with mortals. For a discussion of Gregory's blending terminology, see Hofer, *Christ in the Life and Teaching of Gregory of Nazianzus*, especially 91–121.

as he himself had no need to be purified. We are then to believe rightly in him.

Gregory reviews the details of Christ's nativity to assist us in praising God's salvation in Christ. Many people think of an ox and an ass next to the manger at Christmas, although the Gospel infancy narratives do not mention those animals.[79] Gregory makes this connection for us. He announces the fulfillment of Isaiah's prophecy: "An ox knows its owner, and an ass, its master's manger; but Israel does not know, my people has not understood" (Is 1:3). Gregory proclaims, "Like an ox, recognize your owner—so Isaiah exhorts you—and like an ass, know the manger of the Lord himself."[80] Gregory bids us to join Christ in his mysteries: "Walk uncomplainingly through all the ages and miracles of Christ, as Christ's disciple. Be purified, be circumcised, remove the veil with which you were born!"[81] Again, Gregory takes a comprehensive view of the incarnation in faith, urging us to join Christ in all that he has done. This culminates in being crucified with him, dying with him, and being buried with him "so that you may also rise with him and be glorified with him and reign with him, seeing God, so far as that is attainable, and being seen by him."[82] He who is within the Trinity is revealed to us even now, as far as that is possible while we are in the bonds of mortal flesh. After his mention of the flesh, he concludes his preaching with praise to Christ Jesus our Lord.

Oration 39, On the Lights

Gregory's second contribution in this homiletic series celebrates the Epiphany, a feast honoring the baptism of the Lord,

79 For an overview of this nativity symbolism, see Jody Vaccaro Lewis, "The Inn, the Manger, the Swaddling Cloths, the Shepherds, and the Animals," in *The Oxford Handbook of Christmas*, ed. Timothy Larsen (Oxford: Oxford University Press, 2020), 224–35.

80 *Or.* 38.17 (SC 358, 144; Daley, 126).

81 *Or.* 38.18 (SC 358, 146; Daley, 126).

82 *Or.* 38.18 (SC 358, 148; Daley, 127).

called "the Lights." This oration begins, "Again my Jesus, and again a mystery." Not surprisingly, purification holds a prominent place in this oration that celebrates faith in Christ. At the beginning of this festive work, Gregory preaches that Christ's baptism "sets in motion my own purification and comes to the aid of that light which we received from him as a gift from above, in the beginning, and which we darkened and confused by sin."[83]

Gregory plays on the double use of "light of the world" in the Gospel accounts. In John's Gospel, Jesus says, "I am the light of the world" (Jn 8:12) and in Matthew's account, he says, "You are the light of the world" (Mt 5:14). Gregory employs the metaphor of God's voice echoing, "I am the light of the world," strongly in him and also, perhaps, in his listeners. Christ's light can purify all those participating in his mysteries, which Gregory contrasts with Jewish and pagan rites, with extended descriptions of the latter. Surely, what Christians celebrate is "not a kind of legal, shadowy purification" of a temporal washing found in Jewish observances of the law.[84] Even more distant from the fullness of Christian worship, the pagans hold beliefs and practice rituals that could never purify.

Drawing a contrast to Christ's light, Gregory describes at length the sordid sexual and violent practices of the pagan gods, proof of the diabolical aspects of idolatry. He says of their false worshipers:

> They are disgusting because of their error, still more disgusting in the vileness of what they worship and revere; as a result, they are even more lacking perception than the idols they worship, surpassing what they adore in mindlessness to the same degree as their gods surpass them in worthlessness![85]

83 *Or*. 39.1 (SC 358, 150; Daley, 128 [alt.]).
84 *Or*. 39.1 (SC 358, 150; Daley, 128).
85 *Or*. 39.6 (SC 358, 160; Daley, 130).

The disgust begins with the error of pagan thinking and how such an error leads to such horrible acts of abominable worship.

Gregory praises the gift of escaping from "superstitious error, of living in the company of truth and serving the true and living God."[86] He calls his people to contemplation of the truth, an awesome act that begins in fear of the Lord and observance of his commandments. This fear leads to cleansing, and where there is cleansing there is also illumination. "For this reason," Gregory tells his congregation, "one must first purify oneself, then associate oneself with what is pure, if we are not to undergo what Israel experienced, when it was unable to bear the glory shining on Moses' face, and so demanded a veil."[87]

The Word will come to those who have swept out the unclean, materialistic spirit from their souls by deep knowledge—and put into practice a life of virtue. Then they will be able to proclaim God's wisdom. "Until then, however," Gregory writes, reminding his people of the basics, "let us first purify ourselves, and be initiated into the Word, so that we may do as much good to ourselves as possible, forming ourselves in God's image and receiving the Word when he comes—not only receiving him, in fact, but holding on to him and revealing him to others."[88]

Gregory then articulates the central mystery of the Christian faith to those whose souls have been cleansed by the Word. He observes, "Since the chief point of a feast is the remembrance of God, let us remember God."[89] To remember God is to think of him rightly. Some may suppose that Gregory as "the Theologian" would go into abstruse, technical formulations about the Trinity. They would be mistaken. Gregory is far more concerned with getting the

86 *Or.* 39.8 (SC 358, 162; Daley, 131).
87 *Or.* 39.9 (SC 358, 164; Daley, 131).
88 *Or.* 39.10 (SC 358, 168–70; Daley, 132).
89 *Or.* 39.11 (SC 358, 170; Daley, 132 [alt.]).

realities of the faith right in the mind than quibbling over particular words to use. In a characteristic move, he says:

> And when I speak of God, let yourselves be surrounded with a flash of light which is both one and three: three in properties, or indeed in hypostases, if one wants to call them that, or indeed in "persons"—for we will not become involved in a battle over names, as long as the syllables point towards the same notion—and one with regard to the concept of substance or indeed divinity.... The divinity is one in three, and the three are one—those three in whom the divinity exists, or to put it more accurately, who are the divinity.[90]

Avoiding the opposed errors of the Sabellian aggregation of the three in modalism and the Arian cutting of the three into unequal pieces, Gregory proclaims the Father, the Son, and the Holy Spirit. The Father is without beginning. The Son is not without a beginning, but not in the sense of a beginning in time, as he is beyond all time and is the maker of time. The Holy Spirit comes forth from the Father, not by generation but "by procession (if one must create new terminology for the sake of clarity)."[91] Gregory then continues to develop his theological account of the Trinity, and tops it off with this simple line: "There is one God, then, in three, and the three are one, as we have said."[92]

90 *Or.* 39.11 (SC 358, 170–72; Daley, 132–33). For analysis, see Verna E. F. Harrison, "Illumined from All Sides by the Trinity: Neglected Themes in Gregory's Trinitarian Theology," in *Re-Reading Gregory of Nazianzus*, ed. Beeley, 13–30, at 18–19.

91 *Or.* 39.12 (SC 358, 174; Daley, 133). Moreschini rightly draws attention to Gregory's way of presenting the adverb as a neologism. See SC 358, 175n2. For a study of this passage regarding the *filioque*, see A. Edward Siecienski, *The Filioque: History of a Doctrinal Controversy*, OSHT (New York: Oxford University Press, 2010), 42. With analysis of additional writings of Gregory, Siecienski opines, "Gregory's emphasis on the Father's unique role as cause within the godhead later became *the* theological foundation upon which the East's rejection of the *filioque* was built" (42, original emphasis). I agree with him. For a caution underscoring Gregory's innovation in terminology of the Holy Spirit's procession, see my review of *The Filioque: History of a Doctrinal Controversy* in *Thom* 75, no. 3 (2011): 503–7.

92 *Or.* 39.12 (SC 358, 176; Daley, 133).

Gregory treats the mystery of creation briefly, as he races toward what he most wants all to praise: Christ. Humans were made to God's image, but succumbed to the devil and sin. So, what did God do? In answering this, Gregory celebrates the incarnation in a turn of phrase that would enter the Byzantine and Latin liturgies: "Natures are made anew; God becomes human."[93]

Gregory recalls his previous oration's praise of the feast of Christ's birth, and here concentrates on Christ's baptism. "Christ is full of light: let us shine with him," exclaims Gregory for this celebration.[94] Again, Gregory stresses purification: "He is the pure one, baptized by John, as he begins his signs. What should we learn? How shall we be formed by this?" He continues, "We must be taught to be purified first, to be lowly in our thinking, to proclaim the Gospel in the fullness of spiritual and bodily maturity."[95] Here Gregory has a message concerning not only baptism, but also clergy. He wants people not to rebel against the ministers of the mystery, and, even more, he does not want people to come to trust in themselves after quickly becoming leaders and teachers. Jesus was cleansed by John when he was thirty years old. Gregory therefore asks the young who want to teach: "are you teaching your elders, even before your beard is grown? Do you think you can teach them, without perhaps gaining the respect that comes from maturity or manners?"[96] The young should not make an excuse by resorting to the example of the young Daniel, who was able to teach the elders of Israel regarding the case of Susanna (Dn 13:1–64). An exceptional situation does not count as the Church's law.

93 *Or.* 39.13 (SC 358, 176; Daley, 134). See the first *sticheron* of the Aposticha of Vespers of Christmas Day and the Benedictus antiphon of the feast of January 1 in the Roman liturgy, as explained by Andrew Louth in introducing Maximus the Confessor's comments in his Difficulty 41. See Andrew Louth, *Maximus the Confessor*, ECF (London: Routledge, 1996), 155.

94 *Or.* 39.14 (SC 358, 180; Daley, 134).

95 *Or.* 39.14 (SC 358, 180; Daley, 134).

96 *Or.* 39.14 (SC 358, 180; Daley, 135).

Gregory interprets John the Baptist's "winnowing fan" to refer to purification, and he treats other details of the Baptist's preaching in a similar vein (cf. Mt 3:7–12). This does not mean that purification only prepares for baptism. He names different kinds of baptism, the last of which he calls "the baptism of tears." This is the kind of baptism needed for post-baptismal sin, a baptism of contrition, which was opposed by the Novatianists. Novatus of Carthage was a cleric who rebelled against Cyprian of Carthage (claimed by Gregory as a favorite saint).[97] Novatus fled to Rome, where he became allied with Novatian; unsurprisingly, their names were at times confused in early accounts. As rigorists, the Novatianists denied the Church's ability to forgive idolatry and other grave sins. They wanted to be known as the Pure. It is fitting that Gregory refutes this heresy of the Pure precisely in his exhortation to purification. Gregory, unlike the Novatianists, stresses his humanity and his constant need for mercy:

> I confess to being a human being, a changeable animal with a nature always in flux; I accept this gift eagerly, and adore the one who has given it, and I share it with others; I bear mercy to others before receiving it myself. I know that I, too, am "beset by weakness" (Heb 5:12), and that I will receive "in the measure" with which I measure (Mt 7:2).[98]

The Novatianists only pretend to be pure, suspects Gregory, since in their hypocrisy they will not accept the conversion of David or of Peter. For these heretics, mercy for sin committed is impossible after baptism. Gregory demands, "What is the proof of this? Either show me, or do not condemn! If the case is in doubt, let compassion win the day!"[99] Gregory weeps for these rigorists and speculates that

97 For Gregory's perplexing oration that confuses Cyprian of Carthage with another Cyprian, see *or.* 24, *In Praise of St. Cyprian.*

98 *Or.* 39.18 (SC 358, 188–90; Daley, 137 [alt.]).

99 *Or.* 39.19 (SC 358, 192; Daley, 137).

there may be yet one more baptism, a baptism by fire after death that they will experience.[100] Gregory concludes this oration, not surprisingly, with emphasis on purification, faith in the Trinity, and a customary doxology to Jesus Christ our Lord.

Oration *40*, On Baptism

One day after giving *or.* 39, Gregory preached the long *or.* 40, *On Baptism.* The text is more than the lengths of the two previous orations combined.[101] As a protreptic, its purpose is to persuade people to be baptized. To do this, it frequently stresses the need for purification and right faith. When we listen to the two previous orations as leading to *or.* 40, we understand more vividly how Gregory wants people to experience the mysteries of Christ by having a life submerged in him. He wants his listeners to live out the Christian faith, the baptismal life, in complete conformity to Christ. In the concluding chapters of *or.* 40, we see this focus in earnest as it follows an exhortation for a complete purification. Skipping many chapters of this oration, we will concentrate here on the oration's final chapters on the purification of the whole person and on the faith that Gregory wants to "inscribe" on his listeners.

In *or.* 40.38–40, Gregory speaks of a series of purifications by picking up the immediately preceding chapter's emphasis on baptism as illumination—something we heard also in *or.* 39. He had quoted the great Light, "You are the light of the world" (Mt 5:14),

100 For Gregory on a final baptism by fire within his speculation on the last things, see Brian E. Daley, SJ, *The Hope of the Early Church: A Handbook of Patristic Eschatology* (Grand Rapids, MI: Baker Academic, 2010 [original edition published in 1991 by Cambridge University Press]), 83–85. Cf. *or.* 7.21.

101 A Greek text and French translation of *or.* 40 appear in SC 358, 198–311. For Gregory's commonalities with the other great Cappadocians on baptism, see Everett Ferguson, "Exhortations to Baptism in the Cappadocians," *StPatr* 32 (1997): 121–29, and for commonalities with the Alexandrian tradition on baptism, see Everett Ferguson, "Gregory's Baptismal Theology and the Alexandrian Tradition," in *Re-Reading Gregory of Nazianzus*, ed. Beeley, 67–83. For Ferguson's broader perspective on Gregory on baptism, see Everett Ferguson, *Baptism in the Early Church: History, Theology, and Liturgy in the First Five Centuries* (Grand Rapids, MI: Eerdmans, 2009), 529–602.

and exhorted, "Let us become 'light-bearers in the world offering the Word of life' (Phil 2:15–16), that is, life-giving power for others."[102] He continues in *or.* 40.38: "Let us purify every part, brothers and sisters, let us sanctify every sense. Let there be nothing imperfect in us, nothing of the first birth; let us leave nothing unillumined."[103] This oration offers a goldmine of reflection on the spiritual senses, a topic of increasing importance in theology today.[104] Gregory explores every aspect of the human person for a purification that causes one to experience God in a new life. Gregory wants us to have pure eyes, ears, tongue, smell, touch so that what we experience is not the pleasures of the world, but the goodness of God, who is so much better than the world. He concludes this chapter with an exhortation to delight our taste with "words sweeter than honey" (Ps 19:10 LXX; Ps 119:103 LXX).

Gregory moves on to speak of purifying the different parts of the body, beginning with the head, called the workshop of the senses. He wants his people to hold fast to the head of Christ, "from whom the whole body is fitted and joined together" (Col 2:19). The shoulder needs sanctification and purification in order to carry Christ's cross, which not everyone easily bears. The hands and feet are to be purified, so that the hands may be lifted up in prayer and grasp Christ's teaching and so that the feet may be prepared for the Gospel, as Christ himself washes and purifies the feet. The stomach, heart, loins, and kidneys also receive Gregory's attention. The kidneys, for example, symbolize the faculty of desire, and Gregory wants us to say, "Lord, before you is all my desire" (Ps 37:10 LXX). He explains how each of his listeners is to be "a man of desires" (Dn

102 *Or.* 40.37 (SC 358, 284; Harrison, 133 [alt.]).

103 *Or.* 40.38 (SC 358, 284; Harrison, 133 [alt.]).

104 For an important collection of essays on select Christian writers in history, see *The Spiritual Senses: Perceiving God in Western Christianity*, eds. Paul L. Gavrilyuk and Sarah Coakley (Cambridge: Cambridge University Press, 2012). For the editors' introduction, see pp. 1–19. The collection does not feature Gregory of Nazianzus.

9:23 LXX), i.e., desires of the Spirit. In short, our purification is to enable us to offer ourselves wholly to God. "Let us receive in return the whole," says Gregory, "since to receive purely is this, to be given to God and make our own salvation a sacred offering."[105]

After concluding his exhortation to purification for this sacrificial exchange, Gregory extols the wonder of their shared faith:

> Besides all this and above all, guard for me the good deposit, by which I live and by which I also govern, and which I desire to accompany me in my journey hence, with which I bear everything painful and spit upon every pleasure, the confession of Father and Son and Holy Spirit. I entrust this to you today. With this I will both submerge you [in the water] and raise you up. This I give you as a companion and protector for all your life, the one divinity and power, found in unity in the three, and gathering together the three as distinct.[106]

Gregory details this Trinitarian confession against the various heresies of his day, yet without naming them. For example, he says that the Son is ranked below the Father by those who themselves lie below—a wonderful rhetorical twist to put down those who put down the Son. He similarly shows how the Holy Spirit is degraded, but in fact no person of the Trinity is a creature. "If I still worshipped a creature or was baptized into a creature," Gregory argues, "I would not be divinized, nor would I have transformed my first birth."[107] Gregory thus ties together orthodox faith with salvation, a salvation experienced through the purifying waters of baptism.

Gregory explains the faith for those who have received a different teaching. He knows that some have within them an ill-formed

105 *Or.* 40.40 (SC 358, 292; Harrison, 136).

106 *Or.* 40.41 (SC 358, 292; Harrison, 136–37).

107 *Or.* 40.42 (SC 358, 296; Harrison, 137–38). Gregory should be better known as differing from his friend Basil in acclaiming that the Holy Spirit is God and consubstantial with the Father and the Son. His Pneumatology has been extraordinarily influential in Christian history. See Oliver B. Langworthy, *Gregory of Nazianzus' Soteriological Pneumatology*, STAC 117 (Tübingen: Mohr Siebeck, 2019).

faith. Quoting the Apostle Paul, Gregory says, "'I bear witness before God and the elect angels' (1 Tm 5:21), that you must be baptized with this faith."[108] Calling himself a calligrapher, Gregory is prepared to inscribe the proper faith on the souls of those to be baptized.[109] He identifies himself with Moses as one who is writing with the finger of God a new Decalogue. This set of ten commandments is not what we read in the Pentateuch, such as "Thou shall not steal." Rather, it summarizes what Christian faith communicates to the believing soul.[110] And what is that faith for a pure soul?

Right faith entails first of all belief in God as the creator of all things, both visible and invisible, out of nothing. God guides the entire cosmos by providence toward something better. Evil, as Gregory explains, comes not from the Creator, but from the evil one and from us. The Theologian then moves on to reflect on salvation. The Son of God, the Word before the ages, has become Son of Man for your deification, Gregory proclaims. Gregory loves to give holistic formulae about Christ's offer of salvation to us, such as: "He is a whole human being, and the same is also God, on behalf of the whole sufferer, that salvation may be granted to the whole of you, destroying the whole condemnation of sin."[111] He continues: this One is "impassible in his divinity, passible in what was assumed"—a point that Gregory makes elsewhere in the strongest of terms.[112]

108 *Or.* 40.44 (SC 358, 300; Harrison, 139 [alt.]).

109 For this emphasis on inscribing, see Susanna Elm, "'O Paradoxical Fusion!'"

110 Gregory announces that he is giving a Decalogue. He numbers the tenth article, but the earlier nine are not clearly identified. For one way of counting the ten, see SC 358, 307n4.

111 *Or.* 40.45 (SC 358, 306; Harrison, 140–41).

112 *Or.* 40.45 (SC 358, 306; Harrison, 141 [alt.]). See *ep.* 202.18, to Nectarius. There Gregory instructs his ill-formed successor in Constantinople that the most terrible part of Apollinarian teaching is that "the only-begotten God, the Judge of all, the Author of Life, the Destroyer of Death, is perishable, and underwent suffering in his proper divinity" (my translation). One should not mistake Gregory's teaching of "God crucified" (*or.* 45.29) to mean that Christ's suffering occurred *within the divine nature*. The paradox of the incarnation would collapse for Gregory, if that were the case, as God would not be God. For this hermeneutical key to the Christological controversies of the early Church, see the outstanding Paul L. Gavrilyuk, *The Suffering of the Impassible God: The Dialectics of Patristic Thought*, OECS (Oxford: Oxford University Press, 2004).

And what is the result? "He is as much human because of you as you may become God because of him."[113] On account of our iniquities, he suffered, died, rose, and ascended into heaven in order to bring with him you who lie below. He will come again in his more deiform body, without the heaviness of our frail flesh, remaining God all the while. He will judge and give recompense. Gregory teaches, "And this will be light to those whose mind has been purified, that is God seen and known, in proportion to each one's purity, which indeed we also call the kingdom of heaven."[114] But to others who do not have the light? Gregory says that "it will be darkness to those blinded in their directive faculty, that is estrangement from God."[115] Finally, Gregory bids his people to do what is good (cf. Gal 6:10), acting on this foundation of dogmas, since "faith without works is dead" (Jas 2:10), just as works without faith. With this, Gregory closes out his summary of the faith and promises that more will be revealed by the grace of the Trinity in the people, once they are baptized.

Gregory gives a closing vision in preaching to his people. He sees that, after baptism, the bright and virgin souls will have lamps bright with faith ready for the bridal chamber. Referring to the parable of the wise and foolish virgins (cf. Mt 25:1–13), he encourages the faithful to be ready for the wedding feast. There the Bridegroom will be joined with the souls that have entered with him. "He will be joined with them, in my view," concludes Gregory, "in teaching them things most perfect and most pure. In those things, may even we participate, those who are teaching such things and those learning them, in the same Christ our Lord, to whom be glory unto the ages. Amen."[116]

113 *Or.* 40.45 (SC 358, 306; Harrison, 141 [alt.]).
114 *Or.* 40.45 (SC 358, 306; Harrison, 141).
115 *Or.* 40.45 (SC 358, 306; Harrison, 141).
116 *Or.* 40.46 (SC 358, 310; Harrison, 142 [alt.]).

Conclusion

When we attend to Gregory's life and preaching on faith, we find faith and the need for purification inseparable. More often do we find purification joined to matters of faith in Gregory's preaching than the linking of reason and faith, a pair commonly found in instruction today. The twinning of purification, which certainly includes the cleansing of reason and faith, could have significant repercussions on catechesis and theology today. How can we think or believe rightly without being cleansed of what holds us back from knowing created natures and God? How can we attain what we believe except when we have been made pure, as God is pure? Gregory ceaselessly speaks of purification, because he wants people to experience faith's life-changing transformation. Moreover, while there has been much interest recently in the recovery of the notion of deification, there has not been sufficient attention to the fact that Gregory's proclamation of the deified life for believers means becoming pure spiritually and bodily. Purification enables us to approach rightly the supreme mystery revealed in Christ: God is Father, Son, and Holy Spirit. Gregory takes great pains in his preaching to bring people to think about the Trinity rightly, something that far too many preachers today do not attempt.

A final example of Gregory's preaching can encapsulate his teaching on purification and faith. His *or.* 20, *On Theology and the Appointment of Bishops*, may have been a reworking of what he delivered in Constantinople when he arrived there in the fall of 379. The form in which we possess this oration has parts that are found in other orations (*or.* 2, 27, 28, 29, and 39).[117] It sums up several of Gregory's favorite themes, and so we naturally find his emphasis on purification and faith.

117 Daley, *Gregory of Nazianzus*, 98.

While so many talk endlessly, Gregory begins, he wants rather to live out the philosophy that comes from above, to be with God. Without the purification of ears and intelligence, it is not safe to be a spiritual leader or to do theology. "Knowing that no one is worthy of the great God, who is both victim and high priest," Gregory says, "unless one has first offered oneself to God as a 'living sacrifice' (Rom 12:1), or rather has become a living 'holy temple' (Eph 2:21) of the living God, how should I be hasty to engage myself to speak concerning God, or approve anyone who might engage himself to use such words in a rash way?"[118] Gregory answers that the first requirement is to purify oneself and to associate with the One who is pure. This purity changes our life by giving us heaven's wisdom. Gregory quotes Paul's words, "I live, now no longer I, but Christ lives in me" (Gal 2:20). It was not that Paul was dead, but that he was "alive with a life superior to that of most human beings, since he shared in the true life that knows not the limit of death."[119] Such a life propels one to the Trinity.

Thinking of those unreceptive to his preaching on the Trinity, Gregory makes this admission: "I am constantly repeating the same argument, since I fear for the crude and material style of your thought."[120] He tries to make it as simple as possible:

> For me it is enough to hear that there is a Son, and that he is from the Father, and that the one is Father and the other is Son.... Do you hear mention of a begetting? Do not trouble yourself about how it occurs. Do you hear that the one who proceeds forth from the Father is the Spirit? Do not exercise your curiosity about the manner.[121]

118 *Or.* 20.4 (SC 270, 62; Daley, 99–100 [alt.]).

119 *Or.* 20.5 (SC 270, 66; Daley, 100).

120 *Or.* 20.10 (SC 270, 78; Daley, 103).

121 Or. 20.10–11 (SC 270, 78–80; Daley, 103–4).

After all, can we figure out the mystery of our own being let alone God's being? Gregory asks, "If you, who discuss these things, do not know who you really are, if you do not fully grasp these things, of which your perception is a witness, how do you suppose you can know precisely what and how great God is?"[122]

In his conclusion, Gregory advises, "grasp what you can, and pray to grasp the rest. Love what already abides in you, and let the rest await you in the treasury above. Ascend by the way you live. Through purification, acquire what is pure."[123] The kingdom of heaven, for Gregory, is what is purest and most perfect: the knowledge of God. Gregory ends, as he usually does, with a Trinitarian praise in Christ: "Let us store our treasure there in heaven, so that we may possess this profit of loving labor: the full illumination of the holy Trinity—what are its qualities and its greatness, if I may put it this way—shining in Christ himself, our Lord, to whom be glory and power for the ages of ages. Amen."[124]

Gregory's preaching on purification and faith leads us to the hope of salvation amidst daily struggles. In our next chapter we will study how the Word gives us the hope of salvation through John Chrysostom's life and preaching.

122 *Or*. 20.11 (SC 270, 80; Daley, 104).
123 *Or*. 20.12 (SC 270, 80; Daley, 104 [alt.).
124 *Or*. 20.11 (SC 270, 84; Daley, 104 [alt.]).

CHAPTER 4

JOHN CHRYSOSTOM

The Word in Our Flesh for the Hope of Salvation

The Apostle Paul places a particular importance on hope when speaking about matters of salvation. He exhorts the Thessalonians to be sober, "putting on the breastplate of faith and love and the helmet that is the hope of salvation" (1 Thes 5:8). In Paul's vision of what life in Christ means, Christian hope is precisely a hope *of salvation*—amidst the sufferings of this present world. The Letter to the Romans, for example, underscores this hope several times. In Romans 5, Paul calls us, after stressing faith, to boast "in hope of the glory of God" (Rom 5:2). Hope culminates a list of actions during a life of suffering: "affliction produces endurance, and endurance, proven character, and proven character, hope, and hope does not disappoint" (Rom 5:3–5). Paul later says crisply, "by hope we were saved" (Rom 8:24). While serving the Lord, we are to be "rejoicing in hope, enduring in affliction, and persevering in prayer" (Rom 12:12). All of Scripture, for Paul, should be seen from this stance of hope for us in our present trials: "For whatever was written previously was written for our instruction, that by endurance and by the encouragement of the Scriptures we might have hope" (Rom 15:4).

In a wish that those who listen to him may abound in hope, the Apostle Paul writes, "May the God of hope fill you with all joy" (Rom 15:13). Reflecting on these words, a daily inspirational book quotes the popular American evangelist Billy Graham:

> How often have you found what you were looking for in life, only to realize it didn't bring you the satisfaction you thought it would?
>
> It is life's ultimate frustration—thinking we will find fulfillment in the things of this world. But they can never bring lasting happiness. As one bumper sticker I saw expressed it, "All I want is a little more than I have now."
>
> We look for love, security, and happiness through our jobs, our possessions, our relationships—but if they really brought lasting joy, wouldn't we have testimonies to that effect from millions of people all over the world? Instead, we find emptiness, discontent, and hopelessness.
>
> Try putting Christ first and watch how your life is turned around. You will discover that he alone is the source of love, peace, and joy you have been searching for.[1]

From this Pauline-inspired outreach, with simple questions and an offer of hope in a world of emptiness, discontent and hopelessness, we turn to one of the most popular preachers in the early Church, John Chrysostom (d. 407), for our study of incarnation, deification, and proclamation.

1 Billy Graham, *Hope for Each Day: Words of Wisdom and Faith* (Nashville, TN: Thomas Nelson, 2002), 16.

The Word in John's Flesh for Us

Tradition calls John "Chrysostom," the Golden Mouth, because of his eloquent preaching.[2] When Jerome was writing his catalogue of early Christian writers, *On Illustrious Men*, in 392–93, Chrysostom was known as "John of Antioch," a presbyter who already had authored many works.[3] The only work that Jerome had read of John's was *On the Priesthood*, a dialogue of six books of great importance for preachers that we will examine below. John's productivity throughout his life, especially in preaching, is astounding. We have more than one thousand extant works: 13 treatises, about 240 letters, and more than 800 homilies and scriptural commentaries.[4] The ratio of his exegetical homilies to his other works is 5:1.[5] Additionally, his popularity in tradition is attested by the more than one thousand works falsely ascribed to his name.[6]

Chrysostom in the twentieth century, however, was often passed over in the studies of historical theology on the Trinity and the incarnation in favor of his older contemporaries from Cappadocia (Basil the Great, Gregory of Nazianzus, and Gregory of Nyssa).

2 The first known references to John as Chrysostom are Latin witnesses in the sixth century. See Facundus of Hermiane, *Defense of the Three Chapters* 4.2.26 (SC 478, 158) for a Latin translation rather than transliteration *os aureum* (Golden Mouth). Chrysostomus Baur quotes Pope Vigilius's *Constitution* chap. 60, no. 217, ed. Otto Günther, *Epistulae*, p. 291 (CSEL 35, Pars 1, Vienna 1895); this gives evidence from 553 of a Greek custom: *quem Chrysostomum vocant* (whom they call Chrysostom). See Chrysostomus Baur, OSB, *S. Jean Chrysostome et Ses Oeuvres dans l'Histoire Littéraire. Essai presenté à l'occasion du XV*[e] *centenaire de Saint Jean Chrysostome* (Louvain: Bureaux du Recueil, 1907), 59.

3 Jerome, *On Illustrious Men*, chap. 129 (TU 14, 54).

4 Wendy Mayer, "John Chrysostom," in *The Wiley-Blackwell Companion to Patristics*, ed. Ken Parry (Malden, MA: John Wiley & Sons, 2015), 141–54, at 141.

5 Wendy Mayer, "The Homiletic Audience as Embodied Hermeneutic: Scripture and Its Interpretation in the Exegetical Preaching of John Chrysostom," in *Hymns, Homilies and Hermeneutics*, eds. Sarah Gaydor-Whyte and Andrew Mellas, Byzantina Australiensa (Leiden: Brill, 2021). For an overview of new research on Chrysostom, see Chris L. de Wet and Wendy Mayer, "Approach and Appreciating John Chrysostom in New Ways," in *Revisioning John Chrysostom: New Approaches, New Perspectives*, CAEC 1 (Leiden: Brill, 2019), 1–31.

6 On p. 141, Wendy Mayer refers to Sever J. Voicu, "Johannes Chrysostomus II (Pseudo-Chrysostomica)," *Reallexikon für Antike und Christentum* 18 (1997): 503–15.

Yet, new approaches have been applied to his numerous works, such as through social history's attention to city, family, sex, and wealth, or through recent literary and philosophical theories. In addition, studies of medical matters and emotions as well as reconfigurations of categorizing patristic exegesis provide grounds for significant secondary literature from scholars in the twenty-first century.[7] For preachers, lest it be forgotten, his life offers an extraordinary model.

Besides his own writings, many early reports give information about his life. Among the most significant is a *Funerary Speech*, not as well-known as it should be, delivered by one of John's supporters soon after his death on September 14, 407.[8] To narrate John's life, Sozomen borrows heavily from the account of Socrates Scholasticus, but he supplements that information with the *Funerary Speech* (which Socrates did not use).[9] In another early report, John's friend Palladius contributed his *Dialogue on the Life of St. John Chrysostom* (perhaps written 408–9). We have extant, moreover, in the ninth-century *Bibliotheca* of Patriarch Photius a summary of the acts of the Synod of the Oak (403), a council of great importance for John's tumultuous ministry as Bishop of Constantinople.

Just as Socrates's *Ecclesiastical History* introduces John through his episcopal ordination in Constantinople, so Sozomen's *Ecclesiastical History* features John in Book VIII, beginning with Constantinople's need for a new bishop.[10] The people of Constantinople disagreed over who should be their next bishop,

7 For Wendy Mayer's *Chrysostomica: An Online Bibliography of Scholarship on John Chrysostom and Attributed Writings (last updated in March 2016)*, see http://www.cecs.acu.edu.au/chrysostombibliography.html (accessed August 12, 2020).

8 *Funerary Speech for John Chrysostom*, translated with an introduction by Timothy D. Barnes and George Bevan, TTH 60 (Liverpool: Liverpool University Press, 2013). Sometimes that author is called Pseudo-Martyrius. The critical edition is found in Martin Wallraff, *Oratio Funebris in Laudem Sancti Johannis Chrysostomi. Epittaffio attribuito a Martirio di Antiochia* (BHG 871, CPG 6517), with an Italian translation by C. Ricci (Spoleto, 2007).

9 Barnes and Bevan, *Funerary Speech*, 23.

10 Socrates's account of John begins in his *Ecclesiastical History* 6.2.

and Sozomen relates that thoughts turned to John, a presbyter in Antioch, outstanding in life and wonderful in eloquence. Sozomen reports that when the pagan Libanius, the greatest orator of the age, was asked on his deathbed who should take his place, he replied, "It would have been John had not the Christians taken him from us."[11] Sozomen documents that many who listened to John's preaching were excited to the love of virtue and to the imitation of his life. "For by living a divine life he imparted zeal from his own virtues to his hearers. He produced convictions similar to his own, because he did not enforce them by rhetorical art and strength, but expounded the sacred books with truth and sincerity," records this fifth-century historian. He then gives a standard account of the importance of a life's congruity with teaching: "For a word which is ornamented by deeds customarily shows itself as worthy of belief; but without these the speaker appears as an impostor and a traitor to his own words, even though he teach earnestly." John exemplified the best of what it means to be a preacher, and he was chosen for the episcopal throne in Constantinople on account of this.[12] That is how Sozomen starts his review of John's life, but let us return to John's own beginning.[13]

His life began in Antioch around the year 349 with his father, Secundus, and his mother, Anthusa.[14] According to John's *On the Priesthood*, his mother was widowed soon after his birth.[15] John confesses in that work that in his youth he was often at the law

11 Sozomen, *Ecclesiastical History* 8.2 (GCS Bidez, 350; Hartranft, 399).

12 Sozomen, *Ecclesiastical History* 8.2 (GCS Bidez, 350; Hartranft, 399).

13 Similarly, in his *Dialogue on the Life of St. John Chrysostom*, Palladius begins with Chrysostom's political tumult as Bishop of Constantinople, and then in chap. 5 returns to Chrysostom's early years in Antioch. The *Funerary Speech* delays narrating John's life before Constantinople until chap. 6.

14 Among the secondary sources in their interpretations of the primary sources, most influential for me is J. N. D. Kelly, *Golden Mouth: The Story of John Chrysostom—Ascetic, Preacher, Bishop*. Ithaca, NY: Cornell University Press, 1995. The names of John's parents are preserved only in Socrates, *Ecclesiastical History* 6.3.

15 For Anthusa's plea to John not to be ordained, on account of her widowhood's loneliness and suffering, see *On the Priesthood* 1.5.

courts and attending the theatrical shows—signs of the rhetoric, argumentation, and flair for drama that would forever mark his life. John left the possibility of a stellar career in the world to be baptized, perhaps at Easter 368, and to assist Bishop Meletius of Antioch for about three years. During this time, John was educated alongside Theodore of Mopsuestia by Diodore of Tarsus, both prominent Antiochene theologians who would later be hailed by Cyril of Alexandria and others as harbingers of Nestorius's heresy.[16] Meletius appointed John a lector. After avoiding ordination to the priesthood, in 371/2 John became one of the monks on the mountains outside of Antioch where he received direction from an old man. He dedicated himself to prayer and the reading of Scripture. At some point after about four years of this monastic life, John became a hermit in a cave. Severe fasting during those two years of solitude wreaked havoc on his health. Ill, he had to return to Antioch for care. After further service as a lector, he was ordained a deacon by Meletius, probably in late 380 or early 381. Though at the time deacons were not allowed to preach, John attended his bishop, fulfilled his diaconal ministries in and out of the sanctuary, especially to those in need, and wrote various essays. After Bishop Meletius died while presiding at the First Council of Constantinople (381), Flavian became John's bishop and took great interest in his future ministry.

The first homily John delivered after Flavian ordained him to the priesthood, shortly before Lent in 386, has for its audience in the sermon's title "to himself and to the bishop and to the multitude of people."[17] John's first audience was himself. He began that sermon by expressing his incredulity at being ordained, wondering

16 See John Behr, *The Case against Diodore and Theodore: Texts and Their Contexts*, OECT (Oxford: Oxford University Press, 2011).

17 SC 272, 388.

if he were in a dream at night.[18] After his protestation of sinfulness and unworthiness, he launched into an encomium of Flavian, John's ardent supporter. J. N. D. Kelly underscores the rhetorical devices of praising a subject familiar at that time, and then aptly comments: "But even the modern reader can overhear, rising above the literary conventions, John's authentic voice when, for example, he exclaims that "nothing, nothing so impedes our advance to heaven as wealth and all the evils which flow from it.""[19]

After over a decade of frequent preaching in Antioch, the wildly popular John was whisked away by imperial officials to lead the Church of Constantinople. Nectarius had succeeded Gregory of Nazianzus as Constantinople's bishop in 381, and he reigned in the capital city until his death in September 397. As the new leader of the Church of Constantinople, John wholeheartedly dedicated himself to spreading the Gospel. He directed missions—just as did the apostle Paul—so that peoples still ignorant of Jesus Christ would hear the good news of salvation.[20] He also preached to an extraordinary degree. The *Funerary Speech* yields insight into Chrysostom's preaching in Constantinople: "When this man came, he taught all how great the care of the Lord is for us, how great the raging frenzy of the Devil is against us, what the rewards are of virtue, what the punishments are for wickedness. . . ." This begins a long list of topics of his preaching. Of special mention for homiletic themes are matters of wealth and poverty, oath taking, drunkenness, and

18 See Kelly, *Golden Mouth*, 55.

19 Kelly, *Golden Mouth*, 56 (SC 272, 406). Kelly mistakenly identifies the passage as SC 272, 418.

20 J. N. D. Kelly comments on John's episcopal priorities in Constantinople, "John's great interest in promoting Christianity among barbarians and outside the borders of the empire was at this time unusual, not to say unprecedented." See Kelly, *Golden Mouth*, 144. For an overview of John's direction of missionary labor, see Jonathan P. Stanfill, "John Chrysostom and the Rebirth of Antiochene Mission in Late Antiquity," *CH* 88, no. 4 (2019): 899–924.

fornication. For John, sinners were "exchanging eternal life for a small and useless pleasure."[21]

In Constantinople, Chrysostom was embroiled in severe disputes which shook the empire. He was twice exiled from the city. The first exile occurred shortly after a local synod, held in one of Chalcedon's suburbs called the Oak in 403. During this era's Origenist controversy, John had welcomed Egyptian monks nicknamed, because of their height, "the Tall Brothers." They were reputed to follow Origen's ascetical practices and scriptural interpretation. The leader of the Church of Alexandria, Theophilus, opposed them, and brought several bishops to Constantinople and then to the Oak for John's condemnation. The renowned Cypriot heresy-hunter, Epiphanius, was in league with Theophilus to oppose John.[22] Among those Theophilus brought to the Synod of the Oak was his nephew Cyril, who would later succeed him in leading the Church of Alexandria. A list of twenty-nine charges raised against John at the Synod of Oak include: "(5) that he insulted his clergy as dishonorable, spoiled, good-for-nothings, and workers for a day's wage; (6) that he called Saint Epiphanius a chatterbox and a little devil."[23] The synod deposed John as head of Constantinople's church and exiled him, but he was almost immediately recalled. After the brief first exile following that Synod, John began a homily against his enemy Empress Eudoxia in this way: "Again Herodias raves. (Again she is troubled.) Again she dances. Again she seeks to receive John's head on a platter." Socrates comments, "This, of course, exasperated the empress still more."[24]

21 *Funerary Speech*, 31 (Barnes and Bevan, 57).

22 John and Epiphanius are said to have cursed each other, and both of their curses were fulfilled. For an article that begins with the two of them painted together in iconography, see Young Richard Kim, "An Iconic Odd Couple: The Hagiographic Rehabilitation of Epiphanius and John Chrysostom," *CH* 87, no. 4 (2018): 981–1002.

23 Photius, *Bibliotheca*, Codex 59 (Bekker 18a ; Barnes and Bevan, 154 [alt], cf. Kelly, 299).

24 Socrates, *Ecclesiastical History* 6.18 (GCS Hansen, 341; Zenos, 159 [alt.]). In Mk 6:22 it is the daughter of Herodias who dances, not Herodias. The critical edition of Socrates's *Ecclesiastical History* has *orcheitai*, the Greek present indicative middle/passive third-person

With many in power set against him, John was deposed as Bishop of Constantinople and exiled a second time. This occurred in June 404; he would never see Constantinople again. All his extant letters, including his seventeen letters to the deaconess Olympias (who was also exiled), come from his second exile.[25] In mid-September 407, John was forced to travel when he was deathly ill. He stopped at the shrine of the martyr Basiliscus near Comana in Pontus. After John received the Eucharist, Palladius reports, "he offered his last prayer using his usual formula: 'Glory to God for all things.' Then he signed himself at the last Amen."[26] It was his last proclamation, which typifies the manner of his life of praise.

How should we assess the preaching of this patron of preachers? Wendy Mayer calls Chrysostom's preaching "forthright, entertaining, and accessible."[27] John often poses questions, a hallmark of many early preachers that shows engagement with the people in searching out the things of God and in getting the people to think. Describing what was at the core of his preaching concern, Jaclyn Maxwell states, "Knowledge of the Scriptures offered Christians their only hope of salvation—ignorance of their contents was 'an abyss.'"[28] John wanted his listeners to embody the Word preached

singular verb for *orcheomai*, dance. The active form means causes to dance. In Socrates's rendering of the preaching, John could have changed the subject from Herodias to Herodias's daughter, but that seems unlikely.

25 For an overview of the entire letter collection, see Wendy Mayer, "The Ins and Outs of the Chrysostom Letter-Collection: New Ways of Looking at a Limited Corpus," in *Collecting Early Christian Letters: From the Apostle Paul to Late Antiquity*, eds. Bronwen Neil and Pauline Allen (Cambridge: Cambridge University Press, 2015), 129–53. Anne-Marie Malingrey did the most recent edition of the letters to Olympias in SC 13bis. For an English translation, see *Saint John Chrysostom: Letters to Saint Olympia*, translated by David C. Ford, PPS 56 (Crestwood, NY: St. Vladimir's Seminary Press, 2017). For a recent study of how John consoled Olympias through biblical stories of suffering and divine providence, relevant to his preaching method, see Robert G. T. Edwards, "Healing Despondency with Biblical Narrative in John Chrysostom's *Letters to Olympias*," *JECS* 28, no. 2 (2020): 203–31.

26 Palladius, *Dialogue on the Life of St. John Chrysostom*, chap. 11 (Meyer, 73).

27 Mayer, "John Chrysostom," 142.

28 Maxwell, *Christianization and Communication in Late Antiquity*, 122. She is quoting from *On Lazarus* 3.3 (PG 48:995), and she draws attention to this point, made more positively, in *Homilies on Genesis* 35.1 (PG 53:321–22).

to them. Mayer writes, "For John, perhaps more than for any other preacher of his time, the *telos* of exegetical preaching is to effect, through repeated exposure to the oral interpretation of scripture, the transformation of the listener into a living embodied hermeneutic exemplar."[29] The basis of such an embodied exemplarity in Chrysostom's listeners is the embodied exemplarity of those featured in Scripture: a good preacher tells stories, and Chrysostom loved to tell Scripture's own stories. In Robert Edwards's appraisal, "Chrysostom finds God's characteristic way of working in biblical narratives, especially in his favorite biblical stories: from the Old Testament, the Joseph cycle (cf. Genesis 37–50), Job, the three youths in the fiery furnace (cf. Daniel 3), and, from the New Testament, Lazarus and the rich man (cf. Lk 16:19–31), and narrations of Paul's life, among others."[30] Paul has an outstanding prominence as we will see, but the reason that we should imitate Paul, for John, is that he imitates Christ (cf. 1 Cor 11:1). "Jesus, the Son of the Father of mercies, the Son of the Very God," Chrysostom affirms while preaching on Paul, "has brought every virtue."[31]

After preaching on Paul's image of the helmet as "the hope of salvation" in 1 Thes 5:8, Chrysostom comes to v. 9, "God did not destine us for wrath, but to gain salvation through our Lord Jesus Christ." Chrysostom preaches:

> So much does he desire that we should be saved, that he has given his Son, and not merely given, but given him to death. From these considerations, hope is born. For do not despair of yourself, O man, in going to God, who has not spared even his Son for you. Faint not at present evils. He who gave his

29 Wendy Mayer, "The Homiletic Audience as Embodied Hermeneutic: Scripture and Its Interpretation in the Exegetical Preaching of John Chrysostom," in *Hymns, Homilies, and Hermeneutics in Byzantium*, edited by Sarah Gador-White and Andrew Mellas, ByzAu 25 (Leiden: Brill, 2021), 11–29, at 13.

30 Robert G. T. Edwards, "Divine Providence and Biblical Narrative in the Thought of John Chrysostom," Ph.D. diss., University of Notre Dame, 2020, 21.

31 *Homilies on Ephesians* 23.3 (PG 62:167; Alexander, 166).

> Only Begotten, that he might save you and deliver you from Gehenna, what will he spare for your salvation? Therefore, you must hope for every good thing.[32]

Holding on to what God promises in Christ, John Chrysostom's hope of salvation was the driving force behind his preaching. Without understanding that fervor, we will not make sense of his homilies, his prayers, or his life.

Called in the West the "Doctor of the Eucharist," John knew that the Only Begotten is made present in the Eucharist and consumed so that Christ may be inside us.[33] Listen to how John assumes Christ's voice when preaching on 1 Timothy 5:

> For you I was spit upon, I was scourged. I emptied myself of glory, I left my Father and came to you, who hate me, and turn from me, and are loath to hear my name. I pursued you, I ran after you, that I might overtake you. I united and joined you to myself, "Eat me," I said, "Drink me." Above I hold you, and below I am entwined [*symplekomai*] in you. Is it not enough for you that I have your first fruits above? Does not this satisfy your affection? I descended below: I not only am mingled [*mignymai*] with you, I am entwined [*symplekomai*] in you. I am masticated, broken into minute particles, that the blending together [*anakrasis*], and mixture [*mixis*], and union [*henōsis*] may be more complete. Things united remain yet in their own limits, but I am interwoven [*synyphainomai*] with you. I would have no more any division between us. I will that we both be one thing [*hen*].[34]

32 *Homilies on 1 Thessalonians* 9 (PG 62:451; Broadus, 366 [alt.]).

33 Benedict XVI teaches that John "was also called 'Doctor of the Eucharist' because of the vastness and depth of his teaching on the Most Holy Sacrament. The 'Divine liturgy' which is most frequently celebrated in the Eastern Church and which bears his name as well as his motto: 'a man full of zeal suffices to transform a people', shows the effectiveness of Christ's action through his ministers." See Benedict XVI, Angelus address, Castel Gandolfo, September 18, 2005.

34 Chrysostom, *Homilies on 1 Timothy* 15.4 (PG 62:586; Tweed, 463–64 [alt.]). For analysis, see Ashish J. Naidu, *Transformed in Christ: Christology and the Christian Life in John Chrysostom*, PTMS 188 (Eugene, OR: Pickwick Publications, 2012), 143–44. Cf. *Homilies on the Gospel of John* 46.3: "In order then that we may become this not by love only, but

Chrysostom concludes with the instruction to remember God's great care for us, so that we may not prove ourselves unworthy of the great gift we have received through the loving kindness of Christ Jesus our Lord.

Because of God's loving kindness in the humanity of Christ, Chrysostom had a boundless confidence in divine providence. Robert Edwards writes, "Yielding to God's providence, which at first can sound rather passive, is thus associated with more straightforward positive virtues: patience, endurance, hope, thanksgiving. These are among some of the highest of virtues in Chrysostom's estimation."[35] This reliance on God's providence allowed him to focus on the hope of salvation.

In *The Hope of the Early Church*, Brian Daley comments that John "was intensely concerned to focus his hearers' attention on what awaited them at the end of their histories. Eschatological themes recur constantly in his sermons."[36] Indeed, Chrysostom preaches frequently on hell, and Daley summarizes that he "insists the condemned must remain there forever (*In 1 Thes* 8.4; *In II Cor* 10.4; *In II Thes* 3.1). God's threats of eternal punishment are not empty, nor are they simply stories told for pedagogical effect; 'it is impossible,' he asserts, 'that punishment and Gehenna should not exist' (*In I Thes* 8.4; cf. *In Rom Hom* 25.4–6)." Why? God wants to deter us from sin and to live virtuously, with a human dignity above that of brute animals. "For, say, if he [God] did not call us to account, would human

---

in very deed, let us be blended (*anakerasthōmen*) into that flesh. This comes about by the food that he has freely given us, desiring to show the love which he has for us. On this account, he has mixed up (*anemixen*) himself with us. He has kneaded up (*anephure*) his body with ours, that we might be a certain one thing, like a body joined to a head" (PG 59:260; Stupart, 166 [alt.]).

35 Edwards, "Divine Providence and Biblical Narrative in the Thought of John Chrysostom," 168. Edwards cites Francesca Prometea Barone, "Le vocabulaire de la patience chez Jean Chrysostome: les mots ἀνεξικακία et ὑπομονή," *Revue de philologie, de littérature et d'histoire anciennes* 81, no. 1 (2007): 5–12, and Paula Baudoin, "Makrothymia dans Saint Jean Chrysostome," *StPatr* 22 (1989): 89–97.

36 Daley, *The Hope of the Early Church: A Handbook of Patristic Eschatology,* 105.

life then have endured? Should we not then have fallen into the state of beasts?"[37]

Chrysostom has a reputation for preaching against the accumulation of wealth and for the promotion of almsgiving. His several sermons on the parable of Lazarus and the rich man, as would be expected, exemplify these favorite themes found almost everywhere.[38] But Chrysostom has something even more important than wealth and poverty in mind when he addresses those topics: the hope of salvation is at stake.

Take, for example, the second to last of his popular ninety *Homilies on the Gospel of Matthew*. *Homily* 89 concerns Mt 27:62–28:10, which features Christ's resurrection. Chrysostom parallels the women at the empty tomb with his listeners, urging them to see how they too can experience Christ. The risen Lord greeted the women at the tomb with "Rejoice!" Those listening to John's preaching can also receive the Lord's greeting—in the liturgical mysteries and on the last day. Chrysostom preaches:

> Perchance someone of you would wish to be like the women, to hold the feet of Jesus. You can even now. You who wish can hold not only his feet and his hands, but also that sacred head, when you receive the terrifying mysteries with a pure conscience. But not here only, but also in that day you shall see him, coming with that unspeakable glory, and the multitude of the angels, if you wish to be kind (*philanthrōpoi*); and you shall hear not these words only, *Rejoice* (Mt 28:9), but also those others, *Come you blessed of my Father, inherit the kingdom prepared for you before the foundation of the world* (Mt 25:34).[39]

37 *Homilies on Philippians* 3.2; for analysis, see Daley, *The Hope of the Early Church*, 107–8. For the variety of ways that Chrysostom uses animals in his preaching, see Blake Leyerle, "Locating Animals in John Chrysostom's Thought," in *Revisioning John Chrysostom*, eds. de Wet and Mayer, 276–99.

38 Several of these sermons have been translated in *On Wealth and Poverty*, translated by Catherine P. Roth, PPS 9 (Crestwood, NY: St. Vladimir's Seminary Press, 1984).

39 Chrysostom, *Homilies on the Gospel of Matthew* 89.3 (PG 58:784; Riddle, 527 [alt.]). The translation of humane for *philanthrōpoi* is misleading for Chrysostom's preaching, as God is supremely *philanthrōpos*. Various philosophies and religions in antiquity used

Here Chrysostom quotes Christ twice, first in the simple greeting of "Rejoice" to the women on the day of the resurrection, and second in Christ's metaphor of the separation of the sheep from the goats based upon what people do for his little ones. The latter motivates Chrysostom, here in preaching on the resurrection, to give a lengthy disquisition on the dangers of women wearing gold jewelry. By preferring exterior gold to interior virtue, women endanger their salvation through a slavery to materiality, in all its anxiousness, and they endanger the salvation of others who may be tempted to sins, such as thinking more about the golden jewelry than the liturgy, or falling into greed, envy, lust, etc. They could use their gold to help the poor and thereby work toward their salvation.[40] Chrysostom compares the women of his church who wear golden jewelry to actresses on a stage and to harlots, who are similarly bedecked. Then he contrasts them with the Gospel's women at the empty tomb.[41] "How will you be able to kiss Christ's feet and cling to them, when you are dressed in this way?" Chrysostom asks. He continues to speak for Christ, "From this adornment, he turns away. For this reason, he wanted to be born in the house of the carpenter, or rather not even in that house, but in a shed, and [placed in] a manger."[42] Chrysostom then says that his listeners must not

---

that term, which often meant beneficence. Ti 3:4, as should be kept in mind, uses the term *philanthrōpia* for the appearance of the Savior.

40 Chrysostom gives a deifying role for the mercy of almsgiving. Leyerle writes, "Chrysostom thus can even claim that giving alms is like celebrating the eucharist, and that it 'makes one holier than priests' and 'equal to God.'" See Blake Leyerle, "John Chrysostom on Almsgiving and the Use of Money," *HTR* 87, no. 1 (1994): 29–47, at 47. Leyerle cites *Homilies on 2 Corinthians* 20.3 (PG 61:539–40) and *Homilies on Titus* 6.2 (PG 62:698). For the latter reference, I would translate John's term *homoious* to be "like" rather than "equal to." For analysis of that homily on Titus, see James Daniel Cook, *Preaching and Popular Christianity: Reading the Sermons of John Chrysostom*, OTRM (Oxford: Oxford University Press, 2019), 120.

41 For an exemplary account of Chrysostom's rhetorical use of the theatrical and the sexual, see Blake Leyerle, *Theatrical Shows and Ascetic Lives: John Chrysostom's Attack on Spiritual Marriage* (Berkeley and Los Angeles: University of California Press, 2001).

42 Chrysostom, *Homilies on the Gospel of Matthew* 89.4 (PG 58:768; Riddle, 529 [alt.]).

have that kind of wealth, which is hateful to the Lord, but must be "clothed with virtue."[43]

Some may find it strange to encounter the decrying of women's gold jewelry in the midst of a sermon on the resurrection. Even so, we must recognize that John preaches in this way for a reason. Jaclyn Maxwell goes so far as to say, "Convincing the Christians of Antioch that even the smallest details of life were indeed matters of heaven and hell occupied a great deal of Chrysostom's attention."[44] The hope of salvation drove John to preach that each day, in the all aspects of life, his people should reject the allurements of this world and be united in the virtuous life of Christ.[45] "Let us not betray our own salvation, but hold fast to our hope of what shall be hereafter," preaches Chrysostom after one of his countless exhortations against gold and in favor of almsgiving. He wants both old and young to hold fast to that hope. He wants all to instruct one another: "Knowing this, let wives exhort their husbands, and husbands admonish their wives; let us teach youths and maidens, and all instruct one another, to care not for present things, but to desire those which are to come."[46] All should be impelled by the hope of salvation of others as well as of oneself. "Nothing is colder than a Christian who cares not for the salvation of others," John proclaims.[47] And of all

43 Chrysostom, *Homilies on the Gospel of Matthew* 89.4 (PG 58:768; Riddle, 529).

44 Maxwell, *Christianization and Communication in Late Antiquity*, 153.

45 For the sense of coming together in shared emotional responses, see Peter C. Moore, "Bound Together for Heaven: Mutual Emotions in Chrysostom's Homilies on Matthew for Well-Ordered and Fruitful Community in Anxious Times," *Revisioning John Chrysostom*, eds. de Wet and Mayer, 334–60. For an overview of emotion, see now Blake Leyerle, *The Narrative Shape of Emotion in the Preaching of John Chrysostom*, CLA 11 (Oakland, CA: University of California Press, 2020).

46 *Homilies on the Gospel of John* 47.5 (PG 59:270; Stupart, 172).

47 *Homilies on Acts* 20.4 (PG 60:162; J. Walker, 133 [alt.]). With this homily's conclusion (20.4), Chrysostom repeats, "Do not insult God," concerning those who find it impossible to lead others to become Christian: "It is easier for the sun not to give heat, nor to shine, than for the Christian not to send forth light.... Knowing therefore these things, let us hold fast to virtue, as knowing that it is not possible to be saved otherwise, than by passing through this present life in doing these good works, that we may also obtain the good things which are to come, through the grace and mercy of our Lord Jesus Christ, with

Christians who are to care about others being saved, those ordained to instruct Christ's flock bear a grave responsibility.

The dangers of preaching for salvation in *On the Priesthood*

"I do not think many among the bishops [*hierousi*] will be saved, but many more will perish," speculates John when preaching on Matthias's replacement of Judas, the betrayer among the apostles.[48] That homiletic line is famous, and it succinctly conveys the essence of John's preaching on ordained ministry. In this sermon, he gives the Pauline qualifications for a bishop from 1 Tm 3:2–9 and Ti 1:7–9. And he asserts that the loss of a single unbaptized soul carries with it an unfathomable penalty: "For if the salvation of that soul was such a worth that the Son of God became man, and suffered so much, think how much a punishment must the losing of it bring!"[49] Bishops and priests bear a particularly heavy responsibility for the salvation of souls, and so their offices place their own souls in jeopardy of losing salvation.

In our consideration of Chrysostom as a preacher of the hope of salvation of other preachers, we can do no better than focus on his hugely influential *On the Priesthood*.[50] This dialogue in six books speaks much about the dangers to salvation in priestly ministry.

---

whom to the Father together with the Holy Spirit be glory, might, honor, now and forever and ever. Amen" (PG 60:163–64; Walker, 134 [alt.]).

48 *Homilies on Acts* 3.4 (PG 60:39; Walker, 23 [alt.]). Chrysostom uses the word *hierousi* for priests, but it clearly means bishops here. He distinguishes them from presbyters and deacons a few lines later in this homily.

49 *Homilies on Acts* 3.4 (PG 60:40; Walker, 23 [alt.]).

50 In *Golden Mouth*, Kelly writes that this dialogue relates an occurrence of church authorities wanting to ordain John and his friend Basil priests. Kelly continues, "[T]he widely held view that they were to be consecrated bishops, unlikely in itself, is traceable to John's preoccupation with the episcopal office, in important later sections of the dialogue" (25). Kelly says that the term *hierōsynē*, used in the dialogue's title, is "an inclusive term applying in the appropriate context to both the presbyterate and the episcopate" (26).

It can be read as a text intended to reform clerical ministry and deter the unworthy from seeking ordination. The dialogue takes place between two characters, John and his best friend Basil. Those unfamiliar with this dramatic work may be surprised to learn that John deceives his friend Basil so that Basil is ordained while John is not.[51] After justifying the deception, John wants Basil to accept the model of the risen Lord's dialogue with Simon Peter, "Do you love me?" (cf. Jn 21:15–19).[52] For John, the priest's friendship with Christ reorders all other relationships, including with his best friend and with his mother—the two relationships featured at the beginning of this dialogue.[53] On this basis of a priest's relationship with Christ, much of the rest of the work describes the terrifying tasks priests are called to undertake for the salvation of the flock.

Chrysostom loves the rhetorical device of *synkriseis* (comparisons), such as comparing a shepherd of sheep with a pastor of a rational flock in *On the Priesthood.* If a shepherd loses some sheep due to wolves, robbers, accidents, etc., he might receive a pardon from the flock's owner, but he might need to compensate the owner financially for the loss. A pastor of Christ's flock, on the other hand, "risks a penalty not of money but of his own soul for the loss of the sheep."[54] Who are his enemies? Listen to Paul: "Our wrestling is not against flesh and blood, but against the principalities, against powers, against the world rulers of the darkness, against the spiritual hosts of wickedness in the heavenly places" (Eph 6:12). John quotes from Paul again, from Galatians and 2 Corinthians, to indicate the

51 For the context of deceit and lying in early Christianity, see Boniface Ramsey, OP, "Two Traditions on Lying and Deception in the Ancient Church," *Thom* 49, no. 4 (1985): 504–33.

52 *On the Priesthood* 2.1.

53 For this reordering, see Andrew Hofer, OP, "The Reordering of Relationships in John Chrysostom's *De sacerdotio*," *Augustinianum* 51, no. 2 (2011): 451–71. For a recent complementary analysis, see Pak-Wah Lai, "Reading *On the Priesthood* as Dialogue: Perspectives on John Chrysostom's Ascetic Vision," in *John Chrysostom: Past, Present, Future*, eds. Doru Costache and Mario Baghos (Sydney: AIOCS Press, 2017), 217–34.

54 *On the Priesthood* 2.2 (SC 272, 106; Neville, 54).

evil swarm of enemies that works from within: "Now the works of the flesh are manifest, which are these: fornication, adultery, uncleanness, lasciviousness, idolatry, sorcery, enmities, strifes, jealousies, wraths, factions, backbitings, whisperings, swellings, and tumults."[55] These are only examples; there are, in fact, many more enemies. A sheepfold's enemies will stop when they have taken the sheep, but the enemies of a pastor's flock will not relent until they have destroyed the pastor himself.

John continues to describe the precariousness of salvation through the *synkrisis* of a shepherd to a spiritual pastor. For example, it is evident when sheep are ill, injured, starved, or otherwise being harmed. The flock of the faithful, on the other hand, may not make manifest how they are injured. A shepherd can compel sheep to accept cautery and knife, to shut them up in a pen for a long time, and to modulate their feed and drink. Sure, a pastor may try to apply all sorts of spiritual healing for his flock, if he knows what ails them, but he cannot heal them against their will. Much tact is needed to convince the spiritually ill to submit to treatment—let alone to be thankful for their priests. A priest must be a skillful physician who cuts out what needs to be removed, but if he makes the incision without mercy, the patient may turn away completely from the hope of healing. "I could tell you of many who have been stranded in utter misery," John says, "because they were called to pay the full price of their sins."[56]

John says that the shepherd needs a thousand eyes to examine a soul's condition from every angle. Some in the flock are puffed up in arrogance and do not want spiritual medicine from their pastor; they fall, heedless of their own salvation. Others do not pay the penalty for their sinfulness but go on to commit sins that are even more grievous. While John uses a variety of images from fields such

55 *On the Priesthood* 2.3 (SC 272, 108; Neville, 55).

56 *On the Priesthood* 2.4 (SC 272, 114; Neville 57).

as theatre, law, medicine, and business, he develops in a particularly appropriate way the image of the shepherd. The shepherd is to call out to the wandering sheep, from his concentration, perseverance, and patience. "He cannot drag by force or constrain by fear," John observes, "but must by persuasion lead [the stray] back to the true beginning from which he has fallen away."[57] Persuasion is the work of rhetoric, which John highlights now in priestly preaching. John encourages the priest not to grow despondent or neglect the salvation of those who wander, but instead to recall about his flock that "God may give them the knowledge of the truth and they may be freed from the snare of the devil."[58]

A priest certainly has great responsibility for the salvation of souls, and must think of his charge as did the apostle Paul. No one was endowed with more grace, thinks Chrysostom, than Paul. Yet, Paul was deathly concerned about the precariousness of salvation. Chrysostom wants Paul's words to be the standard for priestly ministry. Only those who can say what Paul said should be priests: "I could wish that I were anathema from Christ for my brethren's sake, my kinsmen according to the flesh" (Rom 9:3). Everything should be done for the salvation of the flock.

John knows that vainglory and a host of other evils afflict him like wild beasts. He catalogs these problems at length:

> anger, dejection, envy, strife, slanders, accusations, lying, hypocrisy, intrigue, imprecations against those who have done no harm, delight at disgraceful behavior in fellow priests, sorrow at their successes, love of praise, greed for preferment (which more than anything else hurls the human soul to destruction), teaching meant to please, slavish wheedling, ignoble flattery, contempt for the poor, fawning on the rich, absurd honors and harmful favors which endanger giver and receiver alike, servile fear fit only for the meanest of slaves, restraint of plain

57 *On the Priesthood* 2.4 (SC 272, 116; Neville 58).

58 *On the Priesthood* 2.4 (SC 272, 116; Neville, 58), cf. 2 Tm 2: 25–26.

> speaking, much pretended and no real humility, failure to scrutinize and rebuke, or more likely doing so beyond reason with the humble while no one dares so much as to open his lips against those who wield power.[59]

Those who are being considered for priestly ministry need to examine their souls for such frightful spiritual dangers. All the disorders of the Church, according to John, are due to the unqualified becoming prelates, who in turn wreak havoc on the Church.[60]

John speaks movingly of the sacramental and liturgical responsibilities of priests. A priest in the sacred liturgy must be as pure as angels, as he partakes of heaven's own worship.[61] John asks, "When you see the Lord sacrificed and lying before you, and the High Priest standing over the sacrifice and praying, and all who partake being tinctured with that precious blood, can you think that you are still among men and still standing on earth?"[62] John cries out with great wonder at the loving kindness of God, that the Son, who sits with the Father, is "at that moment held in our hands, and gives himself to those who wish to clasp and embrace him—which they do, all of them, with their eyes."[63] Priests have a sacramental power beyond what can be reckoned by earthly standards. Their authority is greater than that of angels and archangels, as whatever they bind on earth will be bound in heaven, and whatever they loose on earth will be loosed in heaven. John quotes the Gospel words, "The Father

59 *On the Priesthood* 3.9 (SC 272, 162; Neville, 77–78). Chrysostom list begins with anger and dejection, two opposite vices in Greek (*thymos* and *athymia*), which would have a rhyming cadence in Greek following the word for beasts, *thēria*, which immediately precedes those two vices. This is but one of many examples that could be given of Chrysostom's rhetorical prowess.

60 *On the Priesthood* 3.10.

61 John gives much attention to angels in his writing and preaching, such in comparing the priestly and the ascetic lives to angels. A distinctive and influential trait concerns his emphasis that angels come from heaven to be present and active in the liturgy, as opposed to remaining in heaven and worshiping God there. See Ellen Muehlberger, *Angels in Late Ancient Christianity* (New York: Oxford University Press, 2013), 195–200.

62 *On the Priesthood* 3.4 (SC 272, 142–44; Neville, 70).

63 *On the Priesthood* 3.4 (SC 272, 144; Neville, 71).

has given all judgment to the Son" (Jn 5:22), and comments that the Son has placed it all in the hands of priests.

Beyond *On the Priesthood's* descriptions of priestly governance and liturgical celebration, John devotes extraordinary attention to priestly preaching in Books 4 and 5. We must keep in mind the preacher's awesome priestly authority. Chrysostom develops the *synkrisis* of a physician to a priest regarding treatment. A physician may treat the human body with an assortment of drugs, various medical instruments, and forms of diet. A physician may recommend that the ill relocate to a different climate to improve one's health, for instance, by getting more sleep. A priest, by contrast, does not have that wide range of treatments. "When all is said and done," John states, as we saw in our book's Introduction, "here is one means and only one method of treatment available, and that is teaching through the word."[64] John then calls it the best instrument, the best diet, and the best climate. Without preaching, all else seems useless.

John focuses on the harm that false doctrine does to people's souls and on the healing that true preaching brings. Words are urgently needed both for the sake of the safety of the Church's members and also to ward off the attacks from those outside the Church. "We must take great care, therefore," John says invoking Paul, "that the word of Christ may dwell in us richly" (cf. Col 3:16).[65] All sorts of doctrinal challenges confront priests and their people, and they endanger our salvation. "Do I need to enumerate all the devil's heresies?" asks John.[66] He does specify some. For example, Valentinus and Marcion reject the Old Law given to Moses, whereas the Jewish people try to observe it obstinately. A Christian preacher must steer between these two extremes; if he combats only one, his people may

64 *On the Priesthood* 4.3 (SC 272, 250; Neville, 115 [alt.]).
65 *On the Priesthood* 4.3 (SC 272, 252; Neville, 116).
66 *On the Priesthood* 4.4 (SC 272, 256; Neville, 117).

overreact. Likewise, in Trinitarian teachings, a preacher must navigate between the modalism of Sabellius and the subordinationism of Arius. "We must shun and avoid the impious confusion of the one party and the mad division of the other," John says, "by confessing that the Godhead of the Father and the Son and the Holy Spirit is one, but adding that there are three hypostases."[67]

The answer for Chrysostom is to imitate Paul, who did not claim to be expert in speech, but did claim to have knowledge. And he spoke that knowledge. Preaching, for Chrysostom, is thus not a matter of imitating the great Greek orator Demosthenes, but Paul. Chrysostom says he takes no account of diction or style (a comment that should be understood as coming from one of the best-trained orators of his day). He says, "Let a man's diction be beggarly and his verbal composition simple and artless, but do not let him be inexpert in the knowledge and careful statement of doctrine."[68]

John knows from Paul that of all elders, or presbyters, those who teach and preach deserve double honor (cf. 1 Tm 5:17). He comments, "For this is the ultimate aim of their teaching: to lead their disciples, both by what they do and what they say, into the way of that blessed life which Christ commanded. Example alone is not sufficient instruction."[69] John recalls that such a determination came from the Savior himself, who says, "Whosoever shall do and teach will be called great" (Mt 5:19). John interprets these Gospel words to mean that both action and instruction are necessary. The priest must be able verbally to counter the Church's enemies, lest the people in the congregation doubt what he is saying.

When John describes carrying out the ministry of the word, he says that preaching good sermons "conduces to salvation and to many benefits."[70] Yet there are many challenges. Most people

67 *On the Priesthood* 4.4 (SC 272, 258–60; Neville, 118 [alt.]).
68 *On the Priesthood* 4.6 (SC 272, 270; Neville, 121–22).
69 *On the Priesthood* 4.8 (SC 272, 278; Neville, 125).
70 *On the Priesthood* 5.1 (SC 272, 280; Neville, 127).

refuse to submit to a preacher's authority and instead think of themselves as spectators sitting in on an orator's speech. In doing so, they become divided against one another about a preacher, just as a society is divided in taking different sides about an orator. People criticize sermons because preachers weave the words of others into their own too much or are suspected of doing so when, in fact, they have taken nothing from another. Preachers are not even allowed to repeat their own words too soon, as congregants assume the role of an audience at a play or a concert.

A preacher needs two qualities above all else, according to Chrysostom: the contempt of praise and the power of eloquence. Chrysostom knows that preachers deemed eloquent by the people would be applauded. A preacher must ignore the praise that he receives and be careful about the criticism that comes his way. John wants priests to nip evil suspicions in the bud by convincing their accusers. To put the people's reactions into perspective he proposes that a priest should rule as a father treats very young children.[71] John also admits, "I do not know whether anyone has ever succeeded in not enjoying praise."[72] He knows how dangerous this love is, if disordered. Moreover, even the most skillful of speakers needs to practice and strive to be as good as people expect him to be. John says of the skilled preacher that unless his sermons "always match the great expectations formed of him, he will leave the pulpit the victim of countless jeers and complaints."[73] He says that the priest must compose his sermons to please God, which alone should be the standard of sermons. In this way, the preacher must have contempt for human praise but at the same time strive to be most eloquent.

Book 6, the last book of *On the Priesthood*, concludes the work with various exhortations, such as the need for purity. Again, the

71 For Chrysostom's frequent mentioning of children, especially in adult moral formation, see Blake Leyerle, "Appealing to Children," *JECS* 5, no. 2 (1997): 243–70.

72 *On the Priesthood* 5.4 (SC 272, 290; Neville, 130).

73 *On the Priesthood* 5.5 (SC 272, 292; Neville, 131).

apostle Paul appears as the exemplar, such as through his ability to say, "I live, no longer I, but Christ lives in me" (Gal 2:20). The soul of a priest should be ablaze as the light of the world. In living this kind of life, the priest does everything for "the glory of God and the edification of the Church."[74] John, as an ascetic, thinks that he belongs in his cell, but that Basil his interlocutor needs to be with the beautiful bride of Christ, the Church. She has so many enemies, and she needs the protection of Basil and others who will fight for her. Basil himself becomes frightened at this prospect at the end of the dialogue, so John comforts him by pointing to Christ. "For I trust in Christ," John concludes, "who called you and set you over his own sheep, that you will gain such assurance from this ministry that when I am endangered on that Day, you will receive me into your everlasting habitation."[75] Here we see the culmination of what the priesthood's pastoral care is about for John: bringing others to heaven.

Hoping with the Apostle Paul for Salvation

As we have seen repeatedly, John Chrysostom ceaselessly expresses his hope for salvation through his model preacher, the Apostle Paul.[76]

74 *On the Priesthood* 6.4 (SC 272, 320; Neville, 142).

75 *On the Priesthood* 6.13 (SC 272, 362; Neville, 160 [alt.]).

76 One scholar writes, "I will argue that Chrysostom's soteriology, when understood within its historical and theological context, is nothing less than a doctrine of deification and that his doctrine is both well-illustrated and enriched by the numerous Pauline and non-Pauline portraits presented in his writings." See Pak-Wah Lai, "John Chrysostom and the Hermeneutics of Exemplar Portraits," Ph.D. diss., University of Durham, 2010, at p. 133. Lai responds to Norman Russell's passing over of Chrysostom in his magisterial review of deification in the Greek Fathers, as an Antiochene thinker who never uses deification language and who calls the baptized gods "only in a titular sense." See Russell, *Deification in the Greek Patristic Tradition*, 237. Brian Dunkle notes that John Chrysostom articulates "the commonplace link between Christology and salvation: what Christ is by nature we become by grace." Dunkle gives this example from Chrysostom's comment on Rom 8:29, "For what the Only-begotten was by nature, this they too have become by grace" in *Homilies on Romans* 15.2 (PG 60:541). See Brian Dunkle, SJ, "'The Twofold Affection'": The Background to John Chrysostom's Use of Φύσις and Χάρις," *VC* 75, no. 4 (2021): 355–74, at 368.

Paul shows us what it means to be in Christ. For John, "where Paul was, there also was Christ."[77] Chrysostom dedicates seven homilies to the praises of Paul, over 250 homilies to the letters he identifies as Pauline (including Hebrews), 18 homilies on Pauline passages outside those letters, over 50 homilies on the Acts of the Apostles (which comes to feature Paul), and many other homilies, letters, and treatises where Paul appears.[78] Chrysostom is "undoubtedly the most comprehensive commentator on the Pauline epistles from the patristic era," judges Margaret Mitchell.[79]

As for this chapter's focus on the "hope of salvation" taken from 1 Thes 5:8, Chrysostom frequently uses that expression or, occasionally, a phrase similar to it from that Old Testament sufferer Job, "hope of my salvation."[80] This salvation is bodily. For an extended reflection on how this is so, we turn to John's treatment of 1 Corinthians 15, a single Pauline chapter on our bodily resurrection that John covers in five homilies.[81]

When John begins to preach on 1 Corinthians 15, he recognizes that Paul treats here what is "the most necessary of all things, the subject of the resurrection."[82] Paul was not addressing some matter of morals such as someone being a fornicator, another being covetous, or another not appropriately covering her head—questions

77 *Homily on Romans 16:3, On "Greet Priscilla and Aquila,"* 1 (PG 51:191). For analysis, see Margaret M. Mitchell, "The Archetypal Image: John Chrysostom's Portraits of Paul," *JR* 75, no. 1 (1995): 15–43, at 31; cf. Rylaarsdam, *John Chrysostom on Divine Pedagogy*, 161.

78 Margaret M. Mitchell, *The Heavenly Trumpet: John Chrysostom and the Art of Pauline Interpretation* (Louisville: Westminster John Knox Press, 2002), 2–5.

79 Mitchell, *Heavenly Trumpet*, 5.

80 A TLG search of Chrysostom's texts there yields 78 instances of "hope of salvation" (either *elpi* sōtērias* or *sōtērias elpi**). This search excludes any intermittent words, including the article before "salvation." When the search allows three words between the two terms of *elpi* sōtērias* in any order, we find 130 instances in Chrysostom's texts. In the Septuagint, Job's wife taunts him by quoting back to him what he had said, "Behold, I will hold on a little longer, while awaiting the hope of my salvation" (Jb 2:9 LXX).

81 *Homilies on 1 Corinthians* 38–42. Absent a recent critical edition, see PG 61:321–68. For an English translation, which I have at times altered, see the Chalmers translation in NPNF 1.12, 226–58.

82 *Homilies on 1 Corinthians* 38.1 (PG 61:321; Chalmers, 226 [alt.]).

treated earlier in the letter. Rather, it is "the very sum of all good things" and "all our hope."[83] The devil, John says, was behind people's opposition to the resurrection. The devil causes confusion about this central matter of faith in different ways, such as leading people to oppose it completely or to believe that the resurrection has already happened (cf. 2 Tm 2:7–8). Yet another sinister idea is that the resurrection is only the purification of the soul and not a resurrection of the body. If the devil were to overturn the Christian mind on the resurrection, then he could make believers turn back from the faith as if all our beliefs were fables: "For if they were persuaded that there is no resurrection of bodies, he [the evil one] would have a little later persuaded them that neither was Christ raised. And thereupon he would introduce, going step-by-step in due course, that Christ had not come nor had done what he did."[84] Concerned to teach Pauline pedagogy, which counteracts the devil's own gradual tactics, John shows that Paul does not immediately let his hearers know how disastrous their opinions about the resurrection are. Rather, he builds up to this gradually and gently, finally recalling for them what is of first importance: Christ's death and resurrection according to the Scriptures. Moreover, John emphasizes with Paul that "Christ died for our sins" (1 Cor 15:3).

Following Paul in 1 Corinthians 15, John is at pains to oppose those who have been spiritualizing the Gospel in a Manichean fashion. John's opponents are "enemies of the truth," who "war against their own salvation."[85] They have interpreted Paul on death merely to mean "being in sin" and on resurrection merely to mean "being delivered from sin."[86] But the reality is that Christ took a body, and did die and rise in bodily form. John points out that Paul directs his

83 *Homilies on 1 Corinthians* 38.1 (PG 61:321; Chalmers, 226).

84 *Homilies on 1 Corinthians* 38.1 (PG 61:321; Chalmers, 226 [alt.]).

85 *Homilies on 1 Corinthians* 38.2 (PG 61:324; as 38.3 in Chalmers, 228).

86 *Homilies on 1 Corinthians* 38.2 (PG 61:324; as 38.3 in Chalmers, 228).

readers to the Scriptures, as they are fulfilled by Jesus' death and resurrection. The scriptural prophecies, John adamantly maintains, do not speak of death as sin, when they speak of the Lord's death, but they mean his bodily death, which in turn is followed by his burial and rising from the dead. The literalness of the body must be preserved in the basic Christian proclamation of Christ's death and resurrection. Otherwise, our faith is emptied.

On 1 Cor 15:11, "Whether then it be I or they, so we preach," John has a fascinating digression on grace. In his characteristic humility, Paul credits God for any good done in his life. Paul does this so that "he might signify the mercy of God from every circumstance: from God's having saved him such as he was and, when saved, making him again such as he is."[87] What does this mean for us? John preaches that no one in sin should despair, and no one in virtue should be confident. John steers his listeners away from both despair and slothfulness, making them think with Paul about God's grace for our salvation.

Chrysostom's focus on "If in this life only we have hoped in Christ, we are the most pitiable of all human beings" (1 Cor 15:19) deserves our attention. "What do you say, O Paul?" asks John. He continues, "How in this life only have we hope, if our bodies be not raised, with the soul abiding and being immortal?"[88] Chrysostom ties this to what Paul writes in 2 Corinthians about appearing before Christ's judgment seat so "that everyone may receive the things done in the body, according to what he did whether good or evil" (2 Cor 5:10). Because it is about being in the body, if there is no resurrection of the body, then it seems that the soul abides uncrowned. And if this be the case, "we shall enjoy nothing then at all. And if

87 *Homilies on 1 Corinthians* 38.6 (PG 61:329; as 38.8 in Chalmers, 231).

88 *Homilies on 1 Corinthians* 39.3 (PG 61:335; as 39.4(*bis*) in Chalmers, 235–36 [alt.]).

nothing then, in the present life is our recompense."[89] He shows how the Apostle effectively motivates his people through fear:

> For so when he intends to introduce any of the necessary doctrines, he first shakes thoroughly their hardness of heart by fear: which accordingly he did here, having both above scattered those seeds, and made them anxious, as those who had fallen from all: and now again after another manner, and so as they should most severely feel it, doing this same thing and saying, "we are of all human beings most pitiable," if after so great conflicts and deaths and those innumerable evils, we are to fall from so great blessings, and our happiness is limited by the present life. For in fact all depends on the resurrection.[90]

In another homily on 1 Corinthians 15, Chrysostom invokes the Creed to support Paul's argument. The Creed professes faith in "the forgiveness of sins," and immediately then in "the resurrection of the dead." John comments on their connection: "one leads you by the hand to the other."[91] But he says that even professing faith in the resurrection is not sufficient, as the Creed continues, "and life everlasting." John knows that some were raised from the dead only to die again, such as Jesus's friend Lazarus. The resurrection professed in the Creed is a rising to everlasting life so that "none may any longer have a notion of death after the resurrection."[92]

The Apostle, John points out, does not die daily in order to receive some cheap reward, but rather to receive Christ himself. John returns to Paul's words: "If in this life only we have hoped in Christ, we are the most pitiable of all human beings" (1 Cor 15:19). In truth, John declares, "the great reward is to please Christ at all times."[93] With this emphasis on pleasing Christ, Chrysostom rails

89 *Homilies on 1 Corinthians* 39.3 (PG 61:336; as 39.4(*bis*) in Chalmers, 236).
90 *Homilies on 1 Corinthians* 39.3 (PG 61:336; as 39.4(*bis*) in Chalmers, 236 [alt.]).
91 *Homilies on 1 Corinthians* 40.2 (PG 61:349; Chalmers, 245 [alt.]).
92 *Homilies on 1 Corinthians* 40.2 (PG 61:349; Chalmers, 245).
93 *Homilies on 1 Corinthians* 40.3 (PG 61:351; Chalmers, 246).

against various sins later in this homily—as Paul says in verse 34, "sin not." A corrupt life produces evil doctrines and dismisses the resurrection. John especially targets the sins of the rich and reminds them of their common bodily nature with the poor. Each has only a single belly to fill. If the rich complain that they must also provide for their many servants, why should they have so many? God gave us hands and feet so that we would not need servants. If there was servitude because of Adam's sin, Christ put an end to that. "For in Christ Jesus," John quotes Paul, "there is neither slave nor free" (Gal 3:28). John encourages a tiered policy whereby the rich avoid having many servants (even if they must have two), and train them and let them go free. The rich must not, he insists, scourge them or put them in chains because then it would no longer be a "work of loving kindness" (*philanthrōpias to ergon*).[94] John knows that he disgusts some wealthy listeners, but he insists that they are enslaved by their passions. Wealthy sinners are no better than beggars. In fact, they are worse. For beggars may have imperfections in their bodies that cause them to need assistance, but wealthy sinners have the disease of their own arrogance. To them and to all, John repeats the humble Christ's invitation to find rest for our souls (cf. Mt 11:29), which we may obtain through grace and loving kindness.

When preaching on 1 Cor 15:35–46, John emphasizes that Paul helps those without faith understand what the resurrection of the body is like. Paul anticipates that someone will ask, "How are the dead raised? And with what kind of body will they come?" (1 Cor 15:35). Here, John explains, Paul no longer remains his exceedingly gentle and humble self, but resorts to calling such a person a fool. Paul then gives explanations from nature to correct the foolishness. The seed that we sow dies in order for a plant to rise. Whereas the opponent argues that the death of a body cannot yield life, Paul shows that it is the other way around. Only the dead rise to new

94 *Homilies on 1 Corinthians* 40.5 (PG 61:354, as 40.6 in Chalmers, 248).

life. Just as new life springs from a seed buried and decaying, so too with us. Moreover, Paul has his readers understand the different kinds of bodies, celestial and earthly. Let us consider the celestial bodies. Sun, moon, and stars differ from one another in brightness. In fact, even the stars differ among each other. So too will we at the resurrection of the body. "Although they be all in the kingdom," John comments, "all shall not enjoy the same reward. Although all sinners be in hell, all shall not suffer the same things."[95]

John wants his people to hope that they and their loved ones will be in God's kingdom, and therefore lead a life toward that salvation. Let us bewail not our beloved departed, advises John, but rather those who have ended their life badly. When one of us is buried, it is a sowing that leads from corruption to incorruption. For a voice will come from heaven, and the dead will spring up. The one who rises again "is no more led to a life full of toil, but to a place where anguish and sorrow and sighing flee away."[96]

Chrysostom frequently offers scriptural examples for his people to ponder as demonstrations of God's loving providence and as models for their lives.[97] He also asks them to collect models from the Scriptures and from their present life that will help them to approach death wisely. John mentions Abraham's attitude, devoid of tears and bitter words, in the sacrifice of Isaac. And he gives voice to his people's possible objection: "But he, you say, was Abraham."[98] John encourages them by telling them that they have an even nobler call, and then adduces the example of Job.[99] Job certainly did grieve

95 *Homilies on 1 Corinthians* 41.3 (PG 61:358; as 41.4 in Chalmers, 251 [alt.]).

96 *Homilies on 1 Corinthians* 41.4 (PG 61:360; as 41.7 in Chalmers, 253 [alt.]).

97 For an extended study, see Edwards, "Divine Providence and Biblical Narrative in the Thought of John Chrysostom."

98 *Homilies on 1 Corinthians* 41.4 (PG 61:360; as 41.7 in Chalmers, 253).

99 Job frequently appears in Chrysostom's thought. For a translation of his Job commentary, see *St. John Chrysostom, Commentaries on the Sages*, vol. 1, *Commentary on Job*, translated by Robert Charles Hill (Brookline, MA: Holy Cross Orthodox Press, 2006). For scholarship on Chrysostom on Job, I highly recommend the work of Douglas Finn, see his "Job and His Wife as Exemplary Figures in the Preaching of John Chrysostom," *ZAC* 23, no. 3 (2019):

for his children as is proper for a loving father.[100] What John objects to is the practice of lamenting the faithful departed in ignoring the crown that awaits them. Why should we wish that they still be tossed about in mid-ocean, where we are in this life, when they could be now safely at port?

Chrysostom considers the objection that we ought to mourn a loved one who departed this life in sin. Should we not mourn in that case? No, he preaches. We should rejoice that the departed no longer sins. Also, we can help that loved one "not by tears, but by prayers and supplications and alms and offerings."[101] John reminds his people that mention of the departed is made during the liturgical celebration of the divine mysteries. There God is approached, and the Lamb, who takes away the sin of the world, is beseeched. To make his point, John quotes a liturgical prayer for "all those who sleep in Christ and for those who perform commemorations on their behalf."[102] According to the principle of *lex orandi, lex credendi* (the law of praying is the law of believing), John reasons: "For if there were no commemorations for them, these things would not have been spoken: since ours is not a stage show, God forbid! It is by the ordinance of the Spirit that these things are done."[103]

John then returns to the example of Job for our hope. If the children of Job were cleansed by the sacrifice he made on their

---

479–515, "Job as Exemplary Father according to John Chrysostom," *JECS* 26, no. 2 (2018): 275–305; and "Sympathetic Philosophy: The Christian Response to Suffering according to John Chrysostom's Commentary on Job," in *Suffering and Evil in Early Christian Thought*, ed. Nonna Verna Harrison and David Hunter (Grand Rapids, MI: Baker Academic, 2016), 97–119. Timothy D. Barnes and George Bevan write that perhaps the most significant feature of the *Funerary Speech*, the earliest account of John's life, when compared to later accounts "is the fact that the *Speech* presents John as a modern Job who consistently turned the other cheek and refused to resist the exercise of imperial power, even when he unconsidered it unjust (§§ 3, 27, 30, 83, 109, 127)" See Barnes and Bevan, *Funerary Speech*, 33.

100 For John's multi-faceted approach to sorrow, which more often concerns repentance rather than mourning, see Blake Leyerle, "The Etiology of Sorrow and Its Therapeutic Benefits in the Preaching of John Chrysostom," *JLA* 8, no. 2 (2015): 368–85.

101 *Homilies on 1 Corinthians* 41.4 (PG 61:361; as 41.8 in Chalmers, 253).

102 *Homilies on 1 Corinthians* 41.4 (PG 61:361; as 41.8 in Chalmers, 253 [alt.]).

103 *Homilies on 1 Corinthians* 41.4 (PG 61:361; as 41.8 in Chalmers, 253–54 [alt.]).

behalf, how could there be a doubt that our offering would not give consolation to the departed? We can give aid to the departed through offering and prayer. That is why we pray for the departed in the liturgy, just as we also mention the saints. We are all one body in truth, although some are more glorious than others are. John concludes by questioning: "Why therefore do you grieve? Why mourn when it is your power to gather so much pardon for the departed?"[104] If you have lost a child, consider that the child is asleep, not dead, and has gone to a better place. Say with Job, "The Lord has given, and the Lord has taken away. Blessed be the name of the Lord forever" (Jb 1:21).[105] Be like Job and bless the Lord. Know that God has taken the child. The taking of the child was not the action of an enemy, but of God, who knows what is good and who loves that child more than you do.

When we turn to the last homily on 1 Corinthians 15, we find that Chrysostom continues to attend to Paul's pedagogy of leading his audience in the hope of the resurrection of the body. "Behold, I tell you a mystery," Paul says (1 Cor 15:51). John dramatically shows that Paul is allowing his audience in on a secret. He explains from Paul's text that not all will fall asleep, i.e. die, but all will be changed. It will happen suddenly, in the twinkling of an eye, as bodies corrupted will put on incorruption at the resurrection. John excitedly shows Paul's reaction to Christ's victory over death:

> Do you see his noble soul? How even as one who is offering sacrifices for victory, having become inspired and seeing already things future as things past, he leaps and tramples upon death fallen, and shouts a cry of triumph over its head where it lies, crying out mightily and saying, "O death, where is your sting? O grave, where is your victory? (Hos 13:14) It is gone, it is perished, it is utterly vanished away, and in vain have you done all

104 *Homilies on 1 Corinthians* 41.5 (PG 61:361; as 41.8 in Chalmers, 254).

105 *Homilies on 1 Corinthians* 41.5 (PG 61:362; as 41.9 in Chalmers, 254). John's text here does not have the common Septuagintal reading, and adds "forever."

> those former things." For he [Christ] not only disarmed death and vanquished it, but even destroyed it, and made it wholly cease to exist.[106]

John also places responsibility on each one of his hearers for their own lives, something of particular importance if people were to take the liturgical prayer for the dead as absolving them of responsibility to repent before death. While here John still explicitly states that he does not want his people to be grieved or thrown into despair, he also does not want them to have false hopes in what other people—even someone righteous, a prophet, or an apostle—might do for them after they have died. We must not be slothful. Rather, we all are to do what is expected and so depart from this world with confidence. Then we may all attain "the good things stored up for those who love God."[107] That is the hope of our salvation that will be fully realized in the resurrection of the body.

Conclusion

Sixteen hundred years after John Chrysostom's death, Pope Benedict XVI wrote a letter of commemoration. Benedict gives an overview of John's life and ministry as well as his teachings on communion among Christian leaders and on the Eucharist. After exhorting theologians to return to the sapiential patrimony of the holy Fathers for help in our times, Benedict concludes:

> I would like to end this writing with a final word of the great Doctor, in which he invites his faithful—and also us, of course—to reflect on the eternal values: "For how long will we be nailed to the present reality? How much longer will it be before we can meet with success? How much longer will we

106 *Homilies on 1 Corinthians* 42.2 (PG 61:365; as 42.4 in Chalmers, 257).

107 *Homilies on 1 Corinthians* 42.3 (PG 61:368; as 42.5 in Chalmers, 258 [alt.]).

> neglect our salvation? Let us remember what Christ considered we deserved, let us thank him, glorify him, not only with our faith but also with our effective actions, in order to obtain future goods through the grace and loving tenderness of Our Lord Jesus Christ, for whom and with whom glory be to the Father and to the Holy Spirit, for ever and ever. Amen."[108]

Nowhere does John use the word "hope" in this quoted passage, but his preaching on the Gospel of John here communicates his characteristic emphasis on the hope of salvation. Benedict's emphasis in interpreting Chrysostom resembles the title of Billy Graham's book that sums up the message of Graham's own life: *The Reason for My Hope: Salvation.*[109]

John wants preachers to witness by word and deed to the hope of salvation. Again, "how long will we be nailed to this present reality?" He realizes that the faithful have many struggles and preoccupations that block them from pursuing their everlasting home in heaven. He ceaselessly draws examples from family life, different kinds of work, the theater, and other forms of worldly comfort to redirect his people's attention to the Word of God. By that Word, this preacher lifts his people to the vision of hope that cannot be seen by the eyes of the world.

After reviewing the Word in Chrysostom's life, this chapter focused on the hope of salvation in his *On the Priesthood* and his preaching on 1 Corinthians 15. John wants those charged to preach to remind their people of everlasting salvation, an everlasting bodily reality that should give direction in the midst of the many problems and pleasures of this passing world. Christ is truly risen, and we firmly hope to be.

108 Benedict XVI, "On the Occasion of the 16th Centenary of the Death of St. John Chrysostom," August 10, 2007, quoting *Homilies on the Gospel of John* 46.4 (PG 63:262).

109 Billy Graham, *The Reason for My Hope: Salvation* (Nashville: Thomas Nelson, 2013).

This hope allows us to engage in the greatest Christian act of our fleeting life on earth, which is also the principal activity of the saints in heaven: to love. After all, "God is love" (1 Jn 4:8 and 16). For the Word showing us love, we now turn to Augustine of Hippo in our next chapter.

CHAPTER 5

AUGUSTINE OF HIPPO

The Word in Our Flesh for Love

On the night before he died, Jesus preached his farewell discourse in John's account of the Gospel. He says, "As the Father loves me, so I also love you. Remain in my love. If you keep my commandments, you will remain in my love, just as I have kept my Father's commandments and remain in his love" (Jn 15:9–10). Jesus gives his love to us, just as he has received love from his Father. The Lord invites us to rest in his love. As the incarnate Son, he shows us by word and deed how he has kept his Father's commandments and remained in his love. We are to do likewise, now keeping Christ's commandments and remaining in his love. And so what does he command us to do? "Love one another" (Jn 15:17).

Preaching on Jn 15:17–27, Rowan Williams, the renowned Anglican theologian who served as Archbishop of Canterbury from 2002 to 2012, highlights the distinctive love that God brings:

> The love that is embodied in Jesus Christ and in the friends of Jesus Christ is . . . a love that perseveres when it's not returned, it's a love that is extravagantly poured out on the unlovable,

> and just in case you're wondering, the unlovable in this case is not them, it's us. Jesus is reminding his friends at the table of the Last Supper that God's love is without a cause. God loves a world which is profoundly different from his own eternal radiant blissful being. God has made a world that is radically different from that eternity, and having made it, God loves it without reserve and without condition.[1]

From that reflection on love, we turn in this study of incarnation, deification, and proclamation to an early preacher who has served as a theological inspiration for Williams and for countless others: Augustine of Hippo (d. 430).

The Word in Augustine's Flesh for Us

Like Gregory of Nazianzus, Augustine tells us a lot about his own life. Nowhere more does Augustine so notably recount the Word inside of him than in the *Confessions*. As he writes in Book 10, "You pierced my heart by your Word, and I loved you."[2] In this masterwork written around 397–400/1, Augustine speaks about himself in the first ten books and about Sacred Scripture in the final three books, from the beginning of creation (Gn 1:1) through the Sabbath rest (Gn 2:2).[3] This distinction does not suggest a strict separation

1 Rowan Williams, Sermon on October 28, 2012, Anglican Consultative Council-15, Holy Trinity Cathedral, Auckland, New Zealand. http://aoc2013.brix.fatbeehive.com/articles.php/2669/archbishops-sermon-at-acc-15-on-the-reckless-love-of-god Accessed on April 26, 2020.

2 *Confessions* 10.6.8 (CCL 27, 158; Bourke, 269 [alt.]). I am indebted to Abbot Austin G. Murphy, OSB, for pointing out this powerfully simple line, depicted on his abbatial shield.

3 Augustine divides the work in this way in his *Retractations* 2.6.1 (CCL 57, 94). Readers commonly interpret the first nine books to be about Augustine's life, and the remaining four about themes—without adverting to Augustine's own division. An example of nine-four division of books is in Henry Chadwick, *Augustine*, Past Masters (Oxford: Oxford University Press, 1986), 68. Annemaré Kotzé explains well that "Book Ten is still 'autobiographical' in the sense that Augustine sets out to satisfy requests from those who want to know 'what he is like now' (*conf.* 10.3.4), but there exists a gap of ten years between the events narrated in Book Nine and the 'now' of Book Ten." See her "Augustine on Himself," in *Augustine in Context*, ed. Tarmo Toom (Cambridge: Cambridge University Press, 2017), 22–29, at 23.

of the two topics. One cannot read Augustine's account of his life without finding Scripture nor his account of Scripture without finding him. He begins the work with "Great are you, O Lord, and exceedingly praiseworthy" (Ps 47:2[48:1]; 95[96]:4; 144[145]:3).[4] He concludes with a prayer stating that we see things because God has made them, and they exist because God sees them. Alluding to Matthew 7:7, the final lines read: "From you, it is asked; in you it is sought, for you, it is knocked; thus, in this way it will be granted; in this way it will be found; in this way it will be opened. Amen."[5] Augustine's life is a vivid witness of that scriptural fulfillment.

Because of Augustine's twin interests of life and Scripture, it may not be surprising that preaching has a prominent place in Augustine's famous narrative about the variety of his loves over the course of his life. For example, in the opening of the *Confessions*, soon after the mention of his restless heart, Augustine asks how people can believe in God without a preacher (Rom 10:14). Testifying to his new life in God's re-creation, he prays in faith: "you have breathed into me through the humanity of your Son, through the ministry of your preacher."[6] The connection between Christ's humanity and the preacher's ministry is striking, and suggests the prominent combination of the incarnate One and the preacher for turning Augustine's wayward life around toward God. Here we consider only some highlights from the *Confessions.*

Book 3 of the *Confessions* opens with the teenage Augustine's move to Carthage, in love with loving and wanting to find something to love. He recounts that he went to a church. He does not,

4 Augustine repeats this acclamation at the beginning of the second part of the work, *Confessions* 11.1.1.

5 Mt 7:7 provides the impulse of much patristic prayer, study, and preaching—after Tertullian's denial that a believing Christian continues to ask, seek, and knock. See Tertullian, *Prescription against the Heretics*, chaps. 7–11.

6 *Confessions* 1.1.1 (CCL 27, 1; Bourke, 4 [alt.]). J. J. O'Donnell observes that this preacher, according to various interpretations, could be Christ, Paul, or Ambrose; Augustine prefers to keep the reference ambiguous.

however, inform us about the preaching there. Rather, he tells us that he even dared to indulge in lust during the solemn rites.[7] Also in Book 3, Augustine tells us that he became enraptured by the love of wisdom in Cicero's *Hortensius* and repulsed by the simplicity of Scripture. He underwent a Manichean conversion, becoming one of their hearers and following what he later understood to be lies.[8] As the Manichees rejected the Old Testament, so he derided the prophets. Book 3 closes with a recollection of Monica, who dreamed that where she stood, her son would eventually join her. She asked an unnamed bishop of North Africa, one who had himself been given over at an early age to Manichean thinking because of his mother, to talk with Augustine. The bishop recognized that Augustine was not ready for a conversion to God, but promised his mother that a son of her tears would not be lost.

The close of Book 3 prepares us to see Augustine, some nine years later, in Milan with another bishop, Ambrose, at the end of Book 5. Like the African bishop who helped Monica, Ambrose contrasts with that of Faustus, the Manichean bishop who disappointed Augustine early in Book 5. Ambrose is described immediately as being among the best in the whole world, a devoted worshiper with eloquence. Augustine stresses that he listened to Ambrose for his eloquence, and at first paid no attention to what he said. Only later did the content seep into him, as he felt that style and substance were inseparable in Ambrose's preaching. Ambrose's words and his

7 *Confessions* 3.3.5.

8 Often people interpret Manicheanism through Augustine. For an interpretation of Augustine through Manicheanism, see the work of Jason David BeDuhn, *Augustine's Manichean Dilemma*, vol. 1: *Conversion and Apostasy (373–388 C.E.)*, and vol. 2: *Making a "Catholic" Self, 398–401 C.E*, DRLAR (Philadelphia: University of Pennsylvania Press, 2010 and 2013). For BeDuhn's prior monograph on Manicheanism, see *The Manichean Body in Discipline and Ritual* (Baltimore: Johns Hopkins University Press 2000). BeDuhn's perspective offers a strikingly different portrayal of Augustine. One of the important sources for the study of Manicheanism is the collection of Coptic Homilies, discovered in 1929 as one of the seven Medinet Madi codices. This past century's research has allowed us to have a much more informed understanding of Manicheanism.

life—a celibate life dedicated to pondering and ministering to the Word—made a deep impression on Augustine. After much prayer and struggle, Augustine experienced the power of grace. He, his son Adeodatus, and his friend Alypius were baptized in Milan on April 24, 387. About ten years later, around the time of Ambrose's death and having become the new Bishop of Hippo, Augustine would begin writing his *Confessions*.

As a bishop, Augustine spent much time with the Bible for the sake of his preaching.[9] Less scholarly in its intention, this practice differed from that of Jerome, the greatest Latin biblicist in the first millennium of the Church, whose Vulgate translation and detailed biblical commentaries will forever influence Western Christianity. Augustine tells the priest Jerome:

> I do not have, nor could I have, such great knowledge of the divine scriptures as I see that you have. And if I have some ability in this area, I use it completely for the people of God. But on account of my work for the Church I cannot at all have the leisure for training scholars in more details than the people will listen to.[10]

9 On Augustine as preacher, Hubertus Drobner writes, "What is the subject matter of preaching? Nothing else than God's word. The preacher therefore is nothing else than the interpreter of God's word, not proclaiming his own words." See Hubertus Drobner, "'I would rather not be wearisome to you:' Saint Augustine as Preacher," *MelTheo* 51 (2000): 117–26, at 124.

10 *Ep.* 73.5 (CCL 31A, 47–48; WSA II/1, Teske, 273). Anne-Marie La Bonnardière uses this passage from Augustine's letter when she begins "Augustine, Minister of the Word of God," in *Augustine and the Bible*, edited and translated by Pamela Bright, BA 2 (Notre Dame, IN: University of Notre Dame Press, 1999), 245–51. Augustine does offer multiple commentaries and questions on select Old Testament books, most famously on the beginning of Genesis. As for New Testament exegesis, Augustine's early *Commentary on Galatians* (394–95) is more properly commentarial rather than homiletic. Eric Plumer argues that we should read this commentary in view of Augustine's monastic community and priestly ministry. See Eric Plumer, *Augustine's Commentary on Galatians: Introduction, Text, Translation and Notes*, OECS (Oxford: Oxford University Press, 2003). Within Augustine's monastic and pastoral concerns, even this commentary aims at building up the people of God rather than giving detailed exegesis. Plumer writes, "As a pastor, Augustine approaches Paul's Letter to the Galatians with this question in the forefront of his mind: 'How can we live in the Spirit so as to build up the body of Christ?'" (117).

We have over 900 extant texts in Augustine's sermon corpus. The corpus is traditionally divided into: (1) some 580 *sermones ad populum*, (2) his *tractatus*, which include 124 texts (divided by scholars into 1–54 and 55–124) on the Gospel of John and ten on the First Letter of John, and (3) the 205 treatments covering all 150 Psalms (almost all recorded while Augustine preached), called *enarrationes* by Erasmus of Rotterdam in the sixteenth century.[11] Newer discoveries have increased the extant records, most especially the Dolbeau sermons.[12] When the Benedictine monks of Saint Maur edited the first category in the late seventeenth century, they subdivided the sermons into four collections: on the Scriptures, on the liturgical seasons, on the saints, and on diverse topics.[13] Scholars have too long overlooked his preaching in favor of his substantial treatises, but such a lopsided view is now being corrected in earnest.[14] "St. Augustine was, above all," Brian Daley aptly remarks, "a preacher."[15] Edmund Hill observes that Augustine "wasn't just making speeches, but talking of what he had most at heart to his own people, and it is clear that he loved them and they loved him."[16] In one sermon he complains that their keenness or "violence" in wanting him to preach caused his sermon to be long, which he concluded from the stench that was now in the church because the people had spent

11 Shari Boodts overviews recent scholarship on Augustine's sermons in "Navigating the Vast Tradition of St. Augustine's Sermons: Old Instruments and New Approaches," *Augustiniana* 69, no. 1 (2019): 83–115. For her reckoning of the counts, see p. 86. Boodts writes, "While it is important to be aware of what was lost, it would make no sense to disregard a corpus of over 900 sermons simply because there may have once been over 6000" (94n42).

12 For Edmund Hill's translation of the Dolbeau sermons, see WSA III/11, *Sermons Discovered Since 1990*. For François Dolbeau's brief introduction, see pp. 13–20.

13 See Michele Pellegrino, "General Introduction," in WSA III/1, 13–137, at 15.

14 For an example of studies by many scholars, see *The Cambridge Companion to Augustine's Sermons*, edited by Andrew Hofer, OP (forthcoming).

15 Brian E. Daley, SJ, "Augustine the Preacher: Practicing the Rhetoric of Love," in *The Center Is Jesus Christ Himself: Essays on Revelation, Salvation, and Evangelization in Honor of Robert P. Imbelli*, ed. Andrew Meszaros (Washington, DC: The Catholic University of America Press, 2021), 231–51, at 231.

16 Edmund Hill, OP, "St Augustine as Preacher," *Blackfriars* 416 (1954): 463–71, at 469.

so much time there!"[17] According to John Cavadini's keen analysis, "Augustine notes explicitly that the preacher is above all a listener. It is Augustine's duty to speak, but 'it's a futile preacher outwardly of God's word, who isn't also inwardly a listener.'"[18] Augustine and his people listen together to God. When we pay attention to Augustine's preaching, we experience more of his humanity and the Lord's own humanity given to us through him in love.

In a sermon on Christmas, Augustine cries out in a paean for the incarnation. Hear not only his extraordinary response to how God has loved us, but his attention to our speech:

> What praises, then, should we be singing to God's love, what thanks should we be expressing! I mean, he loved us so much that for our sake he came to be in time, though all times were made through him; and he was prepared to be younger in age than many of his servants in the world, though he is older in eternity than all the world. He loved us so much that he became man though he had made man; that he was created from a mother whom he had created, carried in arms he had fashioned, sucked breasts which he himself filled; that he lay squalling in a manger wordless in infancy, though he is the Word without whom human eloquence would be at a loss for words.[19]

Love led Christ in his human will to die for those who did not love him.[20] In a sermon on the giving back of the Creed—that is, when catechumens profess the Christian faith—Augustine instructs:

17 *Exposition of Psalm* 72.34. Cf. Hill, "St Augustine as Preacher," 469.

18 John C. Cavadini, "Simplifying Augustine," in *Visioning Augustine*, foreword by Mark Therrien, CCT (Hoboken, NJ: Wiley Blackwell, 2019), 81–109, at 85–86.

19 *S.* 188.2 (PL 38:1004; WSA III/6, Hill, 32).

20 See Han-luen Kantzer Komline, *Augustine on the Will: A Theological Account*, OSHT (New York: Oxford University Press, 2019), 146: "More and more over the course of his career, and especially during the Pelagian controversy, Augustine saw the incarnation, whereby God demonstrated the extent of the divine love for the world, as illustrating good human willing." For her explanation, see especially chap. 6, "Christ and the Will," 277–329.

> But *greater love has nobody than this, that one should lay down one's life for one's friends* (Jn 15:13). Nobody, do you think? Absolutely nobody. It's true; Christ said it. Let's question the apostle, and let him answer us: *Christ,* he says, *died for the ungodly.* And again he says, *While we were enemies, we were reconciled with God through the death of his Son* (Rom 5:6, 10). So there you are; in Christ we do find greater love, seeing that he gave up his life not for his friends but his enemies. How great must be God's love for humanity, and what extraordinary affection, so to love even sinners that he would die for love of them! *For God emphasizes his love toward us*—they are the apostle's words—*because while we were still sinners Christ died for us* (Rom 5:8).[21]

It is this same love enfleshed that is known in the Eucharist. Augustine preaches that on the night before he died "Christ was being held in his hands, when he was commending his own body and said, 'This is my body.' For he held that body in his hands."[22] That mystery is the hallowed link between Christ's incarnation and the Christian life of love. "He received his flesh from the flesh of Mary," preaches Augustine while telling us to "adore the Lord's footstool" (Ps. 98[99]). "Because he walked here in that flesh," continues Augustine, "he gave us that same flesh to eat for our salvation. But no one eats it without first having adored it. In this way it is found how the Lord's footstool is adored. Not only do we not sin by adoring it; we would sin if we did not adore."[23] Preaching on John 6 and seeing that Bread of Life discourse in connection with "we being many are made one body" (1 Cor 10:17), Augustine exclaims,

21 *S.* 215.5 (PL 38:1074–75; WSA III/6, Hill, 163). This emphasis on love expresses what Augustine sets as a model for preaching on the incarnation in *On Catechizing the Uninstructed* 4.7–8.

22 *Expositions of the Psalms* 33(1).10 (CCL 38, 381; WSA III/16, Boulding, 21 [alt.]). I am indebted to Joseph T. Lienhard, SJ, "*Sacramentum* and the Eucharist in St. Augustine," *Thom* 77, no. 2 (2013): 173–92.

23 *Expositions of the Psalms* 98.9 (CCL 39, 1385; WSA III/18, Boulding, 474–75 [alt.]).

"O sacrament of piety! O sign of unity! O bond of love!"[24] Indeed, Augustine' preaches that we may all live together with Christ in a Eucharistic bond of love.

Perhaps one sermon most typifies Augustine's preaching on what it means to lead the Church through the ministry of the Word. In his long *Sermon on Pastors* (*s.* 46), which the Roman liturgical tradition features, Augustine gives a highly engaging and personal interpretation of what it means to be a preacher.[25] "Being Christians is for our sake," Augustine tells his people about being pastors, "being in charge is for yours. It is to our advantage that we are Christians, only to yours that we are in charge."[26] He recalls the Scripture: "The straying sheep you have not recalled; the lost sheep you have not sought" (Ez 34:4), in juxtaposition with the admonition of the Apostle: "Preach the word; insist upon it, welcome and unwelcome" (2 Tm 4:2). He takes that as his mandate, and proclaims:

> I *will* call back the straying sheep, I *will* seek the lost one. Whether you like it or whether you don't that's what I'm going to do. Even if the briars of the woods tear at me as I seek, I will all the same squeeze myself through all the thickets, I will search out all enclosures; according to the strength my terrifying Lord gives me, I will roam everywhere in my search. I will

24 *Homilies on the Gospel of John* 26.13 (on Jn 6:41–59) (CCL 36, 266; FC 79, Rettig, 271 [alt.]). For a recent study of Augustine's preaching that highlights this passage, see Kolawole Chabi, "Augustine's Eucharistic Spirituality in His Easter Sermons," *Augustinianum* 59, no. 2 (2019): 475–504.

25 This sermon has long had prominence as a model for preachers. The Roman Rite's Liturgy of the Hours, Office of Readings, Weeks 24–25 offers lessons from it. For a beautiful overview of Augustine's pastoral ministry, see James K. Lee, "'One in the One Shepherd': St. Augustine and Pastoral Ministry," *HeyJ* 63 (2022): 232–44. For emphasis on the ministerial burden, see George P. Lawless, OSA, "Augustine's Burden of Ministry," *Angelicum* 61, no. 2 (1984): 295–315.

26 *S.* 46.2 (CCL 41, 529–30; WSA III/2, Hill, 263). Cf. Augustine's preaching elsewhere on the anniversary of his ordination as a bishop in *s.* 340.1: "Where I'm terrified by what I am for you, I am given comfort by what I am with you. For you I am a bishop, with you, after all, I am a Christian. The first is the name of an office undertaken, the second a name of grace; that one means danger, this one salvation" (PL 38:1483; WSA III/9, Hill, 292).

> call back the stray, I will seek the sheep that is perishing. If you don't want to have to put up with me, don't stray, don't perish.[27]

Possidius, a friend who lived with Augustine for several years in the monastic community of Hippo before becoming Bishop of Calama, wrote Augustine's *Life* some years after his death.[28] Possidius knew him well for nearly forty years, and he shows the intense love at work in Augustine's life. For example, he provides the wonderful detail that Augustine's dinner table had the following words inscribed: "Whoever loves to gnaw by words at the life of one not present should recognize his own life unworthy of this table."[29] Listen to how Possidius wanted to close his account:

> From the writings of this priest (*sacerdos*), so pleasing and dear to God, it is clear, as far as the light of truth allows humans to see, that he led a life of uprightness and integrity in the faith, hope, and love of the Catholic Church. This is certainly acknowledged by those who read his writings on the things of God. I believe, however, that they profited even more who were able to hear him speaking in church and see him there present, especially if they were familiar with his manner of life among his fellow human beings.[30]

We can keep in mind this testimony as we turn to love in one of Augustine's several masterpieces, *On Christian Teaching*. Afterwards, we will consider love in what is arguably some of his finest preaching, the *Homilies on the First Letter of John*.

27 *S.* 46.14 (CCL 41, 541; WSA III/2, Hill, 272).

28 This *Vita* precedes the *Indiculum*, a catalogue of Augustine's works. By pairing the two, Possidius presents Augustine's life and works together. For a study of Possidius, see Erika T. Hermanowicz, *Possidius of Calama: A Study of the North African Episcopate at the Time of Augustine*, OECS (Oxford: Oxford University Press, 2008).

29 *The Life of Saint Augustine*, chap. 22 (PL 32:52): *Quisquis amat dictis absentum rodere vitam, hac mensa indignam noverit esse suam* (my translation).

30 *The Life of Saint Augustine*, chap. 31 (PL 32:64–65; O'Connell, 130).

Love in *On Christian Teaching*

Around 396, when he succeeded Valerius as Bishop of Hippo, Augustine started writing the four-book *On Christian Teaching* and stopped at section 3.25.35. When he was reviewing all his works near the end of his life, around 426/7, he took the work up again and completed it.[31] This four-book work would be one of the most influential works in Western theology, and has great relevance to Augustine's vision of the formation of preachers.[32] *Doctrina*, in the work's title, should be taken in the sense of an active process of teaching rather than as a body of teaching, as Augustine carefully exposits the two activities in teaching: finding and delivering to others what is found.[33]

31 Edmund Hill hypothesizes that Aurelius, the Bishop of Carthage and Primate of Africa, commissioned Augustine to write the work for clergy. Soon after he became Bishop of Hippo, Augustine, with his friend Alypius who became Bishop of Thagaste, writes to Aurelius, to thank him for extending to priests the permission to deliver homilies. This would then occasion the need for *On Christian Teaching*. Augustine also takes this opportunity to say that he is still waiting to hear what Aurelius thinks of the seven rules or keys of Tychonius (*ep*. 41). Augustine might not have wanted to continue Book 3 of *On Christian Teaching* without Aurelius's judgment, as the Bishop of Carthage might have reservations about borrowing from the work of the schismatic Tychonius when the Church in North Africa was so troubled by the Donatist schism. Perhaps Aurelius did not answer Augustine or decided against citing Tychonius. In any case, only near the end of his life, did Augustine resume the work, and without the concern about a negative reaction to using Tychonius's work. See Translator's Note in *Saint Augustine, Teaching Christianity: De Doctrina Christiana*, WSA I/11, Hill, 95–97.

32 Karla Pollmann is right in seeing a broader audience for this text than simply preachers in giving homilies. For example, she notes *On Christian Teaching* 4.18.37, which shows that Augustine has in mind various forms of communication, private and public, oral and written, and among the written, books and letters of varying lengths. See Karla Pollmann, "To write by advancing in knowledge and to advance by writing," *AugStud* 29, no. 2 (1998): 131–37. Her response concludes the journal's book symposium on her *Doctrina Christiana: Untersuchungen zu den Anfängen der christlichen Hermeneutik unter besonderer Berücksichtigung von Augustinus, De doctrina christiana*. Paradosis 41 (Freiburg, Switzerland: Universitätsverlag Freiburg, 1996). For a more recent review of secondary literature on the audience and purpose of *On Christian Teaching*, see James A. Andrews, *Hermeneutics and the Church: In Dialogue with Augustine* (Notre Dame, IN: University of Notre Dame Press, 2012), 23–41.

33 For a valuable collection of essays, see *De Doctrina Christiana: A Classic of Western Culture*, eds. Duane W. H. Arnold and Pamela Bright (Notre Dame, IN: University of Notre Dame Press, 1995). Of special mention for this present study are William S. Babcock, "*Caritas* and Signification in *De doctrina christiana* 1–3" (145–63) and John C Cavadini, "The Sweetness of the Word: Salvation and Rhetoric in Augustine's *De doctrina christiana*" (164–81).

After a preface in which he gives a rationale for providing rules to assist others in approaching the Bible, Augustine begins: "Every treatment [*tractatio*] of the Scriptures rests upon two things: the way of finding [*modus inveniendi*] what must be understood and the way of delivering [*modus proferendi*] what is understood."[34] Notice the unity of these two elements.[35] One without the other would be incomplete in treating Scripture. The first three books are dedicated to "the way of finding," and the fourth book is devoted to "the way of delivering," which includes preaching the Word. Both parts depend utterly on love.

One might think that the two parts are all about understanding, as "what is understood" appears in both. Such an emphasis follows from the prologue. Yet understanding, when taken into the broader Augustinian framework and also as seen in this work, is inadequate for the overall project. Why? A basic Augustinian principle is that you do not love what you do not know. Augustine asks plainly, "Who loves what he does not know?"[36] We can know things we do not love, but we cannot love things we do not know. Our love depends upon knowing some good, ultimately the One who alone is Good, the Supreme Good. However, if we fully comprehend something, as Augustine repeatedly preaches, that cannot be God.[37] Love takes us further than mere understanding, which is a prerequisite.

Moreover, love is meant to be seen in the lives of those who treat Scripture. Augustine concludes the work in this way: "Nevertheless, I give thanks to our God, that in these four books it is not

34 *On Christian Teaching* 1.1.1 (CCL 32, 6; WSA I/11, Hill, 106 [alt.]).

35 For an argument of the unity of *On Christian Teaching*, see Andrews, *Hermeneutics and the Church.* While acknowledging the distinction between Books 1–3 and Book 4, Andrews correctly writes, "Yet, to divide the work strictly, focusing only on discovering the meaning or only on delivering what has been discovered, misses the entire purpose of *De doctrina*: it envisions one act of interpretation comprising two *modi operandi*. . . . The two parts stand and fall together" (24).

36 *On the Trinity* 8.4.6 (CCL 50, 275; McKenna, 250 [alt.]).

37 See the examples of *s.* 52.16 (in a homily on the Trinity, dated 410–12) and *s.* 117.5 (on Jn 1:1–3, dated 418 or after 420).

how I am, to whom many things lack, but how one ought to be who in sound teaching, that is Christian teaching, should be dedicated to labor not only for himself but also for others, however little I have been able to explain by my power."[38] Yes, there are two principal activities in treating the Bible: finding what is to be understood in the Bible and communicating that understanding to others. Augustine emphasizes these precisely in terms of how the one who has the twofold task of treating the Bible should be, a task preeminently about love, as we will now investigate.

On Christian Teaching, Books 1–3, The Way to Learn Love

Early in Book 1 Augustine makes a distinction between things (*res*) and signs (*signa*). He says that all teaching is about these two. Signs are things that signify, or point to, other things. Thus, every sign is a thing, because if it were not a thing, it would be nothing. Rather than concentrating first on how the words of Scripture are signs that point to things, Augustine instead wants his readers to focus on the different categories of things, the subject of Book 1. Augustine dedicates the two subsequent books to signs: Book 2 to understanding the signs in Scripture and Book 3 to understanding, more particularly, difficult ambiguous signs in Scripture. But what are these categories of things in Book 1?

There are three types of things: things meant to be enjoyed; things meant to be used; and things that enjoy and use other things.[39] Things meant to be enjoyed are things that make us happy. Things meant to be used assist us in reaching things that are to be enjoyed. We ourselves fall in the third category of things: those who enjoy and use other things. How does love figure into this? Augustine writes: "*To enjoy* [*Frui*] is to cling to something with love [*amore inhaerere*] for its own sake. *To use* [*Uti*], on the other hand, is to

38 *On Christian Teaching* 4.31.64 (CCL 32, 167; WSA I/11, Hill, 241 [alt.]).

39 *On Christian Teaching* 1.3.3.

refer what has come into a use to what should be obtained that you love [*amas*], provided that it deserves to be loved [*amandum est*]."[40] When we love things, do we love them for their own sake as the source of happiness, or do we refer them in use to those things that should be loved for their own sake? Things loved for their own sake are certainly not signs of other things, but things used can be referred to those things that we enjoy for their own sake.

In expositing the distinction between things and signs, Augustine depicts a journey, his favorite motif for describing life in a world filled with signs of what is to be enjoyed.[41] Today some emphasize the enjoyment of the journey or the fact that the journey itself is the destination. Augustine's thinking, however, is heavily teleological; he is focused on the end or purpose. Moreover, having a love, simply loving something, is not enough—and it can even be to our ruin. In Book 14 of the *City of God*, a later work, Augustine writes, "two loves built the two cities."[42] Both the terrestrial city and the heavenly city are built on love, but vastly different kinds of love. The terrestrial city has a love that can never fulfill us, whereas the heavenly city offers a love that will fulfill. "Our heart is restless until it rests in you," as Augustine prays in the *Confessions*.[43] God knows that we have, during this life on earth, a jumble of loves. What he wants is to have our loves ordered properly—and that is what Scripture teaches. True love, the love that God pours into our hearts through the Holy Spirit (cf. Rom 5:5), can guide the pilgrimage of our life to what can be forever enjoyed.

The things to be enjoyed properly for their own sake are the Father, Son, and Holy Spirit. The Holy Trinity is one supreme thing.

40 *On Christian Teaching* 1.4.4 (CCL 32, 8; WSA I/11, Hill, 107, emphasis added).

41 The literature is abundant. For a recent beautiful book, see Sarah Stewart-Kroeker, *Pilgrimage as Moral and Aesthetic Formation in Augustine's Thought* (Oxford: Oxford University Press, 2017).

42 *City of God* 14.28 (CCL 48, 451).

43 *Confessions* 1.1.1 (CCL 27, 1).

Each of the three is the complete divine substance, and all three are together only that one substance. The Father is neither the Son nor the Holy Spirit, and the Son is neither the Father nor the Holy Spirit. The Holy Spirit is neither the Father nor the Son. All three have the same eternity, unchangeableness, greatness, and power. Augustine treats the central mystery of Christian faith, the Trinity, here so as to sort out our loves.[44] God is not a part of the world, but transcends the things of this world, the things of use, in whom he is also most immanent. This wholeness in loving God above everything else, finding in him alone complete enjoyment, fulfills the greatest commandment found in Dt 6:5. How can we enjoy God who is so beyond us with our whole being, when we have turned toward creatures in place of the one Creator?

Augustine emphasizes that Wisdom, who is the Son of God, has become flesh.[45] Wisdom has taken on the infirmities of our life to make a way for us back to the Father.[46] This journey is not travelled physically but by the affections. Augustine elaborates:

> And it was being blocked, as by a barricade of thorn bushes, by the malice of our past sins. So what greater generosity and compassion could he show, after deliberately making himself the pavement under our feet along which we could return home,

44 *On Christian Teaching* 1.5.5.

45 Austin Murphy rightly observes: "Preaching is an important way in which the Church as an authority teaches and mentors believers in the apprenticeship of wisdom. Augustine connects it directly to the incarnational dynamic in *doc. Chr.* 1.12.11: 'And although to the healthy and pure interior eye [the eternal Wisdom of God] is present everywhere, he deigned to appear also to the fleshly eyes of those whose interior eye is infirm and impure. Indeed, "because in the wisdom of God the world was not able to know God through wisdom, it pleased God to save those who believe through the foolishness of preaching"' [cf. 1 Cor 1:21]." See Austin Gregory Murphy, OSB, "The Bible as Inspired, Authoritative, and True according to Saint Augustine," Ph.D. diss., University of Notre Dame, 2016, p. 447n30.

46 David Meconi comments on this pattern in Augustine's preaching: "The Son's enfleshment perfectly unites divine power with human weakness. In asking his congregants to confess their infirmity, Augustine invites them to see where they need the one true doctor, the one who alone can heal so deeply." See David Vincent Meconi, SJ, "Recapitulative Tropes in Augustine's Sermons," *New Blackfriars* 95 (2014): 689–97, at 695–96.

> than to forgive us all our sins once we had turned back to him, and by being crucified for us to root out the ban blocking our return that had been so firmly fixed in place?[47]

John Cavadini aptly comments that "the sweet Wisdom of God speaks persuasively with her blood, disentangling us from the web of sweetnesses that is our own construction, and forming our affections instead by her charity."[48]

Now that we know that Wisdom incarnate has become our way back to the Father in love, what about the neighbor? Jesus commands, "Love one another as I have loved you" (Jn 15:12). Augustine asks whether we are to love neighbors for their own sake or for the sake of God. Do we "use" our neighbors, or do we "enjoy" them? His nuanced response displays once again how he reads Sacred Scripture. The prophet Jeremiah says, "Cursed is the one who places his hopes in man" (Jer 17:5). If something other than God, even a human being, is loved for its own sake, in this Augustinian sense of "enjoying," then that is selected as one's end or fulfillment. That would be disastrous. Only God should have that place. Our love for our own selves and for our neighbors must be for the sake of God. But once it is for the sake of God, then we can enjoy our neighbors in the Lord as the enjoyment is of God in our neighbors.[49] In Augustine's order of charity, which emphasizes the completeness of enjoyment in God who is to be loved above all things, our neighbors get a special place: "Love your neighbor as yourself" (Lv 19:18). What can get between the soul and the body? Our neighbor must

47 *On Christian Teaching* 1.17.16 (CCL 32, 15; WSA I/11, Hill, 113).

48 Cavadini, "Salvation and Rhetoric," 171.

49 *On Christian Teaching* 1.32.35–33.37. Augustine cites Phlm 20, where Paul says to Philemon, "let me enjoy you in the Lord." For a classic argument that Augustine himself did not and could not later defend the distinction he made in *On Christian Doctrine* Book 1, which puts love of neighbor as a qualified form of "use," see Oliver O'Donovan, "*Usus* and *Fruitio* in Augustine, *De Doctrina Christiana* 1," *JTS* n.s. 33, no. 2 (1982): 361–97. Stewart-Kroeker responds to Oliver O'Donovan's argument about the use-enjoyment distinction in chapter 6 of her *Pilgrimage as Moral and Aesthetic Formation in Augustine's Thought.*

be there, so to speak, as we are bidden never to take our soul away from God in love, and we may be called to give our bodies over for love of neighbor.

The most important foundation for interpreting Scripture is the double-love commandment where Jesus unites Dt 6:5 and Lv 19:18 in the Gospel of Matthew. When with Augustine we read Matthew's account of Jesus's response to the question as to what is the greatest commandment, we find the Scriptures open up for us. Augustine quotes repeatedly from Mt 22:37–40. This account of Christ's pairing of Dt 6:5 with Lv 19:18 gives a particular reason not found in other Gospels: "On these two commandments depends the whole Law and the prophets" (Mt 22:40). In other words, Jesus himself teaches that Scripture depends on these paired commandments to love. For good measure, Augustine adds the Pauline teachings: "the end of the commandment is love" (1 Tm 1:5) and "the one who loves another has fulfilled the Law" (Rom 13:8). These three passages together communicate the Bible's own hermeneutics.[50]

For Augustine, love is essential for the true knowledge of Scripture. He says that those who think that they know what Scripture says, but have not love, have not yet understood Scripture. Likewise, he offers a charming image about those who may err on some scriptural details but still grow in love. It is like, he says, when a vehicle goes off the road but still comes to the destination.[51] Still, these people too should be corrected, lest they eventually go in the wrong direction. In summarizing Augustine's teaching that all of Scripture is about love, Michael Cameron observes: "For Augustine all truly spiritual reading of Scripture radiates from this center. As he later wrote, 'Any idea about salvation, whether conceived by a

50 Pollmann, *Doctrina Christiana*, 143–46.

51 *On Christian Teaching* 1.36.41.

mind or proclaimed by a mouth or carved out of any page of Scripture whatsoever, has no other end than love.'"[52]

Once Augustine has taught about the most important *things* and established that love of God and neighbor is the overarching rule for interpreting Scripture, he can dedicate the next two books of *On Christian Teaching* to understanding the *signs* of Scripture. Not surprisingly, the *signs* are signs of these *things*—and so love must be at the forefront of our understanding. Book 2 pertains to knowing signs in general, and Book 3 takes up the difficult cases of how to know what God wills in Scripture's ambiguous signs.

The signs of Scripture are not as straightforward as some may expect. Divine providence, suggests Augustine, has placed obscurities in Scripture to combat pride through labor and to save the intelligence from boredom.[53] Also, by understanding what God intends through these signs, a delight arises. Augustine knows that the Song of Songs is addressed to the Bride, the Church, and he illustrates his point about signs through a passage from that biblical book: "Your teeth are like a flock of shorn ewes coming up from the washing, which all give birth to twins, and there is not one among them that is barren" (Sg 4:2). Augustine goes through the details of the images and confesses his delight to realize that the shorn ewes coming up from the wash are the baptized, who have let go of their burden of sin and who bear fruitfulness in the twin commandments: love of God and love of neighbor. The Holy Spirit, according to Augustine, has so shaped the Scriptures as to have both clear passages to feed the hungry and obscure passages to drive away boredom. Almost all the obscurities can be explained by the plain reading of other scriptural passages. That is why, it seems, the sheep giving birth to twins can be delightfully thought

52 Michael Cameron, *Christ Meets Me Everywhere: Augustine's Early Figurative Exegesis*, OSHT (New York: Oxford University Press, 2012), 220, citing *Expositions of the Psalms* 140.1.

53 *On Christian Teaching* 2.6.7.

of as an image of the double-love commandment, as that is what all Scripture teaches.

Also, in this second book, Augustine describes a spiritual ascent through the Gifts of the Holy Spirit, beginning with fear of the Lord and arriving at wisdom (cf. Is 11:2–3). Afterwards, Augustine returns to single out the third step, which is knowledge.[54] What do we come to know in Scripture in Augustine's ascent? Only this: "God is to be loved on God's account, and one's neighbor on God's account." Augustine continues, "to love God, indeed, with one's whole heart, with one's whole soul, with one's whole mind, but one's neighbor as oneself, that is to say, that one must refer all the love of one's neighbor, as of oneself, to God."[55] An emphasis on knowledge of signs continues through Book 2, and one should not forget the bedrock principle of knowing the double-love commandment signified throughout all Scripture. Augustine at times invokes the line: "Knowledge puffs up, but love builds" (1 Cor 8:1). He asserts that students of the Scriptures should never stop reflecting on 1 Cor 8:1. When we are built up by love, then we heed Christ's invitation of Mt 11:28–30:

> Come to me, you who labor and are burdened, and I will refresh you. Take my yoke upon you and learn from me, because I am meek and humble in heart. And you will find rest for your spirits. For my yoke is easy and my burden light.

Augustine then asks, "For whom is this so, except those meek and humble in heart, whom knowledge does not puff up, but love builds up?"[56] Augustine later repeats 1 Cor 8:1 at the end of Book 2.[57]

54 *On Christian Teaching* 2.7.11.
55 *On Christian Teaching* 2.7.10 (CCL 32, 37; WSA I/11, Hill, 132).
56 *On Christian Teaching* 2.41.62 (CCL 32, 75; WSA I/11, Hill, 161 [alt.]).
57 *On Christian Teaching* 2.42.63.

Before Book 2's conclusion, Augustine prosecutes his argument about knowing scriptural signs.[58] Augustine emphasizes that those who read Scripture in the fear of God and docile piety should search to know God's will. Augustine wants his readers to know Scripture, preferably committing much of it to memory. God's will is veiled under scriptural signs. Various difficulties arise because some signs are unknown and some are ambiguous. Knowing biblical languages is of value. In fact, Augustine brings so many other matters to bear on our knowledge of the Bible that he must develop an integrative approach to the multiple disciplines. Employing the popular image of "the gold of Egypt," Augustine speaks of how the secular sciences can be used to know God's will in Sacred Scripture, just as the Hebrews took Egyptian gold at God's command when they left Egypt.[59] Augustine says that this is what the Latins Cyprian, Lactantius, Victorinus, Optatus, Hilary and countless Greek writers have done. Moses, after all, was "educated in all the wisdom of the Egyptians" (Acts 7:22).[60] Knowledge from the books of the pagans can be useful, but it pales in comparison to what is found in Sacred Scripture, books so lofty and so humble at the same time. Even so, when we use knowledge from pagans to understand Scripture, we can reap a bountiful harvest.

In Book 3, Augustine treats various sorts of ambiguities, such as how words are phrased in their pronunciation and in their grammatical construction. Most importantly, he distinguishes between figurative or metaphorical expressions and literal or proper expressions. One should not treat the literal as merely a metaphor. So how should the two be distinguished? It is through one singular method

58 He produces a list of the canonical books of Scripture, which should remind us of the debate in the Church over which books were canonical. North African councils during the life of Augustine were helpful in determining the biblical canon. See canon 47 of the Third Synod of Carthage (August 28, 397), which is thought to repeat in substance canon 36 of the October 8, 393 Synod at Hippo Regius (Denzinger, 43rd ed., no. 186).

59 *On Christian Teaching* 2.40.60–42.63.

60 *On Christian Teaching* 2.40.61 (CCL 32, 74).

that he so often emphasizes: "Anything in the divine writings that cannot be referred either to good, honest morals or to the truth of the faith, you must know is said figuratively." He continues:

> Good honest morals belong to loving God and one's neighbor, the truth of the faith to knowing God and one's neighbor. As for hope, that lies in everybody's own conscience, to the extent that you perceive yourself to be making progress in the love of God and neighbor, and in the knowledge of them.[61]

With that principle, ambiguities are always resolved in favor of love. Using a rhyming contrast between love (*caritas*) and greed (*cupiditas*), Augustine says in *On Christian Teaching* that Scripture "commands nothing but love [*caritatem*] and censures nothing but greed [*cupiditatem*], and in this way it gives form to human morals."[62] Indeed, all figurative expressions must be interpreted through this hermeneutical principle.[63] In contrast to enjoying God for his own sake and of self and neighbor for God's sake in *caritas, cupiditas* "is the soul's movement toward the enjoyment of self or neighbor or any bodily thing for reasons other than God (*non propter Deum*)," as William Babcock explains.[64] Later in the book Augustine writes:

> The tyranny of greed being thus overthrown, love reigns supreme with its just laws of loving God for God's sake, and

61 *On Christian Teaching* 3.10.14 (CCL 32, 86; WSA I/11, Hill, 176). Augustine then reminds the reader that what he just wrote formed the subject of Book 1.

62 *On Christian Teaching* 3.10.15 (CCL 32, 87; WSA I/11, Hill, 179 [alt.]).

63 Augustine preaches on love, after recalling Mt 22:39–40: "So if there's no time to pore over all the sacred pages, to leaf through all the volumes of the words they contain, to penetrate all the secrets of the scriptures, hold onto love, on which they all depend. In this way you will hold onto what you have learned there; you will also get hold of what you haven't yet learned. I mean, if you know love, you know something from which that also depends which perhaps you don't yet know; and in whatever you do understand in the scriptures, love is revealed (*charitas patet*); while in the parts you don't understand, love is concealed (*charitas latet*). And so it is that one who holds onto love in action, has a grasp both of what is revealed and of what is concealed in the divine words." See *s.* 350.2 (PL 39:1534, WSA III/10, Hill, 108 [alt.]). Cf. Pellegrino, "General Introduction," 77.

64 Babcock, "*Caritas* and Signification," 155.

> oneself and one's neighbor for God's sake. So this rule will be observed in dealing with figurative expressions, that you should take pains to turn over and over in your mind what you read, until your interpretation of it is led right through to the kingdom of love.[65]

By situating love so centrally, Augustine does not negate other virtues but rather shows the truthfulness and comprehensiveness of love at work in the Scriptures for our good living. For example, Augustine constantly extols the need for another virtue, humility, to guard against pride. He comments, "There is, in fact, almost no page of the holy books in which the lesson does not sound forth, that 'God resists the proud, but gives grace to the humble'" (see Prv 3:34, Jas 4:6, 1 Pt 5:5).[66] Augustine himself towered over others by his intellect and his rhetorical prowess, and so he wanted to put these gifts humbly at the service of what endures: love.

On Christian Teaching, Book 4, The Way of Sharing the Love Learned

In his prologue to *On Christian Teaching*, Augustine writes, "love itself, which ties people to one another by the knot of unity, would have no scope for pouring minds and hearts in together, as it were and blending them with one another, if human beings learned nothing through human beings."[67] In the act of love shown in the

65 *On Christian Teaching* 3.15.23 (CCL 32, 91; WSA I/11, Hill, 179 [alt.]).

66 *On Christian Teaching* 3.23.33 (CCL 32, 97; Hill, 184). Augustine features this proverb at the beginning of his *Confessions* and *City of God*, to name two of his most significant works that illustrate the truthfulness of God's action in human life.

67 *On Christian Teaching*, prologue 6 (CCL 32, 4; WSA I/11, Hill, 103 [alt.]). For Augustine, it seems that all Christians have only one heart, which is the heart of Christ. In Augustine's liturgy, the priest bids the people, *Sursum cor* ("Lift up your heart"), not *Sursum corda* ("Lift up your hearts"). See the Ascension homily of *s.* 265C.1 (cf. *s.* 263A). Augustine's monastic life expresses that early Christian ideal of being in Augustine's reading of Acts 4:32 "one soul and one heart in God." See the Vetus Latina database for the frequency of this formulation. For example, Augustine quotes, while speaking of imitating the angelic life, "because it is written, *There is one soul and one heart toward God, and nobody has any private property, but all things are in common among them.*" See *s.* 198/Dolbeau 26.48 (Dolbeau, 127; WSA III/11, Hill, 217).

very writing this text, Augustine relies on the help of the Lord so that his readers may not only understand what Scripture says, but lead others to understand and live according to the Word in an ever-increasing love. This is how Book 4 is dedicated to handing on what is understood in Scripture.

This communication, Augustine maintains, does not fall within the discipline of rhetoric. Augustine rails against rhetoric, because it is the art of persuading people to accept whatever the speaker wants—be it true or false. Since rhetoric does not concern itself with the truth, a speaker may try to convince people through lies to accept lies. Augustine had a horror of lying and wrote much against it.[68] For Augustine, Scripture does not lie, because God, who is the Truth, does not lie. A preacher, then, is to model how God speaks—namely, truthfully. Also, God himself is the most persuasive speaker, who wins us back through delight.[69] Therefore, the preacher does not simply communicate information, but does so persuasively to convert others to the love of God.

While opposed to rhetoric, Augustine does indeed recommend eloquence for persuasion. Such eloquence can be learned more readily by listening to eloquent speakers than by poring over rules. He likens this to infants learning to speak, or children learning grammar, by what they hear from others. If they hear what is detrimental to their growth, then they will likely imbibe errors. It is important for those who want to preach well to listen to good preachers. Moreover, eloquence must be at the service of wisdom, as it is more important to be wise than eloquent—although Augustine would prefer that those who hand on the Scriptures be both.

68 See especially his two treatises *On Lying* (written in 395) and *Against Lying* (written in 420). For a brief overview, see Boniface Ramsey, OP, *Mendacio, De Contra mendacium*, ATA, 555–57.

69 See especially Mark F. M. Clavier, *Eloquent Wisdom: Rhetoric, Cosmology and Delight in the Theology of Augustine of Hippo*, STT 117 (Turnhout: Brepols, 2014).

Preachers should realize that neither they nor their listeners are blank slates. Augustine forcefully imparts this instruction:

> Therefore, the one who treats and teaches the divine Scriptures [*divinarum Scripturarum tractator et doctor*], the defender of right faith and the hammer of error, has the duty of both teaching what is good and unteaching what is bad. In this task of speaking it is his duty to win over the hostile, to stir up the slack, to point out to the ignorant what is at stake and what they ought to be looking for.[70]

Augustine goes on to name the apostle Paul and the prophet Amos as examples of eloquent wisdom.

Moreover, Augustine devotes considerable space in Book 4 to illustrating three functions of eloquence that he adapts from Cicero's *Orator* for Christian use: to teach, to delight, and to sway.[71] Teaching regards the content of the communication, and it is usually carried out in the low, calm style. To delight and to sway concern how the content is delivered. Delighting is carried out moderately, when the preacher wants to praise or blame. In swaying the preacher carries on in a grand manner so that people may be urged to be converted, their hearts won over by the force of the preaching. In addition to examples from Paul and his two most frequently cited model bishops, Cyprian and Ambrose, Augustine refers to his own experience. He relates an incident of preaching in Caesarea in Mauritania, where the residents would ritually fight one another, even to death. Augustine says that he did not think he was successful when they applauded him, but when he saw them weep, he knew he had won

70 *On Christian Teaching* 4.4.6 (CCL 32, 119; WSA I/11, Hill, 203 [alt.]).

71 Cicero says, "To prove (*Probare*) is of necessity, to please (*delectare*) is of charm, and to sway (*flectere*) is of victory." See *The Orator*, 21.69: (LCL 342, 356; Hubbell, 357 [alt.]). Augustine quotes Cicero as saying "To teach" (*Docere*) rather than "To prove" (*Probare*) for the first of the three requirements. See *On Christian Teaching* 4.12.27 (CCL 32, 135; WSA I/11, Hill, 215).

them over. Years later, he reports, by the graciousness of Christ, they did not return to that wicked way.[72]

Augustine places paramount importance on prayer for delivering over to listeners what is learned from Scripture. He plays on the term *orator*, stemming from the Latin word for mouth, face, or speech: *os, oris*. An *orator* is obviously a speaker or rhetor, but when praying (*orando*) a Christian *orator* should pray for himself and for those he is about to address. By doing so, he becomes "a pray-er before being a speaker" (*orator antequam dictor*).[73] The things that need to be said are matters of faith and love, and those who are to speak about God must turn to God. Certainly, they are to prepare by learning the things are that are to be taught, but at the moment they are to be guided by God. Augustine recalls Mt 10:19–20, about how the Spirit of the Father will be "speaking in you." Augustine questions, "So if the Holy Spirit is speaking in those who are handed over to the persecutors on Christ's account, why not also in those who are handing Christ over to the learners?"[74]

Augustine knows that some, with a false reliance on the Spirit, may seize this opportunity to disregard any rules for teaching. To expose the error of that reasoning, he observes that one could similarly dismiss praying, as the Lord says, "Your Father knows what you need before you ask it of him" (Mt 6:8). Eschewing these false possibilities, Augustine urges his readers to follow the instructions found in Paul's epistles to Timothy and Titus, "three letters of the apostle, by the way, which anyone charged with the role of teacher in the Church ought always to have before his eyes."[75] He includes quotations from these letters several times in his exhortations to preach, such as "Preach the word, persist whether it be welcome

72 *On Christian Teaching* 4.24.53.
73 *On Christian Teaching* 4.15.32 (CCL 32, 138).
74 *On Christian Teaching* 4.15.32 (CCL 32, 139; WSA I/11, Hill, 219).
75 *On Christian Teaching* 4.16.33 (CCL 32, 139; WSA I/11, Hill, 219).

or unwelcome" (2 Tm 4:2). Augustine compares such preaching to medicine. Just as medicine cannot heal a body unless God is at work in the body, so neither can preaching heal the soul unless God is at work in that soul. God can heal a body without medicine, and he can heal a soul without preaching. Yet God chooses to use our works of mercy and good deeds for the healing of others.

After offering more illustrations, Augustine takes up what is more important than style in convincing people: a preacher's life.[76] Granted, people may listen on account of Christ, who says of those with good words but not a good life, "They sit on the chair of Moses" (Mt 23:2). The people can benefit even from corrupt preachers who are constrained by their position still to say what is true. But Augustine finds that these preachers would benefit far more if they themselves practiced what they preached.[77] Preachers who speak good words, but words not reflected in their own lives, are in fact those who steal the words of others.[78]

As he nears his conclusion to Book 4, whether his readers repeat what others say or preach their own composed sermons, Augustine urges them not to forget the importance of prayer so that it may be God who works through their mouths. "After all," he says, "if Queen Esther prayed, when she was going to speak in the king's presence for the temporal salvation of her people, that God might put suitable words into her mouth, how much more should you pray to receive such a favor, when you are toiling in word and teaching for the people's eternal salvation?"[79] Prayer is necessary both before and after preaching, as at the end preachers are to give

76 Hubertus Drobner writes, "Quite undoubtedly Augustine himself, asked what he regarded as the highest and most indispensable quality of a preacher, would have answered: That he acts as he speaks, that he himself gives the first and splendid example of a life according to the truth he proclaims to his flock from the pulpit." See Drobner, "Saint Augustine as Preacher," 118.

77 *On Christian Teaching* 4.27.60.

78 *On Christian Teaching* 4.29.62.

79 *On Christian Teaching* 4.30.63 (CCL 32, 167; WSA I/11, Hill 240).

thanks to God "in whose hand are both we and our words" (Wis 7:16).[80] Preaching gives way to the mystery of the all-loving and sustaining God.

Homilies on 1 John: Preaching on Love

Augustine preached on the First Letter of St. John during the Easter Octave, perhaps in the year 407, but could not finish that preaching within the eight days.[81] We have ten tractates, or homilies, which are considered to be some of his most outstanding preaching. The most famous line of this homiletic set may be "Love, and do what you want."[82] In introducing his preaching on 1 John, Augustine refers to his audience as "Your Holiness" (*Vestra Sanctitas*). Does he have in mind some great prelate in the audience? No, he regularly refers to the faithful who listen to him in exalted terms of holiness and love.[83] This prologue explains that while John said many things in

80 *On Christian Teaching* 4.30.63.

81 *Homilies* 9 and 10 were given after the Easter Octave (cf. *Homilies on 1 John* 9.1), and Augustine stopped his comments in Homily 10 at 1 Jn 5:3, leaving the rest through 1 Jn 5:21 untreated or not extant. Even so, Augustine's work is by far the most complete treatment we have of this letter up through his time. For analysis of this preaching, his preaching on the Psalms of Ascent, and some of the *Homilies on the Gospel of John* understood to be preached between December 406 and the summer of 407, see Adam Ployd, *Augustine, the Trinity, and the Church: A Reading of the Anti-Donatist Sermons*, OSHT (New York: Oxford University Press, 2015). For Augustine's focus on love, see Lewis Ayres, "Augustine, Christology, and God as Love: An Introduction to the Homilies on 1 John," in *Nothing Greater, Nothing Better: Theological Essays on the Love of God*, ed. Kevin J. Vanhoozer (Grand Rapids, MI: Eerdmans, 2001), 67–93.

82 *Homilies on 1 John* 7.8: *Dilige, et quod vis fac* (SC 75, 328; Rettig, 223). In tracing Stoic influences on Augustine, Marcia Colish comments: "the Christian will do whatever he does out of love alone and he will have the discernment to translate his loving intentions into appropriate actions. This doctrine may be regarded as Augustine's most radical Christianization of Stoic ethics." See Marcia L. Colish, *The Stoic Tradition from Antiquity to the Early Middle Ages*, vol. 2 (Leiden: Brill, 1990), 220. For an earlier formulation of this injunction in Augustine, "Love, and say what you like," (*Dilige, et dic quod voles*), see his *Commentary on Galatians*, chap. 57.4 (Plumer 224; Plumer 227).

83 Edmund Hill comments, "Augustine unfailingly treated his audience with courtesy and respect, the respect which servants owe their employers." See Hill, *Saint Augustine as Preacher*, 4. Hill supports this observation with a reference to *s.* 23.1. Augustine says there that his listeners judge him. Paul Agaësse, SJ, notes that Augustine uses the titles *Sanctitas*

his First Letter, nearly everything was about love.[84] Augustine wants his listeners to burn with love, and so he asks us to listen carefully to John's words through his preaching. They are like oil on a flame. If we have but a little bit of a fire of love, that love will grow. But if we do not have any flame, but only kindling, then John's words will provide the fire. Augustine has in mind key virtues that, in tandem with love, make us one. He writes that in some the fire is already being nourished; "in some a fire is set ablaze if there were none, in order that we may rejoice in one love. But where love is, there is peace; and where humility is, there is love."[85] Love bridges humility and peace; Augustine considered peace to be commonly and ardently desired in life, and humility to be foundational in the Christian life.[86] This threefold emphasis on humility, love, and peace also has special relevance to the pastoral need that Augustine identified in the Church of his time.

Augustine preached on 1 John while mindful of the Donatist schism. The Donatists received their name because of Donatus of Carthage, who led a vast movement in North Africa in protest against the sacramental practice of Catholics. They considered themselves the true Christians, who carried on the tradition of the faith of the martyrs of North Africa. Donatus succeeded Majorinus, a bishop who argued that Caecilian's consecration as bishop of Carthage in 312 was invalid or null. Majorinus claimed that one of Caecilian's episcopal consecrators had sinned by earlier handing over sacred books to pagan imperial officials during the Diocletian

---

vestra and *Caritas vestra* because his listeners represent for him the Holy Catholic Church and the charity that unites the Church. See SC 75, 104n1.

84 Augustine later preaches, "What power love has all Scripture makes known, but it is probably not made known anywhere more than in this epistle" (*Homilies on 1 John* 5.13; SC 75, 270; Rettig, 197).

85 *Homilies on 1 John*, prologue (SC 75, 106; Rettig, 120).

86 For an analysis of Augustine on peace within the context of the *City of God*, see Andrew Hofer, OP, "Book 19. The Ends of the Two Cities: Augustine's Appeal for Peace," in *The Cambridge Companion to Augustine's City of God*, ed. David V. Meconi, SJ (Cambridge: Cambridge University Press, 2021), 228–50.

persecution, thus disqualifying Caecilian as the rightful bishop. Majorinus then became a rival bishop to Caecilian, but died soon afterwards. After succeeding Majorinus, Donatus led the opposition for decades.

For Augustine, the Donatist schism offended the Church's unity of love.[87] Augustine says that the Donatists did not recognize non-Donatist Christians as their brothers and sisters by baptism. Whereas the Donatists self-identified as the Church of the martyrs under imperial persecution, claiming the great martyr and bishop Cyprian of Carthage (d. 258) as their inspiration for separation, Augustine claimed Cyprian as a figure of unity in the Church. Augustine repeatedly said, "not punishment, but the cause" (*non poena, sed causa*) makes a martyr.[88] For Augustine, a true martyr needed the cause of love in humility within the peace of the visible body—we might say fleshiness—of the Catholic Church. In 411, an imperially-sponsored conference in Carthage pitted Donatist bishops against Catholic bishops in debate. It was a defining moment in the North African ecclesial division. The Donatists would be known by history as the losers in this contest, but recent scholarship has called into question Augustine's narrative of Donatism and his appeal to love for unity.[89] Maureen Tilley writes, "Donatism did not die in 411 and Donatist studies are not going out of business any

87 Mark Edwards gives this unflattering assessment of Augustine's portrayal: "The Donatist as Augustine represents him is a parochial Pharisee, so besottedly certain of his own rectitude that he cannot hold communion with anyone in whom he perceives a blemish. . . . In short, Augustine's Donatist is a caricature." See Mark Edwards, "The Donatist Schism and Theology," in *The Donatist Schism: Controversy and Contexts*, edited by Richard Miles, TTH, Contexts 2 (Liverpool: Liverpool University Press, 2016), 101–19, at 116–17.

88 *Ep.* 89.2; Teske (WSA II/1) 359. For a study, see Adam Ployd, "*Non poena sed causa*: Augustine's Anti-Donatist Rhetoric of Martyrdom," *AugStud* 49, no. 1 (2018): 25–44.

89 For an argument on the lengthy verbatim conference transcript that challenges the narrative of "systematic state enforcement of the verdict of 411, concerted Catholic enthusiasm for its terms and Donatist demoralization in its wake," see Neil McLynn, "The Conference of Carthage Reconsidered," in *The Donatist Schism*, ed. Miles, 220–48, at 248.

time soon."[90] A Donatist homily, perhaps delivered by Donatus himself in the early fourth century, speaks of the call to unity as Satan's trick to entice more people into his trap: "So the enemy of salvation concocted more subtle conceit to violate the purity of faith. 'Christ,' he said, 'is the lover of unity. Therefore let there be unity.' Those who were already fawning on him and were deserted by God came to be called 'Catholics.' By prejudice in favor of the name, those who refused to communicate with them were called 'heretics.'"[91] When we hear Augustine preaching about love in the Church's unity, we must keep in mind that he does not do so in a vacuum.

While reading all of the *Homilies on 1 John* would be a salutary way of appreciating the life of preaching as embodying love, we must choose a manageable approach here. To that end, we will limit ourselves to three themes. The first study considers the love of bridegroom and bride. The second examines the sacramental significance of baptism for living a life of love. The third treats love of enemies. Nowhere will we find in 1 John the literal terms of "bridegroom," "bride," "sacraments," "baptism," or "enemies." But that does not stop Augustine from finding these themes expressive of 1 John in its teaching on love. These brief studies will demonstrate how Augustine seeks to apply the Scriptures in terms relevant to the needs of his people and to show forth the Word of God in the fleshiness of human love.

Love of Bridegroom and Bride

Augustine repeatedly expounds this Johannine letter's teaching on love in the terms of marriage, whose goodness Augustine

90 Maureen A. Tilley, "Redefining Donatism: Moving Forward," *AugStud* 42, no. 1 (2011): 21–32, at 32.

91 This homily is oddly named *A Sermon on the Passion of Saints Donatus and Advocatus*. See the translation in *Donatist Martyr Stories: The Church in Conflict in Roman North Africa*, translated with notes and introduction by Maureen A. Tilley, TTH 24 (Liverpool: Liverpool University Press, 1996), 51–60, at 54–55.

ardently defended.[92] We see his appropriation of the marital image mostly in the first two homilies of this series. Augustine appeals to the recurring scriptural theme of the Lord's marital covenant with his people and to the "great sacrament" or "great mystery" of the marital bond between Christ and his Church (Eph 5:32).

In *Homily* 1, Augustine begins with the letter's prologue, which mirrors the prologue of John's Gospel. In the Gospel we read, "the Word was made flesh" (Jn 1:14). This epistle begins, "What was from the beginning, what we have heard and what we have seen with our eyes and our hands have handled [*tractaverunt*] concerns the Word of life." Who could handle the Word, unless "the Word was made flesh and dwelled in us?" asks Augustine. In having Christ, we have "Life itself in the flesh" (*ipsa vita in carne*). Augustine then emphasizes how John counts himself among the "martyrs," the witnesses, of this astounding truth: "And we have seen, and we are witnesses" (1 Jn 1:2). In a lovely turn of phrase, Augustine preaches that "God wanted human beings to bear witness so that also human beings may have God as witness."[93] Augustine then turns his attention to the sun, as John bears witness to this manifestation in broad daylight. Following his mentor Ambrose, Augustine applies to the incarnation the Psalm verse: "he has placed his tabernacle in the sun, and proceeding like a bridegroom from his bridal chamber, he

92 Among his writings on marriage, see especially Augustine's *On the Good of Marriage*. For an overview of Augustine on marriage, I recommend the works of John C. Cavadini. More broadly in patristic context, see John C. Cavadini, "The Sacramentality of Marriage in the Fathers," *ProE* 17, no. 4 (2008): 442–63 and, more particularly in Augustine's anti-Pelagian debate with Julian of Eclanum, John C. Cavadini, "Reconsidering Augustine on Marriage and Concupiscence" *AugStud* 48, no. 1–2 (2017): 183–99. In the latter, Cavadini concludes that Augustine, "presents marriage as a human *societas* configured to an economy of gift that makes a good use of the will to power by subverting it even as it is used, relativizing it within a vocabulary it can of itself never learn to speak, and, thus, recovering marriage and associated natural goods as an economy of gift, of grace, and of gratitude" (199). For a study on seeing the Church through the eyes of Christ the bridegroom, with an analysis of the *City of God*, see John C. Cavadini, "Spousal Vision: A Study of Text and History in the Theology of Saint Augustine," *AugStud* 42, no. 1–2 (2012): 127–48.

93 *Homilies on 1 John* 1.2 (SC 75, 114; Rettig, 123 [alt.]).

has rejoiced as a giant to run the way" (Ps 18 [19]:6).[94] This means that the Word and human nature have been conjoined, or married, in the womb of the Virgin Mary.[95] The womb is the bridal chamber where the bridegroom and bride, the Word and the flesh, meet. Augustine sees that the two are in "one flesh" (Gn 2:24), or that they are "not two, but one flesh" (Mt 19:6). Christ then can speak both as bridegroom and as bride, which Augustine understands from Is 61:10, "Like a bridegroom he has placed on me a crown, and like a bride he has bedecked me with a jewel." Augustine comments that "to that flesh the Church is joined, and there comes to be the whole Christ, head and body."[96] This expresses Augustine's principle of the voice of the whole Christ (*vox totius Christi*).[97] We should not overlook the love at work in this union, a mixture that first forms in divinity and humanity's becoming one flesh in Mary's womb, and then in the Church's union thereto.

In *Homily* 2, Augustine returns to the bridal imagery by adding an interpretation of the risen Lord's appearance to the two disciples

94 For Ambrose's hymn *Intende Qui Regis Israel*, see Brian P. Dunkle, SJ, *Enchantment and Creed in the Hymns of Ambrose of Milan*, OECS (Oxford: Oxford University Press, 2016), 120–29. For a study on Augustine's reliance on Ambrose, see Brian E. Daley, SJ, "The Giant's Twin Substances: Ambrose and the Christology of Augustine's *Contra sermonem Arianorum*," in *Augustine: Presbyter Factus Sum*, eds. Joseph T. Lienhard, SJ, Earl C. Muller, SJ, and Roland J. Teske, SJ, CollAug (New York, 1993), 477–95.

95 For a study on this image within the breadth of Augustine's mixture terms for the incarnation, see Andrew Hofer, OP, "Augustine's Mixture Christology," *StPatr*, from the XVIII. International Conference on Patristic Studies, Oxford (2019), vol. 112, ed. Markus Vinzent, vol. 9: *Fourth-Century Christology in Context: A Reconsideration*, ed. Miguel Brugarolas (Leuven: Peeters, 2021), 103–25.

96 *Homilies on 1 John* 1.2 (SC 75, 116; Rettig, 123).

97 For some studies on the *vox totius Christi*, see Michael Fiedrowicz, *Psalmus vox totius Christi: Studien zu Augustins* Enarrationes in Psalmos (Freiburg: Herder, 1997), summarized in his "General Introduction," in *Expositions of the Psalms* (1–32), WSA III/15, 13–66; Kimberly F. Baker, "Augustine's Doctrine of the *Totus Christus*: Reflecting on the Church as Sacrament of Unity," *Horizons* 37, no. 1 (2010): 7–24; and Michael Cameron, *Christ Meets Me Everywhere*, 165–212, and "The Emergence of *Totus Christus* as Hermeneutical Center in Augustine's *Enarrationes in Psalmos*," in *The Harp of Prophecy: Early Christian Interpretations of the Psalms*, eds. Brian E. Daley, SJ, and Paul R. Kolbet, CJA 20 (Notre Dame, IN: University of Notre Dame Press, 2015), 205–26. Also pertinent is J. Patout Burns, "Augustine's Ecclesial Mysticism," in *The Wiley-Blackwell Companion to Christian Mysticism*, ed. Julia A. Lamm (Malden, MA: Wiley-Blackwell, 2013), 202–15.

on the road to Emmaus and to the Eleven. Explicit bridal imagery is as absent there as it is in 1 John. Where the risen Lord interprets the Scriptures that the Christ must suffer, die, and rise again, Augustine alerts his listeners that the bridegroom has been commended. He then urges them to look for the bride. By knowing both bridegroom and bride, we may attend the celebration of their marriage. In this particular case, the bridegroom is both the son of the king and the king. Those who attend the marriage are themselves the bride. This is quite unlike common weddings where one is the bride and others attend. Then, in a phrase that links the Church, as the bride of Christ, to his flesh, Augustine introduces this twist to the scene of the two disciples recognizing the risen Lord in the breaking of the bread:

> For the whole Church is the bride of Christ whose beginning and firstfruits are the flesh of Christ: there the bride is joined to the bridegroom in the flesh. Rightly, when he pointed out the flesh itself, he broke the bread; and rightly, in the breaking of the bread, the eyes of the disciples were opened and they recognized him.[98]

In this same sermon, Augustine recounts to his congregation 1 Jn 2:15–16: "Do not love the world or the things of the world. If any one loves the world, love for the Father is not in him. For all that is in the world, the lust of the flesh and the lust of the eyes and the pride of life, is not of the Father but is of the world." Such a worldly love works to the exclusion of the love of the Father. Here is also the threefold concupiscence: the desire of the flesh, the desire of the eyes, and the ambition of this age. How does Augustine explain this? He has recourse to a bridal image. Augustine speaks of the ring that a bridegroom gives to his beloved. Augustine wants his people to think about their loves. What if a bridegroom made a ring

98 *Homilies on 1 John* 2.2 (SC 75, 154; Rettig, 143 [alt.]).

for his beloved, but she loved the ring more than her bridegroom? Augustine speaks in the person of the bride: "This ring is enough for me; I no longer wish to see his face."[99] Augustine then turns to direct address as if his people are that bride: "You love the gold instead of the man, you love the ring instead of the bridegroom."[100] A ring is a token of the lover's love for his beloved, and the things that the Creator has made are but tokens of his love for us. "God gave you all these things," Augustine continues, "Love him who made them."[101] Augustine then delivers the punch: "There is more that he wishes to give you, that is, himself, who made these things."[102]

This image illustrates in homiletic form the *uti/frui* distinction between loves that we saw in Augustine's *On Christian Teaching*, so that his people may understand how different their love of God should be from their love of anything other than God. We are to use the world in order to enjoy God in complete love, as the world is a pledge of love from the One who alone satisfies. Augustine closes the sermon with the ramification of what we love. We become what we most love, what we really enjoy. "Do you love the earth?" Augustine asks.[103] If so, you will become earth. Augustine then extends the principle further, "Do you love God? What shall I say? Will you be a god? I dare not say this on my own. Let us hear Scripture: 'I have said, "You are gods and sons of the Most High, all of you (Ps 81[82]:6; Jn 10:34)."[104] Augustine then concludes, "If, then, you wish to be gods and sons of the Most High, 'Love not the world, nor the things of this world' (1 Jn 2:15)."[105]

99 *Homilies on 1 John* 2.11 (SC 75, 174; Rettig, 154).

100 *Homilies on 1 John* 2.11 (SC 75, 174; Rettig, 154 [alt.]).

101 *Homilies on 1 John* 2.11 (SC 75, 174; Rettig, 154 [alt.]).

102 *Homilies on 1 John* 2.11 (SC 75, 174; Rettig, 154).

103 *Homilies on 1 John* 2.14 (SC 75, 180; Rettig, 158).

104 *Homilies on 1 John* 2.14 (SC 75, 180; Rettig, 158).

105 *Homilies on 1 John* 2.14 (SC 75, 180; Rettig, 158). For analysis, see David Vincent Meconi, SJ, "Becoming Gods by Becoming God's: Augustine's Mystagogy of Identification," *AugStud* 39, no. 1 (2008): 61–74, at 71. Cf. the superb monograph of David Vincent Meconi,

Baptism and the Life of Love

As we have seen, one of the most pressing pastoral problems of the Church in North Africa during Augustine's time was the Donatist schism. Augustine repeatedly preaches on 1 John to address this problem. One feature of his pastoral solution was to preach on baptism and to distinguish baptism's character, or indelible mark, from the sacrament's fruitfulness in Christian life. After all, how can people be Christians if they do not show forth Christian love in their lives?

Augustine touches upon the sacrament of baptism in *Homilies* 5 and 6. The former homily addresses 1 Jn 3:9–18, where we read, "Everyone who has been born of God commits no sin." The latter homily addresses 1 Jn 3:18–4:3, which says, "Most beloved, do not believe every spirit; but test the spirits if they are of God." For each, Augustine gives a teaching on love in daily life related to baptism.

When treating "perfect love" in *Homily* 5, the love that makes us sinless and impels us to be willing to lay down our lives for our brethren, Augustine asserts that those born of God have such love. After all, 1 John teaches that "everyone who has been born of God commits no sin" (1 Jn 3:9). But its meaning is not clear. Augustine preaches that the baptized have the sacrament of birth, a great, divine, holy, ineffable sacrament. That sacrament makes a new human being through the remission of sins. Augustine wants newly baptized persons to attend to their heart, to see if they really do have love. They assuredly have the character, or mark of baptism, but—to invoke the Roman military understanding of "character" as a brand on soldiers—they may have become deserters. To those who claim, "I have the sacrament," Augustine replies with a form of St. Paul's message to the Corinthians: "If I should know all the sacraments,

---

SJ, *The One Christ: St. Augustine's Theology of Deification* (Washington, DC: The Catholic University of America Press, 2013).

and have all faith so that I could move mountains, but I have not love, I am nothing" (cf. 1 Cor 13:2).[106]

Augustine continues with the observation that the distinctiveness of love is what is most important in Christian life. Love alone, he says, distinguishes the children of God from the children of the devil. All may sign themselves with the cross. All may respond "Amen." All may chant "Alleluia." But that is not what establishes the real difference:

> Let them all be baptized, enter the churches, build the walls of basilicas. The children of God are not distinguished from the children of the devil except by love. They who have love have been born of God. They who do not have it have not been born of God.[107]

Augustine repeatedly stresses this all-important idea. "You, by your deeds, show yourself a Christian," Augustine preaches. "For if you do not show yourself a Christian by your deeds, even if all should call you a Christian, what good does the name do you where the reality [*res*] is not found?"[108] The preacher brings this homily to a conclusion by quoting John, "Little children, let us love not only by word and tongue, but by work and truth" (1 Jn 3:18), with a further exhortation to love.

The following tractate, *Homily* 6, continues on the next day of the Easter octave with that same verse of 1 Jn 3:18 and moves through the letter to 1 Jn 4:3. Augustine gives special attention to "In this we know that he abides in us by the Spirit whom he has given us" (1 Jn 3:24). As he so frequently does, Augustine recalls Rom 5:5, "The love of God has been poured into our hearts through the Holy Spirit given to us," and speaks of the Pentecostal experience

106 *Homilies on 1 John* 5.6 (SC 75, 258; Rettig, 190 [alt.]).
107 *Homilies on 1 John* 5.7 (SC 75, 260; Rettig, 192 [alt.]).
108 *Homilies on 1 John* 5.17 (SC 75, 270; Rettig, 196).

of disciples. Augustine advises: "If you wish to know that you have received the Holy Spirit, question your heart, in case you have the sacrament and do not have the power of the sacrament."[109] The test is whether we really love our brothers and sisters.

Augustine then underscores how this love is an ecclesial love that goes beyond a common faith in the incarnation of the Word to a common love in the Church that avoids all heresies and schisms. Augustine appeals to 1 Jn 4:2–3: "In this the Spirit of God is known. Every spirit that confesses that Jesus Christ has come in the flesh is of God. And every spirit that does not confess that Jesus Christ has come in the flesh is not of God, and this is the Antichrist of whom you have heard that he is going to come, and he is now in this world."[110] Augustine recalls for his people that "the Word was made flesh" is believed by all sort of heretics, whose names may not be commonly known today: Arians, Eunomians [Anomeans], Macedonians [Pneumatomachians], Cataphrygians [Montanists], and Novatians. All of these have John's account of the Gospel. Does that mean that they confess Jesus Christ come in the flesh? No. Why? Because they have severed love in the Church. Augustine reminds his people of the reason for the incarnation: "Love brought him to the flesh. Therefore, whoever does not have love denies that Christ has come in the flesh."[111] Augustine then maps out an interrogation for those heretics who believe in the incarnation, but deny its very purpose, love, by severing themselves from God and the Church:

> Here, right now, question all heretics. Has Christ come in the flesh? "He has come; I believe this, I confess this." No, rather you deny this. "How do I deny? You hear me say this." No, rather

109 *Homilies on 1 John* 6.10 (SC 75, 300; Rettig, 209).

110 For a study on the Antichrist in Augustine's thinking, see Augustine Marie Reisenauer, OP, "Christ Examining, Excommunicating, and Exorcising the Antichrist in Augustine's *Homilies on the First Epistle of John*," in *Praedicatio Patrum: Studies on Preaching in Late Antique North Africa*, eds. Gert Partoens, Anthony Dupont, and Shari Boodts, 315–49.

111 *Homilies on 1 John* 6.13 (SC 75, 308; Rettig, 214).

> I convict you of denying it. You say it with a word, you deny it in your heart; you say it with words, you deny it in acts. "How," you say, "do I deny it in acts?" Because Christ came in the flesh precisely that he might die for us. He died for us precisely because he taught much love. "Greater love than this no one has than that he lay down his life for his friends" (Jn 15:13). You do not have love because for your own honor you divide unity.[112]

Augustine here not only counters those who are outside the Church through their acts of schism and heresy, but also those who seem to be inside, but have not love. "Many within are only seemingly within, but no one is outside unless truly outside."[113] He preaches, as we must remember, that the Church may have many who love in the Word enfleshed.

Love of One's Enemies

"Love, a sweet word but a sweeter act," begins *Homily* 8.[114] Here Augustine expounds on 1 Jn 4:12–16, which includes "No one has ever seen God. Yet, if we love one another, God remains in us, and his love is brought to perfection in us" (1 Jn 4:12). He addresses a seeming omission in the epistle's treatment of love. The epistle speaks much about love of "brother." But what about one's enemy? Augustine tells his people that they have heard from the Lord that they should love their enemies (cf. Mt 5:43–48). How can the epistle teach us about loving our enemies?

As a preacher with a gift for vivid images, Augustine first illustrates love with a fire. A fire extends to what is closest to it. Likewise, in loving our neighbors, we first love those close to us, then those we do not know who are not hostile to us, and then those who are hostile to us. Only gradually can we love those farthest away from us.

112 *Homilies on 1 John* 6.13 (SC 75, 308; Rettig, 214).
113 *Homilies on 1 John* 6.13 (SC 75, 308; Rettig, 214–15).
114 *Homilies on 1 John* 8.1 (SC 75, 338; Rettig, 228).

Augustine also calls to mind how our love of neighbor is not meant to be the kind of love that uses the neighbor for selfish purposes. He adduces the analogy of one who loves to eat a lot and says, "I love thrushes."[115] That one loves those birds in order to consume them. Do we love others as to consume them? Our love is meant to be a kind of benevolence that truly helps our neighbors. When we love the poor, we do not wish that they continue in their poverty. "You give bread to a hungry person," Augustine says, "but it would be better were no one hungry, and you could give it to no one."[116] In this way, we do not want to be over other people in pride, but rather want all to be equal. In fact, you can say that we want the works of mercy to cease, because we want the misery of others to cease. When there is no more need, the fire of love will not cease, but will continue to burn. Clearly for Augustine, we do not selfishly use people when we love rightly, but we want what is best for them. We want them, above all else, to enjoy God.

So how do we love our enemies? Augustine turns to the image of a sculptor using wood. That artist sees the wood as it is as well as its potential to be formed. There is the love for a possibility of what

115 *Homilies on 1 John* 8.5 (SC 75, 348; Rettig, 234).

116 *Homilies on 1 John* 8.5 (SC 75, 348; Rettig, 234). Jennifer Herdt rightly comments that the poor "are very far from being a mere means to sanctification for Augustine." See Jennifer A. Herdt, "Eudaimonism and Dispossession: Augustine on Almsgiving," in *Augustine and Social Justice*, eds. Teresa Delgado, John Doody, and Kim Paffenroth, ACTI (Lanham, MD: Lexington Books, 2015), 97–112, at 109. For more on this allegation, as leveled at Leo the Great, see the following chapter of this book. For more from Augustine's preaching, consider this: "There's this too that I must advise Your Holiness about: you should know that you perform a double work of mercy if you give something to the poor in such a way that you give it yourself. What's called for, you see, is not only the kindness of lavishing assistance, but also the humility of lending a helping hand. I don't know how it is, my brothers and sisters, but the spirit of the person who actually hands something to a poor man experiences a kind of sympathy with common humanity and infirmity, when the hand of the one who has is actually placed in the hand of the one who is in need. Although the one is giving, the other receiving, the one being attended to and the one attending are being joined in a real relationship. You see, it isn't calamity that really unites us but humility" (*s.* 259.5; PL 38:1200; WSA III/7, Hill, 181 [alt.]). Hill's translation has "it isn't calamity that really unites us but humanity." Presumably he read *humanitas* as the sentence's last word, but PL 38:1200 has *humilitas*.

may come to be. This is God's creative love for us sinners.[117] Jesus came not for the healthy, but for the sick so that they might become healthy. Christ himself forgave his enemies from the wood of the cross, loving us creatively so that we might be his friends. By the blood of his cross, the Lord turned his enemies into his friends—and we are to follow this example. A physician does not love the illness afflicting the sick, but works to alleviate the illness. Likewise, we love our enemies creatively. Moreover, this love perfects *us* who are called to love our enemies. "Have you begun to love?" asks Augustine. "God has begun to dwell in you; love him who has begun to dwell in you that by indwelling more perfectly he may make you perfected."[118] We were the ones who were ill, and now the Physician has healed our illness and empowered us to love as he loves.

This mutuality between God and us is radically unequal when we begin to love as God loves. John says, "God is love. And he who abides in love abides in God, and God abides in him." Augustine explains: "They abide mutually in one another, he who holds and he who is held. You dwell in God, but that you may be held; God dwells in you, but that he may hold you; that you may not fall."[119] In other words, God's dwelling within us does not make him subject to us in the way that we are held within a house. If a house is destroyed, those within the house fall. God is not contained like that within us. He is whole if we abandon him, and he is whole if we return to him. God never increases nor needs his creation. Augustine stresses, "He seeks nothing from us, and he sought us when we were not seeking him."[120] He is the Shepherd who has found the lost sheep, rejoices

117 A similar argument is made in *Homilies on 1 John* 9.9 regarding "Let us love because he has first loved us" (1 Jn 4:19). Augustine there speaks of God as always beautiful, as the one who has re-formed us, who were ugly and misshapen, to be beautiful by his love: "The more love increases in you, the more beauty increases; for love itself is the soul's beauty" (SC 75, 398; Rettig, 258).

118 *Homilies on 1 John* 8.12 (SC 75, 366; Rettig, 243).

119 *Homilies on 1 John* 8.14 (SC 75, 368; Rettig, 244).

120 *Homilies on 1 John* 8.14 (SC 75, 370; Rettig, 245).

with it, and carries it on his shoulders. God's creative love propels us, as we see in these *Homilies on 1 John*, to the perfection of loving even our enemies.

Conclusion

With five million extant words from Augustine, who esteemed love to be paramount in Christian life, this chapter has hardly exhausted Augustine's thinking on the power of love. We focused on two texts. In *On Christian Teaching*, we saw that Scripture, so formative for a life of love, must be interpreted by the double-love command. One who treats the Scriptures must always go back to the rule of love to interpret difficult passages and then hand over to others through love what God wants. In the *Homilies on 1 John*, we went back to an Easter Octave when Augustine was troubled by the Donatist schism to hear how Augustine teaches his people to overcome adversities through the love preached in the New Testament. Repeatedly, Augustine turns to love to address all the various needs and desires of the Christian life. Because God is love, that love has been enfleshed so that we might live rightly. As Rowan Williams, one of the most eloquent teachers of Augustine, has written in summarizing Augustine on love: "If we try to love human beings independently of loving God, we ignore what they are."[121]

We conclude this treatment of Augustine with a difficult matter: love amidst scandalous allegations against the clergy and religious. Our own times of scandals is not unique in Christian history. Augustine dealt with several scandals during his episcopal ministry.[122] He himself had been accused of giving some sort of drug

121 Rowan Williams, chap. 11, "Augustinian Love," in his collection *On Augustine* (London: Bloomsbury, 2016), 191–206, at 200.

122 David G. Hunter, "Between Discipline and Doctrine: Augustine's Response to Clerical Misconduct," *AugStud* 51, no. 1 (2020): 3–22. On p. 6, Hunter finds the following principles in Augustine's dealing with misconduct: (1) Decisive action that usually resulted

or love potion to a married woman. A false accusation seems to have been spread by none other than Bishop Megalius of Calama, Primate of Numidia, who consecrated Augustine a bishop. Megalius later apologized for the accusation, but the Donatists seem to have used it among other accusations against Augustine.[123] Clergy, following the apostle Paul, have become "a spectacle to the world" (1 Cor 4:9), and Augustine observes in one homily on his clergy: "those who love us seek what they may praise in us, while those who hate us tear us to pieces."[124] In one scandal, a priest by the name of Boniface accused a monk by the name of Spes of a sexual sin, and Spes (who was seeking an ecclesiastical office) responded by accusing Boniface of sin. Their accusations were made public. The manner in which Augustine dealt with this misconduct, and other forms of clerical/religious misconduct, can serve as a model for today.

Augustine wanted everyone to know the facts that could be shared, including the inability to determine what had happened. He hoped that the Lord would bring to light who the guilty party was

in removal of the offenders from the clergy; (2) Concern for the rights of the victim over clerical privilege; (3) A just hearing for the accused clergyman; (4) Concern for transparency in all proceedings; and (5) Personal accountability of the bishop for the behavior of his clergy. In at least one case, Augustine considered resigning from his position as Bishop of Hippo. The mistake he made was to promote Antoninus of Fussala, a young man who had grown up in his monastery, to be a bishop at the age of 20. Such confidence did not turn out well in this man who became swollen in pride. In *ep.* 209.10, he tells Pope Celestine that he would "consider withdrawing from the office of administering the episcopacy" and devoting himself to lamentations for his mistake (PL 33:956; WSA II/3, Teske, 397). This chapter's conclusion is indebted to Hunter's invaluable and timely research.

123 Peter Brown, *Augustine of Hippo: A Biography*, rev. ed. (Berkeley and Los Angeles: University of California Press, 2000), 198–99; Hermanowicz, *Possidius of Calama*, 35–36. See *Against the Letters of Petilian* 3.16.19: "Let him [Petilian] dishonor the blessed bread [not the Eucharist, but blessed at the liturgy for distribution], distributed simply and joyously, with a term of poisonous wickedness and madness, and let him think so poorly of your intelligence that he would presume that it could be believed to be a love potion given to a woman not only with her husband's knowledge but even with his approval. Let him count against me what the man who was going to ordain me to the episcopacy wrote angrily about me when I was still a presbyter, but that he sought and received pardon from a holy council for having sinned against us in this way he does not wish to count in my favor" (WSA I/21, Tilley and Ramsey, 216).

124 *S.* 356.1, preached in 426 (*Sermones Selecti* 18, Lambot, 132; Hill, 173 [alt.]).

in this sordid case. In dealing with this scandal, he pondered the Matthean verse: "Because injustice will become abundant, the love of many will grow cold" (Mt 24:12). Augustine noted that the Lord continues, "But whoever perseveres up to the end will be saved" (Mt 24:13). Augustine does not want the people's love to grow cold, but at the same time he knows that they must acknowledge the seriousness of the evil confronting them. He says, "Hence, my dearest people, in this scandal because of which some are disturbed about the priest, Boniface, I do not say to you that you should not grieve. For the love of Christ is not present in those who do not grieve over these things."[125] The grief should prompt the people to grow in love—regardless of the scandalous details concerning the priest and the monk. "Grieve over these things because they should be grieved over, still not so that because of that grief your love grows cold in living well, but so that it is inflamed to beseech the Lord," exhorts Augustine.[126] Love is to be inflamed more and more even when people are grieved by scandalous reports concerning those prominently called to give them the Word in life and in speech. The love of Christ allows us to grieve and to take action, especially the action of turning to the Lord.

Now in the next chapter, we see how the Word through Leo the Great turns our attention in love to those in greatest need, the poor and the weak.

125 *Ep.* 78.2 (CCL 31A, 84; WSA II/1, Teske, 308).
126 *Ep.* 78.2 (CCL 31A, 84; WSA II/1, Teske, 304).

CHAPTER 6

LEO THE GREAT

The Word in Our Flesh for Loving the Poor and the Weak

When James, Peter, and John spoke to Paul and Barnabas in Jerusalem, they entered into a partnership so that Paul and Barnabas would go to the Gentiles. Paul then relates to the Galatians the one condition insisted on by James, Peter, and John: "Only, we were to be mindful of the poor, which is the very thing I was eager to do" (Gal 2:10). When Paul wants the Corinthians to give to a collection for the poor, he says: "I say this not by way of command, but to test the genuineness of your love by your concern for others. For you know the gracious act of our Lord Jesus Christ, that for your sake he became poor although he was rich, so that by his poverty you might become rich" (2 Cor 8:8–9).

In proclaiming the joy of the Gospel, Pope Francis teaches, "God's heart has a special place for the poor, so much so that he himself 'became poor' (2 Cor 8:9). The entire history of our redemption is marked by the presence of the poor. Salvation came to us from the 'yes' uttered by a lowly maiden from a small town on the fringes of a great empire." Pope Francis continues:

> The Savior was born in a manger, in the midst of animals, like children of poor families; he was presented at the Temple along with two turtledoves, the offering made by those who could not afford a lamb (cf. Lk 2:24; Lv 5:7); he was raised in a home of ordinary workers and worked with his own hands to earn his bread.

Pope Francis then focuses on Christ's preaching:

> When he began to preach the Kingdom, crowds of the dispossessed followed him, illustrating his words: "The Spirit of the Lord is upon me, because he has anointed me to preach good news to the poor" (Lk 4:18). He assured those burdened by sorrow and crushed by poverty that God has a special place for them in his heart: "Blessed are you poor, yours is the kingdom of God" (Lk 6:20); he made himself one of them: "I was hungry and you gave me food to eat," and he taught them that mercy towards all of these is the key to heaven (cf. Mt 25:5ff.).

The Pope draws this conclusion for us:

> For the Church, the option for the poor is primarily a theological category rather than a cultural, sociological, political or philosophical one. God shows the poor "his first mercy."[1]

Pope Francis's words are in continuity with the Gospel and an ancient tradition of papal preaching. We can, in our work on the incarnation, deification, and proclamation, look back to the evangelistic teaching about loving the poor and the weak by his predecessor of Bishop of Rome at the time of the Council of Chalcedon (451): Leo the Great (d. 461).

1 Pope Francis, *Evangelii Gaudium*, Apostolic Exhortation on the Proclamation of the Gospel in Today's World, November 24, 2013, nos. 197–98.

The Word in Leo's Flesh for Us

"Almsgiving is a work of love, and we know that 'love covers a multitude of sins' (Prv 10:12; 1 Pt 4:8)," preaches Leo the Great.[2] In its emphasis on love of neighbor, early Christian life gave special prominence to assisting those in need. That is, after all, what the merciful God does. In their typically incarnational way of thinking, early Christians believed in Jesus—and so gave to the poor for his sake. Jesus preaches, "If you wish to be perfect, go, sell what you have and give to the poor, and you will have treasure in heaven. Then come, follow me" (Mt 19:21). Basil the Great, Gregory of Nazianzus, and Gregory of Nyssa give eloquent testimony to preaching about the poor in Cappadocia.[3] John Chrysostom may be the most well-known preacher on poverty in early Christianity.[4] Augustine of Hippo proclaimed to his people the line from Mt 25:31–46, "When you did it for one of my least ones, you did it for me." He then commented, "I confess, that in God's Scripture, this has moved me the most."[5] These examples of preaching on loving the poor communicate the heart of the Christian life, as they show

2 *Tr.* 7.1 (CCL 138, 29; Freeland and Conway, 36). A sermon from Leo is customarily known in Latin as a *tractatus*.

3 See Holman, *The Hungry Are Dying*. My favorite instance of Cappadocian preaching about the poor is Gregory of Nazianzus's *or.* 14, *On Love of the Poor*. A translation can be found in Daley, *Gregory of Nazianzus*, 76–97.

4 As we saw in Chapter 4, Chrysostom frequently draws attention to care for the poor in his preaching. Most of *sermons* 1–4 and 6–7 on Lazarus and the rich man are translated in *St. John Chrysostom: On Wealth and Poverty*, translated by Catharine Roth, PPS (Crestwood, NY: St. Vladimir's Seminary Press, 1984).

5 *Sermo* 389.5, edited by C. Lambot in *RevBen* 58 (1948): 43–52, at 49: *quod me fateor in scriptura Dei plurimum mouit*. Cf. Allan D. Fitzgerald, OSA, "Mercy, Works of Mercy," in *Augustine through the Ages: An Encyclopedia*, ed. Allan D. Fitzgerald, OSA (Grand Rapids, MI: Eerdmans, 1999), 557–61. Edmund Hill, OP, translates it differently: "something which I confess has exercised me no little in God's scriptures." See WSA III/10, Hill, 409. For a study, see Andrew Hofer, OP, "Matthew 25:31–46 as an Hermeneutical Rule in Augustine's *Enarrationes in Psalmos*," *DR* 126 (2008): 285–300. For the relevance of this Matthean passage to Mother Teresa within a western tradition, see Andrew Hofer, OP. "Augustine, Aquinas, Thérèse, and the Mysticism of Mother Teresa's Five-Finger Gospel," in *Mother Teresa and the Mystics: Toward a Renewal of Spiritual Theology*, eds. Michael Dauphinais, Brian Kolodiejchuk, MC, and Roger Nutt (Ave Maria, FL: Sapientia Press, 2018), 79–101.

us in a powerful way "faith working through love" (Gal 5:6). They show us how Christ remains present in those who suffer and those who care for them. But no bishop in the early Church dwelt, proportionally in his preaching, as much on almsgiving to the poor as Leo the Great.[6] The significance of his love for the poor has great significance for understanding the Word in his life and his preaching on care for those in need.

Richard Finn writes, "Sermons were the most important way in which promoters of almsgiving advanced their cause."[7] The pervasiveness of the theme of almsgiving in patristic preaching makes it one of the most frequent topics in fourth- and fifth-century sermons. Recognizing the hazards of classifying sermons, which may have elements of more than one category, Finn ventures the following classification, which is helpful for seeing the magnitude and range of the theme of care for the poor in patristic preaching:

> (1) sermons devoted essentially to the promotion of almsgiving;
> (2) sermons on wealth and poverty in which almsgiving is a major theme, but in which the preacher also tackles related issues of avarice and pride;
> (3) other sermons in which almsgiving is one of several important topics;
> (4) sermons in which almsgiving is promoted in conclusion to a sermon on some other topic, such as the need for repentance;
> (5) sermons in which almsgiving is briefly promoted, as it were, in passing.[8]

6 Bernard Green, OSB, *The Soteriology of Leo the Great*, OTRM (Oxford: Oxford University Press, 2008), 85; cf. Finn, *Almsgiving in the Later Roman Empire*, 147–59.

7 Finn, *Almsgiving in the Later Roman Empire*, 137.

8 Finn, *Almsgiving in the Later Roman Empire*, 146.

Of Leo's ninety-seven extant sermons, about forty feature exhortations to this work of charity, while several others mention it in various other ways as Finn outlines above.[9] Those most explicitly dedicated to care for the poor deal with the annual collections (*tr.* 6–11) as well as days of fast in December (*tr.* 12–20), in Lent (*tr.* 39–50), after Pentecost Sunday (*tr.* 75–81), and in September (*tr.* 86–94). But one can find additional references in other groups of sermons, such as on the Passion of the Lord (*tr.* 52–72) or in sermons not united by classification, such as his sermon on the feast of St. Lawrence (*tr.* 85) or his sermon on the Beatitudes (*tr.* 95).

Leo is the first Bishop of Rome whose homilies are preserved.[10] By this preservation, his homilies become a model for future generations, but we should not forget that his preaching on love of the poor communicates his response to the concrete needs of real poor people in Rome. For context, we might recall that Augustine died in 430 while the Vandals were besieging his beloved city of Hippo, which succumbed to them the following year; the great Carthage likewise fell in 439. Italy's not too distant neighbor to the south by Mediterranean voyage, North Africa, had received refugees from Rome around the time of the Visigothic sack of the "Eternal City" in August 410, and regularly provided much grain to Rome. Now, in Leo's time, the North African lands were sending refugees to Rome. Leo became Bishop of Rome on September 29, 440.

Bronwen Neil surmises, "In the first year of his pontificate, then, Leo would have had to deal with the effects of a shortage of food and an influx of North African refugees."[11] Before that first year of his pontificate, Leo the Great had been a deacon whose service would

9 Cf. C. Lepelley, "Saint Léon le Grand et la Cité Romaine," *RevSR* 35 (1961): 130–50, esp. 134, and Green, *Soteriology of Leo the Great*, 85.

10 Geoffrey D. Dunn, "Rhetoric in the Patristic Sermons of Late Antiquity," in *Preaching in the Patristic Era*, eds. Dupont, Boodts, Partoens, and Leemans, 103–34, at 120.

11 Neil, *Leo the Great*, 7.

have especially entailed work for the poor, as he himself preaches about the most famous deacon of Rome, the martyr Lawrence.[12]

Throughout his episcopal ministry, Leo expressed a strong sense of God's presence in all the faithful and especially in the poor. On his first anniversary of becoming a bishop, he preached: "I do not doubt that we are visited by a more abundant grace of the divine presence today, when at the same time are present, and with one light sparkle, so many most beautiful tabernacles of God, so many most excellent members of the body of Christ."[13] His pontificate until his death on November 10, 461 was of incalculable service to protecting the life of Christ in Christian lives. He led with extraordinary strength and showed great solicitude for the vulnerable. Leo was the kind of person who could stand up to Attila the Hun, which he did in 452.

He wanted other preachers to rely on Christ in the face of difficulties. Rusticus, Bishop of Narbonne, had written to Leo about various scandals in the Church. The weight of his office seemed too heavy to Rusticus. He told Leo that he wanted to be freed from his episcopal labors and to live in silence rather than handle such problems. In reply, Leo urged Rusticus not to abandon his duty:

> Christ is our counsel and our strength; without him we can do nothing, through him we can do all things. While confirming the preachers of the Gospel and the ministers of the sacraments, he said: "Behold, I am with you all days, even unto the consummation of the world" (Mt 28:20); and, again, he said: "These things I have spoken to you that in me you may have peace. In the world you will have affliction. But take courage, I have overcome the world" (Jn 16:33). Since these promises have been clearly manifested, we must not be weakened by any scandals. Otherwise, we may seem to be ungrateful for having

12 *Tr.* 85.

13 *Tr.* 2.2 (CCL 138, 8; my translation).

> been chosen by God, whose assistance is as powerful as his promises are true.[14]

As for non-sermon writings from Leo, we have only letters such as this one to Rusticus. 143 letters from Leo are considered genuine; they cover many of the disciplinary and doctrinal matters needing Leo's attention, who often has recourse to arguments of Scripture or the practices found in tradition to address contemporary situations.[15] He frequently corrects errors in liturgical, disciplinary, and doctrinal matters. Leo's letters are perhaps most famous for his teaching and corrections concerning Christological doctrine. His highly influential *Tome to Flavian*, which is his *ep.* 28 (dated June 13, 449), was read out at the Council of Chalcedon (451).[16] After hearing Leo's *Tome*, the Fathers at Chalcedon cried out, "Peter has spoken through Leo." They also cried out such things as "Cyril taught accordingly. Eternal is the memory of Cyril. Leo and Cyril taught the same. Leo and Cyril taught accordingly."[17] The council thought that Leo's faith was the same as Peter's, and Leo certainly saw himself as Peter's unworthy heir as head of the Church of Rome.[18] The council also saw him as continuing the faith of Cyril, who had led the previous ecumenical council, the Council of Ephesus (431). Some scholars would prefer to separate Cyril and Leo as having

14 Leo the Great, *ep.* 167, to Rusticus, Bishop of Narbonne (PL 54:1201–2; Hunt, 290–91 [alt.], cf. Neil, 141).

15 For an overview of Leo's letters, see *St. Leo the Great: Letters*, translated by Edmund Hunt, FC 34 (Washington, DC: The Catholic University of America Press, 1957), 5–11, and Bronwen Neil, "Papal Letters and Letter Collections," in *Late Antique Letter Collections: A Critical Introduction and Reference Guide*, eds. Cristiana Sogno, Bradley K. Storin, and Edward J. Watts (Oakland, CA: University of California Press, 2017), 449–66, especially 455–57.

16 For text and translation, see *DEC* 1, 77–82. For another English translation, see Neil, *Leo the Great*, 96–103.

17 Chalcedon, Second Session, 23 in *The Acts of the Council of Chalcedon*, vol. 2, translated by Richard Price and Michael Gaddis, reprint with minor corrections (Liverpool: Liverpool University, 2007), 24–25.

18 See examples in his sermons on his "birthday" (*dies natalis*), the anniversary of his episcopal ordination as Bishop of Rome: *tr.* 2.2, 3.3–4; 4.2–4; 5.4.

very different Christological teachings, but the conciliar tradition after Chalcedon stressed their unity in communicating the same faith.[19] Leo would continue to write about the mystery of Christ with great effect, especially in his letter to the Palestinian monks, *ep.* 124, written in 453, nearly two years after Chalcedon and taking more fully into account the opposed errors of Nestorianism and Eutychianism.[20]

In his preaching against Manicheanism (which denies the goodness of physical creation and does not believe that the Savior is truly human) and against Eutychianism (which does not recognize a human nature present after the incarnation of the Word), Leo showed great sensitivity to Christ's humanity and to what it means to be human, especially to be humans in Christ. For example, his first sermon on the Nativity of the Lord is renowned. It emphasizes the Christian dignity of being deified:

> Realize, O Christian, your dignity. Once made a "partaker in the divine nature," do not return to your former baseness by an unworthy life. Remember whose head it is and whose body of which you constitute a member.[21]

See, for another instance, how radical an understanding he has of deification, based on his view of the dignity of those to whom he preached:

> Taken up by Christ and taking on Christ, then, we are not the same after the purification of baptism as we were before

19 For an illuminating study that counters scholarship of Cyril and Leo as contrasts, see Daniel A. Keating, "Christology in Cyril and Leo: Unnoticed Parallels and Ironies," *StPatr* 48 (2010): 53–58. For Constantinople III's citing Cyril and Leo together as authorities, see its *Exposition of Faith* in Tanner 1.127 and 129.

20 For a translation, see Neil, *Leo the Great*, 106–12. *Ep.* 124 was later reworked and sent as *ep.* 165, to Emperor Leo.

21 *Tr.* 21.3 (CCL 138, 88; Freeland and Conway, 79 [alt.]).

> it. Instead, the body of the reborn becomes the flesh of the Crucified.[22]

That is an extraordinary recognition of the Christian faithful's dignity and how their lives are so configured to the cross that their bodies become the flesh of the *Crucified.*

In his emphasis on the human body, Leo the Great exemplifies the union of doctrine and pastoral practice. Observing that the tension "often encountered in modern theology between orthodoxy and orthopraxis was annihilated by Leo," Bronwen Neil helpfully summarizes one of the major achievements of Leo's sermons:

> Orthodox faith is useless without practical charity, but practical charity needs to be grounded in orthodox faith if it is to lead to assimilation to the divine. In this way Leo succeeds in uniting the intensely spiritual theology of 'divinisation' which we encounter in Greek writers such as Athanasius of Alexandria and Gregory of Nyssa with the penetrating social vision of a Latin author like Salvian of Marseilles, and so presents us with a theology—and a spirituality—which is simultaneously mystical, dogmatic and thoroughly practical.[23]

Leo's preaching expresses that early Christians gave because they had received from Jesus, so almsgiving (or not) was a test case for their orthodoxy. Not only did serving the poor accompany the claim to right faith in Christ; the allegation of neglect of the poor came with the charge of heresy. Just a few decades after the apostle Paul, Ignatius, Bishop of Antioch, depicted Docetists, who hold that Christ only seemed to be but was in fact not bodily, as neglecting the poor. Ignatius writes to the Smyrneans, "Examine closely those

22 *Tr.* 63.6 (CCL 138A, 387; Freeland and Conway, 276 [alt.]).

23 Bronwen Neil, "Leo Magnus," in *Preaching in the Patristic Era*, eds. Dupont, Boodts, Partoens, Leemans, 327–46, at 341. Neil credits J. Mark Armitage, *A Twofold Solidarity: Leo the Great's Theology of Redemption*, Early Christian Studies, no. 9 (Strathfield: St. Paul's Publications in association with the Centre for Early Christian Studies, 2005), 230. But Neil's own insight should be duly credited.

who are heterodox about the grace of Jesus Christ which has come to us, how opposed they are to the mind of God. For love they care not: not for the widow, not for the orphan, not for the oppressed, not for the captive or for the released, not for the hungry or for the thirsty."[24] As Richard Finn notes about other ancient contexts, early Christians who wanted to be known as doctrinally orthodox promoted almsgiving.[25] Rather than seeing a tension between doctrine and mercy, early Christians considered them both to be of the greatest necessity—and both were about the incarnation and bodily salvation.

Leo's preaching has been described by one eminent scholar as "cold logic and a rather detached presence" with the assessment that "his intellectualism may make good theological reading but perhaps poor stimulation."[26] Francis X. Murphy, on the other hand, writes: "Leo frequently exhibits a joyful enthusiasm in explaining the intricacies of the faith; and in his cautions against the temptations of the evil one, or his stimulation to almsgiving and charity, there is a realism that reveals the depth of his own feelings and the perspicacity of his psychic understanding of human nature."[27] Bronwen Neil insightfully points out that Leo saw his duty as a preacher to show that the mysteries celebrated are present reality for believers.[28] Leo, after all, famously preaches, "What was to be seen of our Redeemer has passed over into the sacraments."[29] Consider, also,

24 Ignatius of Antioch, *Letter to the Smyrneans* 6.2 (LCL 24, 302; my translation, cf. Ehrman, 303).

25 Richard Finn, OP, *Almsgiving in the Later Roman Empire: Christian Promotion and Practice (313–450)*, OCM (Oxford: Oxford University, 2006), 130–31.

26 Dunn, "Rhetoric in the Patristic Sermons of Late Antiquity," 126.

27 Francis X. Murphy, CSSR., "The Sermons of Pope Leo the Great: Content and Style," in *Preaching in the Patristic Age*, ed. Hunter, 183–97, at 185–86.

28 Bronwen Neil, "Leo Magnus," in *Preaching in the Patristic Era*, eds. Dupont, Boodts, Partoens, and Leemans, 327–46, at 332–33.

29 *Tr.* 74.2 (CCL 138A, 456; Freeland and Conway, 326 [alt.]). In this passage, Leo stresses both the exterior authority of *doctrina* and the interior illumination given from heaven.

what Leo says at the beginning of an Epiphany sermon concerning his office as a preacher:

> I must meet your expectations by fulfilling the priestly duty of a sermon [*sacerdotalis sermonis officium*] on this most sacred day. I will try—as much as I can with the help of God's Spirit—to go along the paths of understanding, until we arrive at a realization of the fact that the mystery of this feast pertains to the times of all believers and until that which had been adored of old in the planned arrangement should not in any way be considered remote.[30]

In our retrieval of patristic preaching on loving the poor and the weak, we turn to a serious allegation against Leo's preaching: it dehumanizes the poor.

Is Leo's preaching dehumanizing to the poor?

In an influential 1982 study, Boniface Ramsey offers a critical evaluation of almsgiving in the Latin Church in the late fourth and early fifth centuries: He writes, "Rarely, it seems, do the poor themselves take on a personality in the writings of this period. They exist—so it is frequently stated in one way or another—for the sake of the rich, to offer them opportunities for beneficence or to test them."[31] Ramsey continues: "There are very few sympathetic depictions of the underprivileged, portraying them as human beings with particular needs and desires of their own, as persons in their own right"[32] And he suggests "that the very concept of the identification of Christ and the poor, at least as some of the Fathers develop it, tended to work

30 *Tr.* 38.1 (CCL 138, 205; Freeland and Conway, 162 [alt.]).

31 Boniface Ramsey, OP, "Almsgiving in the Latin Church: The Late Fourth and Early Fifth Centuries," *TS* 43, no. 2 (1982): 226–59, at 252.

32 Ramsey, "Almsgiving in the Latin Church," 253.

against the poor by swallowing them up in him."[33] Though Ramsey concedes that "there is no doubt that this identification, along with the general biblical predisposition to favor the poor and disfavor the rich, served to ennoble the position of the underprivileged considerably," he finds that "in the Church in the West at this time, we are faced with a kind of social monophysitism that failed to give due recognition to the individual nature of the poor over against Christ."[34] Again, Ramsey's important article is about the late fourth and early fifth centuries of the Latin Church—the period just prior to Leo's episcopal ministry—and he makes some qualifications, but Ramsey still presses this serious charge of a social monophysitism that evacuates the humanity of the poor to give way to Christ.[35]

Following Ramsey's evaluation of this early period, Bronwen Neil has written several learned studies about Leo the Great's practice of taking up collections and preaching on almsgiving. Neil observes that Leo has prominence in the tradition of almsgiving: he was "the first bishop in the West to institutionalise giving to the poor through a series of collections throughout the seven regions of the city [of Rome]."[36] Leo himself explains that he was following the Fathers in doing what the apostles established.[37] But Neil finds another motivation for Leo's charitable outreach. To put it bluntly, the rich give to the poor so that the rich can go to heaven. Their so-called gifts are products of "self-interested giving."[38] In this

33 Ramsey, "Almsgiving in the Latin Church," 253.

34 Ramsey, "Almsgiving in the Latin Church," 254.

35 One qualification Ramsey gives is that for the Fathers, "the identification with Christ was the very glory of the poor, as well as a motive for almsgiving. What else, for that matter, constituted the identity of any Christian, to say nothing of the poor? And when the Fathers exaggerated the Christological theme, their intention was, after all, not theoretical so much as practical: to provide for the feeding and clothing of the poor" (259).

36 Neil, *Leo the Great*, 18. Cf. Neil, "Blessed is Poverty: Leo the Great on Almsgiving," *SE* 46 (2007): 143–56, at 148 and Neil, "Leo Magnus," at 338–39.

37 Richard Finn says of Leo's preaching on the collections that they were "no new invention in his own day." Finn, *Almsgiving in the Later Roman Empire*, 48.

38 See Neil, *Leo the Great*, 19.

understanding, for Leo and other Christian bishops of his time, the poor were "vehicles for the salvation of the rich, and they lacked social agency and legal autonomy."[39] According to Neil, in most early Christian texts, the involuntary poor are "objects of charity without any corporeal reality or thoughts and feelings of their own." She calls this a "tendency to dehumanize the poor."[40] Neil occasionally makes qualifications, but she also puts the matter this starkly in a chapter on Leo I concerning poverty: "To the question of whether Leo's poor were real persons, we must answer with a resounding negative. Leo's poor, mentioned by category of need where they are mentioned at all, do not horrify or confront his listeners and readers, nor are they meant to do so."[41]

Many scholars have given Leo a more sympathetic treatment. Gary Anderson, J. Mark Armitage, Peter Brown, Susan Wessel, and Bronwen Neil herself elsewhere speak more favorably about Leo's preaching about poverty. Because of her illuminating book-length study on Leo, I want to focus briefly on Susan Wessel, who skillfully brings out the humanity, in all its emotional fullness, in Christ (as the model of compassion), in Leo's audience, and in the poor

39 Bronwen Neil, "Models of Gift Giving in the Preaching of Leo the Great," *JECS* 18, no. 2 (2010): 225–59, at 258.

40 Neil, "Models of Gift Giving in the Preaching of Leo the Great," 254.

41 See Bronwen Neil, chap. 5 "Leo I on Poverty," in *Preaching Poverty in Late Antiquity: Perceptions and Realities*, eds. Pauline Allen, Bronwen Neil, and Wendy Mayer, AKThG (Leipzig: Evangelische Verlagsanstalt, 2009), 202. Neil continues, "Leo singles out no poor person for special mention—his poor are an anonymous mass, grouped according to their capacity to meet basic needs and their access to, or exclusion from, social networks: for example, the hungry, the sick, orphans, widows, slaves, and refugees." In another work, Neil concludes, "Leo's system of welfare, based on the idea of individual voluntary giving, ultimately did nothing to challenge the status quo whereby the elite exploited the services of a vast and cheap source of labour constituted by the poor and the very poor." See her "'*Blessed is Poverty*' Leo the Great on Almsgiving," 154. Writing on Leo's preaching, Geoffrey Dunn offers this criticism: "The benefit of almsgiving to the poor could have been demonstrated more effectively through their portrayal as real people in desperate need, but it was not, and the benefit to the donors could have been couched in graphic terms of what they stood to lose if they failed to help, but it was not." See Dunn, "Rhetoric in the Patristic Sermons of Late Antiquity," 125.

whom Christ so loves.[42] Wessel summarizes Leo's frank assessment about compassion for the poor: "Those who did not imitate Christ by emulating his humility, weakness, and suffering were not truly Christians."[43] I find this treatment highly insightful. Problematically here, however, she continues an unsatisfactory dichotomy in scholarship. She writes: "As the potential recipients of charity and compassion, the poor became the means by which everyone else might express their devotion to Christ. A delicate balance remained, therefore, between portraying the poor as an abstract class whose state of poverty made them similar to Christ, and for that reason worthy of alms, and acknowledging them as fragile individuals whose physical suffering, in and of itself, demanded a compassionate response."[44] As we will see, Leo does not make the poor merely passive recipients for "everyone else." Nor, will I argue, is Leo's way of showing the poor's conformity to Christ a matter in contrast with his acknowledgment of their individual fragility. In her subsequent writing on Leo, Wessel stresses the mutuality between Christological doctrine and charitable practice:

> There was no tension between the reality of lived experience and the theological ideals that Leo preached. The abiding quest for moral excellence helped Christians imitate Christ, while setting their sights on imitating Christ facilitated moral excellence. Christian perfection was both the grounds for, and the consequence of, acknowledging Christ as an exemplary model.[45]

42 For denial of divinization in Leo's thinking, see Susan Wessel, *Leo the Great and the Spiritual Rebuilding of a Universal Rome*, SuppVC 93 (Leiden: Brill, 2008), 251: "Divinization was not a possibility for Leo because he was committed to the idea that Christ was linked to humanity only through the complete integrity of his human nature."

43 Wessel, *Leo the Great and the Spiritual Rebuilding of a Universal Rome*, 246. Wessel cites Leo, *tr.* 25.6.

44 Wessel, *Leo the Great and the Spiritual Rebuilding of a Universal Rome*, 192.

45 Susan Wessel, *Passion and Compassion in Early Christianity* (New York: Cambridge University Press, 2016), 146.

This latter expression of Wessel's is pitch perfect.

If we continue the work done on Leo, taking this more perspicuous approach, we will be able to see more fully the ramifications of the Word made flesh for the poor according to the mind of Leo. To develop this exposition, I will unveil some principles from Leo's teaching on the incarnation and the poor. I then turn to *sermon* 9, his preaching on the beatitudes, and his preaching on Christ's cross and resurrection. What we will see in Leo's preaching is a kind of deification at work in the humanity of the poor and those, including the poor, who give alms. Against some misunderstandings in the scholarly literature, Daniel Keating has shown Leo's particular emphasis on deification, especially through the "wonderful exchange."[46] We can see further how the "wonderful exchange" between God and man in the incarnation has profound reference to the deification of our common human condition in connection to poverty. This deification does not dehumanize, but rather perfects humanity to share in God's own nature through transformation by his mercy.

Principles on the Incarnation and the Poor

Leo repeatedly describes Christ's humanity by characteristics of the poor: lowliness, humility, weakness, mortality, vulnerability, suffering, death.[47] Among all the poor, the slave or servant occupies a terribly lowly place. And Leo emphasizes that Christ has taken that place. He frequently invokes Philippians 2 to remind his people that the Son of God, who was *in forma Dei*, took on the *forma servi* in the

46 Daniel Keating, "The Wonderful Exchange: Deification in Leo the Great," in *Deification in the Latin Patristic Tradition*, ed. Jared Ortiz (Washington, D.C.: The Catholic University of America Press, 2018), 208–30.

47 E.g., *tr.* 21.2 (CCL 138, 87; Freeland and Conway, 78): "When, therefore, the identity of each substance is preserved and they join in a single Person, majesty takes up humility, strength takes up weakness, eternity takes up mortality. To pay the debt of our condition, his inviolable natures pours forth into a vulnerable one."

incarnation. In his excellent study on Leo, J. Mark Armitage writes, "Leo sees the poor as perhaps the ultimate sign of Christ's human nature, in the sense that the assumption of human *humilitas* by divine *Gloria* represents an assumption not only of human nature, but also of the *forma servi*, of the *status* of lowliness and poverty."[48]

For Leo, not only is Christ "whole in his own condition, and whole in ours" (*totus in suis, totus in nostris*),[49] but Christ is also "rich in his own condition, and poor in ours" (*dives in suis, pauper in nostris*).[50] Put otherwise, the incarnation itself is God's loving-kindness for poor humanity and within poor humanity. Leo says: "Since he made human nature his own, he exempted himself in no way from human lowliness."[51] Consider how Leo describes Christ's agony in the garden, with allusion to 2 Cor 8:9:

> Therefore in us the Lord was fearing with our terror so that he might clothe himself by taking our infirmity and might wrap our inconstancy with the solidity of his virtue. For the tradesman from heaven came into this world rich and merciful, and initiated a salvific exchange by a wondrous transaction, receiving the things that are ours and giving us the things his: honors for insults, health for sorrows, life for death.[52]

Rather than dehumanizing the poor for the sake of the eternal salvation of the rich, Leo preaches almsgiving as a virtue to be practiced by both rich and poor.[53] He does not view the poor as mere receptacles for the rich. Moreover, Leo adduces biblical stories about particular poor individuals and their circumstances.

48 Armitage, *A Twofold Solidarity*, 172.

49 He preaches that phrase in *tr.* 23.2 (CCL 138, 104) and repeats it in his *Tome to Flavian*, *ep.* 28. 3.

50 See *tr.* 91.3 (CCL 138, 567).

51 *Tr.* 10.2 (CCL 138, 42; Freeland and Conway, 44 [alt.]).

52 *Tr.* 54.4 (CCL 138A, 320; Freeland and Conway, 235 [alt.]).

53 Neil recognizes this, as she writes, "Both rich and poor were called to give alms according to their means." See Bronwen Neil, "Blessed are the Rich: Leo the Great and the Roman Poor," *StPatr* 44 (2010): 533–47, at 547.

He exalts the widow's miniscule contribution to the temple treasury in three sermons.[54] He emphasizes the reward for those who give the mere cup of cold water in three sermons ("cold water" for Fathers such as Jerome, Augustine, and Leo indicates that people do not have the money for wood to heat the drink).[55] And he calls attention to the destitute widow of Zarephath in two sermons.[56] The poor are able to help other poor people, and so practicing charity is irrelevant to class.[57] In one sermon from the December fast before Christmas he says, "The widow in the Gospel put two coins in the treasury, and it surpassed the gifts of all the rich. No piety is disdained in the presence of God, no mercy is fruitless. He has given different gifts to humans, but he does not seek different affections."[58] For Leo, the preacher speaks to the poor, whom he loves and means to assist. As Augustine's sermons give witness of direct speech to the poor, so do Leo's—despite the judgment of some scholars that the poorest were not present within the church building.[59] To be clear then, Leo does not preach love of the poor for the salvation of the rich alone.[60]

54 *Tr.* 20.3, 42.2, 44:2; cf. Mk 12:41–44.

55 *Tr.* 14.2, 42.2, 44.2; cf. Mt 10:42. See Ramsey, "Almsgiving in the Latin Church," 236.

56 *Tr.* 12.3, 44.2; cf. 1 Kgs 17:9–16.

57 For an argument that the poor assisted the poor in the first two centuries of Christianity, see Denise Kimber Buell, "'Be not one who stretches out hands to receive but shuts them when it comes to giving': Envisioning Christian Charity When Both Donors and Recipients are Poor," in *Wealth and Poverty in Early Church and Society*, ed. Susan R. Holman (Grand Rapids, MI: Baker Academic, 2008), 37–47.

58 *Tr.* 20.3 (CCL 138, 83; Freeland and Conway, 74 [alt.]).

59 Richard Finn writes, "[I]t would be unsafe to conclude that the poor were usually or mainly absent. Not addressing the destitute may say more about their low status than their absence from the congregation" (*Almsgiving in the Later Roman Empire*, 141). Borrowing from work by Michele Pellegrino, Finn goes on to cite Augustine's *s.* 20A.9 and *Expositions of the Psalms* 51.14.

60 Cf. Helen Rhee, *Loving the Poor, Saving the Rich: Wealth, Poverty, and Early Christian Formation* (Grand Rapids, MI: Baker Academic, 2012). Rhee's book studies Christianity before Constantine's reign, and so does not address Leo the Great.

Also, Leo repeatedly takes the feelings and capabilities of the poor into account. In his compassion, he wants all Christians to experience with the poor what they feel:

> The nature of the rich and the poor is the same. . . . A fragile and doomed mortality should realize itself in all human beings, and for the common condition render a social affection to its own kind: weep with the weeping and lament with the lamentations of the sorrowing, share abundance with the needy, with the good service of a healthy body bend down to the one lying suffering, set out a portion of food for the hungry, and feel cold in the pale nakedness of the shivering.[61]

Thus, all Christians are to share in the feelings that arise from dire poverty.[62]

The poor are not only recipients of charity through which there is a social transformation; they also do what is central to Christian life: they pray. Our life, our salvation, depends on prayer. Leo quotes Sirach's personification of alms, "the alms themselves will pray for you," and then adds that those who receive assistance will also pray.[63] The prayers of the poor, whether of the involuntary poor or of the voluntary poor who have chosen to take up an ascetical life, are of great importance in the Christian tradition.

On account of viewing the poor as Christ, Leo has a motivation to care for the very particular and personal needs of poor individuals. All are related to Christ, and Christ is related to all. The awareness of Christ's presence in the poor can motivate someone to love individual poor persons by putting Leo's preaching to practice. Gary Anderson observes this about Leo's approach: "It is in the concrete act of assisting a poor person that one meets Christ.

61 *Tr.* 11.1 (CCL 138.46).

62 For an excellent discussion on suffering, compassion, and care for the poor in her monograph on Leo, see Wessel, *Leo the Great and the Spiritual Rebuilding of a Universal Rome,* 179–207, especially 195.

63 *Tr.* 10.3.

Taking revulsion at the misery of the poor implied a rejection of God's self–impoverishment in the incarnation. The two were inextricably bound."[64]

In fact, one should not underestimate how Leo united all social classes in his preaching on loving the poor and the weak, which emphasizes commonality: common human nature, common sins, a common Savior who took up humanity described in terms of the poor, a common apostolic tradition, a common right faith, a common bishop who is motivating and directing the care for the poor, a common liturgical celebration, a common timing and location of collections, common virtuous action in charity and mercy, and a common hope. By having this stress on what is common, Leo drew lines of exclusion against the devil, sin (especially pride and greed), and all those outside the right faith. He thus re-envisioned lines of inclusion and exclusion in a society still being transformed by Christian faith and gave a new life to his people through his preaching. This is a social engagement that reaches far wider than a little free-will offering that does not effect structural change.[65] Peter Brown comments thus:

> Through the preaching of Leo, the Christian congregations were actively encouraged to view the poor as fellow members of the same urban community. Entitlement to protection and to supplies of food that had once been associated exclusively with the civic rights of the Roman People to their share in the *annona* [dole of grain and other food for citizens] came to be offered to all distressed Romans by the pope and his clergy.[66]

64 Gary A. Anderson, *Charity: The Place of the Poor in the Biblical Tradition* (New Haven: Yale University, 2013), 9. Anderson cites *tr.* 10. 2.

65 For an argument that liberation theology need not displace the centrality of the Church, but can be seen to flow therefrom, see Ross McCullough, "Christ's Presence in the Poor and the Church: A Traditionalist Liberation Theology," *ProE* 28, no. 3 (20019): 320–32. McCullough does not cite Leo the Great in this brief study.

66 Peter Brown, *Through the Eye of a Needle: Wealth, the Fall of Rome, and the Making of Christianity in the West, 350–550 AD* (Princeton: Princeton University Press, 2012), 468.

For centuries the Roman government had ways of providing for citizens who were in need. What Leo did was show how Christians could give to the poor, including non-citizen beggars, in a way that expressed the transformative power of Christian life. We now look in detail at his Sermon 9 and his preaching on the beatitudes.

On Christ and the Poor in *Sermon 9*

In November 443, Leo preached *sermon* 9 for the annual collections.[67] He introduces his topic by recalling God's greatest kindness, which comes to us through the teaching of Jesus Christ:

> But that no longer should, through ignorance of the truth, the creature made to the image of God might be led to the precipice of everlasting death, he [our Redeemer and Savior] inserted in the pages of the Gospel his judgment's description, which would call back every human being from the snares of the most cunning enemy, since it would now be unknown to no one what rewards should be hoped for by the good and what punishments should be feared by the evil.[68]

The devil, who sinned through pride and envy, tries many tricks to lure human beings away from God into falsehood. On this, Leo comments: "Knowing that God can be denied not only by words, but also by deeds, he [the instigator and author of sin] snatched charity from many whose faith he could not take away."[69]

67 This set of sermons on the annual collections is described by the translators, Freeland and Conway, as having this basic message throughout: "Give as generously as you can to the poor, because in so doing you are actually giving to Christ who will reward you." The translators then provide two examples, the first from *tr.* 6.1 and the second from *tr.* 7.1: "How marvelous this considerate goodness of the Creator! He wanted there to be assistance for two in a single act" and "Almsgiving is a work of love, and we know that 'love covers a multitude of sins.'" See *Sermons*, 35.

68 *Tr.* 9.1 (CCL 138, 32; Freeland and Conway, 38 [alt.]).

69 *Tr.* 9.1 (CCL 138, 33; Freeland and Conway, 39 [alt.]).

Christ's judgment at the end of time, as depicted in Mt 25:31–46, is intended to instruct us to show mercy to others now. Leo preaches: "Let no human being be thought worthless to a human being, nor should that nature which the Creator of things made his own be despised in anyone."[70] This is an amazing statement that runs counter to a throw-away society in every age.[71] Leo wants his people to think that when we show our love to the poor and the weak we already pass into God's heart and can hope for heaven: "since that which God cherishes is loved by a human being, rightly one is taken into his kingdom who is passed into his affection."[72]

Far from disregarding the feelings of the poor, Leo points out in *sermon* 9 that some people are ashamed to ask openly for what they need. They would prefer poverty's misery to public embarrassment. His solution is that people should relieve the poor of their hidden need. Leo preaches, "Therefore they [these poor who would be embarrassed by public generosity to them] must be understood and be relieved from their hidden need, so that for this reason they may rejoice more since both their poverty and their privacy would be considered."[73] Peter Brown observes that in Leo's preaching we see the transition from viewing the poor simply as "others" to seeing them as "brothers." "[Leo] spoke of them," says Brown, "as like the poor of Israel—as self-respecting citizens down on their luck who needed justice and protection quite as much as they needed food."[74] Paul Blowers cites Leo's *sermon* 9 concerning an application of Psalm 40:2: "Blessed is the one who understands about the needy

70 *Tr.* 9.2 (CCL 138, 35; Freeland and Conway, 40 [alt.]).

71 Pope Francis has given insight, by word and deed, to transforming a "throw-away" society. For a comparison between him and Augustine, see Kevin Grove, CSC, "Rhetoric and Reality: Augustine and Pope Francis on Preaching Christ and the Poor," *TS* 80, no. 3 (2019): 530–53. A similar project could be done in comparing Pope Francis and his predecessor Leo the Great.

72 *Tr.* 9.2 (CCL 138, 35; Freeland and Conway, 40 [alt.]).

73 *Tr.* 9.3 (CCL 138, 36; Freeland and Conway, 41 [alt.]).

74 Peter Brown, *Through the Eye of a Needle: Wealth, the Fall of Rome, and the Making of Christianity in the West, 350–550 AD* (Princeton: Princeton University, 2012), 467.

and poor one. On the evil day, the Lord will liberate him." Blowers says that this "'understanding' means penetrating the real needs of those who suffer, which are hidden beneath shame."[75] In doing so, it means understanding the Word, who made himself needy and poor in our flesh.

In his *sermon* 9's interpretation of that Psalm 40 line, Leo uses the word *persona* to describe the presence of Christ in the poor: "Rightly in the one 'needy and poor' is thought the person (*persona*) of our Lord Jesus Christ, who, although he was rich, just as the blessed apostle said, became poor so that he might enrich us by his poverty."[76] This wonderful exchange described in 2 Corinthians 8 is used by some of the Fathers of the Church as a way to speak about the mystery of divinization.[77] For Leo, it functions still, as it did for the Apostle Paul writing to the Corinthians, within the context of giving material support to the poor. The basic intention of this teaching on divinization is to motivate people to give to poor persons in their personal needs.

Furthermore, in an allusion to Mt 25:31–46, Leo sees that he who is one person in two natures, divine and human, remains present to the world through the poor:

> And so that it may seem that his presence be not lacking to us, he so modulated the mystery of his humility and glory so that the one whom we adore as King and Lord in the majesty of the Father is himself the same whom we feed in his poor ones. We are thus 'liberated' on account of this on 'the evil day' from

75 Paul M. Blowers, "Pity, Empathy, and the Tragic Spectacle of Human Suffering: Exploring the Emotional Culture of Compassion in Late Ancient Christianity," *JECS* 18, no. 1 (2010): 1–27, at 22n202.

76 *Tr.* 9.3 (CCL 138, 36–37; Freeland and Conway, 41 [alt.]). Cf. 2 Cor 8:9. The word *persona* can have a range of meanings other than the Boethian "individual substance of a rational nature." Leo regularly speaks about the *persona* of Christ as a result of the incarnation rather than as the eternal *persona* of the Son, one of the Trinity, who became incarnate.

77 For discussion on 2 Cor 8:9 in Irenaeus, see Russell, *The Doctrine of Deification in the Greek Patristic Tradition*, 108.

> everlasting damnation, and admitted into the fellowship of the heavenly kingdom for our care of the poor one 'understood.'[78]

Psalm 40's "Blessed is the one who understands about the needy and poor one. On the evil day, the Lord will liberate him" comes to life in the flesh of our day.

Some might advance the charge that not only do the rich use the poor to get to heaven, but Christ uses the poor to get to earth. The poor are doubly used. Another way of thinking of this, however, is to see that the poor, rather than being dismissed, are the way of salvation. They express how Christ's humanity is the way of salvation. Their dignity is heightened rather than lessened by this identification with Christ. What is more, all people—both rich and poor and those in between—can be counted blessed by Christ when caring for the poor.[79]

On the Beatitudes and Loving the Poor

The beatitudes hold a prominent place in Leo's preaching, which stands to reason, as Christ's preaching on the beatitudes begins the Matthean account of his preaching and inaugurates the kingdom of heaven.[80] While some modern commentators describe Jesus in

78 *Tr.* 9.3 (CCL 138, 36–37; Freeland and Conway, 41 [alt.]).

79 Leo concludes the homily with an appeal to expose Manicheans to priests so that the Manichean enslavement to the devil might end. Such a call seems to various modern interpreters to be in opposition to charity or to be an attempt to have social control. For an argument that Leo is trying to secure power in disciplined watchfulness, see Henri O. Maier, "'Manichee!' Leo the Great and the Orthodox Panopticon," *JECS* 4, no. 4 (1996): 441–60. For Bronwen Neil, "The 'plague' of heresy had to be wiped out, even at the expense of Christian charity." See Bronwen Neil, "A Crisis of Orthodoxy: Leo I's Fight against the 'Deadly Disease' of Heresy," in *Ancient Jewish and Christian Texts as Crisis Management Literature*, Thematic Studies from the Centre for Early Christian Studies, eds. David C. Sim and Pauline Allen (New York: T & T Clark International, 2012), 144–58, at 158. I think the call to expose people is problematic, and it may obscure rather than express the command to love one's neighbor, especially the weak.

80 Bronwen Neil discusses the seven homilies that feature the Matthean beatitudes in "'Blessed is Poverty' Leo the Great on Almsgiving": these are *tr.* 95 (specifically on the

Matthew's Gospel as the "New Moses," Leo the Great sees Jesus on the other side in the giving of the new law in the beatitudes that begin the Sermon on the Mount.[81] He is not one who receives the law and passes it on, but is rather the Lord God, who spoke to Moses on another mount: "It was he himself who had once honored Moses by speaking to him there with a more fearful justice—but here, with a holier mercy."[82] Arguably, this divine, rather than Mosaic, perspective has a greater plausibility for the evangelist who sees that Jesus is "God with us" (Mt 1:23).

Leo finds that Christ's preaching on the beatitudes fulfills Jeremiah's prophecy of the new covenant (Jer 31:31–33). After quoting Jeremiah concerning the Lord's law having been written on the people's minds and hearts, Leo preaches: "What he said to Moses he said also to the apostles, and the swift hand of the Word, writing in the hearts of the disciples, established the precepts of the new covenant."[83]

Helping the poor is preeminent in Leo's understanding of the new covenant written on the hearts of the disciples, especially the beatitudes regarding the poor in spirit and the merciful. While preaching on the first beatitude, "Blessed are the poor in spirit," Leo distinguishes the kind of poverty that is mentioned. He does not want to glorify a condition that oppresses "many" who "suffer in heavy and hard necessity."[84] Rather, he speaks of the spiritual poverty of humility, which the poor may be more likely to attain. The difference is important for several reasons. Most significantly,

beatitudes), and *tr.* 10, 11, 16, 40, 49, and 78. Neil writes elsewhere: "The ideals expressed in the Beatitudes of *Matth.* 5 matched Leo's social vision perfectly." See her "Blessed are the Rich," 547. Also, Leo's preaching on the beatitudes in *tr.* 95 is influential in the Roman liturgical tradition, as it appears in the Roman breviary's Office of Readings from Thursday of the 22nd Week through Monday of the 23rd Week of Ordinary Time.

81 For a prominent example of showing Jesus as the "New Moses" in Matthew's Gospel, see Dale C. Allison, *The New Moses: A Matthean Typology* (Minneapolis: Fortress, 1993).

82 *Tr.* 95.1 (CCL 138A, 583; Freeland and Conway, 395 [alt.]).

83 *Tr.* 95.1 (CCL 138A, 583; Freeland and Conway, 395 [alt.]).

84 *Tr.* 95.2 (CCL 138A, 583–84; Freeland and Conway, 395).

if it is merely by a material or worldly poverty that one attains the kingdom of heaven, one would not work to alleviate it. In fact, Leo instead encourages the poor to hold on to humility (as opposed to holding on to their destitution) and the rich to do works of kindness, for the greatest riches are in spending on "relieving the misery of another's suffering."[85]

After recognizing the primacy of the Lord himself in magnanimous poverty, Leo draws his example from the first disciples. The apostles themselves become poor, sharing in the poverty of Christ and the involuntary poor of those around them. This actualizes Christ's preaching of the Sermon on the Mount, as those who heard Christ preached and practiced what he preached and practiced. Leo recalls how they gave up everything, and led many people to imitate them—promulgating the Gospel by word and deed. The fifth-century pope comments, "When all their goods and possessions were dispersed, the people were enriched in eternal goods through this most holy poverty. Because of the apostles' teaching, they were glad 'to have nothing' in this world but 'to possess all things with Christ.'"[86]

As is so customary in Leo's preaching, the sermon turns directly to St. Peter. Leo recounts how Peter proclaimed the good news to the lame beggar: "Silver and gold I do not have, but what I have I give you. In the name of Jesus Christ the Nazarene, get up and walk" (Acts 4:4). Leo offers this beautiful turn of phrase: "He who did not give the image of Caesar on the coin restored the image of Christ in the man."[87] And Leo later preaches: "The poor Apostle who had nothing to give to the petitioner gave such abundance of divine grace that, just as he had set one man on his feet again, so he

85 *Tr.* 95.2 (CCL 138A, 584; Freeland and Conway, 396).

86 *Tr.* 95.3 (CCL 138A, 584–85; Freeland and Conway, 396).

87 *Tr.* 95.3 (CCL 138A, 585; Freeland and Conway, 396).

healed many thousands of the faithful in their hearts."[88] The greatest miracle is the miracle of true faith in Jesus Christ. It is a miracle that occurred and continues to occur because of the Lord's solidarity with the poor in the incarnation and his disciples' solidarity with the poor in their preaching. In this scene of the lame beggar and the poor apostle, Christ is encountered. In Leo's orthodox preaching, which continues that of Christ and his apostles, the kingdom of God is at hand.

When Leo comes to the beatitude "Blessed are the merciful" in this sermon, he preaches in a way that can make us think of his first Christmas sermon's famous words: "Realize, O Christian, your dignity" (*Agnosce, o christiane, dignitatem tuam*).[89] In that Christmas sermon, he quotes 2 Pt 1:4 about partaking of the divine nature as that dignity. Here he says about this beatitude of mercy: "Realize, O Christian, the dignity of your wisdom" (*Agnosce, Christiane, tuae sapientiae dignitatem*).[90] Leo preaches deification by the beatitudes: "Mercy wants you to be merciful; justice wants you to be just. In this way the Creator will appear in his own creature, and 'the image of God,' expressed through the paths of imitation, may shine in the mirror of the human heart."[91] The poor thus need not only mercy, the subject of the beatitude, but also justice. They have been treated

88 *Tr.* 95.3 (CCL 138A, 585; Freeland and Conway, 397).

89 *Tr.* 21.3 (CCL 138; Freeland and Conway, 79).

90 *Tr.* 95.7 (CCL 138A, 588; Freeland and Conway, 398). The three other uses of *agnosce* in Leo's preaching are also pertinent: *tr.* 27.6: "Wake up then, O human being, and realize the dignity of your nature. Recall that you have been made according to the image of God. This nature, although it had been corrupted in Adam, has nevertheless been refashioned in Christ (CCL 138, 137; Freeland and Conway, 144 [alt.]); *tr.* 6.1: "Those who feed Christ in the poor store up their treasure in heaven. Realize the kindness in this and the thoughtfulness of how God has arranged things. He willed that you should have an abundance so that through you another might not be wanting" (CCL 138, 27; Freeland and Conway, 35 [alt.]; *tr.* 87.4: "'What you have done to one of these, you have done to me.' Realize who says this, and, free from anxiety, recognize with the clear eyes of faith into whose hands you are placing your wealth" (CCL 138A, 545; Freeland and Conway, 372 [alt.]). Leo wants his people to know the greatness of life in Christ.

91 *Tr.* 95.7 (CCL 138A, 588; Freeland and Conway, 398–99).

unjustly, as well as unmercifully, and Leo expresses the Lord's concern for them and for all by proclaiming the beatitudes.

Moreover, it should not be overlooked that Leo nearly equates the beatitude of mercy with assisting the poor. Listen to his sermon from 445 on the annual collections:

> What hope would lift up the fallen, what medicine heal the wounded, if almsgiving did not remit faults, and needs of the poor did not become remedies for sin? So by saying, "Blessed are the merciful, for God will have mercy on them," the Lord made it clear that the entire scale on which he is going to judge the whole world when he appears in his majesty would be tilted while hanging from the following balance: Only the quality of good works directed toward the destitute would determine the sentence (for the ungodly to burn with the devil, for the generous to reign with Christ).[92]

For Leo, the entire judgment of Christ, the very purpose of the Son of God taking the form of a slave and winning the victory in that form, can be summarized in loving the poor. In his preaching on our care for the poor, we see the image of Christ radiantly in the preacher and his hearers.

The Mysteries of the Cross and the Resurrection for the Needy

Because Leo so closely identifies Christ's humanity with the humanity of the poor, we can especially see how his preaching of the cross and the resurrection is good news for the poor, so often excluded from social assistance. In the Roman Empire, poor noncitizens did not qualify for the dole and other public benefits. Leo provides a space wherein God's mercy is at work for all who

92 *Tr.* 11.1 (CCL 138, 45; Freeland and Conway, 46).

accept it in faith—regardless of an earthly citizenship. Christ's victory in the paschal mysteries is for all but especially for those who know themselves to be weak and wounded. In a sermon preached on Wednesday of Holy Week in 443, Leo imagines what Christ's words, "When I have been lifted up, I shall draw all to myself" (Jn 12:32), mean. Christ, in Leo's sermon, speaks thus: "I will deal with the whole condition of humanity and will call back to integrity the nature lost long ago. In me will all weakness be abolished, in me will all wounds be healed."[93] Can you imagine how the poor Christians of fifth-century Rome would receive that good news? In his Good Friday sermon from April 10, 453, Leo preaches, "To no one among the infirm has that victory of the Cross been denied."[94] And he is preaching to all who look for mercy:

> Has that taking on of our substance in the divinity—by which "the Word became flesh and dwelt in us"—left any person outside his mercy except an unbeliever? Besides, who is there whose nature is not one with Christ if Christ has received him by taking our nature and if he has been born again of that Spirit from which Christ was begotten? Who then does not recognize the stages of his own life in him? Who does not see that his taking of food, his rest in sleep, his anxiety in sorrow, and his tear of compassion made his form that of a servant?[95]

Leo also motivates his hearers to imitate God in his mercy. In his Good Friday preaching of 444, he quotes and meditates on a line from the great Philippian hymn that Paul records: "Perceive this also in yourselves, just as in Christ Jesus. Being in the form of God . . ." Leo then repeats the entire hymn, all the way to "every tongue should confess that Jesus Christ is Lord to the glory of God the Father." Leo wants his people to understand this "mystery of

93 *Tr.* 57.4 (CCL 138A, 336; Freeland and Conway, 246).

94 *Tr.* 66.3 (CCL 138A, 403; Freeland and Conway, 288).

95 *Tr.* 66.4 (CCL 138A, 404; Freeland and Conway, 289, [alt.]).

great devotion" (1 Tm 3:16) in themselves. He preaches, "No rich person should reject his humility, no noble person should scorn it. Indeed, no human good fortune whatsoever may be brought to such a height that people might consider as shameful for themselves something which he, remaining God in the form of God, did not consider to be such."[96] Leo then applies this Christological principle of compassion to his hearers:

> Imitate what he did. Love what he loved. Since you have discovered the grace of God in yourselves, respond by loving your own nature in him. As he did not lose riches in his poverty, nor diminish glory in his humility, nor lose eternity in his death, so you, following in his footsteps to the same degree, scorn earthly things in order that you might attain to heavenly ones.[97]

In another sermon on Good Friday, Leo makes a striking statement of the continuity of the Lord's passion: "Our Lord's passion has been drawn out to the end of the world. He himself is honored in his saints, he himself is loved, he is also fed in the poor, he is clothed."[98] Think about it: *Our Lord's passion has been drawn out to the end of the world.* Leo carries this forward by calling to mind those persecuted for the sake of righteousness. He begins the sermon on the next day, Holy Saturday, with these words: "In the last sermon, most beloved, we brought up our participation in the Cross of Christ—not inappropriately I think—so that the very lives of believers might incorporate the Paschal Mystery in themselves, and so that what has been honored by a feast might be celebrated through our conduct."[99] The deification that Leo proposes is one

96 *Tr.* 72.4 (CCL 138A, 445–46; Freeland and Conway, 319 [alt.]). Whereas the Empire excluded non-citizens who were poor, Leo excludes the non–believing poor—and he wanted non–believers, whatever their social status, to become believers.

97 *Tr.* 72.5 (CCL 138A, 446; Freeland and Conway, 319).

98 *Tr.* 70.5 (CCL 138A, 430; Freeland and Conway, 309).

99 *Tr.* 71.1 (CCL 138A, 434; Freeland and Conway, 311 [alt.]).

whereby Christ's mysteries are lived out by the faithful—and especially by those who suffer.

Christ's resurrection, then, causes much joy. Linking Christ's rising from the dead to his solidarity with our feeble humanity, Leo proclaims, "We must rejoice a great deal over this transformation by which we are taken from earthly coarseness to heavenly dignity through that ineffable mercy of the one who descended to our state in order to lift us up to his."[100] For Leo, because Christ has risen and ascended into glory, he is even more present to us now by his divinity.[101] How can we know Christ's presence, especially when we experience the snares of the devil? Leo concludes a homily on the Ascension with these words:

> Nothing is stronger, most beloved, against the wiles of the devil than the kindness of mercy and the generosity of love, through which every sin is either avoided or conquered. But the sublimity of this virtue is not gained until what is contrary to it has been broken down. What is so inimical to the works of mercy and charity as greed, from which root the seed of all evil comes? . . . Let us resist then, most beloved, this rankling evil, and strive after charity, without which no virtue can shine. Through this way of love, by which Christ descended to us, we also can ascend to him, to whom are honor and glory with God the Father and with the Holy Spirit forever and ever. Amen.[102]

Conclusion

Let us return to the charge of a foremost scholar of Leo the Great at work today: "To the question of whether Leo's poor were real persons," Bronwen Neil writes, "we must answer with a resounding

100 *Tr.* 71.2 (CCL 138A, 435; Freeland and Conway, 312).
101 Cf. *tr.* 74.4.
102 *Tr.* 74.5 (CCL 138A, 460–61; Freeland and Conway, 329 [alt.]).

negative. Leo's poor, mentioned by category of need where they are mentioned at all, do not horrify or confront his listeners and readers, nor are they meant to do so." This is mystifying to me. Must we answer with a resounding negative? It is true that the poor are mentioned by category of need, but they are also mentioned by particular biblical examples. Recall how the apostle Peter is a model poor person for Leo. Does Leo mention the rich by name or single out particular rich persons in his preaching? I cannot think of any.

Moreover, if seeing Christ in the poor is derogatory to the poor, is seeing Peter in Leo derogatory to Leo? He wants his people to see Peter in him, as he preaches "so that he [Peter] may be understood in the person of my lowliness (*ut in persona humilitatis meae ille intellegatur*)."[103] Did the cry at the Council of Chalcedon after hearing Leo's Tome, "Peter has spoken through Leo," suggest that Leo had no separate humanity? Or does it instead show some sort of investment of Petrine presence in this lowly successor in Rome? In one sermon, Leo says that after Christ's resurrection, Mary Magdalene was bearing the person of the Church (*personam Ecclesiae gerens*).[104] Does Leo's prosopology, i.e., his understanding of the *persona*, person, or voice of a scriptural figure, denigrate Mary Magdalene in seeing her express the Church? If the answer is no, perhaps we should answer similarly when seeing Leo express himself as Simon Peter or when the poor express Jesus Christ. In each case, it is a recognition of what God has done. Among these cases, would not the most important one be a matter of Christ's presence—in the poor?

Furthermore, if the conditions of the poor were to horrify Leo's listeners, would that ultimately make the poor more real as persons? Recall that Leo does want us to feel cold with those who are shivering. We should feel the terrible plight of the poor, and Leo

103 *Tr.* 3.4 (CCL 138, 13).
104 *Tr.* 74.4 (CCL 138A, 458).

speaks of fasting as a way of sharing a little in what others frequently experience. But if my personhood is dependent on your feeling, rather than on my being made to the image of God, then there is something woefully inadequate. I would think that a greater sense of personhood would emerge if Christians thought that the poor were equally human as the rich and even comparatively privileged in their closeness to Christ—ideas that Leo frequently propounds. Could there be improvements in Leo's thinking about the humanity of the poor? Certainly, there can be additional insights into what it means to be a person, to be human, and to be poor. But for Leo, following Mt 25:31–46, the poor—without losing their humanity, which prompted the incarnation to occur in the first place—are accorded arguably the highest recognition that could have been imagined: they have Christ present in them. The humanity of the poor, rather than being eliminated by Christ's presence, is revealed as precious, exemplary, and loved by God, and it is found in individual poor persons in mid-5th century Rome—and here and now. Another Bishop of Rome, in his Message for the First World Day of the Poor, writes:

> [W]e touch with our own hands the *flesh of Christ* [original emphasis]. If we truly wish to encounter Christ, we have to touch his body in the suffering bodies of the poor, as a response to the sacramental communion bestowed in the Eucharist. The Body of Christ, broken in the sacred liturgy, can be seen, through charity and sharing, in the faces and persons of the most vulnerable of our brothers and sisters.[105]

105 Pope Francis, Message of the First World Day of the Poor, November 19, 2017, no. 3. Interestingly, Pope Francis has inaugurated two annual World Days relevant to this chapter. The World Day of the Poor is the 33rd Sunday of Ordinary Time, the Sunday before the Solemnity of Christ the King, which is the last Sunday before the end of the liturgical year. Also, Pope Francis declared that the 3rd Sunday of Ordinary Time would be the Sunday of the Word of God. See his motu proprio *Aperuit Illis*, Instituting the Sunday of the Word of God, September 30, 2019. In its conclusion (no. 15), Pope Francis writes, "The poor are not blessed because they are poor; they become blessed if, like Mary, they believe in the fulfilment of God's word. A great disciple and master of sacred Scripture, Saint Augustine, once wrote: 'Someone in the midst of the crowd, seized with enthusiasm, cried out:

As a preacher, Leo wanted his listeners to recognize in all human persons a common nature, created by God, assumed in the incarnation, and redeemed by his blood. Christ has come to be with us precisely in weak human nature understood in the weakness of the poor. Without an understanding of that weak human nature, Leo's listeners would not be able to understand the sublime majesty of the incarnation or its effect in transforming our humanity to share in Christ's divinity through the practice of the virtues.

In our final chapter, we hear Gregory the Great, a later Bishop of Rome, saying that preachers, after their great deeds of preaching such as for the weak, must never forget their own weakness in Christ. In a sense, the last chapter can also remind us of the first two chapters: our goal of holiness, with the help of Origen's life and preaching, and the first virtue considered, humility, in the example and speech of Ephrem. Preachers must end where the beginning of our salvation lies: repentance in the humble recognition of the holiness of the eternal Word who comes down to our flesh in order to redeem us by his blood.

"Blessed is the womb that bore you" and Jesus replied, "Rather, blessed are they who hear the word of God and keep it." As if to say: My mother, whom you call blessed, is indeed blessed, because she keeps the word of God. Not because in her the Word became flesh and dwelt among us, but because she keeps that same word of God by which she was made and which, in her womb, became flesh'" (*Tractates on the Gospel of John*, 10, 3).

CHAPTER 7

GREGORY THE GREAT

The Word in Our Flesh for Acceptance of Our Weakness

Having considered the topic of loving others in their weakness in Chapter 6, we turn in this final chapter to preachers accepting their own weakness in Christ. All of us are pitifully weak from the point of view of God's all-powerful mercy, and the most deified of preachers are no exception. Christians are deified by picking up their cross and following Jesus. Preachers who bear the Word within them are offered an intense experience of living out Christ's own life in obedience until death. He accepted our weakness for our salvation. But can we accept our weakness? We should never forget that it is on account of our weakness that the Word has come to us—and can be proclaimed by us. "God chose the weak of the world," St. Paul tells the Corinthians (1 Cor 1:27), and says to them, "I came to you in weakness" (1 Cor 2:3).

The great Pope John Paul II (Bishop of Rome from 1978 to 2005) showed the world in a particularly powerful way the necessity of preaching during his frail final years. Reflecting on the weakness at the heart of the Gospel, he writes, "Suffering, in fact, is always *a trial*—at times a very hard one—to which humanity is subjected." He then illustrates Christian suffering from the apostle Paul:

> The gospel *paradox of weakness and strength* often speaks to us from the pages of the Letters of Saint Paul, a paradox particularly experienced by the Apostle himself and together with him experienced by all who share Christ's sufferings. Paul writes in the Second Letter to the Corinthians: "I will all the more gladly boast of my weaknesses, that the power of Christ may rest upon me" (2 Cor 12:9). In the Second Letter to Timothy we read: "And therefore I suffer as I do. But I am not ashamed, for I know whom I have believed" (2 Tm 1:12). And in the Letter to the Philippians he will even say: "I can do all things in him who strengthens me" (Phil 4:13).

Pope John Paul continues:

> Those who share in Christ's sufferings have before their eyes the Paschal Mystery of the Cross and Resurrection, in which Christ descends, in a first phase, to the ultimate limits of human weakness and impotence: indeed, he dies nailed to the Cross. But if at the same time in this *weakness* there is accomplished his *lifting up,* confirmed by the power of the Resurrection, then this means that the weaknesses of all human sufferings are capable of being infused with the same power of God manifested in Christ's Cross.[1]

One early Christian preacher who underscored the truth that preachers encounter God's power in their own weakness is Gregory I, the Bishop of Rome from 590 until his death in 604. For our final chapter's interest in incarnation, deification, and proclamation, we turn to Gregory.

1 John Paul II, *Salvifici Doloris,* Apostolic Letter on the Christian Meaning of Human Suffering, February 11, 1984, no. 23.

The Word in Gregory's Flesh for Us

Posterity calls Gregory I—like Leo I, his predecessor a century and a half earlier—"the Great." He first received the title not from a fellow Latin, but from a Greek author in the early seventh century.[2] The Greek Christian East venerates him as the Dialogist.[3] In the West, Boniface VIII numbered him in 1298 among the four most illustrious Latin Doctors of the Church with Ambrose, Jerome, and Augustine.[4] Repeatedly in liturgical and scholarly contexts, many—but not all—have lauded Gregory's exemplary greatness. Adolf von Harnack, the liberal historian of dogmas, characterizes Gregory as having produced nothing more than crude "work-religion (*ergismus*)":

2 John Moschus calls Gregory "the Great" in introducing John the Persian's story of encountering Gregory in Rome. See *Spiritual Meadow*, chap. 151 in *The Spiritual Meadow (Pratum Spirituale)*, introduction, translation, and notes by John Wortley, CSS 139 (Kalamazoo, MI: Cistercian Publications, 1992), 124. For a study on Gregory's connections to the Greek East, see Phil Booth, "Gregory and the Greek East," in *A Companion to Gregory the Great*, eds. Bronwen Neil and Matthew Dal Santo, BCCT vol. 47 (Leiden: Brill, 2003), 109–31. For Gregory's reception in Byzantium, with a focus on Paul Evergetinus's *Synagōgē*, see Andrew Louth, "Gregory the Great in the Byzantine Tradition," in *A Companion to Gregory the Great*, eds. Neil and Dal Santo, 343–58. For an analysis of Gregory as "the Great" in the West, see Conrad Leyser, "Late Antiquity in the Medieval West," in *A Companion to Late Antiquity*, ed. Philip Rousseau, with the assistance of Jutta Raithiel (Chichester: Wiley-Blackwell, 2009), 29–42, at "The Making of Gregory 'the Great'," 39–41.

3 He is called the Dialogist because of the fame of his *Dialogues*, translated by Pope Zacharias (741–52) into Greek. Francis Clark argued against the authenticity of Gregory's authorship of the *Dialogues*. But Gregory's authorship has been vigorously defended, by scholars such as Paul Meyvaert in his "The Authentic *Dialogues* of Gregory the Great," *SE* 43 (2004): 55–129. For a more recent defense, drawing especially upon connections with Gregory's writing of four miracles of St. Andrew in *ep.* 11.26, see Matthew Dal Santo, "The Shadow of a Doubt? A Note on the *Dialogues* and *Registrum Epistolarum* of Pope Gregory the Great (590–604)," *JEH* 61, no. 1 (2010): 3–17.

4 The Roman tradition commemorates these doctors with a Mass introit taken from Sir 15:5 (Vulgate) that was used also for the feast of John the Evangelist:

In medio ecclesiae aperuit os eius
ei implevit eum dominus spiritu sapientiae et intellectus;
stolam gloriae induit eum
In the midst of the Church, he opened his mouth,
And the Lord filled him with the Spirit of wisdom and understanding;
he clothed him in a robe of glory.

> Gregory has nowhere uttered an original thought; he has rather at all points preserved, while emasculating, the traditional system of doctrine, reduced the spiritual to the level of a coarsely material intelligence, changed dogmatic, so far as it suited, into technical directions for the clergy, and associated it with popular religion of the second rank.[5]

Whether people praise him or blame him, what Gregory most emphasized about himself was that he was a weak sinner—reliant on the prayers of others and on the mercy of God.

From one of Rome's noble families with a remarkable religious tradition, Gregory was born around the year 540. His great-great-grandfather was Pope Felix III (483–92). His father was an official in the Church of Rome, and three of Gregory's aunts were nuns, although one abandoned the monastic life to marry. The family-owned land on the Caelian Hill in Rome and vast tracts of land in Sicily. Gregory became prefect of the city of Rome in 573, administering the city that had lost much of its secular glory.[6] Many wars and plagues ravaged the Italian peninsula in the sixth century, and Gregory could not find what he wanted in the world. Upon his father's death, he converted his family home on the Caelian Hill into a monastery dedicated to St. Andrew, and he founded several more monasteries on his family's Sicilian properties. Gregory entered St. Andrew's Abbey. He was called out of the monastery to serve the city, however, this time as one of Rome's seven deacons.

In 579 or 580, Pope Pelagius II sent Gregory the deacon to Constantinople as the *apocrisiarius*, or papal legate/nuncio at the imperial court, where he served for about six years. During this period of diplomatic work, he found time to deliver many spiritual

5 Adolph von Harnack, *History of Dogma*, vol. 5, translated from the third German edition by James Millar, Theological Translation Library (Oxford: Williams and Norgate, 1898), 262. For an analysis of this infamous assessment, see John Moorhead, *Gregory the Great*, ECF (New York: Routledge, 2005), 36–37.

6 For a recent assessment of scholarship on what Gregory's high civic title was, see DelCogliano, *Gregory the Great: On the Song of Songs*, 8n20.

talks on the Book of Job, talks he later revised to cover the entire book. One of the longest works of the patristic era, running to about 1,800 pages in the 3-volume critical edition, the *Moralia in Job* is divided into 35 books.[7] Mindful of his bodily and spiritual weaknesses, Gregory seems naturally to have focused on Job, a model of one who suffers. Gregory writes in his dedicatory letter:

> Perhaps this was a plan of Divine Providence so that I might comment on the stricken Job after having been stricken myself, and so that I might the better understand the soul of the one whipped through the lashes I myself received.[8]

During his ministry in Constantinople, Gregory engaged in his only recorded theological debate, one very much related to Job 19:25–26 and the weakness of this flesh. In his *Moralia*, Gregory comments on Job's words, "I know that my Redeemer lives, and that I shall rise on the last day from the earth. And I shall again be encompassed with my skin." Here Gregory records that he opposed the elderly Constantinopolitan patriarch Eutychius who taught that the resurrected body would be impalpable.[9] Gregory debated with him from the scriptural witness of Christ's own resurrected flesh and the promise of ours, which will have the flesh of our nature but not the "flesh" that is reckoned as sin. Emperor Tiberius Constantine sided with Gregory and ordered Eutychius's book to be burned. Both Gregory and Eutychius fell ill after their debate, as we read in the *Moralia*. Gregory recovered to find that Eutychius had died, but only after witnesses reported that Eutychius had recanted. He

7 *S. Gregorii Magni Moralia in Job*, ed. Marcus Adriaen, CCL 143, 143A, 143B (Turnhout: Brepols, 1979–85). For a new six-volume English translation, see *Gregory the Great: Moral Reflections on the Book of Job*, translated by Brian Kerns, OCSO (Collegeville, MN: Liturgical Press, 2014–2022).

8 *Letter to Leander*, Prologue to *Moralia on Job*.5 (Kerns, 1.54).

9 *Moralia on Job* 14.72–74 (Kerns 3.195–98).

would take hold of his hand's skin and say to others, "I confess that we will all arise with this flesh."[10]

After his service in Constantinople, Gregory returned to St. Andrew's and lived a monastic life that in retrospect seemed ideal to him.[11] Pope Pelagius II died of the plague in 590, and Gregory reluctantly became Bishop of Rome on September 3 of that year. He was the first monk to become Pope. Gregory set out an ascetical agenda for Rome's clergy, who did not seem to have been devoted to his memory and work after his death.[12] England would be the place that most fondly remembered him, thanks especially to the mission headed by Augustine of Canterbury, who was sent to England by Gregory. Gradually, what the Rule of St. Benedict became for Western monasticism, Gregory's *Pastoral Rule* became for Western clergy.[13] Many of his preserved letters also communicate his instruc-

10 *Moralia on Job* 14.74 (Kerns 3.198). For a recent consideration of this, see Janet Sidaway, "The reception of Chalcedon in the West: a case study of Gregory the Great," *SJT* 73, no. 4 (2020): 307–17, at 316–17. Sidaway recommends Yves-Marie Duval, 'La discussion entre L'apocrisiare Grégoire et le patriarche Eutychios au sujet de la resurrection de la chair,' *Grégoire le Grand*, 347–65.

11 Scholars have different views on Gregory's role at St. Andrew's Abbey after he returned from Constantinople. George Demacopoulos writes, "In 585, Gregory returned to Rome and St. Andrews, where he quickly assumed the office of abbot." See Demacopoulos, *Five Models of Spiritual Direction in the Early Church* (Notre Dame, IN: University of Notre Dame Press, 2007), 129. Demacopoulos also writes, "In 585 Gregory returned to Rome and St. Andrews, where he may have assumed the role of abbot." See Demacopoulos, *Gregory the Great: Ascetic, Pastor, and First Man of Rome* (Notre Dame, IN: University of Notre Dame, 2015), 4. Mark DelCogliano states, "Gregory was never the abbot." See DelCogliano, *Gregory the Great: On the Song of Songs*, 10. For an overview of Gregory on the monastic life, see Barbara Müller, "Gregory the Great and Monasticism," in *A Companion to Gregory the Great*, eds. Neil and Dal Santo, 83–108.

12 Cf. Jacob A. Latham, "Inventing Gregory 'the Great': Memory, Authority, and the Afterlives of the *Letania Septiformis*," *CH* 84, no. 1 (2015): 1–31. Demacopoulos writes, "Even though the idea of a Gregorian counterinitiative is plausible, there is little direct evidence of a contemporaneous anti-Gregorian clerical faction." See Demacopoulos, *Gregory the Great: Ascetic, Pastor, and First Man of Rome*, 121. Demacopoulos underscores the anti-monastic, clerical battle over Gregory's immediate legacy in Rome, in that book and in his *Invention of Peter*, 167. For an account of his immediate successor's envy of Gregory and lack of concern for the people, see chap. 28 of *The Earliest Life of Gregory the Great by an Anonymous Monk of Whitby*, text, translation, and notes by Bertram Colgrave (Cambridge: Cambridge University Press, 1968), 126–27.

13 DelCogliano supports Drobner's comment: "What Benedict's Rule was to monks of the Middle Ages, the Pastoral Rule of Gregory the Great was to the clergy of the world." See

tion on the clerical life. He wrote to a fellow bishop something that all preachers should keep in mind:

> We know that the first virtue is the recognition of one's weakness, and thus we gather that you are able to carry out the ministry undertaken by you with success, in that we see you recognizing your own weakness through your humility. For we are all weak, but that man is weaker who is not able to perceive his own weakness. But you, most blessed brethren, are strong since, not trusting your own fortitude, you put your trust in the strength of almighty God.[14]

Scholars differ in how they portray Gregory's thought and action as pope, depending on the emphasis of their interpretation of one who had a penchant for holding polarities together. Gregory evinces an uneasy tension that indicates both the saving power of the Word and the frailty of the flesh at work in one's life: contemplation and ministry; heaven and earth; perfection and imperfection. Here we emphasize one recurring theme: preachers must accept their weakness.

Weakness as the Meeting Point between Divinity and Humanity

For Gregory, our weakness is precisely where we meet God and proclaim him. Preaching on the blind man encountered by Christ along the way to Jericho, Gregory the Great says: "The blind man came to the light when our Creator drew near Jericho, because when divinity undertook the disability of our flesh [*defectum nostrae carnis*], the human race received the light which it had lost. For

---

Hubertus Drobner, *The Fathers of the Church: A Comprehensive Introduction* (Peabody, MA: Hendrickson, 2007), 518 and DelCogliano, *Gregory the Great: On the Song of Songs*, 22.

14 *Ep.* 7.4, Gregory to Cyriacus, Bishop of Constantinople, October 598 (Martyn 2.453).

when God suffers human things, then humanity is raised to divine things [*Unde enim Deus humana patitur, inde homo ad divina sublevatur*]."[15] Gregory then connects this Gospel miracle with our need for Jesus: "If anyone recognizes the darkness of his blindness, if anyone understands that the light of eternity is wanting in him, let him cry out from the bottom of his heart, let him cry out with his whole mind, let him say: *Jesus, son of David, have mercy on me*!"[16]

Similarly, in a Christmas homily on the beginning of Luke 2, Gregory recalls Isaiah's words, "All flesh is grass" (Is 40:6). In the incarnation, the Word has turned that grass of ours into wheat. That is why he was placed in a manger—namely, so that believers would not be empty of the food of heavenly knowledge. Preaching on the angelic proclamation of Christ's birth, Gregory says:

> Since the king of heaven took upon himself the "earth" of our flesh, the company of angels on high no longer despises our weakness. . . . [The angels] now honor as their companions those whom previously they had despised as weak and despicable. . . . They no longer dared to reject as weak and beneath them what they honored as above themselves in heaven's king, nor did they disdain to have [as their companion] a human being when they worshipped the human being who was God above themselves. . . . Human beings indeed have been called gods. Therefore, O human being, protect the dignity of God that is yours against vices, because for your sake God became a human being."[17]

In one of his *Homilies on Ezekiel*, he gives in poetic fashion the great exchange that takes place in the incarnation: The Word assumes our weakness and we are deified in receiving his power:

15 Homily to the people in the basilica of St. Peter, Apostle, *Homilies on the Gospels* 2.2 (CCL 141, 13; *Hom.* 2 = *Hom.* 13 in Hurst, 95 [alt.]).

16 *Homilies on the Gospels* 2.2 (CCL 141, 14; Hurst, 96 [alt.]).

17 Homily to the people in the basilica of the Blessed Virgin Mary, *Homilies on the Gospels* 8 (CCL 141, 55–56; *Hom.* 8 = *Hom.* 7 in Hurst, 52–53 [alt.]).

He became flesh that he might make us spiritual.
He kindly bowed down that he might lift us up.
He went out that he might lead us in.
He appeared visible that he might reveal the invisible.
He bore the lashes that he might heal us.
He suffered dishonor and derision that he might free us from eternal dishonor.
He died that he might give us life.
Therefore let us give thanks to him who gives life, although dead,
and gives life the more because he died. . . .
He who in his own nature always remains incomprehensible deigned to be
comprehended in our nature and to be flogged,
because if he had not assumed the things of our weakness he could never have
raised us to the power of his strength.[18]

In his sermon on Pentecost, Gregory gives several insights about deification and the weakness of preachers set aflame by the Holy Spirit for their mission:

> Teachers possess fiery tongues, because when they preach out of love for God they enflame the hearts of their hearers. A word of teaching is useless if it cannot provide the flame of love. Those who said: *Were not our hearts burning within us as he spoke to us on the road and explained the scriptures to us* received this fire of teaching from the mouth of Truth himself. When words are clearly heard the mind is set on fire, numbness and cold recede, the heart becomes solicitous in its desire for heavenly things on high and strange to earthly desires.[19]

18 *Homilies on Ezekiel* 1.4.20 (CCL 142, 272; Tomkinson, 331–32 [alt.]).

19 To the people in the basilica of St. Peter, apostle, *Homilies on the Gospels* 30.5 (CCL 141, 261; Hurst, 241 [alt.]).

Recall those to whom the Spirit came on that Pentecost Day in Acts 2. Gregory calls them "the holy preachers"—a favorite phrase of his. But they were afraid of suffering. When the Spirit came down upon them, they were raised. Because they were raised to such a height, Gregory asks, "What can I say but that [the Spirit] made the minds of earthly human beings heaven?"[20] Gregory twins the Son's coming in the flesh with the Spirit's coming at Pentecost as the two poles of incarnation and deification:

> In the one, certainly, God by his appointing accepted [*suscepit*] humanity into himself; in the other, truly, human beings accepted [*susceperunt*] God come down from above. In the one, God became human by nature; in the other, human beings became gods by adoption. Therefore, if we do not want to remain fleshbound in death, most beloved brethren, let us love this life-giving Spirit.[21]

Gregory wanted all preachers to experience the fire of the Holy Spirit in order to set others on fire with divine love.[22] This divine love in the heart reorders us. Preachers, like all Christians, are to experience a compunction, or piercing, of the heart, reminiscent of the sinful woman who did not cease kissing the feet of Christ (cf. Lk 7:45), an act greater than pastoral service.[23] By looking to God's love, preachers must not lose sight of their human weakness in Christ where mercy is found.[24]

20 *Homilies on the Gospels* 30.9 (CCL 141, 266; Hurst, 245 [alt.]).

21 *Homilies on the Gospels* 30.9 (CCL 141, 266; Hurst, 245 [alt.]).

22 In comparing Gregory with Augustine, Robert Markus writes, "[Gregory's] references to sacramental rites in the life of the Church are rare," and "his emphasis [is] very much heavier on preaching." See Markus, *Gregory the Great and His World*, 49. Gregory does, at times, emphasize the Eucharist, such as in the *Dialogues*.

23 Gregory comments on Sg 1:1–2A, with an allusion to Lk 7:44–45: "the woman who kisses is preferred to the pastor because whoever amid desire for the Lord feels compunction in interior ardor of mind is preferred to the one who provides exterior goods" (SC 314, 98: DelCogliano, 123).

24 Bernard Green concludes a study on Gregory's Christology, soteriology, and ecclesiology with this apt summary: "The striving after perfection that Gregory urged upon his

We now turn to preachers' acceptance of their weakness in two of Gregory's major works: the *Book of Pastoral Rule* and the *Homilies on Ezekiel.*[25] In the former, we will focus on the preacher's weakness in the last book, the very brief Book IV. In the latter, we will see Gregory's emphasis on weakness in the prophet Ezekiel, through whom, as Gregory says, the order of preachers is designated (*per prophetam praedicatorum ordo*).[26] Like Ezekiel, who not only spoke but also enacted the prophecy that God wanted to communicate to the people, preachers are to embody the Word. Yet, precisely because preachers realize that they have the Word, they also must continually accept that they themselves are human and weak until the end.

Weakness in the *Book of Pastoral Rule*

The *Book of Pastoral Rule,* sometimes rendered the *Pastoral Rule,* communicates the most thorough treatment of pastoral care from the early Church. Gregory was inspired in part by Gregory of Nazianzus's *or.* 2, *On His Flight.* That earlier Gregory is the sole non-scriptural authority cited by Gregory the Great in this work (not counting quotations of his own *Moralia in Job*). The *Pastoral Rule* is Gregory the Great's only "systematic" work, that is, a work governed by a logical order for instruction rather than following the order of presentation given in a particular biblical book. Bruno Judic says that this work has many functions, but the first is as a

audience was a journey through humility to union with Christ, in whose humility human and divine were made one." See Bernard Green, OSB, "The Theology of Gregory the Great: Christ, Salvation and the Church," in *A Companion to Gregory the Great,* eds. Bronwen Neil and Matthew J. Dal Santo (Leiden: Brill, 2013), 135–56, at 156.

25 Other works of Gregory, especially his *Moralia* and his *Forty Homilies on the Gospel,* could also be featured. The *Commentary on First Kings* (i.e., First Samuel), attributed to Gregory, has been shown by Adalbert de Vogüé to be spurious. See his edition of *Grégoire le Grand (Pierre de Cava): Commentaire sur le Premier Livre des Rois,* SC 351, 391, 432, 449, 469, 482 (Paris: Cerf, 1989–2004).

26 *Homelies on Ezekiel* 1.9.29 (CCL 142, 138).

manual for preachers.[27] As such, the *Pastoral Rule* is not recording an act of preaching but rather a guide for bishops and others with the "burdens of pastoral care" (*pastoralis curae pondera*).[28] *Pondus,* the singular of *pondera,* was used by Augustine in his unforgettable line *Pondus meum amor meus*—"My love is my weight."[29] In the *Confessions,* Augustine explains how things tend toward their proper places because of their different "weights." A stone is borne downwards, and a fire is borne upwards. With God's gift of inflamed hearts, Augustine and others are borne up to heaven. Later, Augustine would bemoan his duty of episcopal preaching with this tricolon: *magnum onus, magnum pondus, magnum labor*—"a great responsibility, a great weight, a great labor."[30] Gregory's term of *pondera,* now in the plural, accents burdens—the difficulties that load him and other pastors down.[31] Like his namesake from Nazianzus, Gregory the Great wanted to point out the care of souls as the most difficult "art of arts" at the beginning of ministry—after expressing a desire to flee from its burdens.[32]

27 Bruno Judic, "Structure et Fonction de la *Regula Pastoralis,*" in *Grégoire le Grand,* Chantilly, Centre culturel Les Fontaines 15–19 septembre 1982, eds. Jacques Fontaine, Robert Gillet, Stan Pellistrandi (Paris: Éditions du Centre National de la Recherche Scientifique, 1986), 409–17, at 414.

28 The phrase *pastoralis curae pondera* appears in the opening phrase of the dedicatory letter to John of Ravenna. See SC 381, 124. For a review of secondary literature on the *Pastoral Rule* audience, see Brendan Lupton, "Reexamining Gregory the Great's Audience for the *Pastoral Rule,*" *DR* 133 (2015):178–204. The audience could include priests, abbots, and other Christian leaders called to speak for the salvation of souls. For an adaptation of the *Pastoral Rule* for ministers today, see Thomas C. Oden, *Care of Souls in the Classic Tradition* (Philadelphia: Fortress Press, 1984).

29 Augustine, *Confessions* 13.9.10 (CCL 27, 246; Bourke, 416 [alt.]).

30 Augustine, *s.* 339.4. Here Augustine gives, and repeats, the memorable line, "The gospel terrifies me." WSA III/9, Hill, 282. Cf. Lawless, "Augustine's Burden of Ministry."

31 For first-century non-Christian use of the phrase *curarum pondera,* see Lucan, *Pharsalia* 9.951 (LCL *The Civil War,* Books I–X, 576); see also Statius, *Thebaid* 4.39 (LCL Statius I, 508). For an example of Gregory's idea that only by going down in compassion to our neighbor may we rise, see *Homilies on the Gospels* 39.10 (CCL 141, 391–92; Hurst, 367–68).

32 For a study of the phrase's history before Gregory, see Hofer and Piper, "Retracing the 'Art of Arts and Science of Sciences' from Gregory the Great to Philo of Alexandria."

Gregory uses words with the stem *infirm** some 55 times in his *Pastoral Rule. Infirmitas,* weakness, is a word with rich philosophical and theological significance. For example, in Gregory's Latin Bible, he reads Paul's words to the Corinthians, *Quis infirmatur, et ego non infirmor?* ("Who is not weak, and I am not weak?"). He quotes this phrase twice in the *Pastoral Rule.*[33] Gregory would have read, through Rufinus's translation of *or.* 2, this summation of Gregory of Nazianzus's encomium to Paul: "Therefore, Paul glories, but he does so in infirmities and tribulations."[34] Like the *Pastoral Rule,* the contemporaneous early letters of his pontificate are "heavy with the language of weakness," to borrow Robert Markus's observation.[35] At the beginning of his episcopal ministry, Gregory wanted to emphasize his weakness and the weakness of all who hold an office of preaching.

One should not think that Gregory denied or obscured his office or maintained preaching to be a "non-institutional" activity.[36] In the dedicatory preface to John of Ravenna, in February 591,

33 2 Cor 11:29; *Pastoral Rule* 1.5, *Pastoral Rule* 2.10.

34 *Or.* 2.55. Rufinus has in his Latin translation: *Gloriatur ergo Paulus, sed in infirmitatibus ac tribulationibus suis.* See CSEL 46, ed. Augustus Engelbrecht, 45. Similar terms in meaning abound in the *Pastoral Rule.* For example, the stem *humil** appears 93 times.

35 Robert A. Markus, *Gregory the Great and His World* (Cambridge: Cambridge University Press, 1997), 14. One should not think that only the early letters have this stress on weakness. Gregory later complains a great deal about sickness, tied to his sinfulness. For example, he writes in July 600 that "the second year has now almost ended of my confinement to my wretched bed," see *ep.* 10.14. The complaints are in a long series, as exemplified in *ep.* 11.18, 11.20, and 11.21. G. R. Evans comments, "[F]rom 598 until his death in 604 he was largely confined to bed by acute pain, although he got up when he could to celebrate Mass. He worked on indefatigably to the end." See Gillian R. Evans, *The Thought of Gregory the Great* (Cambridge: Cambridge University Press, 1986), 5.

36 I am puzzled by Conrad Leyser's comment that "[t]he *praedicatores* embody Gregory's radically non-institutional vision of the Church in the last days" (*Authority and Asceticism,* 157). Leyser supports this statement by appealing to Gregory's reference to Felicity, a martyred mother who preaches to her seven sons. See *Homilies on the Gospels* 3.3. Gregory, however, gives anything but a non-institutional vision of the Church in his letters. Also, *praedicare* has a wider semantic range than liturgical preaching. Felicity preaches to her sons by communicating the Gospel to them, and so becomes a "mother of Christ" in accordance with Mt 12:46–50. Gregory sees her as a model of the Church. Instead of Rome's Felicity (the first woman martyr named in the Roman canon of the Mass), Equitius

Gregory refers to the burdens of pastoral care that he now has.[37] He has the office of bishop, an experience quite different from monastic contemplation. The letter's inscription seems clear about the episcopal setting: "Gregory, to the Most Reverend and Holy Brother John, a Fellow Bishop." In this way, he accords titles of holiness to his correspondent, but not to himself, out of humility. In the *Pastoral Rule,* Gregory applies a variety of names to the pastor, whom he describes most prominently as *rector.*[38] They all refer in various ways to a Christian office, and rector emphasizes that one leads others by duty. In fact, Gregory worked to ensure that occupants of high offices are worthy of their holy stations.

Gregory organizes the *Pastoral Rule* into four books. The first regards how one should come to the burdens of pastoral care, beginning with attention to its heaviness to deter, purify, and prepare ministerial candidates. "No one does more harm in the Church," says Gregory, "than he who has the title or rank of holiness and acts perversely." Gregory continues:

> No one presumes to contradict such a delinquent. Moreover, because such a sinner is honored by the dignity of his rank, his offenses spread considerably by way of example. And yet everyone who is unworthy would flee from such a great burden of guilt if, with the attentive ear of the heart, he pondered the saying of the Truth: "He that scandalizes one of these little ones who believes in me, it would be better for him that a millstone

(*Dialogue* 1.4) and Benedict (*Dialogue* 2) could be pointed to as examples in Gregory's writing of non-ordained persons engaging in preaching; but they are abbots.

37 Demacopoulos says, "Gregory sent his *Liber regulae pastoralis*, or *Book of Pastoral Rule*, to John, archbishop of Ravenna, in 590 at the beginning of his pontificate." See Demacopoulos, *St. Gregory the Great: Book of Pastoral Rule*, 13. I prefer the dating of February 591, given for his *ep.* 1.24a, to John of Ravenna (Martyn 1.146–47).

38 Gregory's choice of emphasizing the term *rector* may indicate the influence of Gregory of Nazianzus, *or.* 2, through Rufinus's Latin translation. See Robert A. Markus, "Gregory the Great's *Rector* and His Genesis," in *Grégoire le Grand*, eds. Fontaine, Gillet, and Pellistrandi, 137–46. For Gregory, synonyms, or near synonyms, include: *magister*, *doctor*, and *praedicator*.

> were hung around his neck and that he were cast into the depth of the sea" (Mt 18:6).[39]

Gregory then encourages those who should take on this *pastorale magisterium* of preaching but who are tempted to refuse it in preference of their own meditation.[40] To these people he gives the model of the only begotten Son of the Father, who came from the bosom of the Father for the benefit of the multitude.

He also speaks about the episcopacy explicitly. In chapter 8 of Book 1, Gregory quotes Paul's teaching that "if one desires the episcopate, he desires a good work" (1 Tm 3:1); and then devotes that chapter to explicating the meaning of that phrase. When Paul wrote Timothy, Gregory explains, whoever led the people would be the first to be martyred. Gregory knows that in his own time, in the absence of such an impending danger of death, some are emboldened to lead for selfish reasons:

> Therefore, he who seeks not the good work of the ministry, but only the glory of honor, testifies against himself that he does not desire the office of a bishop [*episcopatum*]. For a man does not love the sacred office, nor does he even understand it, if by craving a position of spiritual leadership he is nourished by the thought of subordinating others, rejoices at being praised, elates his heart by honor, or exalts in the abundance of his affluence.[41]

The next two books in the *Pastoral Rule* address the worthy who humbly take upon themselves the great burdens of pastoral care. Gregory concentrates on the pastor's life in Book 2 and on

39 *Pastoral Rule* 1.2 (SC 381, 134–36; Demacopoulos, 32 [alt.]). Demacopoulos interprets Gregory's use of *nullus* to be "no layperson," but here Gregory seems more broadly to mean that "no one at all presumes to contradict" an errant preacher.

40 Gregory uses the phrase *pastorale magisterium* in *Pastoral Rule* 1.1 and 1.11. See especially *Pastoral Rule* 1.5 for a selfish preference for silent meditation over preaching.

41 *Pastoral Rule* 1.8 (SC 381, 156; Demacopoulos, 41).

the pastor's speech in Book 3.[42] In Book 2, it is made clear that the pastor should be pure in thought, outstanding in action, discrete in silence, useful in word, singularly compassionate as one close to others, raised above all by contemplation, a companion through humility to those who do good, and upright against the vices of the recalcitrant. The pastor must be attentive to his inner life without failing to provide for the needs of others.[43] Take this example of his counsel about how to live. In Gregory's own words, the leader, or preacher, should be:

> a compassionate neighbor to everyone and superior to all in contemplation so that he may transfer the weaknesses of others to himself by means of his intense piety and transcend even his own aspirations for invisible things through the loftiness of his meditation. Otherwise, in pursuing high things he will despise the weaknesses of his neighbors, or by adapting himself to the weaknesses of his neighbors he will abandon the pursuit of high things.[44]

Moreover, rulers must rule over themselves before ruling over others:

> Supreme rule, then, is well administered when the one who presides has dominion over the vices rather than his brothers.

42 This twofold treatment of life and ministry is of the greatest importance. Cf. the Second Vatican Council's *Presbyterorum Ordinis, Decree on the Ministry and Life of Priests* (1965), with its three chapters: (1) The Priesthood in the Ministry of the Church; (2) The Ministry of Priests; and (3) The Life of Priests. For Gregory, life precedes ministry.

43 Book 2 is essentially what Gregory gave as his Synodical Letter to the four Eastern patriarchs. See Bruno Judic, "Preaching according to Gregory the Great," in *Preaching in the Patristic Era*, at 235.

44 *Pastoral Rule* 2.5 (SC 381, 196; Demacopoulos, 58 [alt.]). Benedict XVI notes *Pastoral Rule* 2.5 in his encyclical on love: "Saint Gregory speaks in this context of Saint Paul, who was borne aloft to the most exalted mysteries of God, and hence, having descended once more, he was able to become all things to all men (cf. 2 Cor 12:2–4; 1 Cor 9:22). He also points to the example of Moses, who entered the tabernacle time and again, remaining in dialogue with God, so that when he emerged he could be at the service of his people. "Within [the tent] he is borne aloft through contemplation, while without he is completely engaged in helping those who suffer: *intus in contemplationem rapitur, foris infirmantium negotiis urgetur*." See Benedict XVI, *Deus Caritas Est*, Encyclical on Christian Love, December 25, 2005, no. 7.

> But when superiors correct the delinquents among the laity, it is necessary for them to be careful that when they attack the sin through due discipline, they should still acknowledge themselves, as an exercise of humility, to be the equals of those they correct. And it is fitting that in our silent thoughts, we even prefer those whom we correct to ourselves. For their vices are literally destroyed by the vigor of our discipline, whereas our own vices are not even wounded by the words of anyone.[45]

In Book 3, Gregory offers his most detailed exposition of the work in thirty-six pairs of audiences of the "diversity in the art of preaching."[46] The pairs begin with men versus women, then young versus old, and end with those who do evil secretly and good openly versus those who hide the good they do and allow themselves to be despised. This third book offers a treasure of pastoral sensitivity to the complexity of audiences, arranged according to Gregory's penchant for holding opposites together.

Whereas Book 3, with forty chapters, is the longest of the four parts, Book 4 is the shortest, and has no chapter subdivision. Gregory dedicates this last part to the instruction that "the preacher, after he has done everything that is required, should return to himself so that he does not take pride in his life or preaching."[47] This observation on the preacher's returning to himself and knowing his own weakness recapitulates the intention of this work. Gregory does not want the preacher to swell with pride after living for God and preaching the Word. He gives the model of the prophet Ezekiel, whose book along with the Psalms provide the only direct quotations from the Bible in this fourth part. Gregory accentuates the fact that the Lord calls Ezekiel "the son of man"—a title that occurs over ninety times in the Book of Ezekiel—to teach that the preacher should know his own humanity.

45 *Pastoral Rule* 2.6 (SC 381, 210; Demacopoulos, 65).

46 *Pastoral Rule* 3.1: *Quanta debet esse diversitas in arte praedicationis* (SC 382, 262).

47 This is the title of *Pastoral Rule* 4 (SC 382, 534; Demacopoulos, 209).

Gregory tells his reader: "recognize yourself as a human being" when you have finished preaching to others. This implicitly recalls in Book 2 of what the apostle Peter says to Cornelius, when he had stooped down to honor Peter's feet: "I am also a human being" (Acts 10:26).[48] Gregory concludes the work these words: "I am trying to point others to the shore of perfection, as I am tossed back and forth by the waves of sin. But in the shipwreck of this life, I beg you to sustain me with the plank of your prayers, so that your merit-filled hands might lift me up, since my own weight causes me to sink."[49] Moreover, it is typical of Gregory to display his own weakness in his dependence on the help of those he deems to be holy. A good leader, for Gregory, has the discernment to exercise his humility when he is with the holy but wield his authority when he is with the recalcitrant. More fundamental than all other audiences is God, and preachers must always return to know their weakness before the all-holy God. Gregory's development of this theme in the *Pastoral Rule* also clarifies his treatment of the same theme in his sermons on Ezekiel, "the son of man," who points to Christ and serves as a model for preachers.

Weakness in the *Homilies on Ezekiel*

Gregory's preaching on Ezekiel provides applications of what we find in the *Pastoral Rule*. Conrad Leyser aptly notes, "[A]s Gregory finishes the *Pastoral Rule*, he discovers his next exegetical project.

48 See *Pastoral Rule* 2.6. Demacopoulos uses this in his *The Invention of Peter: Apostolic Discourse and Papal Authority in Late Antiquity*, DRLAR (Philadelphia: University of Pennsylvania Press, 2013), 136–37. Gregory pairs Peter's reaction to Cornelius, who falls at Peter's feet in homage, with Peter's reaction to Ananias and Sapphira, who fall at Peter's feet in death, because they had kept back property and lied to him (Acts 5:1–11). For Gregory, the two cases in Acts together illustrate Peter's discernment. Incidentally, Peter's feet have a prominence that could be better recognized (cf. Jn 13:1–11).

49 *Pastoral Rule* 4 (SC 382, 540; Demacopoulos, 212). The sea commonly symbolized the fragility of life in antiquity.

It is through the book of Ezekiel that he will continue to speak."[50] Gregory preached his *Homilies on Ezekiel* in two books, the first commenting on the beginning of the biblical book through Ezekiel 4:3. Gregory tells his fellow bishop Marinianus in the work's preface that these homilies were delivered eight years earlier before the people (*coram populo*).[51] After the first set of twelve homilies, he relates in a preface to Book II (a set of ten homilies) that he has been asked to explain the prophet's vision of the city built on a mountain, which is the New Temple in Ezekiel 40.[52] He explains his double difficulty caused by the text's obscurity and by Agilulphus, King of the Lombards. The Lombards had crossed the Po and were quickly moving to attack Rome. Ezekiel, a prophet of the Babylonian captivity, could model preachers faithful to the Word in Gregory's turbulent times.

Gregory writes that he does not presume on his own virtue, but on him who "makes the tongues of infants eloquent" (Wis 10:21), that is Christ as the Almighty God.[53] He concludes his first homily on Ezekiel with these words: "For the Almighty God is the speech (*sermo*) of the Almighty Father, and those who desire to speak of

50 Conrad Leyser in *Gregorio Magno e il Suo Tempo. XIX Incontro di studiosi dell'antichità Cristiana in collaborazione con l'École Française de Rome*, Roma, 9–12 maggio 1990. I. Studi storici (Rome: Institutum Patristicum Augustinianum, 1991), 169–82, at 180.

51 *Homilies on Ezekiel* 1.preface (CCL 142, 3). In this preface, Gregory compares his work of despicable water to those of the profound streams of blessed fathers Ambrose and Augustine. In doing so, he shows his humility—and invites comparison to the most highly praised Latin Christian preachers.

52 Scott DeGregorio comments about Gregory's work: "These twenty-two homilies contain some of his most profound exegesis." See Scott DeGregorio, "Gregory's Exegesis: Old and New Ways of Approaching the Scriptural Text," in *A Companion to Gregory the Great*, eds. Neil and Dal Santo, 270–90, at 280. DeGregorio aptly observes, "The Bible formed the natural context for everything that Gregory wrote" (273).

53 *Homilies on Ezekiel* 1.1.19 (CCL 142, 15). Critical editions sometimes do not make fully apparent Gregory's extensive scriptural quotations and allusions in his preaching. This citation of Wis 10:21 (Vulgate), *linguas infantium fecit disertas*, is not given in CCL 142, 15 (cf. *Homilies on Ezekiel* 1.2.4; CCL 142, 19). Similarly, no note appears in Tomkinson's translation, 40. Wis 10:21 is featured in *Mor.* preface.2 in striking similarity to *Homilies on Ezekiel* 1.1.19 in beginning a major work. Cf. the Christological use of Wis 10:21 in Augustine, *Confessions* 8.5.10.

him will in no way be mute in him. For the Almighty Word will give useful words, he who became incarnate for us lives and reigns with the Father in the unity of the Holy Spirit, God, forever and ever. Amen."[54] In other words, the Word still speaks through his preachers.

Like several Fathers of the Church before him, Gregory makes comparisons among different states of life and especially to highlight the category of preachers. An objective ranking does not indicate the subjective holiness of any individual in a state of life.[55] In these homilies, Gregory stresses that not only does the Church have the states of celibates and married, the Church also has preachers (*praedicatores*). For example, concerning Ezekiel 40:10, where Gregory reads "all three were of one measure," he interprets the three rooms around the East gate of the Temple to represent these three states of the married, celibate, and preachers. The preachers have the greatest merit, since they not only restrain themselves but also lead others in a zeal for the good life of conversion. But the three states are all of "one measure," because all have the same faith in this life and all will enjoy the same blessedness in the many mansions of the next life (cf. Jn 14:2 and Mt 20:9).[56]

Gregory repeatedly brings out the significance of what Ezekiel means for preachers. Bruno Judic comments:

54 *Homilies on Ezekiel* 1.1.19 (CCL 142, 15–16; Tomkinson, 40 [alt.]).

55 In the fourth century, Jovinian and Vigilantius were considered heretics for not recognizing that some states and actions were objectively holier than others—such as virginity over married life. On the other hand, the early Church repeatedly rejected as heresy the position of those who denied the holiness of Christian marriage. Augustine, for one, upheld the objective superiority of some states over others (see his treatment of Jovinianism in *On Heresies*, chap. 82), and emphasized the charity and humility at work within souls as more important for salvation than states of life. See, for example, his *On Holy Virginity*.

56 *Homilies on Ezekiel* 2.4.6 (CCL 142, 262–63; Tomkinson, 321); cf. *Homilies on Ezekiel* 2.7.3. For the Augustinian background to the three categories in the Church, see G. Folliet, A.A., "Les trois categories de chrétiens: Survie d'un theme augustinien," *L'Année théologique augustiniénne* 14 (1954): 81–96.

> In many instances, Gregory utilized Ezekiel's example in order to stress the duties of preachers. He stressed this most clearly in *Homily* 11 (mainly) and *Homily* 12 of book 1, where it is easy to see the correspondence between *Homily* 11 and the *Regula Pastoralis*. Gregory uses the same scriptural quotations, the theme of *speculator* [watchman], the conditions for preaching, and even techniques of preaching with a clear reference to rhetoric.[57]

In his *Homilies on Ezekiel*, Gregory repeatedly underscores his weakness and the weakness of other preachers who strive to be like Christ to move their listeners to imitate him Let us now consider three homilies as examples: *Homilies on Ezekiel* 1.2, 11, and 12. In Gregory's preaching, weakness provides a contrast to the power of God at work through preachers who must, to the very end, accept their weakness in order for them to praise God.

Homilies on Ezekiel 1.2

In his second homily on Ezekiel, Gregory underscores Ezekiel's dignity on account of the prophetic call he received. Gregory preaches, "If indeed the intention is to define some mystery in the actual expression of his age, it is not absurd that the prophet show forth the Lord, whom he proclaims in words, also in the very time of his age."[58] Here he makes explicit how Ezekiel, at the age of 30 in this vision near the river Chebar, approximates the age of Christ at the river Jordan, when he was baptized and the heavens opened (Lk 3:23). In interpreting the details of the prophetic book, Gregory depicts Ezekiel as a figure of Christ, either directly or as someone who conveys the Word. Gregory observes that we similarly find a figure of Christ in the disciple whom Jesus loved when we read John's Gospel, and we likewise encounter one conveying the word

57 Judic, "Preaching according to Gregory the Great," 246.

58 *Homilies on Ezekiel* 1.2.5 (CCL 142, 19; Tomkinson, 44 [alt.]).

of the Lord in Paul, through whom Christ speaks, as recorded in the Apostle's letters.[59]

With close attention on "likeness" in Ez 1:5, which appears twice in the Vulgate's edition for "the likeness of the four creatures" (*similitudo quatuor animalium*) and "the likeness of a man" (*similitudo hominis*), Gregory shows the importance of resembling Christ in this second homily. He does this first with the four living creatures, next with the Apostle Paul, then with all the holy ones and particularly with those called the "holy preachers." The four holy living creatures of Ezekiel's vision resemble Christ, for "they would not have been holy if they had not possessed the likeness of this man."[60] For the Apostle, Gregory quotes 1 Cor 4:16, "Be imitators of me, just as I am of Christ" and recalls Paul's teaching that we are to bear the image of the heavenly man (1 Cor 15:47–49). Gregory comments: "For every saint is led toward the likeness of this man, insofar as he imitates the life of his redeemer."[61] He then maps out how holy preachers imitate, though not perfectly, their redeemer, who is always greater. Preachers lament over transgressors, but Jesus as head over all weeps over Jerusalem (Lk 19:41–44). They love those who do right, but Jesus loves even more the rich man who does not give up his riches (Mt 19:16–22, Mk 10:17–22).[62] Holy preachers bear insults, but Christ even heard it said that he had a demon (Jn 8:48–49). They guard their humility, but Jesus is meek and humble of heart (Mt 11:29). Holy preachers love their persecutors, but Jesus prays for his even on the cross (Lk 23:34). Preachers suffer for their brothers and sisters, but the Author of life surrendered himself to death (Acts 3:15). In each case, the conformity of preachers to Christ comes especially through a sharing in his greater weakness

59 *Homilies on Ezekiel* 1.2.8 (CCL 142, 21–22); cf. John 21:20 and 2 Cor 13:3.

60 *Homilies on Ezekiel* 1.2.8.19 (CCL 142, 28; Tomkinson, 54 [alt.]).

61 *Homilies on Ezekiel* 1.2.19 (CCL 142, 29; Tomkinson, 54 [alt.]).

62 Gregory calls the rich man an *adolescens* and reports his statement that he kept the commandments *a iuventute*, conflating Mt 19:16–30 with Mk 10:17–31/Lk 18:18–30.

recorded in Scripture: weeping, bearing insults, humility, loving persecutors, and suffering. This attention to "likeness" continues through the sermon.

Reflecting on the meaning of "the likeness of a man" in Ez 1:15, Gregory preaches this summary concerning the holy living creatures of Ezekiel's vision: "whatsoever is holy, whatsoever is wonderful, this in them derives from the semblance of likeness, that is, from the power of imitation."[63] Gregory makes sure that his listeners understand the implication for their contemplation. We are to perceive the life of the redeemer, our head, in our contemplation and imitate him. Considering the ways of the Lord in our heart, we mold within ourselves the image of the "new man." Because this constantly occurs in the hearts of the holy ones, it is rightly said of the living creatures that there is the likeness of a man in them. Gregory questions, "For he who considers the ways of the Lord silently in his heart, what else does he refashion within himself but the image of a new man?" He draws a conclusion that applies for all the holy ones: "Because this constantly occurs in the hearts of the saints, it is now rightly said of the creatures, 'There was the likeness of a man in them' (Ez 1:5)."[64]

Gregory next treats the likeness of glory in the resurrection. He recounts for the people: "We are now the children of God, and it has not yet appeared what we will be. We know that when he will appear, we will be like him, because we will see him as he is" (1 Jn 3:2). On this, Gregory teaches that the saints in glory imitate the divine essence. First, he establishes from Ex 3:14 and Jas 1:17 that God's essence is eternal and immutable. Then he concludes that because we will be like God when we see him, we will no longer be mutable or subject to death and corruption.

63 *Homilies on Ezekiel* 1.2.19 (CCL 142, 29; Tomkinson, 55 [alt.]).

64 *Homilies on Ezekiel* 1.2.19 (CCL 142, 30; Tomkinson, 56 [alt.]).

Gregory sees how the likeness of God will be in our bodies. Following Phil 3:20–21, Gregory preaches that the Lord Jesus Christ will transform our bodies and make them like his own. Although we cannot have a glory equal to his, we will have a likeness. A likeness of life is already at work now in the conduct of the chosen ones. Therefore, we can expect that in the resurrection of the dead a great likeness will be in the mind and in the body.[65] Gregory concludes this sermon with confidence in having a Helper in Christ, who lives and reigns with the Father in the unity of the Holy Spirit. Our weakness leads to ultimate glory.

Homilies on Ezekiel 1.11

This first book's eleventh homily, on Ez 3:15–28, gives a lesson for the preacher, as we saw in Bruno Judic's observation above. The passage opens with Ezekiel going to the river Chebar to sit among the exiles, mourning in silence for seven days. Only then does the Lord's speech come to the prophet. "It must be noted," preaches Gregory, "with what compassion the holy prophet unites with the captive people, and joins in their sorrow by sitting with them mourning."[66] Why? Gregory explains, "The root of the word is the power of the deed."[67] In other words, a prophet's compassion needs to be seen by the people; otherwise how would they accept the preacher's teaching in their time of sorrow? Moreover, the silence of preachers provides time for them to grow in humility, and speech must flow from silence. "A time for being silent, and a time for speaking," from Eccl 3:7, gives the proper order: silence first, then speech. Gregory underscores how although the prophet was sent precisely to speak, he must begin with days of silent humility and mourning. After that necessary preparation, the prophet will hear,

65 *Homilies on Ezekiel* 1.2.21.

66 *Homilies on Ezekiel* 1.11.2 (CCL 142, 169; Tomkinson, 214 [alt.]).

67 *Homilies on Ezekiel* 1.11.2 (CCL 142, 169; Tomkinson, 214 [alt.]).

"Son of Man, I have given you as a watchman for the house of Israel" (Ez 3:17).

As a watchman, the preacher must be on a height, according to Gregory, to see and to be seen.[68] No watchman can be in the depths. For Gregory, this naturally means that a preacher must be at the summit of virtue and stand at the height of life in order to see what is to come and what those below him are doing. To attain this place, he needs to set his own spirit on things above. Here, Gregory makes a personal confession:

> O how hard these things for me to say because I strike myself by speaking. I whose tongue does not hold the preaching, as is fitting, nor suffices to hold that life follows the tongue. I who am often entangled in idle words and, lazy and negligent, default from the exhortation and edification of my neighbors. I who in the sight of God become mute and verbose, mute in essentials, verbose in idle matters. But behold, God's saying about the life of the watchman compels me to speak. I cannot be silent [*Tacere non possum*] and yet fear to hurt myself by speaking.[69]

He then presents a startling image of the Word of God as a sword that must cut through him to pierce his neighbor, as he himself must be cut for his sinfulness. He knows that he must be hurt:

> Let me speak, let me speak so that the sword of God's speech passes through me to pierce the heart of my neighbor. Let me speak, let me speak so that God's speech even against me sounds through me. I do not deny that I myself am a defendant;

68 The Roman Rite's Liturgy of the Hours has a selection from *Homilies on Ezekiel* 1.11.4–6 (CCL 142, 170–72) for the second reading of the Memorial of St. Gregory the Great on September 3.

69 *Homilies on Ezekiel* 1.11.5 (CCL 142, 171; Tomkinson, 215–16 [alt.]). The phrase *Tacere non possum*, so powerful in indicating the necessity of preaching, appears in Gregory's account of the holy Abbot Equitius (d. c. 570) in *Dial.* 1.4.8. Equitius was asked why he preached, since he was not ordained and thus did not have a mandate from the Bishop of Rome under whose authority he lived. The Italian abbot replied that a young man touched his lips with a blood-letting instrument. Equitius continues, "And so from that day, even if I should want to, I cannot be silent [*tacere non possum*] about God."

> I see my own listlessness and negligence. Perhaps before a kind judge the very recognition of guilt will be the obtainment of pardon.[70]

Gregory frequently expresses longing for his former monastic life, when he did not have episcopal responsibilities and thus could devote himself more readily to contemplation. In his many responsibilities among various sorts of people, Gregory admits his weakness of being allured by idle speech and then committing all sorts of infractions. "Who therefore am I, or what kind of watchman am I?" asks Gregory; "I do not stand on the hill of action but still lie in the valley of weakness. But the Mighty Creator and Savior of the human race, gives efficacy to my tongue and altitude to my life, to unworthy me, and so for his love I do not spare myself in his eloquence."[71] After this turn to the Savior, Gregory observes how every watchman must lead a life on high so as to attract his hearers to the heights and, "by speaking, kindle their minds to love of the heavenly kingdom." "But," Gregory continues, "he acts rightly when his tongue has caught fire from his life."[72]

70 *Homilies on Ezekiel* 1.11.5 (CCL 142, 171; Tomkinson, 216 [alt.]). Tomkinson's translation omits translating the second sentence with "Let me speak, let me speak": *Dicam, dicam, ut etiam contra me sermo Dei sonet per me*. See PL 76:907D–908A, the text she uses, as well as the same words found in CCL 142, 171. Cf. Conrad Leyser, "'Let me speak, let me speak': Vulnerability and Authority in Gregory's Homilies on Ezekiel," in *Gregorio Magno e il Suo Tempo. XIX Incontro di studiosi dell'antichità Cristiana in collaborazione con l'École Française de Rome*, Roma, 9–12 maggio 1990. I. Studi storici (Rome: Institutum Patristicum Augustinianum, 1991), 169–82.

71 *Homilies on Ezekiel* 1.11.6 (CCL 142, 172); Tomkinson, 216–17 [alt.]).

72 *Homilies on Ezekiel* 1.11.7 (CCL 142, 172; Tomkinson, 217 [alt.]). Gregory loves vivid images. Benedict XVI says of Gregory: "In these *Homilies on Ezekiel* is also found that beautiful expression according to which 'the preacher must dip his pen into the blood of his heart; then he can also reach the ear of his neighbor.' Reading his homilies, one sees that Gregory truly wrote with his life-blood and, therefore, he still speaks to us today." See Benedict XVI, General Audience of June 4, 2008. No citation is given; the closest passage I have found is this: "For the one who considers his own life interiorly, and builds others up exteriorly by his warning example, is like one who dips the pen of his tongue in his heart, and writes outwardly with it by the hand of speaking to his neighbors." See *Homilies on Ezekiel* 1.10.13 (CCL 142, 150; Tomkinson, 189 [alt.]).

For Gregory, the preacher's faithfulness to the vocation of being a watchman is a matter of life and death for himself and his people. This follows upon the Lord's words to the prophet in Ez 3:17–21: If the preacher does not rebuke the people for the evil they committed, not only will they die, but the preacher will be held responsible for their sin. If the preacher gives the warning, and they still do not repent, they will die, but the preacher will live.[73] But if the preacher gives the warning, and they do repent, both the preacher and the people will live.

Gregory has much more to say in this sermon about the details of Ezekiel 3 for the benefit of preachers, but let us go to his conclusion. Whereas the emphasis in Ezekiel is the dependence of the people on the prophet, Gregory concludes this sermon by depending on the people listening to him. He begs those who hear his preaching for their intercession:

> Therefore, it is necessary for me not only to expound the words of the prophet but also now to lament my own wretchedness before you. And so I seek that your prayer make me such that I avail to benefit myself and you as well. He is powerful through your intercession to bestow such gifts on me unworthy and weak [*indigno mihi et infirmo*], he who deigned from his own righteousness to become weak for us [*pro nobis dignatus est infirmari*]. For he is the Power and Wisdom of God who assumed our weakness [*nostram infirmitatem*] so that he could

73 Leyser writes, "Gregory refused to contemplate the possibility that the spiritually weak would not accept correction from those strong in virtue. He had faith not only in the boundlessness of *caritas*, but also in *peritia* as an inexhaustible resource. If the strong were both fully committed and truly expert, even the most stubbornly pusillanimous would receive *admonitio* at their hands." See Leyser, "Expertise and Authority in Gregory the Great: The Social Function of *Peritia*," in *Gregory the Great: A Symposium*, ed. John C. Cavadini, NDST 2 (Notre Dame, IN: University of Notre Dame Press, 1995), 38–61, at 49. Leyser primarily notes *Pastoral Rule* 3.8 about advising the forward and the pusillanimous. About the latter, Gregory says "we are more likely [*aptius*] to return the timid to good living. . . ." See SC 382, 292; Demacopoulos, 101. Leyser further supports this by pointing to the apostle Paul in *Homilies on Ezekiel* 1.11.18; cf. *Moralia on Job* 24.16.41 as well as in *Pastoral Rule* 3.27 and *ep.* 5.51. For a counter position, where more than a preacher's strength of virtue is needed to move others, see *Homilies on Ezekiel* 1.12, analyzed below.

> from his strength make us strong, Jesus Christ our Lord, who lives and reigns with God the Father in the unity of the]Holy Spirit, forever and ever. Amen.[74]

Homilies on Ezekiel 1.12

The final homily of the first book of *Homilies on Ezekiel* treats the details of Ezekiel's call to go to the plain where the Lord will speak to him—and will tell him to return to his house where he will be bound and be made mute (Ez 3:22–27). It then considers the image of Ezekiel from the beginning of chapter 4, where Ezekiel is told to draw the city of Jerusalem on a clay tablet, have the tablet besieged, and put an iron pan between that drawing and the prophet. Ezekiel is a prophet not only by his words, but also by his deeds. His very life serves as a sign to the house of Israel. Gregory takes the opportunity to propose Ezekiel as the model preacher—showing forth in word and deed what God does to the preacher and to his hearers.

When Ezekiel on the plain encounters the glory of the Lord—a glory such as he saw by the river Chebar—he fell on his face. Gregory preaches:

> The glory of the Lord being manifest, the prophet falls on his face because although a human being is raised to the understanding of the sublime yet, through the contemplation of the majesty of God, he realizes the weakness of his own condition and, as it were, has no standing, he who sees himself as dust and ashes before the eyes of God.[75]

In Ezekiel's case, the Spirit entered him and set him upon his feet (Ez 3:24). Gregory then elucidates what this means for preachers:

74 *Homilies on Ezekiel* 1.11.29 (CCL 142, 184; Tomkinson, 231 [alt.]).

75 *Homilies on Ezekiel* 1.12.4 (CCL 142, 186; Tomkinson, 234 [alt.]).

> When we humbly prostrate before God, when we know ourselves to be dust and ashes, when we ponder the weakness of our proper condition and do not adopt a stance of rigidity and pride [*statum rigiditatis et superbiae*], Almighty God through his Spirit raises us and sets us upon our feet, so that we who humbly from the awareness of our weakness lay and are lying prostrate, afterward in good works, as it were, stand upon our feet through righteousness.[76]

Gregory understands God's order for the prophet to go to the plain to mean that God sends the preacher to those God wants to correct. Gregory says, "And there he sees the glory of the Lord because the more abundantly he perceives the grace of doctrine, the more he extends himself in the labor of preaching from the love of his neighbors."[77]

Once the Spirit had entered Ezekiel the prophet, he was instructed to be shut within his house (cf. Ez 3:24). Gregory understands the prophet's withdrawal to be symbolic of the preacher's: "But because the preacher must always run back to his mind, to preserve inward humility and purity, after the plain it is needful that he return to the house so that he may recognize in the words which he speaks what manner of person he himself is within his conscience."[78] Gregory wants the preacher to resist transitory praise of himself. Similar to the Lord's command to the prophet to go to his house, in Gregory's judgment, is the Lord's command to the healed paralytic, "Pick up your mat and go into your house" (Mk 2:11). Gregory asks whether it means anything other than: "bear the trials of the flesh [*tentationes carnis*] in which you lay until now and return to your conscience in order that you may see what things you have done."[79] Gregory does not tire of stressing this basic point. For instance, he

76 *Homilies on Ezekiel* 1.12.5 (CCL 142, 186; Tomkinson, 234).
77 *Homilies on Ezekiel* 1.12.10 (CCL 142, 188; Tomkinson, 237).
78 *Homilies on Ezekiel* 1.12.10 (CCL 142, 189; Tomkinson, 237).
79 *Homilies on Ezekiel* 1.12.11 (CCL 142, 189; Tomkinson, 238).

interprets Ez 3:25, regarding the prophet's being bound and held back from the people, with this meaning: "So when each preacher is led back to the conscience of his own house, bonds are put upon him and he is bound with them because the more he examines himself in thought the more he realizes with what great infirmities of his mortality the soul of a righteous one is bound."[80]

Gregory then comments on the passage, "I will make your tongue stick fast to the roof of your mouth; and you shall be mute, and not as a man that reproves: because they are a provoking house" (Ez 3:26). He describes in intricate detail the withdrawing of preaching—but with a remarkable twist. Not only does Gregory explore how preaching may fall silent due to the sin of the hearers, as "they are a provoking house," but it may also be due to the sin of the preacher. He offers four scenarios of what God has done at different times:

> Preaching is taken away from good teachers because of evil hearers (Acts 22:18 and Acts 16:6).
>
> Preaching is given to evil teachers because of good hearers (Mt 23:3).
>
> Preaching is given to good teachers for the justification of teachers and hearers (Mt 28:18).
>
> Preaching is taken away from both teachers and hearers unworthy of it (1 Sm 2:27–3:18).[81]

What would be the advantage of knowing the different reasons for the giving and taking away of preaching? Gregory holds that because the reason for granting or removing preaching cannot easily be known, humility is to be preserved. If we hold on to humility,

80 *Homilies on Ezekiel* 1.12.13 (CCL 142, 190; Tomkinson, 239 [alt.]).

81 For these four aspects, see *Homilies on Ezekiel* 1.12.16.

even should preaching depart, it might return through this grace of humility.[82]

In the image of the frying pan (Ez 4:3), Gregory finds that the pan represents the preacher's suffering the frying of his heart to protect the people. Gregory volunteers this beautiful comment: "Indeed no sacrifice to Almighty God is like zeal for souls. Hence the Psalmist said: 'Zeal for your house has consumed me.'"[83] Gregory urges preachers not only to be sacrifices to God, but whole burnt offerings (*holocausta*) so that they be ablaze with spiritual love.[84] "Therefore," exhorts Gregory, "let us take up the iron pan and place it as a wall of iron between us and the city, that is, let us assume strong zeal and set between us and the soul of our hearer what will presently be a strong bulwark. For we shall find this wall of iron then if we now hold it firmly, namely by teaching, by guarding, by persuading, by rebuking, by soothing, by frightening, by acting sometimes mildly and sometimes indeed more severely."[85] Even when the preacher needs to appear harsh for his hearers' benefit, he is to have great love and no disdain for them.

Again, Gregory concludes his homily with a doxology for the incarnation. He preaches that a soul must realize that it cannot be snatched from evil traps by its own power. Rather, the soul:

82 *Homilies on Ezekiel* 1.12.17.

83 *Homilies on Ezekiel* 1.12.30 (CCL 142, 201; Tomkinson, 251 [alt.]).

84 For Gregory's most famous treatment of preachers as whole burnt offerings, see *Homilies on Ezekiel* 2.8.16: "But when he shall devote to Almighty God everything he has, everything he lives, everything he knows, it is a holocaust" (CCL 142, 348; Tomkinson, 410 [alt.]). Thomas Aquinas uses this passage at least thirteen times to describe vowed religious. For a study of Aquinas's appreciation of this Gregorian image, including its Origenistic background, and his comparison of it to the three sets of human goods (exterior goods, goods of the body, and goods of the soul) identified in Aristotle, *Nicomachean Ethics* 1, chap. 8 (1098b), see Andrew Hofer, OP, "Aquinas's Use of Patristic Sources in His Theology of Religious Life," in *Reading the Church Fathers with Thomas Aquinas*, edited by Piotr Roszak and Jörgen Vijgen, Bibliothèque de l'École des Hautes Études, Sciences Religieuses 189 (Turnhout: Brepols, 2021), 295–338, at 329–31.

85 *Homilies on Ezekiel* 1.12.30 (CCL 142, 202; Tomkinson, 252 [alt.]).

> must hope for the Help who can, through the mystery of his redemption, even beyond the spirits that are without flesh, strengthen us living in corruptible flesh, Jesus Christ our Lord, who lives and reigns with the Father, in the unity of the Holy Spirit, God, for ever and ever. Amen.[86]

Conclusion

When John Paul II wrote his post-synodal apostolic exhortation on the bishop, he cited Gregory the Great only once—but he did so to show Gregory's typical emphasis on the weakness of the pastor from his personal experience. John Paul writes, "Spiritual realism enables us to see that the Bishop is called to live out his vocation to holiness in a context of difficulties within and without, amid his own weaknesses and those of others, in daily contingencies and personal and institutional problems." He continues:

> This is a constant feature of the life of pastors, as Saint Gregory the Great acknowledged when he admitted with regret: "After having laid upon my heart the burden of the pastoral office, my spirit has become incapable of frequent recollection, because it remains divided among many things. I am obliged to judge the cases of Churches and monasteries; often I am called to involve myself in the lives and actions of individuals ... And so with my mind pulled and torn, forced to think of so many things, when can it recollect itself and concentrate totally on preaching, without withdrawing from the ministry of proclaiming the word? ... The life of the watchman must always be on high and on guard."[87]

86 *Homilies on Ezekiel* 1.12.33 (CCL 142, 203; Tomkinson, 253 [alt.]).

87 John Paul II, *Pastores Gregis*, Post-Synodal Apostolic Exhortation on the Bishop, Servant of the Gospel of Jesus Christ for the Hope of the World, October 16, 2003, no. 23, quoting Gregory, *Homilies on Ezekiel* 1.11 (PL 76:908).

As John Paul teaches from Gregory's *Homilies on Ezekiel,* Gregory wants preachers never to forget their weakness—their mortality, their sinfulness, their ignorance, their utter reliance on what God gives to them.

What Gregory says in his *Pastoral Rule* and in his *Homilies on Ezekiel* is consistent with what he says elsewhere about preachers accepting their own weakness. In preaching on Lk 10:1–7, the Lord's commissioning of the seventy-two disciples two-by-two, Gregory offers a summary on preaching:

> Then we truly preach what is right to others, if we show our words in our actions, if we ourselves are pierced [*compungimur*] by divine love, and if we wash away with our tears the stains of human life that we daily acquire, since we cannot live without sin. Then do we truly feel remorse if we diligently ponder the deeds of our ancestors so that when we have regarded their glory, our own lives may appear base in our eyes.[88]

The great exemplars of the past help Gregory, and can help us, to know how we fail to live up to the Word we have received.

Moreover, what Gregory writes in his letters about his weakness in his pontificate is not merely posturing for the sake of his personal power or his Church; rather, it expresses what he inculcates in preachers on many occasions: They are not to rely on themselves, but on the Lord. By doing so, they will find that the Word is enacted in their lives as preachers; the Word will be thus enfleshed. We must not be confident in ourselves, but only in God. "Seek God's help and pray for his grace," Gregory tells the newly elected Bishop of Constantinople, Cyriacus, "for without God, we are nowhere without fault. And with him, nowhere without righteousness."[89] Because of

88 *Homiles on the Gospel* 17.10 (CCL 141, 124; *Hom.* 17=*Hom.* 19 in Hurst, 141 [alt.]).

89 *Ep.* 7.7 (CCL 140, 450; Straw [alt.]) in Carole Straw, "Gregory's Politics: Theory and Practice," in *Gregorio Magno e il Suo Tempo.* XIX Incontro di studiosi dell'antichità Cristiana in collaborazione con l'École Française de Rome, Roma, 9–12 maggio 1990. I. Studi storici (Rome: Institutum Patristicum Augustinianum, 1991), 47–63, at 47.

that yearning for God, Gregory became great in grace.[90] The epitaph given to Gregory after his death provides a summary of the ideal correspondence between life and speech: "He fulfilled by act whatever he taught by word" (*Implebatque actu quidquid sermone docebat*)—something that Gregory would not claim for himself.[91]

Nearing the end of his *Homilies on Ezekiel* Gregory gives a heart-wrenching account of current events. He speaks of being surrounded by danger of death on every side: "Some return to us with mutilated hands, others are reported captured, others slain."[92] In the midst of this violence and fear of the evil that may come, Gregory recalls what is most important: his divine adoption. He concludes his preaching on Ezekiel by referring all that he and his hearers experience to God:

> He who created us also became a Father to us through the Spirit of adoption whom he gave. And sometimes he nourishes his children on bread, sometimes he corrects them with the lash, because through sorrows and wounds and gifts he instructs them for their perpetual inheritance. Therefore, glory be to our almighty Lord Jesus Christ, who lives and reigns with the Father in the unity of the Holy Spirit, God, forever and ever. Amen.[93]

When current events make us sorrowful and distressed, we can imitate Gregory. In accepting responsibility for our sinfulness and

90 John Moorhead astutely closes the introduction to his book on Gregory with this observation: "Many people in the contemporary West are attracted to Buddhism, and seek to eradicate desire from their lives. The spiritual tradition from which Gregory speaks points in the reverse direction. In the midst of transience and turbulence, it was yearning that enabled him to keep functioning, in the hope that that which now was unattainably distant would in the end be the object of his loving contemplation, face to face." See Moorhead, *Gregory the Great*, 48.

91 Robert A. Markus used this line of Gregory's epitaph for the epigraph of his *Gregory the Great and His World*. For the full epitaph written by Peter Oldradus of Milan, and recorded by John the Deacon, see John the Deacon, *Vita Gregorii* (PL 75:221B–C), translated in DelCogliano, *Gregory the Great: On the Song of Songs*, 25.

92 *Homilies on Ezekiel* 2.10.24 (CCL 142, 397; Tomkinson, 458).

93 *Homilies on Ezekiel* 2.10.24 (CCL 142, 397–98; Tomkinson, 458–59 [alt.]).

accepting our sorrows and wounds, we can know ourselves as having received the Spirit of adoption from the Father. God accepts us as an everlasting inheritance; and we can turn everything over to the Lord Jesus Christ, the Word made flesh, in endless praise.

CONCLUSION

THE POWER OF PATRISTIC PREACHING

The Word in Our Flesh

In 386, in a basilica surrounded by imperial soldiers in persecution of him and his flock, Ambrose of Milan preached a stirring homily against Auxentius, an anti-Nicene bishop at Milan's imperial court.[1] Ambrose says that his own weapons are his tears, and he recounts at one point a story of St. Peter. At a time of persecution, Christians begged Peter to withdraw in order to save himself so that he would later be able to instruct and confirm them in the faith. At night, as he was leaving near the city gate, he saw Christ enter the city. "Lord, where are you going?" Peter asked. Christ replied, "I am going to be crucified again." Ambrose explains,

1 This Auxentius should not be confused with the anti-Nicene Bishop of Milan, also named Auxentius, immediately before Ambrose's episcopacy. Neil McLynn calls this largely improvised preaching by Ambrose "a sermon which ranks among the masterpieces of antique political rhetoric." See Neil B. McLynn, *Ambrose of Milan: Church and Court in a Christian Capital*, TCH 22 (Berkeley and Los Angeles: University of California Press, 1994), 203. McLynn writes, "As has long been recognized, this speech cannot be understood without reference to the audience's participation. The sudden shifts of direction, occasionally amounting to a complete reversal, reflect the punctuation of their roars of approval or protest, while the staccato bursts in the final paragraphs seem to represent items offered up for popular ratification" (206).

"Peter understood the response to pertain to his own cross."[2] Peter knew that as to Christ's death, "he died to sin once and for all; as to his life he lives for God" (Rom 6:10). "Therefore," Ambrose says, "Peter understood that Christ would be crucified in his little servant [*servulo*] and so he willingly returned." Ambrose then gives the point of the Petrine story for him and his people suffering: "You see, then, that Christ wishes to suffer in his little servants [*servulis*]."[3] Preaching against a heresy that denied the full divinity of the Word with the Father, Ambrose makes present for his people's contemplation both the incarnation of the Word and the Word's dwelling within our own lives.[4] The two are inextricably linked as a single mystery in the Spirit. The sharp division between the modern disciplines of "Christology" and "moral theology" should not blind us to the unity of the Trinity's plan of salvation. This single mystery is

2 *Sermon against Auxentius* 12–13 (PL 16:1010C–11A; de Romestin, 432 [alt.]).

3 *Sermon against Auxentius* 14 (PL 16:1011B; de Romestin, 432 [alt.]). In explaining the Christian faith, Ambrose says elsewhere: "If we soberly hold to those things which be worthy of the Son of God, we ought to understand him to have been sent in such a way that the Word of God, out of the incomprehensible and ineffable mystery of the depths of his majesty, gave himself for comprehension to our minds, so far as we could lay hold of him, not only when *he emptied himself* (Phil 2:7), but also when he dwelt in us, as it is written, *I will dwell in them* (2 Cor 6:16)." See *On the Faith*, 5.7.99 (PL 16:668B–C; de Romestin, 296 [alt.]); cf. Ambrose, *On the Holy Spirit* 3.12.91. For an overview of deification in Ambrose, see Brian Dunkle, SJ, "Beyond Carnal Cogitations: Deification in Ambrose of Milan," in *Deification in the Latin Patristic Tradition*, ed. Ortiz, 132–52.

4 Michael Williams claims, "Whether or not Auxentius was an 'Arian' is beside the point: what is significant is that even here, in what might seem an open-and-shut case, Ambrose goes out of his way to avoid making specific accusations of heresy. He is content to conjure up an impression of 'Arian' hostility, without ever committing himself to the claim that his opponents are really 'Arian' heretics." See Michael Stuart Williams, "No Arians in Milan? Ambrose on the Basilica Crisis of 385/6," *Historia* 67, no. 3 (2018): 346–65, at 360. In his monograph on Ambrose, Williams similarly writes: "Ambrose consistently misrepresented as 'Arian' a range of doctrinal beliefs which modern scholars would label 'Homoian', and which in the west at this time remained wholly consistent with the prevailing definition of orthodoxy as set out at Rimini." See Michael Stuart Williams, *The Politics of Heresy in Ambrose of Milan: Community and Consensus in Late Antique Christianity* (Cambridge: Cambridge University Press, 2017), 221. The *Sermon against Auxentius* expresses what Michael Williams says earlier of Ambrose's hymns, which are mentioned in *Sermon against Auxentius* 34: "Ambrose's hymns in particular may be thought of as emphasizing a didactic and doctrinal purpose in order to encourage or even inculcate a popular resistance to Arianism in Milan." See Michael Stuart Williams, "Hymns as Acclamations: The Case of Ambrose of Milan," *JLA* 6, no. 1 (2013): 108–34, at 133.

lived by preachers and those who listen to them, as all are to receive and communicate the Word in their lives.[5]

In patristic preaching, we find the Word in our flesh. That has been the overarching principle of this book through a consideration of incarnation, deification, and proclamation. We Christians, as different as we are from one another, belong to the Word as branches on the vine, to be pruned and bear abundant fruit, lest we be cut off (cf. Jn 15:1–17). We are blessed to know intimately him who is beyond all knowledge. In the icon of Christ the True Vine, which graces this book's cover, the Lord Jesus holds the Book of the Gospels open to John 15, and the apostles and evangelists surround him as not only going out from him, but in a sense growing out from him. They never leave him, as he remains in them. By holding onto scrolls and books, they reveal the Word as his branches. Like the apostles and evangelists, early Christian preachers in diverse and definite ways show in their lives and words the life and words they drew from Jesus. They communicate the deified life for their contemporary listeners and for those who read their words today. Through these preachers, we find hope in the midst of our suffering, a hope that exists because the Word has taken our flesh. He did so once in that singular union within the womb of the Virgin Mary, and he does so repeatedly in incorporating us into his body through preaching and the sacraments by the power of the Spirit. Consequently, with the Spirit's overshadowing, the Word was not only made flesh, but also is made manifest in our flesh. We embody the same Word that caused both suffering and sustenance to Jeremiah:

5 Monica may have been one of those listening to Ambrose's preaching against Auxentius. See Augustine, *Confessions* 9.7.15: "The faithful people stayed night and day in the church, preparing to die with their bishop, your servant. My mother, your servant, was one of the leaders in these cares and vigils, living on prayers" (CCL 27, 141–42; Bourke, 220 [alt.]). John Peter Kenney comments, "The fact that Monica was a 'martyr,' or witness in the face of death is often neglected, perhaps because her Arian persecutors were themselves Christians." See John Peter Kenney, *Contemplation and Classical Christianity: A Study in Augustine*, OECS (Oxford: Oxford University Press, 2013), 152n57.

"The Word of the Lord has brought me reproach and derision all day long. I say I will not mention him, I will no longer speak in his name. But then it is as if fire is burning in my heart, imprisoned in my bones; I grow weary holding back, I cannot" (Jer 20:8–9).

Augustine knew well how we, so flesh-bound, need to be strengthened. For that reason, when preaching on a Psalm verse—"From the morning watch even until night, my soul has hoped in the Lord"—Augustine says the following:

> Some people say, "Well, yes, the Lord rose again, but is that any reason for me to hope that I can rise too?" Yes, precisely. For that reason, the Lord rose in what he received from you. He could not have risen unless he had first died, and he could not have died unless he had borne flesh. What did the Lord receive from you? Flesh. What was he in himself, he who came to us? The Word of God, which existed before all beings, through which all beings were made.

Augustine then introduces the theme of sacrifice:

> But in order to receive something from you, *the Word was made flesh, and dwelt in us* (Jn 1:14). He took from you something that he could offer for you, just as a priest takes from you something which he will offer on your behalf when you want to appease God for your sins. That was what happened with Christ, exactly that. Our priest took from us what he was to offer for our sake. He received flesh from us, and in that flesh he became a victim, he became a holocaust, he was made into a sacrifice. In his passion he became our sacrifice, but in his resurrection he restored to newness the flesh that had been slain and gave it back to God as the first-fruits of your humanity.

And he concludes by speaking in Christ's own voice:

> He says to you, "See now, everything that is yours is consecrated, because these first-fruits of your nature have been dedicated to God. Hope, therefore, that what has been done in

advance with respect to your first-fruits will come to completion in yourself one day."[6]

The Word speaks through Augustine to let people know that what began when Christ took flesh from the Virgin Mary, overshadowed by the Spirit, is to be completed in our own flesh. That expresses the apostolic faith. In his life of preaching, the apostle Paul knew this well in terms of his suffering on earth: "I am filling up what is lacking in the afflictions of Christ on behalf of his body, which is the church, of which I am a minister in accordance with God's stewardship given to me to bring to completion for you the word of God" (Col 1:24–25). He also had hope of a resurrection: "He will change our lowly body to conform with his glorified body by the power that enables him also to bring all things into subjection to himself" (Phil 2:21). But during this life of fragility, Paul came to hear from the Lord, "My grace is sufficient for you, for power is made perfect in weakness" (2 Cor 12:9). Early Christian preachers continued this apostolic life and preaching by having lives of the Word in their flesh.

In each chapter of this book, we considered a basic biblical aspect of Christian life—helpful in the times of those preachers and in our own—that combines reflection on the incarnation, deification, and proclamation. In the incarnation, the Word gives us holiness in the flesh, shows humility in the flesh, purifies and gives us faith in the flesh, grants hope amidst the daily struggles in the flesh, loves in the flesh, cares for the poor and the weak in the flesh, and displays weakness in the flesh. By the power of the Holy Spirit and with the Virgin Mary's consent, the Word took our flesh once and for all. That singular incarnation leads by the Spirit to a continual enfleshment in us through grace, a sacramental incorporation into Christ, until the end of time. All of us dedicated to evangelization

6 *Expositions of the Psalms* 129.7 (CSEL 95/3, 258–59; WSA III/20, Boulding, 5.133 [alt.]).

are to proclaim nothing less than that same Word—in *our* flesh. In *our* flesh, the Word shows holiness. In *our* flesh, the Word shows humility. In *our* flesh, the Word purifies and communicates faith. In *our* flesh, the Word gives hope. In *our* flesh, the Word loves. In *our* flesh, the Word cares for the poor and the weak. In *our* flesh, the Word accepts weakness. He heals and raises us up to do what he does.

This deification comes about because of the grace of the Word, who takes our flesh and shows his mysteries in our virtuous actions and speech. Since all of us who proclaim the Word are called to serve others, we become instruments for what the Word wants to do in the lives of others. All Christians are called by the power of the Spirit in the sacramental life to be bearers of the Word, allowing him to be expressed in action and speech to the glory of God most high. Preachers are to lead the way by life and speech.

At this time in Christian history many are agreed that we need renewal, far reaching renewal that shines forth as light for the world, from the transparency of our lives. In age after age and place after place, Christian renewal has occurred through preachers preaching what is most important: "Faith comes from what is heard, and what is heard is through the utterance of Christ" (Rom 10:17).[7] Although they did not have perfection in every way and at all times, the Fathers of the Church exemplify a renewal through the basics of the transformed Christian life. They do so in intelligent and faith-filled ways that express with power the divine mysteries celebrated, especially in the Eucharist. Through their graced lives and words, the Fathers become icons of the Word made flesh that we can behold. The power of patristic preaching, in its rich variety,

7 Two recent collections of sermons, with exemplary relevance to the recovery of patristic preaching, are Hans Boersma, *Sacramental Preaching: Sermons on the Hidden Presence of Christ*, foreword by Eugene H. Peterson (Grand Rapids, MI: Baker Academic, 2016) and J. Augustine Di Noia, OP, *Grace in Season: The Riches of the Gospel in Seventy Sermons*, foreword by Aquinas Guilbeau, OP (Providence, RI: Cluny Media, 2019).

allows us to experience "the glory of God on the face of Jesus Christ" (2 Cor 4:6). "But," we must recall, "we hold this treasure in earthen vessels, that the surpassing power may be of God and not from us" (2 Cor 4:7). We praise *the Word in our flesh.*

As we have seen repeatedly, many patristic homilies conclude with thanks and praise that follow upon faith in the incarnation, opening us up to the mystery of the most holy Trinity. This is not accidental; preaching itself is doxology. The Latin verb *praedicare,* for instance, means both to glorify and to preach. In each sense, we make known the mighty deeds of the One who has called us "out of darkness into his wonderful light" (1 Pt 2:9). Glorifying God now in the flesh prepares us for what we are called to be after the resurrection of the body: wholly deified to the glory of God. Could Christians, afflicted by the evils of sin, scandal, and confusion in a world that is passing away, return to the power of patristic preaching that leads a priestly people to turn away from evil and in a life of deifying virtue give thanks and praise in the flesh on account of the Word made flesh? In response to that question, we can conclude with the prayer that, it is said, Augustine expressed at the end of his sermons:

> Let us turn to the Lord God, the almighty Father,
> and from a pure heart render to him the highest and most sincere thanks
> that our puny strength allows.
> Let us entreat him with our whole spirit
> so that in his unique gentleness he may accord a favorable hearing to our prayers.
> May he in his power
> cast out the enemy from our actions and thoughts,
> increase our faith,
> guide our minds,

grant us spiritual thoughts,
and bring us at last to his beatitude.
Through his Son, Jesus Christ our Lord, who lives and reigns with him in the unity of the Holy Spirit, God, forever and ever. Amen.[8]

8 Augustine, *Expositions of the Psalms* 150.8 (CSEL 95/5, 304n25; WSA III/20, Boulding 6.515 [alt.]). Maria Boulding notes how concluding prayers are mentioned in *Expositions of the Psalms* 80.22; 86.9; 128.13; 143.19.

BIBLIOGRAPHY

Ancient Sources: Texts and Translations

Ambrose

De Officiis. Edited with an introduction, translation, and commentary by Ivor J. Davidson. 2 vols. OECS. Oxford: Oxford University Press, 2002.

Ep. 2. PL 16:879A–888A. Translated in part in ICEL, "From a letter by Saint Ambrose, bishop," Office of Readings, December 7, *The Liturgy of the Hours*. Vol. 1, 1218–19.

Intende Qui Regis Israel. Text and translation in Dunkle, *Enchantment and Creed in Ambrose of Milan*, 224.

On the Faith. Translated by H. de Romestin, NPNF, second series, vol. 10, 201–314.

On the Holy Spirit. Translated by Roy J. Deferrari. FC 44, 35–214. Washington, DC: The Catholic University of America Press, 1963.

Sermon against Auxentius. PL 16:1007–18. Translated by H. de Romestin, NPNF, second series, vol. 10, 430–36.

Anonymous Monk of Whitby

The Earliest Life of Gregory the Great by an Anonymous Monk of Whitby. Text, translation, and notes by Bertram Colgrave. Cambridge: Cambridge University Press, 1968.

Apollinarius of Laodicea

Apollinaris von Laodicea und seine Schule. Texte und Untersuchungen. Edited by Hans Lietzmann. Hildesheim: Georg Olms Verlag, 1970.

Aristotle

Nicomachean Ethics. With an English translation by H. Rackham. Rev. ed. LCL 73. Cambridge, MA: Harvard University Press, 1934.

Rhetoric. With an English translation by John Henry Freese. LCL 193. Cambridge, MA: Harvard University Press, 1926.

Athanasius

Ep. 61, to Maximus. PG 26:1085–89.

Augustine of Hippo

Letters

Epistulae I – LV. Edited by Kl. D. Daur. CCL 31. Turnhout, Brepols, 2004.

Epistulae LVI – C. Edited by Kl. D. Daur. CCL 31A. Turnhout, Brepols, 2005.

Ep. 209. PL 33:953–57.

Letters. WSA II/1–4. Translated by Roland Teske, SJ. Hyde Park, NY: New City Press, 2001–2005.

Sermons

Augustine d'Hippone: Vingt-Six Sermons au People d'Afrique. Edited by François Dolbeau. Collection des Études Augustiennes. Série Antiquité 147. Paris: Institut d'Études Augustiniennes, 1996.

Expositions of the Psalms. 1–32. Edited by C. Weidmann. CSEL 93/1A-B (2003, 2011); *51–60.* Edited by H. Müller. CSEL 94/1 (2004). *61–70.* Edited by H. Müller. CSEL 94/2 (2020). *101–109.* Edited by F. Gori, with the assistance of C. Pierantoni. CSEL 95/1 (2011). *110–118.* Edited by F. Gori, with the assistance of A. De Nicola. CSEL 95/2 (2015). *119–133.* Edited by F. Gori. CSEL 95/3 (2001). *134–140.* Edited by F. Gori, with the assistance of F. Recanatini (2002). *141–150.* Edited by F. Gori, with the assistance of J. Spaccia. CSEL 95/5 (2005). For the edition of the *Expositions of the Psalms* not yet published by CSEL, see CCL 38–40 (1956). Translated by Maria Boulding, OSB. WSA III/15–20. Hyde Park, NY: New City Press, 2000–04.

Homilies on 1 John. Edited by Paul Agaësse. SC 75. Paris: Cerf, 1994. Translated by John W. Rettig. FC 92, 119–277. Washington, DC: The Catholic University of America Press, 1995.

Homilies on the Gospel of John. Edited by Augustinus Mayer. CCL 36. Turnhout: Brepols, 1954. Translated by John W. Rettig. FC 78, 79, 88, 90, 92. 1988–95.

Sermons 1–50. Edited by C. Lambot, OSB. CCL 41. Turnhout: Brepols, 1961.

Sermons 51–70A. Edited by P.-P. Verbraken, OSB, et al. CCL 41Aa. Turnhout: Brepols, 1961.

S. 188. PL 38:1003–5.

S. 215. PL 38:1073–76.

S. 340. PL 38:1482–84.

S. 350. PL 39:1533–35.

S. 356. Edited by C. Lambot, OSB, SPM, 132–43. Utrecht: Spectrum, 1950.

S. 389. Edited by C. Lambot, OSB, *RevBen* 58 (1948): 43–52.

Sermons to the People. Translated by Edmund Hill, OP. WSA III/1–11. Hyde Park, NY: New City Press, 1990–97.

Other

Against the Letters of Petilian. Translated by Maureen Tilley and Boniface Ramsey. WSA I/21, 54–264. Hyde Park, NY: New City Press, 2019.

City of God. Edited by Bernardus Dombart and Alphonsus Kalb. CCL 47 and 48. Turnhout: Brepols, 1955.

Commentary on Galatians. Introduction, text, translation, and notes by Eric A. Plumer. OECS. Oxford: Oxford University Press, 2003.

Confessions. Edited by Lucas Verheijen, OSA. CCL 27. Turnhout: Brepols, 1981. Translated by Vernon J. Bourke. FC 21. New York: Fathers of the Church, 1953.

Enchiridion on Faith, Hope, and Love. Edited by E. Evans. CCL 46, 49–114. Turnhout: Brepols, 1969. Translated by Bruce Harbert. WSA I/8, 265–343. Hyde Park, NY: New City Press, 2005.

On Catechizing the Uninstructed. Edited by I. B. Bauer. CCL 46, 121–78. Turnhout: Brepols, 1969. Translation, Introduction and Notes by Raymond Canning. Edited by Boniface Ramsey. WSA. Hyde Park, NY: New City Press, 2006.

On Christian Teaching. Edited by Joseph Martin. CCL 32, 1–167. Turnhout: Brepols, 1962. Translated by Edmund Hill, OP. WSA I/11. Hyde Park, NY: New City Press, 1996.

On Heresies. Edited by R. Vander Plaetse and C. Beukers. CCL 46, 286–345. Turnhout: Brepols, 1969. Translated by Roland J. Teske, SJ. WSA I/18, 31–77. Hyde Park, NY: New City Press, 1995.

On Nature and Grace. Translated by Roland J. Teske, SJ. WSA I/23, 225–75. Hyde Park, NY: New City Press, 1997.

On the Trinity. Edited by W. J. Mountain, with the assistance of Fr. Glorie. CCL 50 and 50A. Turnhout: Brepols, 1968. Translated by Stephen McKenna, CSSR. FC 45. Washington, DC: The Catholic University of America Press, 1963.

Retractationes. Edited by Almut Mutzenbecher. CCL 57. Turnhout: Brepols, 1984.

Cicero

The Orator. With a translation by H. M. Hubbell. LCL 342, 306–509. Cambridge, MA: Harvard University Press, 1939.

Clement of Alexandria

Stromateis. Book 7, edited by Alain le Boulluec. SC 428. Paris: Cerf, 1997.

Cosmas of Jerusalem

Commentarii in Gregorii Nazianzeni Carmina. Edited by G. Lozza, Cosma di Gerusalemme. Commentario ai Carmi di Gregorio Nazianzeno. ST 12. Naples: M. D'Auria, 2000.

Cyril of Alexandria

Third Letter to Nestorius. Translated in McGuckin, *Saint Cyril of Alexandria and the Christological Controversy.*

Homily given at Ephesus on St. John the Evangelist's Day, in *Homiliae Diversae* II. PG 77:985D–987A. Translated in McGuckin, *Saint Cyril of Alexandria and the Christological Controversy.*

Cyril of Jerusalem

Mystagogical Catecheses. Edited by Auguste Piédagnel. SC126bis. 2nd ed. Paris: Cerf, 2009. Translated by Leo P. McCauley, SJ, and Anthony A. Stephenson. FC 64, 153–203. Washington, DC: The Catholic University of America Press, 1970.

Ephrem the Syrian

Commentary on Exodus. Translated by Edward G. Mathews, Jr. and Joseph P. Amar. FC 91, 221–65. Washington, DC: The Catholic University of America Press, 1994.

Commentary on Genesis. Translated by Edward G. Mathews, Jr. and Joseph P. Amar. FC 91, 67–213. Washington, DC: The Catholic University of America Press, 1994.

Diatessaron. *Saint Ephrem's Commentary on Tatian's Diatessaron, An English Translation of* Chester Beatty *Syriac MS 709 with Introduction and Notes,* Journal of Semitic Studies Supplement 2. Oxford University Press, 1993 (2000 reprint).

Homily on Our Lord. Translated by Edward G. Mathews, Jr. and Joseph P. Amar. FC 91, 273–332. Washington, DC: The Catholic University of America Press, 1994.

Hymns against Heresies. Excerpts translated in Sidney H. Griffith, "'Denominationalism' in Fourth-Century Syria: Readings in Saint Ephraem's *Hymns against Heresies, Madrāshê* 22–24." In *The Garb of Being: Embodiment and the Pursuit of Holiness in Late Ancient Christianity,* eds. Georgia Frank, Susan R. Holman, and Andrew S. Jacobs, 79–100. OCCT. New York: Fordham University Press, 2020, and in Sidney H. Griffith, "Setting Right the Church of Syria: Saint Ephraem's *Hymns against Heresies.*" In *The Limits of Ancient Christianity: Essays on Late Antique Thought and Culture in Honor of R. A. Markus,* edited by William E. Klingshirn and Mark Vessey, 97–114. Ann Arbor, MI: The University of Michigan Press, 1999.

Hymns on Faith. Translated by Jeffrey T. Wickes. FC 130. Washington, DC: The Catholic University of America Press, 2015.

Hymns on the Nativity. Translated by Kathleen McVey, *Ephrem the Syrian: Hymns.* CWS, 61–217. New York and Mahwah, NJ: Paulist Press, 1989.

Hymns on Paradise. Translated by Sebastian Brock, *Saint Ephrem: Hymns on Paradise.* PPS. Crestwood, New York: St. Vladimir's Seminary Press, 1990.

Hymns on Virginity and the Symbols of the Lord. Translated by Kathleen McVey, *Ephrem the Syrian: Hymns.* CWS, 259–468. New York and Mahwah, NJ: Paulist Press, 1989.

Letter to Publius. Translated by Edward G. Mathews, Jr. and Joseph P. Amar. FC 91, 338–55. Washington, DC: The Catholic University of America Press, 1994.

Nisibene Hymns. Translated by J. T. Sarsfield Stopford. NPNF, second series, vol. 13, 165–219.

Eunapius

The Lives of the Philosophers and Sophists. With translation by Wilmer Cave Wright. LCL 134, 342–565. Cambridge, MA: Harvard University Press, 1921.

Eusebius of Caesarea

Ecclesiastical History. Edited by Eduard Schwartz. EW vol. 2. Leipzig: Hinrich, 1903. Translated by G. A. Williamson. New York: Dorset Press, 1965.

Facundus of Hermaine

Defense of the Three Chapters. Edited by J.-M. Clément, OSB, and R. Vander Plaetse. SC 471, 478, 479, 487, 499. Paris: Cerf, 2002–06.

Gregory the Great

Book of Pastoral Rule. Edited by Floribert Rommel, OSB. SC 381 and 382. Paris: Cerf, 1992. Translated with an introduction by George E. Demacopoulos. PPS. Crestwood, NY: St. Vladimir's Seminary Press, 2007.

Commentary on the First Book of Kings (1 Samuel), by Pseudo-Gregory. Edited by Adalbert de Vogüé. SC 351, 391, 432, 449, 469, 482. Paris: Cerf, 1989–2004.

Commentary on the Song of Songs. Translated by Mark DelCogliano. Collegeville, MN: Liturgical Press, 2012.

Homilies on the Gospels. Edited by Raymond Étaix. CCL 141. Turnhout: Brepols, 1999. Translated by David Hurst, OSB. CSS 123. Kalamazoo, MI: Cistercian Publications, 1990.

Homilies on Ezekiel. Edited by Marcus Adriaen. CCL 142. Turnhout: Brepols, 1971. Translated by Theodosia Tomkinson. With an Introduction by Archbishop Chrysostomos of Etna. 2d ed. Etna, CA: Center for Traditionalist Orthodox Studies, 2008.

Letters. Edited by Dag Norberg. CCL 140 and 140A. Turnhout: Brepols, 1982. Translated by John R. C. Martyn. 3 vols. MST 40. Toronto: Pontifical Institute of Mediaeval Studies, 2004.

Moralia on Job. Edited by Marcus Adriaen. CCL 143, 143A, 143B. Turnhout: Brepols, 1979–85. Translated by Brian Kerns, OCSO, *Gregory the Great: Moral Reflections on the Book of Job*. CSS. Collegeville, MN: Liturgical Press, 2014–2022.

Gregory of Nazianzus

Letters

Epistolary Collection. Edited by Paul Gallay. 2 vols. Paris: Les Belles Lettres, 1964 and 1967. Translated by Bradley K. Storin. Oakland, CA: University of California Press, 2019.

Theological Epistles. *Ep.* 101, 102 and 202. Edited by Paul Gallay with the collaboration of Maurice Jourjon. SC 208. Paris: Cerf, 1974. *Ep.* 101 and 102 translated by Williams and Wickham, *On God and Christ*, 155–72. *Ep.* 202 translated by Browne and Swallow, NPNF, second series, vol. 7, 438–39.

Orations

Or. 1, *On Pascha*. Edited by Jean Bernardi. SC 247, 72–82. Paris: Cerf, 1978. Translated by Harrison, *Festal Orations*, 57–60.

Or. 2, *On His Flight*. Edited by Jean Bernardi. SC 247, 84–240. Paris: Cerf, 1978. Latin translation by Rufinus Rufinus's translation of Gregory of Nazianzus, *or*. 2. Edited by Augustus Engelbrecht. CSEL 46. English translation by Browne and Swallow in NPNF, second series, vol. 7, 204–27. French translation by Philippe Molac. *Discours sur le sacerdoce de Grégoire de Naziance. La dignité du prêtre selon S. Grégoire de Nazianze.* Paris: Artège Lethielleux, 2018.

Or. 4, *First Invective against Julian*. Edited by Jean Bernardi. SC 309, 86–292. Paris: Cerf, 1983.

Or. 6, *First Oration on Peace*. Edited by Marie-Ange Calvet-Sebasti. SC 405, 120–78. Paris: Cerf, 1995. Translated by Vinson, *Select Orations*, 3–20.

Or. 7, *Funeral Oration on His Brother Caesarius*. Edited by Marie-Ange Calvet-Sebasti. SC 405, 180–244. Paris: Cerf, 1995. Translated by Browne and Swallow, NPNF, second series, vol. 7, 229–38.

Or. 11, *For Gregory, Basil's Brother, Present after the Ordination*. Edited by Marie-Ange Calvet-Sebasti. SC 405, 328–46. Paris: Cerf, 1995. Translated by Vinson, *Select Orations*, 30–35.

Or. 14, *On the Love of the Poor*. PG 35:857–909. Translated by Daley, *Gregory of Nazianzus*, 76–97.

Or. 15, *In Praise of the Maccabees*. PG 35:912–33. Translated by Vinson, *Select Orations*, 72–84.

Or. 16, *On His Silent Father*. PG 35:933–64. Translated by Browne and Swallow. NPNF, second series, vol. 7, 247–54.

Or. 18, *Funeral Oration on His Father*. PG 35:985–1044. Translated by Browne and Swallow, NPNF, second series, vol. 7, 255–69.

Or. 19, *On Julian the Taxcollector*. PG 35:1043–64. Translated by Vinson, *Select Orations*, 95–106.

Or. 20, *On Theology and the Appointment of Bishops*. Edited by Justin Mossay, with the collaboration of Guy Lafontaine. SC 270, 56–84. Paris: Cerf, 1980. Translated by Daley, *Gregory of Nazianzus*, 99–104.

Or. 21, *On Athanasius, Bishop of Alexandria*. Edited by Justin Mossay, with the collaboration of Guy Lafontaine. SC 270, 110–92. Paris: Cerf, 1980. Translated by Browne and Swallow, NPNF, second series, vol. 7, 269–80.

Or. 23, *Second Oration on Peace*. (Also called *Third Oration on Peace*.) Edited by Justin Mossay, with the collaboration of Guy Lafontaine. SC 270, 280–310. Paris: Cerf, 1980. Translated by Vinson, *Select Orations*, 131–41.

Or. 24, *On Cyprian*. Edited by Justin Mossay, with the collaboration of Guy Lafontaine. SC 284, 40–84. Paris: Cerf, 1981. Translated by Vinson, *Select Orations*, 142–56.

Or. 25, *On Hero the Philosopher*. Edited by Justin Mossay, with the collaboration of Guy Lafontaine. SC 284, 156–204. Paris: Cerf, 1981. Translated by Vinson, *Select Orations*, 157–74.

Or. 26, *Second Oration on Himself*. Edited by Justin Mossay, with the collaboration of Guy Lafontaine. SC 284, 224–72. Paris: Cerf, 1981. Translated by Daley, *Gregory of Nazianzus*, 105–16.

Or. 27, *Preliminary Oration against the Eunomians. First Theological Oration*. Edited by Paul Gallay, with the collaboration of Maurice Jourjon. Translated by Williams and Wickham, *On God and Christ*, 25–35.

Or. 35, *On the Martyrs and against the Arians*. Edited by Claudio Moreschini. SC 318, 228–38. Paris: Cerf, 1985. Translated by Vinson, *Select Orations*, 216–19.

Or. 37. *On the Gospel Passage, "When Jesus Finished These Words."* Edited by Claudio Moreschini. SC 318, 270–318. Paris: Cerf, 1985. Translated by Browne and Swallow, NPNF, second series, vol. 7, 338–44.

Or. 38, *On the Theophany*. Edited by Claudio Moreschini. SC 358, 104–48. Paris: Cerf, 1990. Translated by Daley, *Gregory of Nazianzus*, 117–27.

Or. 39, *On the Lights*. Edited by Claudio Moreschini. SC 358, 150–96. Paris: Cerf, 1990. Translated by Daley, *Gregory of Nazianzus*, 128–37.

Or. 40, *On Baptism*. Edited by Claudio Moreschini. SC 358, 198–310. Paris: Cerf, 1990. Translated by Harrison, *Festal Orations*, 99–142.

Or. 41, *On Pentecost*. Edited by Claudio Moreschini. SC 358, 312–54. Paris: Cerf, 1990. Translated by Harrison, *Festal Orations*, 143–59.

Or. 42, *The Farewell Address*. Edited by Jean Bernardi. SC 384, 48–114. Paris: Cerf, 1992. Translated by Daley, *Gregory of Nazianzus*, 139–54.

Or. 43. *Funeral Oration on the Great Basil*. Edited by Jean Bernardi. SC 384, 116–306. Translated by Browne and Swallow, NPNF, second series, vol. 7, 395–422.

Or. 44, *For New Sunday*. PG 36:608–21. Translated by Daley, *Gregory of Nazianzus*, 155–61.

Or. 45, *On Holy Pascha*. PG 36:624–64. Translated by Harrison, *Festal Orations*, 161–90.

Poems

Poem 1.2.34, *Inexact Definitions*. PG 37:945–64. Excerpt translated by Daley, *Gregory of Nazianzus*, 52.

Poem 2.1.1, *On His Own Affairs*. PG 37:969–1017. Translated by Meehan, *Three Poems*, 25–45.

Poem 2.1.11, *On His Own Life*. PG 37:1029–66. Translated by Meehan, *Three Poems*, 77–130.

Poem 2.1.12, *On Himself and the Bishops*. PG 37:1166–1227. Translated by Meehan, *Three Poems*, 49–74.

Poem 2.2.66–102, *Epitaphs on His Mother*. PG 38:44–63.

Gregory of Nyssa

Homilies on the Song of Songs. Translation, introduction, and notes by Richard A Norris, Jr. *Gregory of Nyssa: Homilies on the Song of Songs*. WGRW 13. Atlanta: Society of Biblical Literature, 2012.

Hilary of Poitiers

On the Trinity. Edited by P. Smulders. CCL 62 and 62A. Turnhout: Brepols, 1979–80. Translated by Stephen McKenna, CSSR. FC 25. New York: Fathers of the Church, Inc. 1954.

Ignatius of Antioch

Letters. With a translation by Bart D. Ehrman. LCL 24, 218–321. Cambridge, MA: Harvard University Press, 2003.

Irenaeus

Against Heresies. Edited by Adelin Rousseau and Louis Doutreleau, SJ. SC 100, 152, 153, 210, 211, 263, 264, 293, 294. Paris: Cerf, 1965–82.

Jacob of Serug

A Metrical Homily on Holy Mar Ephrem by Mar Jacob of Serug. Edited and translated by Joseph P. Amar. PO 47. Turnhout: Brepols, 1995.

Jerome

Commentary on Galatians. Translated by Andrew Cain. FC 121. Washington, DC: The Catholic University of America Press, 2010.

On Illustrious Men. Edited by Ernest Cushing Richardson. TU 14, 1–56. Translated by Thomas P. Halton. FC 100. Washington, DC: The Catholic University of America Press, 1999.

John Chrysostom

Homilies

Homilies on the Acts of the Apostles. PG 60:13–384. Translated by J. Walker, et al. NPNF, first series, vol. 11. Peabody, MA: Hendrickson, 1995.

Homilies on the Epistles of Paul the Apostle. PG 60:391–682, PG 61:11–682, PG 62:7–718 (omitting PG 61:681–894). Translated by J. B. Morris, W. H. Simcox, et al. NPNF, first series, vols. 11–14. Peabody, MA: Hendrickson, 1995.

Homilies on the Gospel of John. PG 59:23–482. Translated by G. T. Stupart, et al. NPNF, first series, vol. 14. Peabody, MA: Hendrickson, 1995.

Homilies on the Gospel of Matthew. PG 57 and 58. Translated by M. B. Riddle. NPNF, first series, vol. 10. Peabody, MA: Hendrickson, 1995.

Homilies on Lazarus and the Rich Man. Most translated in *On Wealth and Poverty*. Translated by Catherine P. Roth. PPS 9. Crestwood, NY: St. Vladimir's Seminary Press, 1984.

Other

Commentary on Job. Translated by Robert Charles Hill. In *St. John Chrysostom: Commentary on the Sages*. Vol. 1. Brookline, MA: Holy Cross Orthodox Press, 2006.

Letters to Saint Olympia. Translated by David C. Ford. PPS 56. Crestwood, NY: St. Vladimir's Seminary Press, 2017.

On the Priesthood. Edited by Anne-Marie Malingrey. SC 272. Paris: Cerf, 1980. Translated by Graham Neville. PPS. Crestwood, NY: St. Vladimir's Seminary Press, 1996.

Julian the Emperor

The Works of the Emperor Julian. 3 Vols. With a translation by Wilmer Cave Wright. LCL 13, 29, and 157. Cambridge, MA: Harvard University Press, 1913.

Justin Martyr

Justin, Philosopher and Martyr: Apologies. Edited with a commentary on the text by Denis Minns and Paul Parvis. Oxford: Oxford University Press, 2009.

Leo the Great

Letters

Letters. PL 54:593–1213. Many translated by Edmund Hunt. FC 34. Washington, DC: The Catholic University of America Press, 1957. Some translated by Bronwen Neil, *Leo the Great*. ECF. London: Routledge 2009.

Tome to Flavian (*ep*. 28). Tanner, *Decrees of the Ecumenical Councils*, 1.77–82.

Sermons

Sancti Leonis Magni Romani Pontificis Tractatus Septem et Nonaginta. Edited by Antoine Chavasse. CCL 138 and 138A. Turnhout: Brepols, 1973. Almost all translated by Jane Patricia Freeland, CSJB, and Agnes Josephine Conway, SSJ. FC 93. Washington, DC: The Catholic University of America Press, 1996. Some translated by Neil, *Leo the Great*.

Lucan

Pharsalia (*The Civil War*). With translation by J. D. Duff. LCL 220. Cambridge, MA: Harvard University Press, 1957.

Origen

Homilies

Homilies on Genesis and Exodus. Edited by Louis Doutreleau. SC 7bis. Paris: Cerf, 1976. Translated by Ronald E. Heine, *Origen: Homilies on Genesis and Exodus.* FC 71. Washington, DC: The Catholic University of America Press, 1981.

Homilies on Leviticus. Edited Marcel Borret, SJ. SC 286–87. Paris: Cerf, 1981. Translated by Gary Wayne Barkley. FC 83. Washington, DC: The Catholic University of America Press, 1990.

Homilies 20–28 on Numbers. Edited by Louis Doutreleau, SJ. SC 461. Paris: Cerf, 2001. Translated by Thomas P. Scheck. ACT. Downers Grove, IL: IVP Academic, 2009.

Homilies on Jeremiah. Translated by John Clark Smith. *Origen: Homilies on Jeremiah and 1 Kings 28.* FC 97. Washington, DC: The Catholic University of America Press, 1998.

Homilies on the Psalms. Ed. Lorenzo Perrone, with Marian Molin Pradel, Emanuela Prinzivalli, and Antonio Cacciari, *Die neuen Psalmenhomilien: Eine kritische Edition des Codex Monacensis Graecus 314.* GCS, new series 19. OW 13. Berlin: De Gruyter, 2015. Translated by Joseph W. Trigg, *Origen, Homilies on the Psalms: Codex Monacensis Graecus 314.* FC 141. Washington, DC: The Catholic University of America Press, 2020.

Homilies on Luke. Translated by Joseph T. Lienhard, SJ. FC 94. Washington, DC: The Catholic University of America Press, 1996.

Other

Exhortation to Martyrdom in *Origen,* translation and introduction by Rowan A. Greer, preface by Hans Urs von Balthasar, CWS, 41–79. New York: Paulist Press, 1979.

On First Principles. Edited and translated by John Behr. 2 vols. OECT. Oxford: Oxford University Press, 2017.

The Philocalia of Origen. Edited by Marguerite Harl. SC 302. Paris: Cerf, 1983. Translated by George Lewis. Edinburgh: T & T Clark, 1911.

Palladius

Dialogue on the Life of St. John Chrysostom. Translated by Robert T. Meyer. ACW 45. New York: Newman Press, 1985.

Philo

On the Special Laws. With a translation by F. H. Colson. LCL 320, 100–607. Cambridge, MA: Harvard University Press, 1937.

Philostratus

Lives of the Sophists. With a translation by Wilmer Cave Wright. LCL 134, 2–315. Cambridge, MA: Harvard University Press, 1921.

Plato

The Apology. With a translation by Harold North Fowler, *Plato: Euthyphro, Apology, Crito, Phaedo, Phaedrus*. LCL 36. Cambridge, Mass: Harvard University Press, 2014 [reprint].

Phaedrus. With a translation by Harold North Fowler, *Plato: Euthyphro, Apology, Crito, Phaedo, Phaedrus*. LCL 36. Cambridge, Mass: Harvard University Press, 2014 [reprint].

The Republic. With a translation by Paul Shorey. LCL 2 vols. Cambridge, MA: Harvard University Press, 1946.

Plotinus

Enneads. With a translation by A. H. Armstrong. 7 vols. LCL 440–45 and 468. Cambridge, MA: Harvard University Press, 1966–88.

Possidius

The Life of Saint Augustine. PL 32:33–66. Translated by Matthew O'Connell. Augustinian Series, vol. 1. Introduction and notes by Cardinal Michele Pellegrino. Villanova, PA: Augustinian Press, 1988.

Pseudo-Dionysius

Ecclesiastical Hierarchy. Edited by Günther Heil and Adolf M. Ritter. PTS 67, 61–132. Berlin: De Gruyter, 2012. Translated by Colm Luibheid. *Pseudo-Dionysius: The Complete Works*, CWS, 195–259. New York: Paulist Press, 1987.

Pseudo-Martyrius

Funerary Speech for John Chrysostom. Edited by Martin Wallraff and Italian translation by C.

Ricci, *Oratio Funebris in Laudem Sancti Johannis Chrysostomi. Epittaffio attribuito a Martirio di Antiochia*. BHG 871, CPG 6517. Spoleto, 2007. Translated and introduced by Timothy D. Barnes and George Bevan. TTH 60. Liverpool: Liverpool University Press, 2013.

Quintilian

Institutio Oratoria. Translated by Donald Andrew Russell. *Books 11–12*. LCL 494. Cambridge, MA: Harvard University Press, 2014.

Rufinus

Praefatio atque Epilogus in Explanationem Origenis super Epistulam Pauli ad Romanos. Edited by Manlio Simonetti. *Tyrannii Rufini Opera*. CCL 20. Turnhout: Brepols, 1961.

Socrates Scholasticus

Ecclesiastical History. Edited by Günther Christian Hansen. GCS. Berlin: Akademie Verlag, 1995. Translated by A. C. Zenos. NPNF, second series, vol. 2, 1–178.

Sozomen

Ecclesiastical History. Edited by Joseph Bidez. GCS. Berlin: Akademie Verlag, 1960. Translated by Chester D. Hartranft. NPNF, second series, vol. 2, 239–427.

Statius

Thebaid. With translation by J. H. Mozley. LCL 207 and 498. Cambridge, MA: Harvard University Press, 1928 [reprint].

Tertullian

On Baptism. With translation by Ernest Evans. London: S.P.C.K., 1964.

Prescription against the Heretics. Translated by S. L. Greenslade. *Early Latin Theology*. The Library of Christian Classics, vol. 5, 31–73.

Vigilius

Constitution. *Ep*. 83 to Justinian. Edited by Otto Günther. CSEL 35, Pars 1, 230–320. Vienna, 1895.

Other

The Acts of the Council of Chalcedon. Translated by Richard Price and Michael Gaddis, reprint with minor corrections. 3 vols. TTH. Liverpool: Liverpool University, 2007.

Decrees of the Ecumenical Councils, vol. 1: *Nicaea I to Lateran V*, edited by Norman P. Tanner. Washington, DC: Georgetown University Press, 1990.

Denzinger, Heinrich. *Compendium of Creeds, Definitions, and Declarations on Matters of Faith and Morals*. Revised, enlarged, and, in collaboration with Helmut Hoping, edited by Peter Hünermann for the original bilingual edition, and edited by Robert Fastiggi and Anne Englund Nash for the English edition, 43rd ed. San Francisco: Ignatius Press, 2012.

Donatist Martyr Stories: The Church in Conflict in Roman North Africa. Translated with notes and introduction by Maureen A. Tilley. TTH 24. Liverpool: Liverpool University Press, 1996.

Epistle of Barnabas. In *The Apostolic Fathers: Greek Texts and English Translations*, edited and translated by J. B. Lightfoot and J. R. Harmer, rev. and updated, Michael W. Holmes. Grand Rapids, MI: Baker, 1999.

History of Shimeon Kepha the Chief of the Apostles. In *The Ancient Martyrdom Accounts of Peter and Paul*, translated with an introduction and notes by David L. Eastman. SBL 39. Atlanta: SBL Press, 2015.

The Sayings of the Desert Fathers: The Alphabetical Collection. Translated by Benedicta Ward, Rev. ed. Kalamazoo, MI: Cistercian Publications, 1984.

The Syriac Fathers on Prayer and the Spiritual Life, translated by Sebastian Brock. Kalamazoo, MI: Cistercian Publications Inc., 1987.

The Syriac Vita *Tradition of Ephrem the Syrian*. Edited and translated by Joseph P. Amar. CSCO 629–30. Leuven: Peeters, 2011.

Other Sources

Allison, Dale C. *The New Moses: A Matthean Typology*. Minneapolis: Fortress, 1993.

Anatolios, Khaled. *Deification through the Cross: An Eastern Christian Theology of Salvation*. Grand Rapids, MI: Eerdmans, 2020.

Anderson, Gary A. *Charity: The Place of the Poor in the Biblical Tradition*. New Haven: Yale University, 2013.

Andrews, James A. *Hermeneutics and the Church: In Dialogue with Augustine*. Notre Dame, IN: University of Notre Dame Press, 2012.

Armitage, J. Mark. *A Twofold Solidarity: Leo the Great's Theology of Redemption*. Early Christian Studies 9. Strathfield: St. Paul's Publications in association with the Centre for Early Christian Studies, 2005.

Armstrong, Jonathan. "Ephrem the Syrian: Preaching Christ through Poetry and Paradox." In *A Legacy of Preaching*. Vol. 1, *Apostles to the Revivalists*. Foreword by Timothy George, edited by Benjamin K. Forrest, et al., 95–110. Grand Rapids, MI: Zondervan Academic, 2018.

Arnold, Duane W. H. and Pamela Bright, eds. *De Doctrina Christiana: A Classic of Western Culture*. Notre Dame, IN: University of Notre Dame Press, 1995.

Ayres, Lewis. "Augustine, Christology, and God as Love: An Introduction to the Homilies on 1 John." In *Nothing Greater, Nothing Better: Theological Essays on the Love of God*, edited by Kevin J. Vanhoozer, 67–93. Grand Rapids, MI: Eerdmans, 2001.

———. *Nicaea and its Legacy: An Approach to Fourth-Century Trinitarian Theology*. Oxford: Oxford University Press, 2004.

———. "Seven Theses on Dogmatics and Patristics in Catholic Theology." *Modern Theology* 38, no. 1 (2022): 36–62.

Baker, Kimberly F. "Augustine's Doctrine of the *Totus Christus*: Reflecting on the Church as Sacrament of Unity." *Horizons* 37, no. 1 (2010): 7–24.

Balthasar, Hans Urs von. "Priestly Existence." In *Explorations in Theology II: Spouse of the Word*, translated by Brian McNeil, C.R.V., 373–419. San Francisco: Ignatius Press, 1991.

Barkley, Gary Wayne. Introduction to *Origen: Homilies on Leviticus 1–16*, 21–25. The Fathers of the Church: A New Translation 83. Washington, DC: The Catholic University of America Press, 1990.

Barone, Francesca Prometea. "Le vocabulaire de la patience chez Jean Chrysostome: les mots ἀνεξικακία et ὑπομονή." *Revue de philologie, de littérature et d'histoire anciennes* 81, no. 1 (2007): 5–12.

Bartholomew. "Participants of Abundant Life," Holy Pascha, 2010. In *Speaking the Truth in Love: Theological and Spiritual Exhortations of Ecumenical Patriarch Bartholomew*, edited and with introduction by John Chryssavgis, 47–49. New York: Fordham University Press, 2011.

Baudoin, Paula. "Makrothymia dans Saint Jean Chrysostome." *Studia Patristica* 22 (1989): 89–97.

Baur, Chrysostomus. *S. Jean Chrysostome et Ses Oeuvres dans l'Histoire Littéraire. Essai presenté* à *l'occasion du XV*[e] *centenaire de Saint Jean Chrysostome*. Louvain: Bureaux du Recueil, 1907.

Beck, Edmund. Introduction to *Sermo de Domino nostro*, i. Corpus Scriptorum Ecclesiasticorum Orientalium 271.

BeDuhn, Jason David. *Augustine's Manichean Dilemma*. Vol. 1, *Conversion and Apostasy (373–388 C.E.)* and vol. 2, *Making a "Catholic" Self, 398–401 C.E.* Divinations: Rereading Late Ancient Religion. Philadelphia: University of Pennsylvania Press, 2010 and 2013.

———. *The Manichean Body in Discipline and Ritual*. Baltimore: Johns Hopkins University Press, 2000.

Beeley, Christopher A. *Gregory of Nazianzus on the Trinity and the Knowledge of God: In Your Light We See Light*. Oxford Studies in Historical Theology. New York: Oxford University Press, 2008.

Behr, John. *The Case against Diodore and Theodore: Texts and Their Contexts*. Oxford Early Christian Texts. Oxford: Oxford University Press, 2011.

Benedict XV. *Principi Apostolorum Petro*. October 5, 1920. In *The Papal Encyclicals 1903–1939*, edited by Claudia Carlen, 195–201. Raleigh, NC: McGrath Publishing Company, 1981.

Benedict XVI. Angelus address. Castel Gandolfo. September 18, 2005.

———. *Deus Caritas Est*. Encyclical on Christian Love. December 25, 2005.

———. General Audiences. April 25, 2007, May 2, 2007, June 4, 2008, and April 13, 2011.

———. "On the Occasion of the 16th Centenary of the Death of St. John Chrysostom." August 10, 2007.

———. *Sacramentum Caritatis*. Post-Synodal Apostolic Exhortation on the Eucharist as the Source and Summit of the Church's Life and Mission. February 22, 2007.

Blowers, Paul M., ed. *Moral Formation and the Virtuous Life*. Ad Fontes: Early Christian Sources. Minneapolis: Fortress Press, 2019.

———. "Pity, Empathy, and the Tragic Spectacle of Human Suffering: Exploring the Emotional Culture of Compassion in Late Ancient Christianity." *Journal of Early Christian Studies* 18, no. 1 (2010): 1–27.

———. *Visions and Faces of the Tragic: The Mimesis of Tragedy and the Folly of Salvation in Early Christian Literature*. Oxford Early Christian Studies. Oxford: Oxford University Press, 2020.

Boersma, Hans. *Sacramental Preaching: Sermons on the Hidden Presence of Christ*. Foreword by Eugene H. Peterson. Grand Rapids, MI: Baker Academic, 2016.

———. *Scripture as Real Presence: Sacramental Exegesis in the Early Church*. Grand Rapids, MI: Baker Academic, 2017.

Bonner, Gerald. *St. Augustine: Life and Controversies*. 3rd ed. Norwich: Canterbury, 2002.

Boodts, Shari. "Navigating the Vast Tradition of St. Augustine's Sermons: Old Instruments and New Approaches." *Augustiniana* 69, no. 1 (2019): 83–115.

Booth, Phil. "Gregory and the Greek East." In *A Companion to Gregory the Great*, edited by Bronwen Neil and Matthew Dal Santo, 109–31. Brill's Companions to the Christian Tradition 47. Leiden: Brill, 2003.

Bou Mansour, Tanios. *La Pensée Symbolique de Saint Ephrem le Syrien*. Bibliothèque de l'Université Saint-Esprit 16. Kaslik, Lebanon: Bibliothèque de l'Université Saint-Esprit, 1988.

Bright, Pamela. "Priesthood." In *The Westminster Handbook to Origen*, edited by John Anthony McGuckin, 179–81. Louisville, KY: Westminster John Knox Press, 2004.

Brilioth, Yngve. *A Brief History of Preaching*. Philadelphia: Fortress Press, 1965.

Brinton, Alan. "Quintilian, Plato, and the 'Vir Bonus.'" *Philosophy & Rhetoric* 16, no. 3 (1983): 167–83.

Brock, Sebastian P. *The Luminous Eye: The Spiritual World Vision of Saint Ephrem the Syrian*. Cistercian Studies Series 124. Kalamazoo, MI: Cistercian Publications, 1985.

———. "Poetry." In *Gorgias Encyclopedic Dictionary of the Syriac Heritage*. Edited by Sebastian P. Brock, Aaron M. Butts, George A. Kraz, and Lucas Van Rompany. Digital edition prepared by David Michelson, Ute Possekel, and Daniel L. Schwartz. Gorgias Press, 2011; online ed. Beth Mardutho, 2018. https://gedsh.bethmardutho.org/Poetry.

———. *Singer of the Word of God: Ephrem the Syrian and his Significance in Late Antiquity*. Sebastianyotho 1. Piscataway, NJ: Gorgias Press, 2020.

Brown, Peter. *Augustine of Hippo: A Biography*. Rev. ed. Berkeley and Los Angeles: University of California Press, 2000.

———. *Power and Persuasion in Late Antiquity: Towards a Christian Empire*. Madison, WI: University of Wisconsin Press, 1992.

———. "The Rise and Function of the Holy Man in Late Antiquity, 1971–1997." *Journal of Early Christian Studies* 6, no. 3 (1998): 353–76.

———. "The Rise and Function of the Holy Man in Late Antiquity." *Journal of Roman Studies* 61 (1971): 80–111.

———. "The Saint as Exemplar in Late Antiquity." *Representations* 2 (Spring 1983): 1–25.

———. *Through the Eye of a Needle: Wealth, the Fall of Rome, and the Making of Christianity in the West, 350–550 AD*. Princeton: Princeton University Press, 2012.

Buell, Denise Kimber. "'Be not one who stretches out hands to receive but shuts them when it comes to giving': Envisioning Christian Charity When Both Donors and Recipients are Poor." In *Wealth and Poverty in Early Church and Society*, edited by Susan R. Holman, 37–47. Grand Rapids, MI: Baker Academic, 2008.

Burghardt, Walter J., SJ. *Preaching: The Art and the Craft*. Mahwah, NJ: Paulist Press, 1987.

Burns, J. Patout. "Augustine's Ecclesial Mysticism." In *The Wiley-Blackwell Companion to Christian Mysticism*, edited by Julia A. Lamm, 202–15. Malden, MA: Wiley-Blackwell, 2013.

Cameron, Averil. *Christianity and the Rhetoric of Empire: The Development of Christian Discourse*. Berkeley and Los Angeles: University of California Press, 1991.

Cameron, Michael. *Christ Meets Me Everywhere: Augustine's Early Figurative Exegesis*. Oxford Studies in Historical Theology. New York: Oxford University Press, 2012.

———. "The Emergence of *Totus Christus* as Hermeneutical Center in Augustine's *Enarrationes in Psalmos*." In *The Harp of Prophecy: Early Christian Interpretations of the Psalms*, edited by Brian E. Daley, SJ, and Paul R. Kolbet, 205–26. Christianity and Judaism in Antiquity 20. Notre Dame, IN: University of Notre Dame Press, 2015.

Cantalamessa, Raniero, OFM Cap. *Easter in the Early Church: An Anthology of Jewish and Early Christian Texts*. Edited and translated by James M. Quigley, SJ, and Joseph T. Lienhard, SJ. Collegeville, MN: Liturgical Press, 1993.

Carroll, Thomas K. *Preaching the Word*. Message of the Fathers of the Church 11. Wilmington, DE: Michael Glazier, Inc., 1984.

Catholic Church. *Code of Canon Law* (1983).

Cavadini, John C. "From Letter to Spirit: The Multiple Senses of Scripture." In *The Oxford Handbook of Early Christian Biblical Interpretation*, edited by Paul Blowers and Peter Martens, 455–72. Oxford: Oxford University Press, 2019.

———. "Reconsidering Augustine on Marriage and Concupiscence" *Augustinian Studies* 48, no. 1–2 (2017): 183–99.

———. "The Sacramentality of Marriage in the Fathers." *Pro Ecclesia* 17, no. 4 (2008): 442–63.

———. "Spousal Vision: A Study of Text and History in the Theology of Saint Augustine." *Augustinian Studies* 42, no. 1–2 (2012): 127–48.

———. *Visioning Augustine*. Foreword by Mark Therrien. CCT. Hoboken, NJ: Wiley Blackwell, 2019.

Chabi, Kolawole, OSA. "Augustine's Eucharistic Spirituality in His Easter Sermons." *Augustinianum* 59, no. 2 (2019): 475–504.

Chadwick, Henry. *Augustine*. Past Masters. Oxford: Oxford University Press, 1986.

Clark, Patrick M. *Perfection in Death: The Christological Dimension of Courage for Aquinas*. Washington, DC: The Catholic University of America Press, 2015.

Clavier, Mark F. M. *Eloquent Wisdom: Rhetoric, Cosmology and Delight in the Theology of Augustine of Hippo*. Studia Traditionis Theologiae 117. Turnhout: Brepols, 2014.

Colish, Marcia L. *The Stoic Tradition from Antiquity to the Early Middle Ages*. 2 vols. Leiden: Brill, 1990.

Congar, Yves, OP. *True and False Reform*. Translated by Paul Philibert, OP. Collegeville, MN: Liturgical Press, 2011.

Congregation for Catholic Education. *Instruction on the Study of the Fathers of the Church in the Formation of Priests*. November 10, 1989.

Congregation for Clergy. *Directory for the Ministry and Life of Priests*. New Edition. February 11, 2013.

———. *Ratio Fundamentalis Institutionis Sacerdotalis*. "The Gift of the Priestly Vocation." December 8, 2016.

Congregation for Divine Worship and the Discipline of the Sacraments. *Homiletic Directory*. June 29, 2014.

Conybeare, Catherine. "Augustine's Rhetoric in Theory and Practice." In *The Oxford Handbook of Rhetorical Studies*, edited by Michael J. MacDonald, 301–11. Oxford: Oxford University Press, 2017.

Cook, James Daniel. *Preaching and Popular Christianity: Reading the Sermons of John Chrysostom*. Oxford Theology and Religion Monographs. Oxford: Oxford University Press, 2019.

Cooper, Kate. "Ventriloquism and the Miraculous: Conversion, Preaching, and the Martyr Exemplum in Late Antiquity." In *Signs, Wonders, and Miracles*, edited by Kate Cooper and Jeremy Gregory, 22–45. Studies in Church History 41. Woodbridge: Boydell and Brewer, 2005.

Crawford, Matthew R. "Diatesseron, a Misnomer? The Evidence from Ephrem's Commentary." *Early Christianity* 4, no. 3 (2013): 362–85.

———. "Resolving Genealogical Ambiguity: Eusebius and (ps-) Ephrem on Luke 1.36." *Aramaic Studies* 14 (2016): 83–97.

Crouzel, Henri, SJ. *Origen: The Life and Thought of the First Great Theologian*. Translated by A.S. Worrall. San Francisco: Harper & Row, 1989.

Cunningham, Agnes, SSCM. "Women and Preaching in the Patristic Age." In *Preaching in the Patristic Age: Studies in Honor of Walter J. Burghardt, SJ*, edited by David G. Hunter, 53–72. New York: Paulist Press, 1989.

Cunningham, Mary B. and Pauline Allen, eds. *Preacher and Audience: Studies in Early Christian and Byzantine Homiletics*. Leiden: Brill, 1998.

Daley, Brian E., SJ. "Augustine the Preacher: Practicing the Rhetoric of Love." In *The Center Is Jesus Christ Himself: Essays on Revelation, Salvation, and Evangelization in Honor of Robert P. Imbelli*, edited by Andrew Meszaros, 231–51. Washington, DC: The Catholic University of America Press, 2021.

———. "Building a New City: The Cappadocian Fathers and the Rhetoric of Philanthropy." *Journal of Early Christian Studies* 7, no. 3 (1999): 431–61.

———. "Christ and Christologies." In *The Oxford Handbook of Early Christian Studies*, edited by Susan Ashbrook Harvey and David G. Hunter, 886–905. Oxford: Oxford University Press, 2008.

———. Foreword to *The Fathers of the Church in Christian Theology*, by Michel Fédou, translated by Peggy Manning Meyer. Washington, DC: The Catholic University of America Press, 2019.

———. "The Giant's Twin Substances: Ambrose and the Christology of Augustine's *Contra sermonem Arianorum*." In *Augustine: Presbyter Factus Sum*, edited by Joseph T. Lienhard, SJ, Earl C. Muller, SJ, and Roland J. Teske, SJ, 477–95. Collectanea Augustiniana. New York, 1993.

———. *God Visible: Patristic Christology Reconsidered*. Changing Paradigms in Historical and Systematic Theology. Oxford: Oxford University Press, 2018

———. "'Heavenly Man' and 'Eternal Christ': Apollinarius and Gregory of Nyssa on the Personal Identity of Christ." *Journal of Early Christian Studies* 10, no. 4 (2002): 469–88.

———. *The Hope of the Early Church: A Handbook of Patristic Eschatology*. Grand Rapids, MI: Baker Academic, 2010 [original edition published in 1991 by Cambridge University Press].

———. "Life after Richard McBrien: Q&A with Father Brian Daley, SJ." Interview by Sean Salai, SJ. *America*, January 28, 2015. https://www.americamagazine.org/content/all-things/life-after-richard-mcbrien-qa-father-brian-daley-sj.

———. "Saint Gregory of Nazianzus as Pastor and Theologian." In *Loving God with our Minds: Essays in honor of Wallace M. Alston*, edited by Michael Welker and Cynthia A. Jarvis, 106–19. Grand Rapids, MI: Eerdmans, 2004.

———. "Saint Paul and the Fourth-Century Fathers: Portraits of Christian Life." *Pro Ecclesia* 18, no. 3 (2009): 299–317.

———. "Using the 'Art of Arts': Preaching as Spiritual Leadership in the Early Church." In *Preaching as Spiritual Leadership: Guiding the Faithful as Mystic and Mystagogue*, edited by Michael E. Connors, CSC, 34–50. Chicago: Liturgy Training Publications, 2021.

———. "Walking through the Word of God: Gregory of Nazianzus as a Biblical Interpreter." In *The Word Leaps the Gap: Essays on Scripture and Theology in Honor of Richard B. Hays*, edited by J. Ross Wagner, C. Kavin Rowe, and A. Katherine Grieb, 514–31. Grand Rapids, MI: Eerdmans, 2008.

Dal Santo, Matthew. "The Shadow of a Doubt? A Note on the *Dialogues* and *Registrum Epistolarum* of Pope Gregory the Great (590604)." *Journal of Ecclesiastical History* 61, no. 1 (2010): 3–17.

Daly, Robert J., SJ. "Sacrificial Soteriology in Origen's Homilies on Leviticus." *Studia Patristica* 17 (1979): 872–78.

Daniélou, Jean. *Origen*. Translated by Walter Mitchell. New York: Sheed and Ward, 1955.

Dawson, John David. *Christian Figural Reading and the Fashioning of Identity*. Berkeley: University of California Press, 2002.

DeGregorio, Scott. "Gregory's Exegesis: Old and New Ways of Approaching the Scriptural Text." In *A Companion to Gregory the Great*, edited by Bronwen Neil and Matthew J. Dal Santo, 270–90. Leiden: Brill, 2013.

de Lubac, Henri, SJ. *History and Spirit: The Understanding of Scripture according to Origen*. Translated by Anne Englund Nash, with Greek and Latin translation by Juvenal Merriell of the Oratory. San Francisco: Ignatius Press, 2007.

Demacopoulos, George. *Five Models of Spiritual Direction in the Early Church*. Notre Dame, IN: University of Notre Dame Press, 2007.

———. *Gregory the Great: Ascetic, Pastor, and First Man of Rome.* Notre Dame, IN: University of Notre Dame, 2015.

———. *The Invention of Peter: Apostolic Discourse and Papal Authority in Late Antiquity.* Divinations: Rereading Late Ancient Religion. Philadelphia: University of Pennsylvania Press, 2013.

de Wet, Chris L. and Wendy Mayer, eds. *Revisioning John Chrysostom: New Approaches, New Perspectives.* Critical Approaches to Early Christianity 1. Leiden: Brill, 2019.

Di Noia, J. Augustine, OP, *Grace in Season: The Riches of the Gospel in Seventy Sermons.* Foreword by Aquinas Guilbeau, OP. Providence, RI: Cluny Media, 2019.

DiNardo, Daniel. "Preaching with the Fathers of the Church." The Annual Carl J. Peter Lecture, January 13, 2013, North American College, Rome, www.pnac.org/the-seminary/the-carl-j-peter-lecture/cardinal-dinardos-lecture/. Accessed June 27, 2021.

Dively Lauro, Elizabeth Ann. *The Soul and Spirit of Scripture within Origen's Exegesis.* The Bible in Ancient Christianity 3. Boston: Brill, 2005.

Dolbeau, François. Introduction to Works of Saint Augustine: A Translation for the 21st Century. III/11, *Sermons Discovered Since 1990,* 13–20. Hyde Park, NY: New City Press, 1997.

Douglas, Mary. *Leviticus as Literature.* Oxford: Oxford University Press, 1999.

———. *Purity and Danger.* London: Routledge, 1966.

Drewery, Benjamin. "Deification." In *Christian Spirituality: Essays in Honour of Gordon Rupp,* edited by Peter Brooks, 33–62. London: SCM Press, 1975.

Driscoll, Jeremy, OSB. "Preaching in the Context of the Eucharist: A Patristic Perspective." *Pro Ecclesia* 11, no. 1 (2002): 24–40.

Drobner, Hubertus. *The Fathers of the Church: A Comprehensive Introduction.* Peabody, MA: Hendrickson, 2007.

———. "'I would rather not be wearisome to you:' Saint Augustine as Preacher." *Melita Theologica* 51 (2000): 117–26.

Dunkle, Brian P., SJ. "Beyond Carnal Cogitations: Deification in Ambrose of Milan." In *Deification in the Latin Patristic Tradition*, edited by Jared Ortiz, 132–52. Washington, DC: The Catholic University of America Press, 2018.

———. *Enchantment and Creed in the Hymns of Ambrose of Milan*. Oxford Early Christian Studies. Oxford, 2016.

———. "The Twofold Affection": The Background to John Chrysostom's Use of Φύσις and Χάρις," *VC* 75, no. 4 (2021): 355–74.

Dunn, Geoffrey D. "Aristotle and the Art of Preaching." *Worship* 72, no. 3 (1998): 220–35.

———. "Cicero and the Sermon: Further Reflections on the Art of Preaching." *Australasian Catholic Record* 97, no. 1 (2020): 45–58.

———. "Rhetoric in the Patristic Sermons of Late Antiquity." In *Preaching in the Patristic Era: Sermons, Preachers, and Audiences in the Latin West*, edited by Anthony Dupont, Shari Boodts, Gert Partoens, and Johann Leemans, 103–34. Leiden: Brill, 2018.

Dunn-Wilson, David. *A Mirror for the Church: Preaching in the First Five Centuries*. Grand Rapids, MI: Eerdmans, 2005.

Dupont, Anthony, Shari Boodts, Gert Partoens, and Johann Leemans, eds. *Preaching in the Patristic Era: Sermons, Preachers, and Audiences in the Latin West*. Leiden: Brill, 2018.

Duval, Yves-Marie. 'La discussion entre L'apocrisiare Grégoire et le patriarche Eutychios au sujet de la resurrection de la chair.' In *Grégoire le Grand*, edited by Fontaine, Gillet, and Pellistrandi, 347–65. Paris: Éditions du Centre National de la Recherche Scientifique, 1986.

Eastman, David L. *The Many Deaths of Peter and Paul*. Oxford Early Christian Studies. Oxford: Oxford University Press, 2019.

Edwards, Mark. "The Donatist Schism and Theology." In *The Donatist Schism: Controversy and Contexts*. Translated Texts for Historians, Contexts 2. Edited by Richard Miles, 101–19. Liverpool: Liverpool University Press, 2016.

Edwards, Robert G. T. "Divine Providence and Biblical Narrative in the Thought of John Chrysostom." Ph.D. diss., University of Notre Dame, 2020.

———. "Healing Despondency with Biblical Narrative in John Chrysostom's *Letters to Olympias*." *Journal of Early Christian Studies* 28, no. 2 (2020): 203–31.

Elm, Susanna. "The Diagnostic Gaze: Gregory of Nazianzus' Theory of the Ideal Priest in His Orations 6 (*De Pace*) and 2 (*Apologia de Fuga Sua*)." In *Orthodoxie, Christianisme, Histoire*, edited by Susanna Elm, Éric Rebillard, and Antonella Romano, 83–100. Rome: École française de Rome, 2000.

———. "Inventing the 'Father of the Church': Gregory of Nazianzus' 'Farewell to the Bishops' (Or. 42) in its Historical Context." In *Vita Religiosa im Mittelalter: Festschrift für Kaspar Elm zum 70. Geburtstag*, edited by Franz J. Felten and Nikolas Jaspert, 3–20. Berlin: Duncker & Humblot, 1999.

———. "'O Paradoxical Fusion:' Gregory of Nazianzus on Baptism and Cosmology (*Or.* 38–40)." In *Heavenly Realms and Earthly Realities in Late Antique Religions*, edited by Ra'anan S. Boustand and Annette Yoshiko Reed, 296–315. New York: Cambridge University Press, 2004.

———. *Sons of Hellenism, Fathers of the Church: Emperor Julian, Gregory of Nazianzus, and the Vision of Rome*. Transformations of the Classical Heritage 49. Berkeley and Los Angeles: University of California Press, 2012.

Evans, Gillian R. *The Thought of Gregory the Great*. Cambridge: Cambridge University Press, 1986.

Ferguson, Everett. *Baptism in the Early Church: History, Theology, and Liturgy in the First Five Centuries*. Grand Rapids, MI: Eerdmans, 2009.

———. "Exhortations to Baptism in the Cappadocians." *Studia Patristica* 32 (1997): 121–29.

———. "Gregory's Baptismal Theology and the Alexandrian Tradition." In *Re-Reading Gregory of Nazianzus*, edited by Christopher Beeley, 67–83. Washington, DC: The Catholic University of America Press, 2012.

Fiedrowicz, Michael. Introduction to *Expositions of the Psalms* (1–32), Works of Saint Augustine: A Translation for the 21st Century, III/15, 13–66. Hyde Park, NY: New City Press, 2000.

———. *Psalmus vox totius Christi: Studien zu Augustins* Enarrationes in Psalmos. Freiburg: Herder, 1997.

Finn, Douglas. "Job and His Wife as Exemplary Figures in the Preaching of John Chrysostom." *Zeitschrift für Antikes Christentum* 23, no. 3 (2019): 479–515.

———. "Job as Exemplary Father according to John Chrysostom." *Journal of Early Christian Studies* 26, no. 2 (2018): 275–305.

———. "Sympathetic Philosophy: The Christian Response to Suffering according to John Chrysostom's Commentary on Job." In *Suffering and Evil in Early Christian Thought*, edited by Nonna Verna Harrison and David Hunter, 97–119. Grand Rapids, MI: Baker Academic, 2016.

Finn, Richard, OP. *Almsgiving in the Later Roman Empire: Christian Promotion and Practice (313–450)*. Oxford Classical Monographs. Oxford: Oxford University, 2006.

Fitzgerald, Allan D. 'Mercy, Works of Mercy.' In *Augustine through the Ages: An Encyclopedia*, edited by Allan D. Fitzgerald, OSA, 557–61. Grand Rapids, MI: Eerdmans, 1999.

Folliet, G. "Les trois categories de chrétiens: Survie d'un theme augustinien." *L'Année théologique augustiniénne* 14 (1954): 81–96.

Förster, Hans. *Die Anfänge von Weihnachten und Epiphanias: Eine Anfrage an die Entstehungshypothen*. Studien und Texte zu Antike und Christentum 46. Tübingen: Mohr Siebeck, 2007.

Francis. *Evangelii Gaudium*. Apostolic Exhortation on the Proclamation of the Gospel in Today's World. November 24, 2013.

———. Message of the First World Day of the Poor. November 19, 2017.

Fulford, Ben. "Gregory of Nazianzus and Biblical Interpretation." In *Re-Reading Gregory of Nazianzus*, edited by Christopher Beeley, 31–48. Washington, DC: The Catholic University of America Press, 2012.

Gavrilyuk, Paul L. *The Suffering of the Impassible God: The Dialectics of Patristic Thought.* Oxford Early Christian Studies. Oxford: Oxford University Press, 2004.

Gavrilyuk, Paul L. and Sarah Coakley, eds. *The Spiritual Senses: Perceiving God in Western Christianity.* Cambridge: Cambridge University Press, 2012.

Gavrilyuk, Paul L., Andrew Hofer, OP, and Matthew Levering, eds. *The Oxford Handbook of Deification.* Forthcoming.

Gemeinhardt, Peter. "Teaching the Faith in Early Christianity: Divine and Human Agency." *Vigiliae Christianae* 74, no. 2 (2020): 129–64.

Graham, Billy. *Hope for Each Day: Words of Wisdom and Faith.* Nashville, TN: Thomas Nelson, 2002.

———. *The Reason for My Hope: Salvation.* Nashville: Thomas Nelson, 2013.

Green, Bernard, OSB. *The Soteriology of Leo the Great.* Oxford Theology and Religion Monographs. Oxford: Oxford University Press, 2008.

———. "The Theology of Gregory the Great: Christ, Salvation and the Church." In *A Companion to Gregory the Great,* edited by Bronwen Neil and Matthew J. Dal Santo, 135–56. Leiden: Brill, 2013.

Griffith, Sidney H. "'Faith Seeking Understanding' in the Thought of St. Ephraem the Syrian." In *Faith Seeking Understanding: Learning and the Catholic Tradition,* edited by George C. Berthold, 35–55. Selected papers from the Symposium and Convocation celebrating the Saint Anselm College Centennial. Manchester, New Hampshire: Saint Anselm College Press, 1991.

———. "Setting Right the Church of Syria: Saint Ephraem's *Hymns against Heresies.*" In *The Limits of Ancient Christianity: Essays on Late Antique Thought and Culture in Honor of R. A. Markus,* edited by William E. Klingshirn and Mark Vessey, 97–114. Ann Arbor, MI: The University of Michigan Press, 1999.

———. "'Spirit in the Bread; Fire in the Wine': The Eucharist as 'Living Medicine' in the Thought of Ephraem the Syrian," *MoTh* 15, no. 2 (1999): 225–46.

———. "A Spiritual Father for the Whole Church: the Universal Appeal of St. Ephraem the Syrian." *Hugoye* 1, no. 2 (1998 [2010]): 197–220.

Grove, Kevin, CSC. "Rhetoric and Reality: Augustine and Pope Francis on Preaching Christ and the Poor." *Theological Studies* 80, no. 3 (2019): 530–53.

Hadot, Pierre. *Plotinus or the Simplicity of Vision.* Translated by Michael Chase. Introduction by Arnold I. Davidson. Chicago: University of Chicago Press, 1993.

Hanson, R. P. C. *Allegory & Event: A Study of the Sources and Significance of Origen's Interpretation of Scripture.* Introduction by Joseph W. Trigg. Louisville, KY: Westminster John Knox Press, 2002.

Harnack, Adolph von. *History of Dogma.* Vol. 5. Translated by James Millar from the third German edition. Theological Translation Library. Oxford: Williams and Norgate, 1898.

Harrison, Carol. *The Art of Listening in the Early Church.* Oxford: Oxford University Press, 2013.

———. "Worship as the Beginning and End of Preaching." In *Praedicatio Patrum: Studies on Preaching in Late Antique North Africa,* edited by Gert Partoens, Anthony Dupont, and Shari Boodts, 201–17. Instrumenta Patristica et Mediaevalia 75. Turnhout: Brepols, 2017.

Harrison, Verna E. F. "Illumined from All Sides by the Trinity: Neglected Themes in Gregory's Trinitarian Theology." In *Re-Reading Gregory of Nazianzus,* edited by Christopher Beeley, 13–30. Washington, DC: The Catholic University of America Press, 2012.

Hartung, Blake. "The Authorship and Dating of the Syriac Corpus attributed to Ephrem of Nisibis: A Reassessment." *Zeitschrift für Antikes Christentum* 22, no. 2 (2018): 296–321.

Harvey, Susan A. "Patristic Worlds." In *Patristic Studies in the Twenty-First Century,* edited by Brouria Bitton-Ashkelony, Theodore de Bruyn, and Carol Harrison, 25–53. Turnhout: Brepols, 2015.

———. "Revisiting the Daughters of the Covenant: Women's Choirs and Sacred Song in Ancient Syriac Christianity." *Hugoye* 8, no. 2 (2005[2009]): 125–49.

Hayes, Andrew. "Ephrem the Syrian's Use of Beatitudes." *Zeitschrift für Antikes Christentum* 24, no. 3 (2020): 509–48.

Hayman, A. P. "The Image of the Jew in the Syriac Anti-Jewish Polemical Literature." In *To See Ourselves as Others See Us: Christians, Jews, and "Others" in Late Antiquity*, edited by Jacob Neusner and Ernest S. Frerichs, 423–41. Chico, CA: Scholars Press, 1985.

Herdt, Jennifer A. "Eudaimonism and Dispossession: Augustine on Almsgiving." In *Augustine and Social Justice*, edited by Teresa Delgado, John Doody, and Kim Paffenroth, 97–112. Augustine in Conversation: Tradition and Innovation. Lanham, MD: Lexington Books, 2015.

Hermanowicz, Erika T. *Possidius of Calama: A Study of the North African Episcopate at the Time of Augustine*. Oxford Early Christian Studies. Oxford: Oxford University Press, 2008.

Hill, Edmund, OP. Translator's Note to *Saint Augustine, Teaching Christianity: De Doctrina Christiana*, 95–97. Works of Saint Augustine: A Translation for the 21st Century I/11. Hyde City, NY: New City Press, 1996.

———. "St Augustine as Preacher." *Blackfriars* 416 (1954): 463–71.

Hofer, Andrew, OP. "Augustine, Aquinas, Thérèse, and the Mysticism of Mother Teresa's Five-Finger Gospel." In *Mother Teresa and the Mystics: Toward a Renewal of Spiritual Theology*, edited by Michael Dauphinais, Brian Kolodiejchuk, MC, and Roger Nutt, 79–101. Ave Maria, FL: Sapientia Press, 2018.

———. "Augustine's Mixture Christology." *Studia Patristica*. vol. 112: Papers presented at the Eighteenth International Conference on Patristic Studies, Oxford (2019), edited by Markus Vinzent, vol. 9: *Fourth-Century Christology in Context: A Reconsideration*, edited by Miguel Brugarolas, 103–25. Leuven: Peeters, 2021.

———. "Book 19. The Ends of the Two Cities: Augustine's Appeal for Peace." In *The Cambridge Companion to Augustine's City of God*, edited by David V. Meconi, SJ, 228–50. Cambridge: Cambridge University Press, 2021.

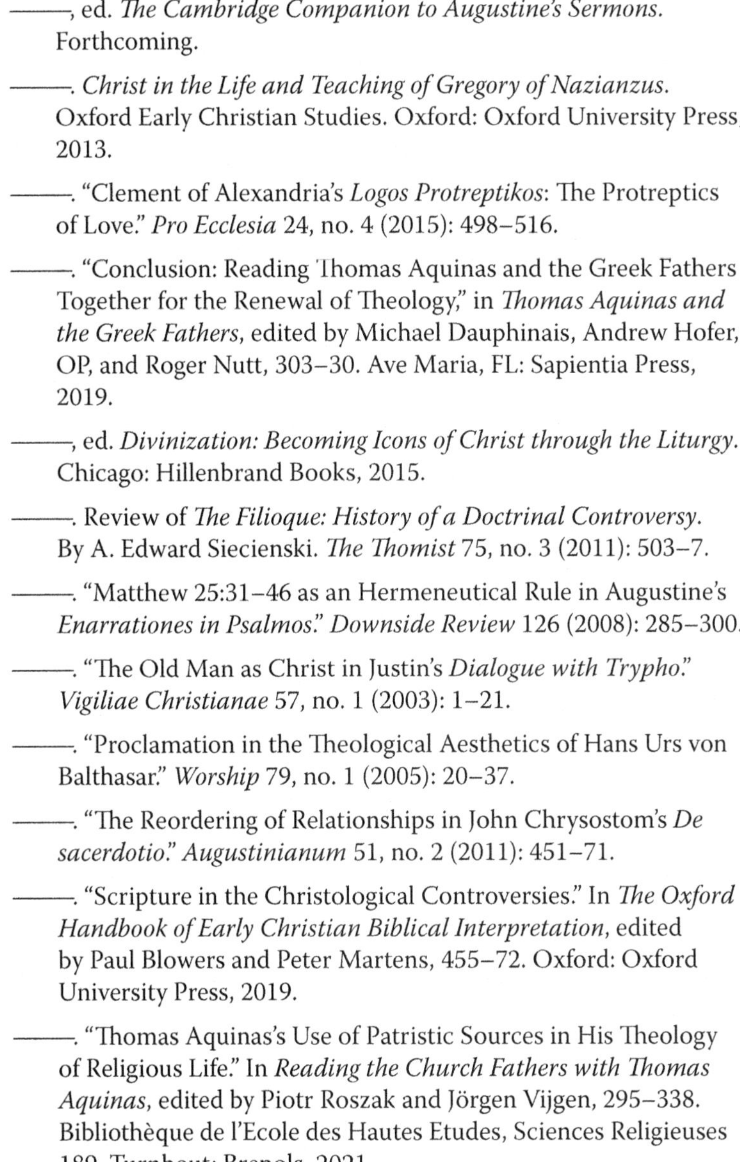

———, ed. *The Cambridge Companion to Augustine's Sermons*. Forthcoming.

———. *Christ in the Life and Teaching of Gregory of Nazianzus*. Oxford Early Christian Studies. Oxford: Oxford University Press, 2013.

———. "Clement of Alexandria's *Logos Protreptikos*: The Protreptics of Love." *Pro Ecclesia* 24, no. 4 (2015): 498–516.

———. "Conclusion: Reading Thomas Aquinas and the Greek Fathers Together for the Renewal of Theology," in *Thomas Aquinas and the Greek Fathers*, edited by Michael Dauphinais, Andrew Hofer, OP, and Roger Nutt, 303–30. Ave Maria, FL: Sapientia Press, 2019.

———, ed. *Divinization: Becoming Icons of Christ through the Liturgy*. Chicago: Hillenbrand Books, 2015.

———. Review of *The Filioque: History of a Doctrinal Controversy*. By A. Edward Siecienski. *The Thomist* 75, no. 3 (2011): 503–7.

———. "Matthew 25:31–46 as an Hermeneutical Rule in Augustine's *Enarrationes in Psalmos*." *Downside Review* 126 (2008): 285–300.

———. "The Old Man as Christ in Justin's *Dialogue with Trypho*." *Vigiliae Christianae* 57, no. 1 (2003): 1–21.

———. "Proclamation in the Theological Aesthetics of Hans Urs von Balthasar." *Worship* 79, no. 1 (2005): 20–37.

———. "The Reordering of Relationships in John Chrysostom's *De sacerdotio*." *Augustinianum* 51, no. 2 (2011): 451–71.

———. "Scripture in the Christological Controversies." In *The Oxford Handbook of Early Christian Biblical Interpretation*, edited by Paul Blowers and Peter Martens, 455–72. Oxford: Oxford University Press, 2019.

———. "Thomas Aquinas's Use of Patristic Sources in His Theology of Religious Life." In *Reading the Church Fathers with Thomas Aquinas*, edited by Piotr Roszak and Jörgen Vijgen, 295–338. Bibliothèque de l'Ecole des Hautes Etudes, Sciences Religieuses 189. Turnhout: Brepols, 2021.

Hofer, Andrew, OP, and Alan Piper, OP. "Retracing the 'Art of Arts and Science of Sciences' from Gregory the Great to Philo of Alexandria." *Journal of the History of Ideas* 79, no. 4 (2018): 507–26.

Holman, Susan R. *The Hungry Are Dying: Beggars and Bishops in Roman Cappadocia*. Oxford Studies in Historical Theology. New York: Oxford University Press, 2001.

Hunt, Hannah. *Clothed in the Body: Asceticism, the Body and the Spiritual in the Late Antique Era*. Ashgate Studies in Philosophy & Theology in Late Antiquity. London: Routledge, 2016.

Hunter, David G. "Between Discipline and Doctrine: Augustine's Response to Clerical Misconduct." *Augustinian Studies* 51, no. 1 (2020): 3–22.

Hunter, David G., ed. *Preaching in the Patristic Age: Studies in Honor of Walter J. Burghardt, SJ*. New York: Paulist Press, 1989.

Iwas, Ignatius Zakka I. "Meekness and Humility." Message of January 20, 2007. Accessed on April 25, 2020. https://www.malankara.com/node/2846.

Jacobs, Andrew S. *Christ Circumcised: A Study in Early Christian History and Difference*. Divinations: Rereading Late Ancient Religion. Philadelphia: University of Pennsylvania Press, 2012.

James, Mark Randall. *Learning the Language of Scripture: Origen, Wisdom, and the Logic of Interpretation*. Studia Traditionis Theologiae 24. Leiden: Brill, 2021.

John Paul II. *Pastores Gregis*. Post-Synodal Apostolic Exhortation on the Bishop, Servant of the Gospel of Jesus Christ for the Hope of the World. October 16, 2003.

———. *Salvifici Doloris*. Apostolic Letter on the Christian Meaning of Human Suffering. February 11, 1984.

Johnson, Aaron P. "Early Christianity and the Classical Tradition." In *The Oxford Handbook of the Second Sophistic*, edited by Daniel S. Richter and William A. Johnson, 625–38. Oxford: Oxford University Press, 2017.

Johnson, Samuel. "The Sacrifice of the Law in Origen's Homilies on Leviticus." In *Origeniana Duodecima: Origen's Legacy in the Holy Land–A Tale of Three Cities: Jerusalem, Caesarea, and Bethlehem*, edited by Brouria Bitton-Ashkelony, Oded Irshai, Aryeh Kofsky, Hillel Newman, and Lorenzo Perrone, 603–16. Bibliotheca Ephemeridum Theologicarum Lovaniensium 302. Leuven: Peeters, 2019.

Judic, Bruno. "Preaching according to Gregory the Great." In *Preaching in the Patristic Era: Sermons, Preachers, and Audiences in the Latin West*, edited by Anthony Dupont, Shari Boodts, Gert Partoens, and Johann Leemans. Leiden: Brill, 2018.

———. "Structure et Fonction de la *Regula Pastoralis*." In *Grégoire le Grand*. Chantilly, Centre culturel Les Fontaines 15–19 septembre 1982, edited by Jacques Fontaine, Robert Gillet, Stan Pellistrandi, 409–17. Paris: Éditions du Centre National de la Recherche Scientifique, 1986.

Junod, Éric. "Wodurch unterscheiden sich die Homilien des Origenes von seinen Kommentaren?" Translated from French by Marianne Mühlenberg. In *Predigt in der Alten Kirche*, edited by Ekkehard Mühlenberg and J. van Oort. Kampen, 50–81. The Netherlands: Kok Pharos Publishing House, 1994.

Kantzer Komline, Han-luen. *Augustine on the Will: A Theological Account*. Oxford Studies in Historical Theology. New York: Oxford University Press, 2019.

Kazan, Stanley. "Isaac of Antioch's Homily against the Jews." *Oriens Christianus* 45 (1961): 30–53; 46 (1962): 87–98; 47 (1963): 89–97; 49 (1965): 57–78.

Keating, Daniel A. "Christology in Cyril and Leo: Unnoticed Parallels and Ironies." *Studia Patristica* 48 (2010): 53–58.

———. "The Wonderful Exchange: Deification in Leo the Great." In *Deification in the Latin Patristic Tradition*, edited by Jared Ortiz, 208–30. Washington, DC: The Catholic University of America Press, 2018.

Kelly, J. N. D. *Golden Mouth: The Story of John Chrysostom—Ascetic, Preacher, Bishop*. Ithaca, NY: Cornell University Press, 1995.

Kennedy, George. *Greek Rhetoric under Christian Emperors*. Princeton: Princeton University Press, 1983.

Kenney, John Peter. *Contemplation and Classical Christianity: A Study in Augustine*. Oxford Early Christian Studies. Oxford: Oxford University Press, 2013.

Kiger, David Wesley. "Fire in the Bread, Life in the Body: The Pneumatology of Ephrem the Syrian." Ph.D. diss., Marquette University, 2020.

Kim, Angela Y. "Signs of Ephrem's Exegetical Techniques in his *Homily on Our Lord*." *Hugoye* 3, no. 1 (2000 [2010]): 55–70.

Kim, Young Richard. "An Iconic Odd Couple: The Hagiographic Rehabilitation of Epiphanius and John Chrysostom." *Church History* 87, no. 4 (2018): 981–1002.

Kolbet, Paul R. *Augustine and the Cure of Souls: Revising a Classical Ideal*. Notre Dame, IN: University of Notre Dame Press, 2010.

Kotzé, Annemaré. "Augustine on Himself." In *Augustine in Context*, edited by Tarmo Toom, 22–29. Cambridge: Cambridge University Press, 2017.

Kunzelmann, A. "Die Chronologie der Sermones des hl. Augustinus." In Vol. 2, *Miscellanea Agostiniana*, 417–520. Rome: Studi Agostiniani, 1931.

La Bonnardière, Anne-Marie. "Augustine, Minister of the Word of God." In *Augustine and the Bible*, edited and translated by Pamela Bright, 245–51. The Bible through the Ages 2. Notre Dame, IN: University of Notre Dame Press, 1999.

Lagrange, Marie-Joseph, OP. "Julian the Apostate: Priestly Retreat Master." Translated by Philip Neri Reese, OP. *Dominicana* (Summer 2014): 78–85. [Translation of Marie-Joseph Lagrange. "Julien l'Apostat prédicateur de retraites sacerdotales." *La Vie Spirituelle, supplément* 17 (1928): 242–48.]

Lai, Pak-Wah. "John Chrysostom and the Hermeneutics of Exemplar Portraits." Ph.D. diss., University of Durham, 2010.

———. "Reading *On the Priesthood* as Dialogue: Perspectives on John Chrysostom's Ascetic Vision." In *John Chrysostom: Past, Present, Future*, eds. Doru Costache and Mario Baghos, 217–34. Sydney: AIOCS Press, 2017.

Langworthy, Oliver B. *Gregory of Nazianzus' Soteriological Pneumatology*. Studien und Texte zu Antike und Christentum 117. Tübingen: Mohr Siebeck, 2019.

———. "Theodoret's Theologian: Assessing the Origin and Significance of Gregory of Nazianzus' Title." *Journal of Ecclesiastical History* 70, no. 3 (2019): 455–71.

Laporte, Jean. "Sacrifice in Origen in the Light of Philonic Models." In *Origen of Alexandria: His World and His Legacy*, edited by Charles Kannengiesser and William L. Petersen, 250–76. Christianity and Judaism in Antiquity 1. Notre Dame, IN: University of Notre Dame Press, 1988.

Latham, Jacob A. "Inventing Gregory 'the Great': Memory, Authority, and the Afterlives of the *Letania Septiformis*." *Church History* 84, no. 1 (2015): 1–31.

Lawless, George P., OSA, "Augustine's Burden of Ministry." *Angelicum* 61, no. 2 (1984): 295–315.

Ledegang, F. *Mysterium Ecclesiae: Images of the Church and Its Members in Origen*. Translated by F. A. Valken. Bibliotheca Ephemeridum Theologicarum Lovaniensium 156. Leuven: Leuven University Press, 2001.

Lee, James K. "'One in the One Shepherd': St. Augustine and Pastoral Ministry." *Heythrop Journal* 63 (2022): 232–44.

Lepelley, C. "Saint Léon le Grand et la Cité Romaine." *Revue des Sciences Religieuses* 35 (1961): 130–50.

Lettieri, Gaetano. "Omelia I: Il sacrificio del Logos." In *Omelie sul Levitico: Lettura origeniana*, edited by Mario Maritano and Enrico dal Covolo, 15–47. Biblioteca di Scienze Religiose 181. Rome: Libreria Ateneo Salesiano, 2003.

Levering, Matthew. "Retrievals in Contemporary Theology." In *The Oxford Handbook of Early Christian Biblical Interpretation*, edited by Paul Blowers and Peter Martens, 723–40. Oxford: Oxford University Press, 2019.

Leyerle, Blake. "Appealing to Children." *Journal of Early Christian Studies* 5, no. 2 (1997): 243–70.

———. "The Etiology of Sorrow and Its Therapeutic Benefits in the Preaching of John Chrysostom." *Journal of Late Antiquity* 8, no. 2 (2015): 368–85.

———. "John Chrysostom on Almsgiving and the Use of Money." *Harvard Theological Review* 87, no. 1 (1994): 29–47.

———. "Locating Animals in John Chrysostom's Thought." In *Revisioning John Chrysostom: New Approaches, New Perspectives*, edited by Chris L. de Wet and Wendy Mayer, 276–99. Critical Approaches to Early Christianity 1. Leiden: Brill, 2019.

———. *The Narrative Shape of Emotion in the Preaching of John Chrysostom*. Christianity in Late Antiquity 11. Oakland, CA: University of California Press, 2020.

———. *Theatrical Shows and Ascetic Lives: John Chrysostom's Attack on Spiritual Marriage*. Berkeley and Los Angeles: University of California Press, 2001.

Leyser, Conrad. "Expertise and Authority in Gregory the Great: The Social Function of *Peritia*." In *Gregory the Great: A Symposium*, edited by John C. Cavadini, 38–61. Notre Dame Studies in Theology 2. Notre Dame, IN: University of Notre Dame Press, 1995.

———. "Late Antiquity in the Medieval West." In *A Companion to Late Antiquity*, edited by Philip Rousseau, with the assistance of Jutta Raithel, 29–42. Chichester: Wiley-Blackwell, 2009.

———. "'Let me speak, let me speak': Vulnerability and Authority in Gregory's Homilies on Ezekiel." In *Gregorio Magno e il Suo Tempo. XIX Incontro di studiosi dell'antichità Cristiana in collaborazione con l'École Française de Rome*, Roma, 9–12 maggio 1990, 169–82. Vol. I. Studi storici. Rome: Institutum Patristicum Augustinianum, 1991.

Lienhard, Joseph T., SJ. "Origen as Homilist." In *Preaching in the Patristic Age: Studies in Honor of Walter J. Burghardt, SJ*, edited by David G. Hunter, 36–52. New York: Paulist Press, 1989.

———. "*Sacramentum* and the Eucharist in St. Augustine." *The Thomist* 77, no. 2 (2013): 173–92.

Litfin, Bryan M. *Getting to Know the Church Fathers: An Evangelical Introduction*. Grand Rapids, MI: Brazos Press, 2007.

Lizzi, Rita. "Ambrose's Contemporaries and the Christianization of Northern Italy." *Journal of Roman Studies* 80 (1990): 156–73.

Louth, Andrew. "Gregory the Great in the Byzantine Tradition." In *A Companion to Gregory the Great*, edited by Bronwen Neil and Matthew Dal Santo, 343–58. Brill's Companions to the Christian Tradition 47. Leiden: Brill, 2003.

———. *Maximus the Confessor*. ECF. London: Routledge, 1996.

———. "St. Gregory the Theologian and Byzantine Theology." In *Re-Reading Gregory of Nazianzus*, edited by Beeley, 252–66. Washington, DC: The Catholic University of America Press, 2012.

Lupton, Brendan. "Reexamining Gregory the Great's Audience for the *Pastoral Rule*." *Downside Review* 133 (2015): 178–204.

MacIntyre, Alasdair. *Ethics in the Conflicts of Modernity: An Essay on Desire, Practical Reasoning and Narrative*. New York: Cambridge University Press, 2016.

Maier, Henri O. "'Manichee!' Leo the Great and the Orthodox Panopticon." *Journal of Early Christian Studies* 4, no. 4 (1996): 441–60.

Markus, Robert A. *Gregory the Great and His World*. Cambridge: Cambridge University Press, 1997.

———. "Gregory the Great's *Rector* and His Genesis." In *Grégoire le Grand*, edited by Fontaine, Gillet, and Pellistrandi, 137–46. Paris: Éditions du Centre National de la Recherche Scientifique, 1986.

Martens, Peter W. "Ideal Interpreters." In *The Oxford Handbook of Early Christian Biblical Interpretation*, edited by Paul Blowers and Peter Martens, 149–65. Oxford: Oxford University Press, 2019.

———. *Origen and Scripture: The Contours of the Exegetical Life*. Oxford Early Christian Studies. Oxford: Oxford University Press, 2012.

———. Review of *Die neuen Psalmenhomilien: Eine kritische Edition des Codex Monacensis Graecus 314*, edited by Lorenzo Perrone, together with Marian Molin Pradel, Emanuela Prinzivalli, and Antonio Cacciari. *Journal of Early Christian Studies* 24, no. 4 (2016): 628–30.

Matz, Brian J. *Gregory of Nazianzus*. Foundations of Theological Exegesis and Christian Spirituality. Grand Rapids, MI: Baker Academic, 2016.

Maxwell, Jaclyn L. *Christianization and Communication in Late Antiquity: John Chrysostom and His Congregation in Antioch*. New York: Cambridge University Press, 2006.

Mayer, Wendy. "Catecheses and Homilies." In *The Oxford Handbook of Early Christian Biblical Interpretation*, edited by Paul Blowers and Peter Martens, 242–54. Oxford: Oxford University Press, 2019.

———. *Chrysostomica: An Online Bibliography of Scholarship on John Chrysostom and Attributed Writings. Last updated March, 2016.* http://www.cecs.acu.edu.au/chrysostombibliography.html.

———. "The Homiletic Audience as Embodied Hermeneutic: Scripture and Its Interpretation in the Exegetical Preaching of John Chrysostom." In *Hymns, Homilies, and Hermeneutics*, edited by Sarah Gaydor-Whyte and Andrew Mellas, 11–29. Byzantina Australiensa 25. Leiden: Brill, 2021.

———. "Homiletics." In *The Oxford Handbook of Early Christian Studies*, edited by Susan Ashbook Harvey and David G. Hunter, 565–83. Oxford: Oxford, 2006.

———. "The Ins and Outs of the Chrysostom Letter-Collection: New Ways of Looking at a Limited Corpus." In *Collecting Early Christian Letters: From the Apostle Paul to Late Antiquity*, edited by Bronwen Neil and Pauline Allen, 129–53. Cambridge: Cambridge University Press, 2015.

———. "John Chrysostom." In *The Wiley-Blackwell Companion to Patristics*, edited by Ken Parry, 141–54. Malden, MA: John Wiley & Sons, 2015.

———. "The Persistence in Late Antiquity of Medico-Philosophical Psychic Therapy." *Journal of Late Antiquity* 8, no. 2 (2015): 337–51.

McCullough, Ross. "Christ's Presence in the Poor and the Church: A Traditionalist Liberation Theology." *Pro Ecclesia* 28, no. 3 (2019): 320–32.

McGuckin, John A. *St. Gregory of Nazianzus: An Intellectual Biography*. Crestwood, NY: St. Vladimir's Seminary Press, 2004.

McLaughlin, R. Emmet. "The Word Eclipsed? Preaching in the Early Middle Ages." *Traditio* 46 (1991): 77–122.

McLynn, Neil B. *Ambrose of Milan: Church and Court in a Christian Capital*. Transformations of the Classical Heritage 22. Berkeley and Los Angeles: University of California Press, 1994.

———. "Among the Hellenists: Gregory and the Sophists." In *Gregory of Nazianzus: Images and Reflections*, edited by Jostein Børtnes and Tomas Hägg, 213–38. Copenhagen: Museum Tusculanum Press, 2006.

———. "The Conference of Carthage Reconsidered." In *The Donatist Schism: Controversy and Contexts*, edited by Richard Miles, 220–48. Translated Texts for Historians, Contexts 2. Liverpool: Liverpool University Press, 2016.

———. "Gregory Nazianzen's Basil: The Literary Construction of a Christian Friendship." *Studia Patristica* 37 (2001): 178–93.

Meconi, David Vincent, SJ. "Becoming Gods by Becoming God's: Augustine's Mystagogy of Identification." *Augustinian Studies* 39, no. 1 (2008): 61–74.

———. *The One Christ: St. Augustine's Theology of Deification*. Washington, DC: The Catholic University of America Press, 2013.

———. "Recapitulative Tropes in Augustine's Sermons." *New Blackfriars* 95 (2014): 689–97.

Melina, Livio. *Sharing in Christ's Virtues: For a Renewal of Moral Theology in Light of Veritatis Splendor*. Translated by William E. May. Washington, DC: The Catholic University of America Press, 2001.

Meyvaert, Paul. "The Authentic *Dialogues* of Gregory the Great." *Sacris Erudiri* 43 (2004): 55–129.

Miles, Richard. *The Donatist Schism: Controversy and Contexts*. Translated Texts for Historians. Contexts 2. Liverpool: Liverpool University Press, 2016.

Milgrom, Jacob. *Leviticus: A Book of Ritual and Ethics*. A Continental Commentary. Minneapolis, MN: Fortress Press, 2004.

Miller, Patricia Cox. "Poetic Words, Abysmal Words: Reflections on Origen's Hermeneutics." In *Origen of Alexandria: His World and His Legacy*, edited by Charles Kannengiesser and William L. Petersen, 165–78. Christianity and Judaism in Antiquity 1. Notre Dame, IN: University of Notre Dame Press, 1988.

Mitchell, Margaret M. "The Archetypal Image: John Chrysostom's Portraits of Paul." *Journal of Religion* 75, no. 1 (1995): 15–43.

———. *The Heavenly Trumpet: John Chrysostom and the Art of Pauline Interpretation*. Louisville: Westminster John Knox Press, 2002.

———. "Origen and the Text-Critical Dilemma: An Illustration from One of His Newly Discovered Greek Homilies on the Psalms." *Biblical Research* 62 (2017): 61–82.

———. "'Problems and Solutions' in Early Christian Biblical Interpretation: A Telling Case from Origen's Newly Discovered Greek Homilies on the Psalms (*Codex Monacensis Graecus* 314)." *Adamantius* 22 (2016): 40–55.

Moore, Peter C. "Bound Together for Heaven: Mutual Emotions in Chrysostom's Homilies on Matthew for Well-Ordered and Fruitful Community in Anxious Times." In *Revisioning John Chrysostom: New Approaches, New Perspectives*, edited by Chris L. de Wet and Wendy Mayer, 334–60. Critical Approaches to Early Christianity 1. Leiden: Brill, 2019.

Moorhead, John. *Gregory the Great*. ECF. New York: Routledge, 2005.

Moschus, John. *The Spiritual Meadow (Pratum Spirituale)*. Introduction, translation, and notes by John Wortley. CSS 139. Kalamazoo, MI: Cistercian Publications, 1992.

Moss, Candida. *The Other Christs: Imitating Jesus in Ancient Christian Ideologies of Martyrdom*. New York: Oxford University Press, 2010.

Mosser, Carl. "The Earliest Patristic Interpretations of Psalm 82, Jewish Antecedents, and the Origin of Christian Deification." *Journal of Theological Studies* 56, no. 1 (2005): 30–74.

Muehlberger, Ellen. *Angels in Late Ancient Christianity*. New York: Oxford University Press, 2013.

Müller, Barbara. "Gregory the Great and Monasticism." In *A Companion to Gregory the Great,* edited by Bronwen Neil and Matthew Dal Santo, 83–108. Brill's Companions to the Christian Tradition 47. Leiden: Brill, 2003.

Murphy, Austin Gregory, OSB. "The Bible as Inspired, Authoritative, and True according to Saint Augustine." Ph.D. diss., University of Notre Dame, 2016.

Murphy, Francis X. "The Sermons of Pope Leo the Great: Content and Style." In *Preaching in the Patristic Age: Studies in Honor of Walter J. Burghardt, SJ,* edited by David G. Hunter, 183–97. New York: Paulist Press, 1989.

Murray, Robert. *Symbols of Church and Kingdom: A Study in Early Syriac Tradition.* Cambridge: Cambridge University Press, 1975.

Naidu, Ashish J. *Transformed in Christ: Christology and the Christian Life in John Chrysostom.* Princeton Theological Monograph Series 188. Eugene, OR: Pickwick Publications, 2012.

Nautin, Pierre. *Origène: Homélies sur Jérémie.* Vol. 1 (Homilies 1–11) Sources Chrétiennes 232. Paris: Éditions du Cerf, 1976.

Neil, Bronwen. "Blessed are the Rich: Leo the Great and the Roman Poor." *Studia Patristica* 44 (2010): 533–47.

———. "Blessed is Poverty: Leo the Great on Almsgiving." *Sacris Erudiri* 46 (2007): 143–56.

———. "A Crisis of Orthodoxy: Leo I's Fight against the 'Deadly Disease' of Heresy." In *Ancient Jewish and Christian Texts as Crisis Management Literature,* edited by David C. Sim and Pauline Allen, 144–58. Thematic Studies from the Centre for Early Christian Studies. New York: T & T Clark International, 2012.

———. "Hagiography." In *The Oxford Handbook of Early Christian Biblical Interpretation,* edited by Paul Blowers and Peter Martens, 303–14. Oxford: Oxford University Press, 2019.

———. "Leo I on Poverty." In *Preaching Poverty in Late Antiquity: Perceptions and Realities,* edited by Pauline Allen, Bronwen Neil, and Wendy Mayer, Arbeiten Kirchen, 171–208. Und Theologiegeschichte. Leipzig: Evangelische Verlagsanstalt, 2009.

———. "Leo Magnus." In *Preaching in the Patristic Era: Sermons, Preachers, and Audiences in the Latin West*, edited by Anthony Dupont, Shari Boodts, Gert Partoens, and Johann Leemans, 327–46. Leiden: Brill, 2018.

———. "Models of Gift Giving in the Preaching of Leo the Great," *Journal of Early Christian Studies* 18, no. 2 (2010): 225–59.

———. "Papal Letters and Letter Collections." In *Late Antique Letter Collections: A Critical Introduction and Reference Guide*, edited by Cristiana Sogno, Bradley K. Storin, and Edward J. Watts, 449–66. Oakland, CA: University of California Press, 2017.

Newman, John Henry. *The Idea of a University*. Introduction by Don Briel and afterword by Christopher O. Blum. Tacoma, WA: Cluny Media, 2016.

Noret, Jacques. "Grégoire de Nazianze, l'auteur le plus cité après la Bible, dans la littérature ecclésiastique byzantine." In *II. Symposium Nazianzenum (Louvain-la-Neuve, 25–28 août, 1981): Actes du Colloque International*, edited by Justin Mossay, 259–66. Studien zur Geschichte und Kultur des Altertums, Neue Folge 2, Forschungen zu Gregor von Nazianz. Paderborn: Schöningh, 1983.

Norris, Frederick W. *Faith Gives Fullness to Reasoning: The Five Theological Orations of Gregory Nazianzen*. Texts translated by Lionel Wickham and Frederick Williams. Supplements to *Vigiliae Christianae* 13. Leiden: E.J. Brill, 1991.

O'Connell, Peter A. "Homer and His Legacy in Gregory of Nazianzus' 'On His Own Affairs.'" *Journal of Hellenic Studies* 139 (2019): 147–71.

Oden, Thomas C. *Care of Souls in the Classic Tradition*. Philadelphia: Fortress Press, 1984.

O'Donovan, Oliver. "*Usus* and *Fruitio* in Augustine, *De Doctrina Christiana* 1." *Journal of Theological Studies* n.s. 33, no. 2 (1982): 361–97.

Palmer, Andrew. "A Lyre without a Voice, the Poetics and the Politics of Ephrem the Syrian," *ARAM* 5 (1993): 371–99.

Pellegrino, Michele. Introduction to *Works of Saint Augustine: A Translation for the 21st Century III/1, Sermons on the Old Testament (1–19)*, edited by John E. Rotelle, OSA, 13–137.

Perrone, Lorenzo. "Codex Monacensis Graecus 314: 29 Psalmhomilien des Origenes." In Origenes Werke 13. Berlin: De Gruyter, 2015.

———. "'Et l'homme tout entier devient dieu': La déification selon Origène à la lumière des nouvelles *Homélies sur les Psaumes*." *Teología y Vida* 58, no. 2 (2017): 187–220.

Pius XII. *Humani Generis*. 1950. *Acta Apostolicae Sedis* 42 [1950].

Ployd, Adam. *Augustine, the Trinity, and the Church: A Reading of the Anti-Donatist Sermons*. Oxford Studies in Historical Theology. New York: Oxford University Press, 2015.

———. "*Non poena sed causa*: Augustine's Anti-Donatist Rhetoric of Martyrdom." *Augustinian Studies* 49, no. 1 (2018): 25–44.

Plumer, Eric. *Augustine's Commentary on Galatians: Introduction, Text, Translation and Notes*. Oxford Early Christian Studies. Oxford: Oxford University Press, 2003.

Pollmann, Karla. *Doctrina Christiana: Untersuchungen zu den Anfängen der christlichen Hermeneutik unter besonderer Berücksichtigung von Augustinus, De doctrina christiana*. Paradosis 41. Freiburg, Switzerland: Universitätsverlag Freiburg, 1996.

———. "To write by advancing in knowledge and to advance by writing." *Augustinian Studies* 29, no. 2 (1998): 131–37.

Possekel, Ute. *Evidence of Greek Philosophical Concepts in the Writings of Ephrem the Syrian*. Corpus Scriptorum Ecclesiasticorum Orientalium 580; *Subsidia* tom. 102. Leuven: Peeters, 1999.

Quiroga Puertas, Alberto J. "Preaching and Mesmerizing: The Resolution of Religious Conflicts in Late Antiquity." In *The Role of the Bishop in Late Antiquity: Conflict and Compromise*, edited by Andrew Fear, José Fernández Ubiña, and Mar Marcos, 189–208. London: Bloomsbury Academic 2013.

Rahner, Hugo, SJ. *A Theology of Preaching*. New York: Herder & Herder, 1968.

Ramsey, Boniface, OP. "Almsgiving in the Latin Church: The Late Fourth and Early Fifth Centuries." *Theological Studies* 43, no. 2 (1982): 226–59.

———. "Two Traditions on Lying and Deception in the Ancient Church." *The Thomist* 49, no. 4 (1985): 504–33.

Raven, Charles E. *Apollinarianism: An Essay on the Christology of the Early Church.* Cambridge: Cambridge University Press, 1923.

Reisenauer, Augustine Marie, OP. "Christ Examining, Excommunicating, and Exorcising the Antichrist in Augustine's *Homilies on the First Epistle of John.*" In *Praedicatio Patrum: Studies on Preaching in Late Antique North Africa*, edited by Gert Partoens, Anthony Dupont, and Shari Boodts, 315–49. Instrumenta Patristica et Mediaevalia 75. Turnhout: Brepols, 2017.

Rhee, Helen. *Loving the Poor, Saving the Rich: Wealth, Poverty, and Early Christian Formation.* Grand Rapids, MI: Baker Academic, 2012.

Rusch, William G. "Preaching." In *The Westminster Handbook to Origen*, edited by John Anthony McGuckin, 177–78. Louisville, KY: Westminster John Knox Press, 2004.

Russell, Norman. *The Doctrine of Deification in the Greek Patristic Tradition.* Oxford Early Christian Studies. Oxford: Oxford University, 2004.

Russell, Paul S. "Ephrem the Syrian on the Utility of Language and the Place of Silence." *Journal of Early Christian Studies* 8, no. 1 (2000): 21–37.

———. "St. Ephraem, the Syrian Theologian." *Pro Ecclesia* 7, no. 1 (1998): 79–90.

Rylaarsdam, David. *John Chrysostom on Divine Pedagogy: The Coherence of his Theology and Preaching.* Oxford Early Christian Studies. Oxford: Oxford University Press, 2014.

Satterlee, Craig A. "Patristic Principles for Post-Christendom Preaching." *Liturgy* 25, no. 4 (2010): 18–29.

Schütz, Werner. *Der christliche Gottesdienst bei Origenes.* Calwer Theologische Monographien. Stuttgart: Calwer Verlag, 1984.

Scully, Ellen. "The Assumption of All Humanity in Saint Hilary of Poitiers' *Tractatus super Psalmos.*" Ph.D. diss., Marquette University, 2011.

Second Vatican Council. *Presbyterorum Ordinis, Decree on the Ministry and Life of Priests*. 1965.

Sheerin, Daniel. "The Role of Prayer in Origen's Homilies." In *Origen of Alexandria: His World and His Legacy*, edited by Charles Kannengiesser and William L. Petersen, 200–14. Christianity and Judaism in Antiquity 1. Notre Dame, IN: University of Notre Dame Press, 1988.

Shemunkasho, Aho. *Healing in the Theology of Saint Ephrem*. Gorgias Dissertations Near Eastern Studies 1. Piscataway, NJ: Gorgias Press, 2002.

Shepardson, Christine. "Anti-Jewish Rhetoric and Intra-Christian Conflict in the Sermons of Ephrem Syrus." *Studia Patristica* 35 (2001): 502–7.

Shoemaker, Stephen J. *Mary in Early Christian Faith and Devotion*. New Haven, CT: Yale University Press, 2015.

Sidaway, Janet. "The reception of Chalcedon in the West: a case study of Gregory the Great." *Scottish Journal of Theology* 73, no. 4 (2020): 307–17.

Siecienski, A. Edward. *The Filioque: History of a Doctrinal Controversy*. Oxford Studies in Historical Theology. New York: Oxford University Press, 2010.

Simonetti, Manlio. "Omelia XVI: Origene inventore di parole." In *Omelie sul Levitico: Lettura origeniana*, edited by Mario Maritano and Enrico dal Covolo, 135–47. Biblioteca di Scienze Religiose 181. Rome: Libreria Ateneo Salesiano, 2003.

Smith, J. Warren. *Ambrose, Augustine, and the Pursuit of Greatness*. Cambridge: Cambridge University Press, 2020.

———. *Christian Grace and Pagan Virtue: The Theological Foundation of Ambrose's Ethics*. Oxford Studies in Historical Theology. New York: Oxford University Press, 2010.

Solheid, John. "Scripture and Christian Formation in Origen's *Fourth Homily on Psalm 77(78)*." *Journal of Early Christian Studies* 27, no. 3 (2019): 417–42.

Stanfill, Jonathan P. "John Chrysostom and the Rebirth of Antiochene Mission in Late Antiquity." *Church History* 88, no. 4 (2019): 899–924.

Steven, Luke. *Imitation, Knowledge, and the Task of Christology in Maximus the Confessor*. Eugene, OR: Wipf and Stock, 2020.

Stewart-Kroeker, Sarah. *Pilgrimage as Moral and Aesthetic Formation in Augustine's Thought*. Oxford: Oxford University Press, 2017.

Stock, Brian. *Listening for the Text: On the Uses of the Past*. Baltimore: Johns Hopkins Press, 1990.

Storin, Bradley K. "Autohagiobiography: Gregory of Nazianzus among His Biographers." *Studies in Late Antiquity* 1, no. 3 (2017): 254–81.

———. *Self-Portrait in Three Colors: Gregory of Nazianzus's Epistolary Autobiography*. Christianity in Late Antiquity 6. Oakland, CA: University of California Press, 2019.

Straw, Carole. "Gregory's Politics: Theory and Practice." In *Gregorio Magno e il Suo Tempo*. XIX Incontro di studiosi dell'antichità Cristiana in collaborazione con l'École Française de Rome, Roma, 9–12 maggio 1990, 47–63. Vol. I. Studi storici. Rome: Institutum Patristicum Augustinianum, 1991.

Thomas, Gabrielle. *The Image of God in the Theology of Gregory of Nazianzus*. Cambridge: Cambridge University Press, 2019.

Thurston, H. and D. Attwater, eds. *Butler's Lives of the Saints*. Revised edition. New York: 1956.

Tilley, Maureen A. "Redefining Donatism: Moving Forward." *Augustinian Studies* 42, no. 1 (2011): 21–32.

Torjesen, Karen Jo. *Hermeneutical Procedure and Theological Method in Origen's Exegesis*. Patristische Texte und Studien 28. Berlin: De Gruyter, 1985.

Trigg, Joseph W. "Being and Becoming God in Origen's *Homilies on the Psalms*." Presentation to the North American Patristics Society. Unpublished manuscript, 2016.

———. *Origen*. ECF. London: Routledge, 1998.

Tugwell, Simon, trans. *Early Dominicans: Selected Writings*. Classics of Western Spirituality. New York: Paulist Press, 1982.

Urbano, Arthur P. "Jesus' Dazzling Garments: Origen's Exegesis of the Transfiguration in the Commentary on Matthew." In *The Garb of Being: Embodiment and the Pursuit of Holiness in Late Ancient Christianity*, edited by Georgia Frank, Susan R. Holman, and Andrew S. Jacobs, 35–56. New York: Fordham University Press, 2020.

———. *The Philosophical Life: Biography and the Crafting of Intellectual Identity in Late Antiquity*. Patristic Monograph Series 21. Washington, DC: The Catholic University of America Press, 2013.

———. "Sizing-Up the Philosopher's Cloak: Christian Verbal and Visual Representations of the Tribon." In *Dressing Judeans and Christians in Antiquity*, edited by Kristi Upson-Saia, Carly Daniel-Hughes, and Alicia J. Batten, 175–94. Burlington, VT: Ashgate, 2014.

———. "Tailoring Rhetoric: Verbalizing Philosophical Dress in the Second Sophistic." In *"The One Who Sows Bountifully": Essays in Honor of Stanley K. Stowers*, edited by Caroline Johnson Hodge, Saul M. Olyan, Daniel Ullucci, and Emma Wasserman, 243–54. Brown Judaic Studies 356. Providence, Rhode Island: Brown Judaic Studies, 2013.

Vaccaro, Jody L. "Digging for Buried Treasure: Origen's Spiritual Interpretation of Scripture." *Communio: International Catholic Review* 25, no. 4 (1998): 757–75.

———. "The Inn, the Manger, the Swaddling Cloths, the Shepherds, and the Animals," in *The Oxford Handbook of Christmas*, edited by Timothy Larsen, 224–35. Oxford: Oxford University Press, 2020.

Vaggione, Richard Paul. *Eunomius of Cyzicus and the Nicene Revolution*. Oxford Early Christian Studies. Oxford: Oxford University Press, 2000.

Valavanolickal, Kuriakose Antony. *The Use of the Gospel Parables in the Writings of Aphrahat and Ephrem*. Studies in the Religion and History of Early Christianity 2. Frankfurt am Main: Peter Lang, 1996.

Van Dam, Raymond. *Kingdom of Snow: Roman Rule and Greek Culture in Cappadocia*. Philadelphia: University of Pennsylvania Press, 2002.

Vijgen, Jörgen. "Aquinas's Reception of Origen: A Preliminary Study." *Thomas Aquinas and the Greek Fathers*, edited by Michael Dauphinais, Andrew Hofer, OP, and Roger Nutt, 30–88. Ave Maria, FL: Sapientia Press, 2019.

Voicu, Sever J. "Johannes Chrysostomus II (Pseudo-Chrysostomica)." *Reallexikon für Antike und Christentum* 18 (1997): 503–15.

Vööbus, Arthur. *Literary, Critical, and Historical Studies in Ephrem the Syrian*. Papers of the Estonian Theological Society in Exile 10. Stockholm: Etse, 1958.

Wallace Ruddy, Deborah. "A Christological Approach to Virtue: Augustine and Humility." Ph.D. diss., Boston College, 2001.

Wessel, Susan. *Leo the Great and the Spiritual Rebuilding of a Universal Rome*. Supplements to *Vigiliae Christianae* 93. Leiden: Brill, 2008.

———. *Passion and Compassion in Early Christianity*. New York: Cambridge University Press, 2016.

Whitmarsh, Tim. *The Second Sophistic*. Greece & Rome: New Surveys in the Classics 35. Oxford: Oxford University Press, 2005.

Wickes, Jeffrey. "Between Liturgy and School: Reassessing the Performative Context of Ephrem's Madrāšê." *Journal of Early Christian Studies* 26, no. 1 (2018): 25–51.

———. *Bible and Poetry in Late Antique Mesopotamia: Ephrem's Hymns on Faith*. Christianity in Late Antiquity 5. Oakland. CA: University of California Press. 2019.

Widok, Norbert. "Die kerygmatische Dimension der Lehre von der Menschwerdung in der *Rede 38* des Gregor von Nazianz." *Zeitschrift für Antikes Christentum* 11, no. 2 (2007): 335–47.

Wilken, Robert Louis. "Origen's *Homilies on Leviticus* and *Vayikra Rabbah*." In *Origeniana Sexta: Origen and the Bible*, edited by Gilles Dorival and Alain le Boulluec, 81–91. Acts from the Sixth Origenian Colloquium, Chantilly, 1993. Leuven: University Press, 1995.

———. *The Spirit of Early Christian Thought: Seeking the Face of God*. New Haven: Yale University Press, 2003.

Williams, Michael Stuart. "Hymns as Acclamations: The Case of Ambrose of Milan." *Journal of Late Antiquity* 6, no. 1 (2013): 108–34.

———. "No Arians in Milan? Ambrose on the Basilica Crisis of 385/6." *Historia* 67, no. 3 (2018): 346–65.

———. *The Politics of Heresy in Ambrose of Milan: Community and Consensus in Late Antique Christianity.* Cambridge: Cambridge University Press, 2017.

Williams, Rowan. *On Augustine.* London: Bloomsbury, 2016.

———. Sermon on October 28, 2012, Anglican Consultative Council-15, Holy Trinity Cathedral, Auckland, New Zealand. Accessed on April 26, 2020. http://aoc2013.brix.fatbeehive.com/articles.php/2669/archbishops-sermon-at-acc-15-on-the-reckless-love-of-god.

Winterbottom, Michael. "Quintilian and the *vir bonus*." In *Papers on Quintilian and Ancient Declamation,* edited by Michael Winterbottom, Antonio Stramaglia, Francesca Romana Nocchi, and Giuseppe Russo, 3–15. New York: Oxford University Press, 2019.

Witvliet, John D. "Pedagogical Reflections on Changing Uses of the Term 'Worship.'" *Worship* 95, no. 1 (2021): 4–11.

Young, Frances M. *Biblical Exegesis and the Formation of Christian Culture.* Peabody, MA: Hendrickson Publishers, 2002.

———. *The Use of Sacrificial Ideas in Greek Christian Writers from the New Testament to John Chrysostom.* Patristic Monograph Series 5. Cambridge, MA: The Philadelphia Patristic Foundation, Ltd., 1979.

Zagzebski, Linda Trinkaus. *Exemplarist Moral Theory.* New York: Oxford University Press, 2017.

BIBLICAL CITATIONS

Mark

Luke

John

Acts

Romans

1 Corinthians

2 Corinthians

Galatians

Ephesians

Philippians

Colossians

1 Thessalonians

1 Timothy

2 Timothy

Titus

Philemon

Hebrews

James

1 Peter

2 Peter

1 John

INDEX

B

D

E

F

G

H

I

J

K

L

M

N

O

P

T

V

W

X

Y

Z

Also in the Patristic Theology series

Bede the Theologian:
History, Rhetoric, and Spirituality
John P. Bequette; Foreword by John C. Cavadini
"For someone who has always wanted to learn more about Bede the Venerable, this is the book." — *American Benedictine Review*

Cross and Creation:
A Theological Introduction to Origen of Alexandria
Mark E. Therrien
"This is an excellent book, a rare introductory text at the same time accessible to advanced undergraduates and profitable for long-time specialists.... Highly recommended." — *Catholic Books Review*

Also from Catholic University of America Press

The Art of Preaching
Daniel Cardo; Foreword by Timothy Gallagher, OMV

The Fathers of the Church in Christian Theology
Michel Fédou, SJ; Foreword by Brian E. Daley, SJ

Preaching to Latinos:
Welcoming the Hispanic Moment in the U.S. Church
Michael I. Kueber; Foreword by Hosffman Ospino

Mysteries of the Lord's Prayer: Wisdom from the Early Church
John Gavin, SJ; Foreword by George Weigel

Athanasius: A Theological Introduction
Thomas G. Weinandy, OFM Cap.

Deification in the Latin Patristic Tradition
Edited by Jared Ortiz
CUA Studies in Early Christianity

Augustine in His Own Words
Edited by William Harmless

The Holy Mass
Edited by Mike Aquilina; Foreword by Thomas G. Weinandy, OFM Cap.
Sayings of the Fathers of the Church